Frontier Forts Under Fire

ALSO BY PAUL WILLIAMS
AND FROM McFARLAND

*Jackson, Crockett and Houston
on the American Frontier: From
Fort Mims to the Alamo, 1813–1836* (2016)

*The Last Confederate Ship at Sea:
The Wayward Voyage of the CSS* Shenandoah,
October 1864–November 1865 (2015)

*Custer and the Sioux, Durnford and the Zulus:
Parallels in the American and British Defeats
at the Little Bighorn (1876) and Isandlwana (1879)* (2015)

Frontier Forts Under Fire

*The Attacks on
Fort William Henry (1757)
and Fort Phil Kearny (1866)*

Paul Williams

McFarland & Company, Inc., Publishers
Jefferson, North Carolina

ISBN (print) 978-1-4766-7093-5 ♾
ISBN (ebook) 978-1-4766-2956-8

LIBRARY OF CONGRESS CATALOGUING DATA ARE AVAILABLE

BRITISH LIBRARY CATALOGUING DATA ARE AVAILABLE

© 2017 Paul Williams. All rights reserved

No part of this book may be reproduced or transmitted in any form or by any means, electronic or mechanical, including photocopying or recording, or by any information storage and retrieval system, without permission in writing from the publisher.

Front cover: *Montcalm trying to stop the massacre,* Albert Bobbett engraving (Library of Congress)

Printed in the United States of America

McFarland & Company, Inc., Publishers Box 611, Jefferson, North Carolina 28640 www.mcfarlandpub.com

Acknowledgments

I would like to thank a number of helpful organizations, in particular the Albany Public Library; British Library, London; National Archives, U.K.; National Army Museum, U.K.; Fort William Henry Museum; Nebraska State Historical Society; Billings Public Library; Denver Public Library; and the Library of Congress. Also, I would like to thank those who have gone before with their own research and publications, both in print and online, covering the stories of the French and Indian War and Red Cloud's War.

Table of Contents

Acknowledgments   v
Preface   1

1. Sabbath Day Point   3
2. Disaster on the Monongahela   9
3. Revenge at Lake George   20
4. The French Strike Back   27
5. Fire and Ice: The Winter Raid   35
6. Fort William Henry Aware   40
7. Montcalm Arrives   45
8. The Siege Tightens: Webb Nowhere in Sight   53
9. A Demand for Surrender   59
10. We Must Fall into the Hands of Our Enemies   64
11. Massacre   70
12. Outrage   75
13. Carnage at Fort Carillon   81
14. The Death Throes of Fort Duquesne   88
15. Québec   94
16. England, Mistress of Canada   100
17. Dakota Territory, 1866   103
18. On the Bozeman Trail   114
19. Fort Phil Kearny Takes Shape   122
20. A Summons to Duty   132
21. A Forgotten Battalion   142
22. Fetterman Arrives   149
23. Over Lodge Trail Ridge   159

24.	Preparation for an Unparalleled Defense	168
25.	Fixing the Blame	175
26.	One and All Gloried in Abuse	180
27.	The Disaster Probed	187
28.	Red Cloud's Resolve	192
29.	The Wagon Box Fight	198
30.	Finale	203

Appendix: Henry Carrington's Report of January 3, 1867 — 211
Chapter Notes — 215
Bibliography — 225
Index — 231

Preface

Frontier forts. Those two words conjure up one enduring image—the wooden stockade, a sentry tower, the solid blockhouse—a remote outpost of European civilization in the vast forests and open plains of North America. Although most "forts" west of the Mississippi during the final decades of frontier expansion were, in fact, military structures with no stockade wall, the film industry saw to it that a more formidable and romantic image prevailed. But the stockaded fort did exist, both West and East, especially during the early days of colonization when European powers fought for supremacy and the native population could outnumber the Europeans—or invaders—who arrived. The frontier fort often included a trading post where white hunters and native Indians exchanged animal pelts for clothing, blankets, pots, kettles, powder and guns.

But in times of conflict such structures were vulnerable and many fell to attack. In 1729 the French Fort Rosalie fell to the Natchez Indian tribe; more than 200 men, women and children died, and many more were taken captive. The most effective storming of a frontier post by Indians was Fort Mims in 1813 when more than 400 soldiers and settlers were killed by Creek warriors bent on reclaiming native lands.

Better known, however, are the "massacres" that occurred near Fort William Henry in 1757 and Fort Phil Kearny in 1866. Both posts had brief lives, two years from first earth being turned to their wooden walls going up in flames.

The Fort William Henry Massacre occurred in New York during the French and Indian War. James Fenimore Cooper's famous novel *The Last of the Mohicans* portrayed the event and several movie adaptations have appeared over the decades. In violation of surrender terms, the British garrison was attacked by Indians allied to the French shortly after marching from the post. The British, understandably, were enraged. And so too were the French allies of the Indians who executed the assault.

But did these "civilized" European powers have the right to such self-righteous indignation? Were the British and French not capable of similar crimes?

A little over a hundred years later, Colonel Henry Carrington, commander of Fort Phil Kearny, Montana Territory, went through similar trials. A detachment of 80 men under the command of Captain William Fetterman was lured into a trap by Indians only five miles from the fort. The outcome is well known; not one white man survived to tell the tale. This too was called a "massacre," but such was not the case. In 1866 a state of war existed between the Powder River tribes and the United States. Chief Red Cloud had declared war at Fort Laramie seven months before. Unlike Fort William Henry, there had been no surrender or cease fire. The Indians had outfoxed the U.S. Army in a fair fight.

Captain Fetterman has been branded as an arrogant officer who underestimated the enemy and disobeyed orders. Historians in more recent times, however, have had a closer look. William Fetterman had, in fact, an excellent track record, which is at odds with the image that has emerged. But what about his second-in-command, Lieutenant George Grummond? He had a history of rash decisions and insubordination—and he commanded Fetterman's cavalry squad. Based on the trail of the dead and Indian testimony, it would appear that Grummond first disobeyed orders and led the "charge" over Lodge Trail Ridge.

Or did he?

There were others with Fetterman's command who were even less likely to be bound by military orders. The time has come for a still closer look.

Margaret, the wife of Colonel Carrington, and Frances, the widow of Lieutenant Grummond, both wrote books that blamed Fetterman for disobeying orders. It has been claimed that they unfairly set the stage for Fetterman to appear as an irresponsible glory-seeker in an attempt to absolve Colonel Carrington from blame. What orders did Fetterman actually receive? Were these women allowed to reshape history because the word of genteel ladies was taken as gospel in Victorian times?

This book examines the traumatic events at Fort William Henry and Fort Phil Kearny with a dispassionate eye, the people involved, and the results that flowed through the following decades.

Note: The spelling and grammar in quotations from the two periods involved are often incorrect, but so numerous that the customary "sic" has been excluded. The reader will understand.

1

Sabbath Day Point

July 23, 1757. Dawn broke over the oaks, maples and pines lining the rugged forest shore of Lake George, New York. With a splash of oars three whale boats set out from the leafy western bank. Those onboard peered warily to the south. A flotilla of small craft could just be discerned through the early morning mist. The approaching craft carried 360 British colonial troops well armed and ready for action—or so their commander Colonel John Parker thought. Through his telescope, Parker peered at the men in the three advance boats and recognized the blue coats of his men, the New Jersey provincials. All appeared to be going to plan. One day earlier, the flotilla had cast off from the British stronghold of Fort William Henry and were now moving towards the French Fort Carillon at the northern end of Lake George. Parker's "purpose was to test our advanced post and take prisoners," recalled Captain Louis Antoine de Bougainville of the French Army.[1] France and Britain were at war; vast tracts of North America were the prize.

Fearing ambush, Parker had dispatched the three advance boats before dawn to scout the waters and shoreline ahead. All appeared well as the occupants beckoned them on. Parker had previously passed safely through the island-studded "crooked and intricate channels"[2] of the narrows, the most likely place to be ambushed by the French and their numerous Indian allies.

Sabbath Day Point, a wooded promontory, appeared on their left. Suddenly a flash shook the foliage as a withering blast of gunfire erupted, musket balls smashing into British boats and men alike. Fifty birch bark canoes launched from the shore. The war-painted and howling warriors paddled furiously to cut Parker's boats off from retreat to the south. Parker yelled orders to return fire, but too soon. The blast of panicked musketry had little effect as the balls whizzed harmlessly over the warriors' heads through a cloud of mist and smoke.[3]

All discipline was lost as the undaunted warriors closed in. The British, terrified by their bloodcurdling yells, strained at the oars in an attempted to escape. But their clumsy boats, "high on the side and strongly built," could "not approach, by a great deal, the fleetness of a bark canoe; this glides—or, rather, it flies—over the water with the rapidity of an arrow," recalled Father Pierre Roubaud, a French priest watching from the shore. "Therefore the English were soon overtaken."[4]

Some boats made a dash for safety while men in other craft raised their arms in surrender, their flintlock muskets, with no time to reload, discarded. Seeing no mercy in their savage foes, some jumped overboard in an attempt to swim for shore. Captain Woodard, "terribly wounded," was one, and he drowned in the attempt.[5] Amidst the din and cries, "The Indians jumped into the water and speared them like fish," recalled Bougainville, "and also sinking the barges by seizing them from below and capsizing them…. The English,

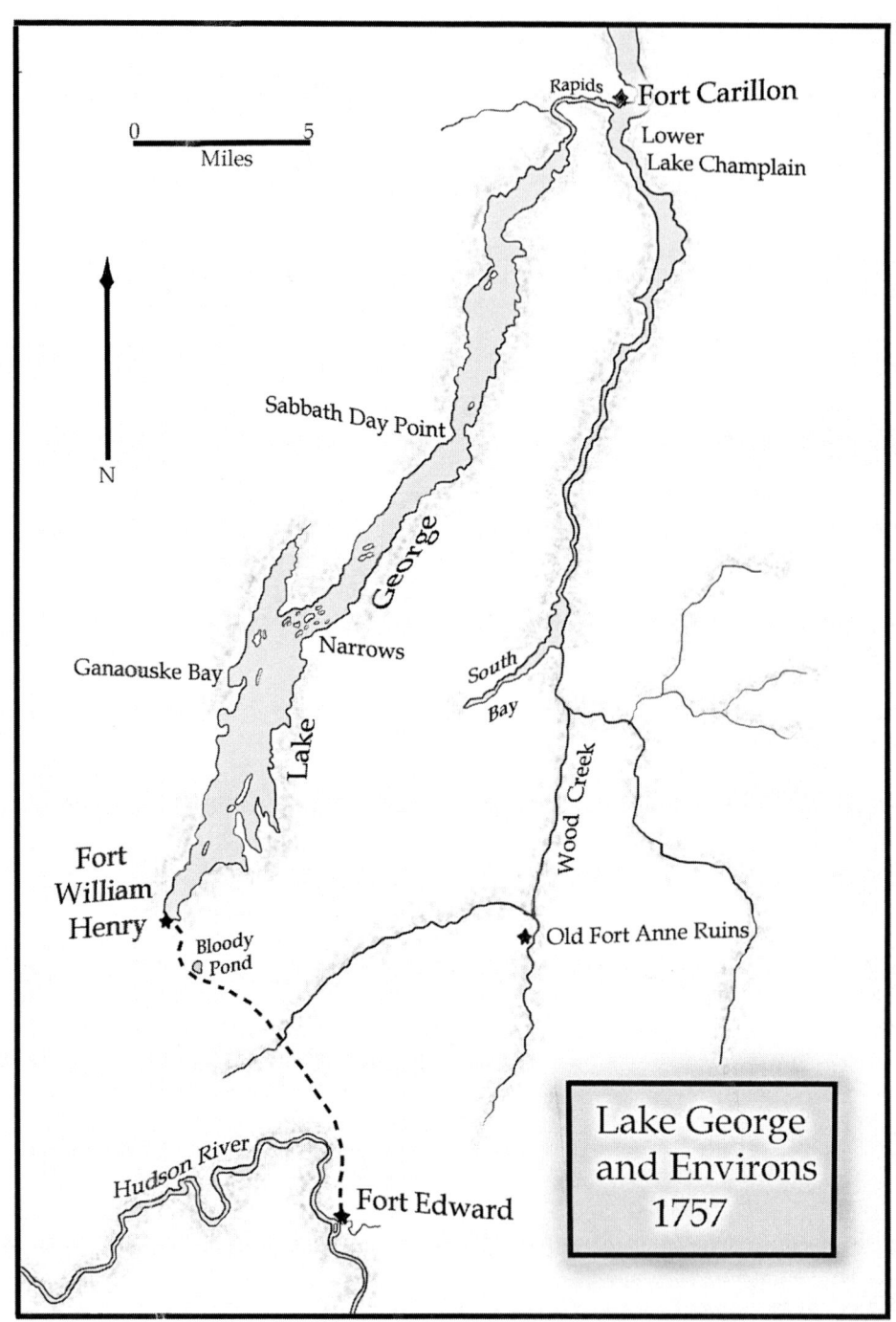

Map by the author.

terrified by the shooting, the sight, the cries, and the agility of these monsters, surrendered almost without firing a shot."[6]

Those swimmers who avoided either drowning and being speared staggered onto the hostile shore where most found little safety. "The woods are the element of the Savage, they run through them with the swiftness of a deer," recalled Roubaud.[7] The fugitives were cut down with war club and hatchet as they ran through the undergrowth and trees. Colonel Parker's boat and three others, however, managed to turn back before being overwhelmed. They made their way through the encircling Indian canoes, disappearing into the mist and safety with 80 men on board. One other boat manned by New York provincials followed and made it through, but Captain McGinnis' boat was spotted amidst the smoky haze. The Indians, having reloaded, opened fire with deadly effect. McGinnis, though wounded, was the only man to survive the volley.[8] Canoes pulled alongside and warriors clambered aboard to scalp the dead and take the officer prisoner.

Aboard some boats the victors were delighted to find an unexpected bonus: barrels of rum. What better way to celebrate their great victory over the despised English than get rip-roaring drunk? Many braves were intoxicated even before making it back to shore.

The savage attack on British troops by Indians at Sabbath Day Point was a prelude to later events at Fort William Henry (author's rendition).

The ambush had been executed by force of 450 French regulars, Canadian militia and Indians under Ensign de Corbiere. They had captured the three scout boats dispatched earlier, and the prisoners, under threat of torture, had revealed Parker's plans. Ottawa warriors wearing their uniforms had rowed out and lured the British craft to destruction.

Jesuit missionary Father Pierre Roubaud, 33, had been assigned to the Abenaki mission at St. François-de-Sales on the St. Lawrence River. He had arrived at Fort Carillon the day before with a party of Abenaki braves to join an army of 8,000 French and Canadian regulars, militia and Indians mustering for an assault on Fort William Henry. As the prisoners were brought in, Roubaud saw some who were "presented to me in a very wretched state, their eyes bathed in tears, their faces covered with perspiration and even with blood, and with ropes around their necks." Roubaud was pleased with an easy victory, their own casualties only four wounded, but was appalled with the captives' treatment.[9] "The rum with which their new masters were filled had excited their brains," he recalled, "and increased their natural ferocity. I feared each instant to see some prisoner, a victim to both cruelty and drunkenness, murdered before my eyes and falling dead at my feet; so that I hardly dared to raise my head, for fear of meeting the gaze of some one of these unfortunate victims. I was very soon compelled to be witness of a spectacle much more horrible than what I had hitherto seen." He returned to his tent amidst the Ottawas, a tribe from the distant Great Lakes region. They were not under the influence of French missionaries who had, in general, induced more merciful values among many Indians. The priest saw warriors about a large cooking pot and "the remains of an English body, more than half stripped of the skin and flesh. I perceived a moment after, these inhuman creatures eating, with a famished avidity, this human flesh; I saw them taking large spoonfuls of this detestable broth, without being able to satiate themselves.... The saddest thing was, that they had placed near them about ten Englishmen, to be spectators of their infamous repast." He attempted to intervene, but a young warrior replied, "Thou hast French taste; me Savage, this meat good for me." Roubaud offered no argument, but when offered a piece of "English roast ... you may easily imagine with what horror I rejected it."

Roubaud approached an aging Ottawa who held an English officer prisoner. He attempted to purchase his release, but the old warrior "was worst than a ferocious beast.... No, said he in a thundering and threatening tone,—well fitted to fill me with dread."[10]

Roubaud described the Indians as "savages adorned with every ornament most suited to disfigure them in European eyes, painted with vermillion, white green, yellow, and black made of soot and the scrapings of pots.... The head is shaved except at the top, where there is a small tuft, to which are fastened feathers, a few beads of wampum, or some such trinket.... Pendants hang from the nose and also from the ears ... a shirt bedaubed with vermillion, wampum collars, silver bracelets, a large knife hanging on the breast, moose-skin moccasins, and a belt of various colors always absurdly combined. The sachems (head chiefs) and war-chiefs are distinguished from the rest: the latter by a gorget, and the former by a medal, with the king's portrait on one side, and the other Mars and Bellona joining hands, with the advice, *Virtus et Honor*."[11]

The following morning, Louis-Joseph de Montcalm-Gozon, Marquis de St.-Veran, commander of the French army in North America, discussed the fate of the captives with his Indian allies. Many chiefs wanted the French to take the prisoners in exchange for a ransom. They had achieved what they came for—a great victory over the English, prisoners, scalps and plunder. It was now time to go home. Montcalm's aide-de-camp Bougainville recalled that they felt "it was tempting the Master of Life" to continue this warfare after such a "beautiful affair as they had just accomplished." But then some chiefs wished to take the prisoners north to the French colony of Montréal. "Finally," recalled Bougainville, "everybody wanted something, everyone came at the same time, everyone shouted at once."

As the debate continued the alcohol wore off and the Indians' temperament softened. "They made very touching visits to their prisoners," recalled Bougainville, "caressing them, taking them white bread, wishing to see they lacked nothing." Perhaps, however, they were merely preparing the fatted calf, as "just the same, they ate one of them up at this camp. It is impossible to stop them.... No moderation at all in these barbarians, either unheard of cruelties or the best treatment that they can think of."[12]

The uneasy bargaining went on. This was a trial for Montcalm, a European general used to a disciplined chain of command. But such was the reality of warfare in the American wilderness where the cooperation of Indians was considered essential. "Here, in the forests of America," Bougainville recalled, "we can do no more without them than without cavalry on the plain."

That afternoon the Indians finally agreed that Montcalm would take charge of the prisoners and send them to Montréal. Preparations were under way when, two hours later, the Indians had a change of heart. More haggling was required and at midnight the talk reconvened. After much discussion it was agreed that the prisoners would be taken to Montréal providing that the French would provide a written receipt for the captives and the Indians would be provided with bread and blankets by the governor of New France, Pierre François de Rigaud, Marquis

Top: French commander the Marquis de Montcalm found himself in conflict with the Canadian governor as well as the British. *Bottom:* Louis Antoine de Bougainville, Montcalm's faithful aid, would survive the war to become the first Frenchman to circumnavigate the globe (Library of Congress).

de Vaudreuil-Cavagnial. Those prisoners not sold or ransomed by the French by the end of the campaign against Fort William Henry would be returned to the Indians.

On July 26, badly wounded prisoners were taken to nearby Fort Carillon for treatment, while the remainder set out for Montréal. Montcalm held another council with the Indians to explain his plans for the campaign against Fort William Henry and what was expected of them. Suddenly the air was rent with the crack of snapping timber, then leaves and branches flew as a great tree crashed down amidst the nearby foliage. Montcalm pointed to the fallen tree. This was a great omen for the fall of Fort William Henry, he said. The Ottawa chief Pennahouel replied, "Father, I who of all the Indians have seen the most revolutions of Tibickigros (the moon) thank thee in the name of all the nations and in my own for the good words thou hast just given us. I approve them, and no one has ever spoken better to us than thou. It is the war Manitou which inspires thee."[13]

Twenty-five miles to the south, meanwhile, the sentries behind the earth and timber ramparts at Fort William Henry were surprised as a few ragged, exhausted survivors appeared from the woods. They told horrific stories of the savage attack, the numbers of warriors multiplying as the story was retold. "On the whole, only Parker and Ogden escaped with about 70 men, all the remainder, being about 280, are killed or taken," a volunteer wrote home. "What could the enemy be doing there? They certainly were on some great design, by being there in so large a body, as is judged 1000 men at least."[14]

Lieutenant Colonel George Monro, commanding Fort William Henry, now realized his post was under threat. But his commanding officer, General Daniel Webb, was at Fort Edward with more troops just 12 miles to the southeast. Monro put pen to paper with an urgent request. If substantial reinforcements were not received, the post may well fall to a determined French assault.

2

Disaster on the Monongahela

The first permanent English settlement on the North American continent, Jamestown, took root in 1607. During the following decades 13 separate British colonies were established from Nova Scotia in the north to Georgia in the south.

The French had their own imperial designs on the New World, and in 1608 Samuel de Champlain sailed up the St. Lawrence River to found the colony of Québec, the capitol of New France. Pushing further inland, his expedition began exploration of the Great Lakes region where they made contact with the Algonquin-speaking natives: the Fox, Ottawa, Nipissing, Miami, Potawatomi, Huron, Chippewa and Sauk tribes. To gain their support Champlain agreed to take part in a raid into the territory of the aggressive and dominant Iroquois confederation: the Mohawk, Oneida, Seneca, Onondaga and Cayuga tribes.[1] Throughout the previous century the Iroquois and Algonquin had raided each other to take booty, prisoners and scalps.

Champlain and his Algonquin allies encountered a raiding party of Iroquois. The enemy braves were astonished when the firearms of Champlain and his men came into play. Three Iroquois fell and the remainder were put to flight. As a result, an enduring alliance between the Algonquin and the French was established.[2] The following year a clash with Iroquois Mohawk saw firearms decide the fight once more, all the braves either killed or captured. Despite other Iroquois tribes forming alliances with the French in future, the Mohawk would consider them the enemy, come what may.

Despite these clashes, the French favored assimilation with the Indians and treating them as equals. As settlers arrived missions were established and many Algonquin, including the Abenaki tribe, were converted to the Roman Catholic faith. While the French government claimed vast tracts of territory, the colonists of Montréal and Québec were more interested in profiting from trade than pushing the Indians aside and taking their land. The English, on the other hand, under pressure from far more immigrants, pushed inland in a quest for territorial expansion, often leading to conflict with the native tribes.

The Dutch, meanwhile, had also arrived. In 1624 their settlements appeared along the Hudson River where they enjoyed a lucrative fur trade with the Indians of the Iroquois Confederacy. In 1664 the colony of Nieuw Amsterdam saw four English men-o'-war arrive. Outgunned, the Dutch authorities wasted little time in hoisting the white flag. Nieuw Amsterdam was renamed New York and Beverwijck renamed Albany as the English took control of the Dutch forts and villages. The Indians had come to rely on European trade goods, and Albany became the center where they exchanged beaver pelts for muskets, knives, tomahawks, kettles, pots and pans. As the Iroquois decimated the beaver in their own hunting grounds, they pushed into Algonquin territory, and villages of the Potawatomi, Huron and Nipissing tribes were destroyed during what became known as the Beaver Wars of 1638–1701. The colonists of New France inevitably came into conflict with the English and raids along the obscure and contested border were carried out by both French and English with Indian allies. A gruesome affair, small settlements went up in flames, the raiders returning with prisoners, booty and scalps.[3]

By the 1740s New France encompassed territory from Cape Breton Island in the north, southwest along the St. Lawrence River to the Great Lakes, then south along the Mississippi River to the Gulf of Mexico. The territory was divided into three separate colonies: Canada, Acadia, and Louisiana. Each had its own administration, although there was a governor-general for all in Québec. But there were only about 75,000 French in residence throughout this vast domain, while the 13 British colonies, occupying far less territory, supported a population of over one million.[4]

The War of Austrian Succession, 1740–48, saw fighting not only in Europe, but between French and British forces in North America. This included the capture of the French *Forteresse de Louisbourg* in Nova Scotia. The massive citadel was handed back at war's end in exchange for territory captured by France in Europe and India. The American colonists were infuriated at the loss, having captured the fortress with the support of the British Navy.

By the 1750s the French had begun building a series of forts as part of a chain of communication between Canada and Louisiana. The name Canada was derived from the Huron word "kanata" meaning "village" or "settlement."[5] But English outposts intruded on what the French considered their domain. On June 21, 1752, Charles de Langlade, of mixed French

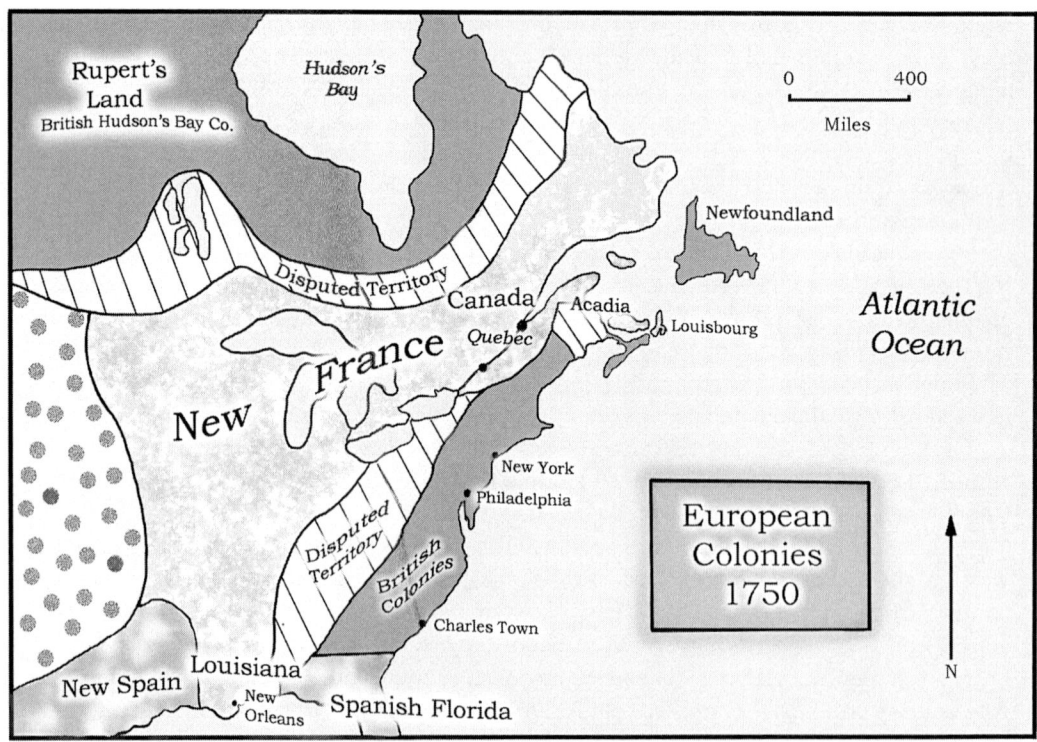

Map by the author.

A young George Washington helped ignite the French and Indian War, and a global conflict followed (Library of Congress).

and Ottawa blood, led a French backed Indian raid on the Miami village and British trading post at Pickawillany on the Great Miami River, a tributary of the Ohio. The stockade and post were burned to the ground and British fur traders scurried back east. The British had no intention, however, of relinquishing their claim to the Ohio River region. Both traders and military parties continued to probe to the west.

Thirty-five-year-old Canadian Ensign Joseph Coulon de Villiers de Jumonville was ordered to lead a force of 35 Canadian regular soldiers southwest into the disputed territory. He was to report any British movements back to Québec. On the morning of May 28, 1754, the Canadians were encamped in a secluded glen. A noise was heard from the wooded heights; they were not alone. As they scrambled for muskets, a shot echoed down the glen. Who fired that first shot, which would escalate into a global war, is not known.[6] What happened next is obscure, the details contradictory, but Virginian Private John Shaw later heard first-hand accounts. He stated that, following the first shot, 22-year-old Virginia militia officer George Washington "gave the Word for all his Men to fire. Several of them (the French) being killed, the rest betook themselves to flight, but our Indians having gone around the French ... they fled back to the English and delivered up their arms." An Indian chief, Tanaghrisson, allied to the British, "took his Tomahawk and split the head of the French Captain having first asked if he was an Englishman.... He then took his Brains and washed his Hands with them and then scalped him."[7] Washington would be accused by the French of having condoned this, which he would deny. Thirteen Canadians had been killed and 21 taken prisoner. Washington had lost only one killed and a few wounded.

One Canadian had escaped and reported news of the fight. Jumonville's brother, Louis Coulon de Villiers, was promptly ordered out from Montréal to re-establish French control. The expedition included Algonquin allies from the Huron, Abenaki and Nipissing tribes. Moving swiftly in a fleet of canoes they arrived at the French outpost of Fort Duquesne 12 days after Washington's attack.[8] Fort Duquesne had been built earlier the same year where the Allegheny and Monongahela Rivers join to form the Ohio. In Algonquin, "ohi:yo" meant "Good River." This had been used by Indians for thousands of years as a major trading and transportation route. A small British fort on the same site had been forced to surrender before being demolished and the stronger Fort Duquesne built.[9] The fortifications included trenches around massive log walls 12 feet high backed with earth and four corner bastions mounted with small cannon. Entrance to the barracks, guardhouse and other buildings was through a gate and drawbridge on the east wall. Outside were additional cabins where the forest had been cleared beyond musket range and food crops were grown.[10] Duquesne was one of a string of French forts, Machault, Le Boeuf and Presque Isle, that stretched north to Lake Erie. This strategic location would make the post a major objective in the savage struggle about to erupt.

Villiers set out from Duquesne and his men beat their way through woods dripping with constant rain. Two weeks later he reached the battle site to see the decomposing bodies of dead Canadians lying about. George Washington was only two miles away in a natural clearing called Great Meadows where his command had constructed a circular stockade protected by trenches. They had been hacking a road through the woods for following British troops. Washington knew the French would be out not only to reclaim the area for France, but also to seek revenge. "We may be attacked by a considerable force," he told his men.[11] Fort Necessity, as the crude structure was called, had been reinforced with troops from the Virginia Regiment since the gunfight in the glen. They brought with them nine small swivel guns which were mounted on the walls. Washington's Indian allies, refusing any further assistance, returned to their homes, but with the arrival of 100 fresh British regulars from South Carolina, he had about 300 men under his command.

On the cloudy morning of July 3 about 700 French and Indians appeared from the woods. Villiers was determined to drive the intruders out. An exchange of gunfire took place and the French fell back amidst the trees. Washington paraded his men in line,

2. Disaster on the Monongahela

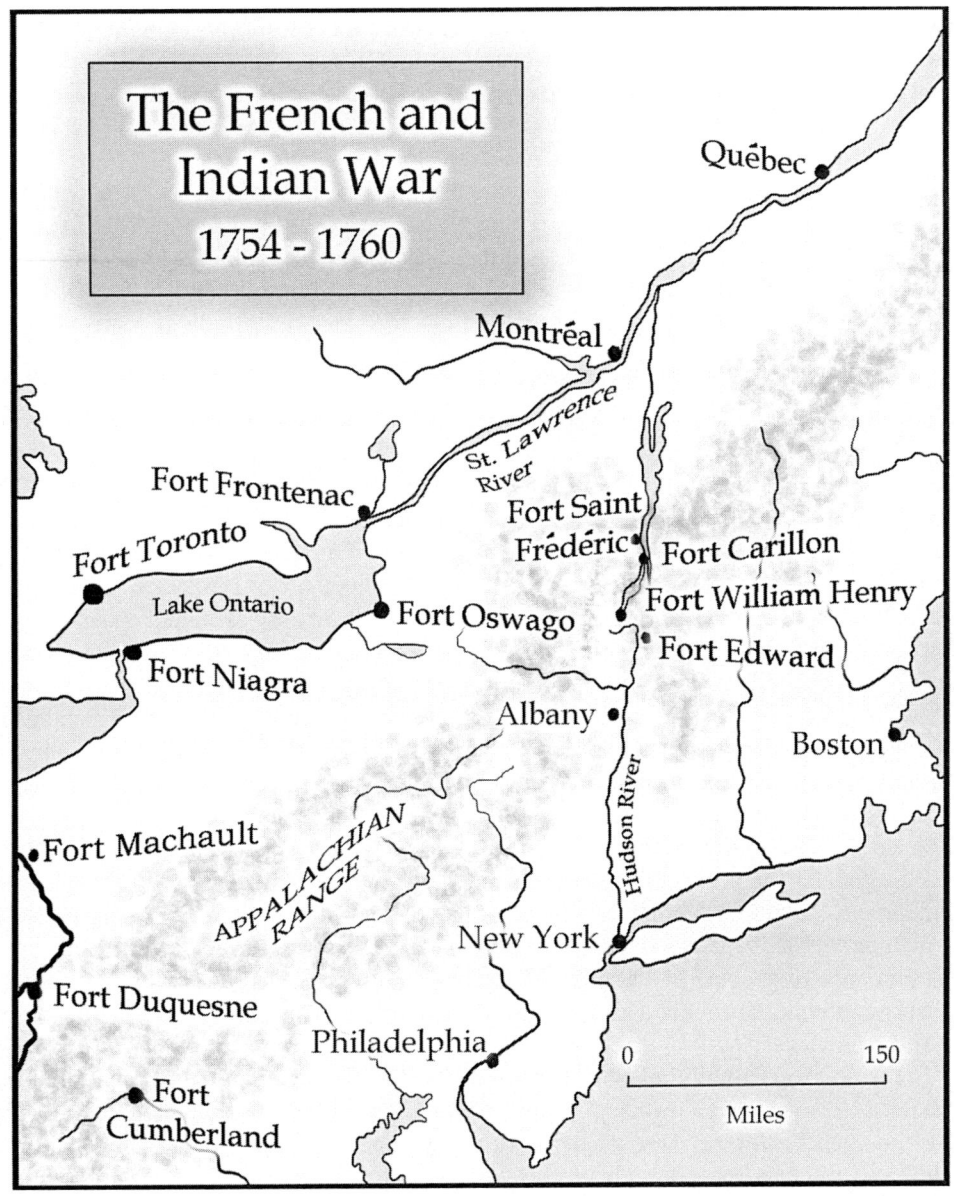

Map by the author.

preparing to charge, but Villiers promptly ordered his own attack. The French bolted from the woods and the Virginian militia promptly broke ranks, scrambling back into the fort and trenches. The 100 disciplined redcoats held their ground but, badly outnumbered, Washington ordered them to retreat. With the enemy now entrenched, Villiers ordered his men fall back into the hills overlooking the stockade. From the protection of the woods they poured musket fire into the British position and men dropped as 30 were killed and 70 wounded. "We continued this unequal fight," reported Washington, "with the Enemy sheltered behind the trees, ourselves without shelter in Trenches full of Water in a settled

Rain, and enemy galling us on all sides incessantly from the woods."[12] At eight o'clock that evening the French showed a flag of truce. Washington sent out two officers and a parley took place. Villiers said he would withdraw his assault if the British agreed to march back to home territory, keeping their arms, and his force would retire to Fort Duquesne. Feeling this upheld British honor, Washington accepted.

The following day the garrison marched out to the beat of drums, their flags held high. But more Indians arrived and, seeking plunder, looted their baggage which, to avoid bloodshed, the British did not resist. On June 17 the young officer handed his report of the melancholy affair to Lieutenant Governor Robert Dinwiddie in Williamsburg, then the capitol of Virginia. Although expecting a rebuke for what could only be seen as failure, Washington received instead a vote of thanks from the House of Burgesses. The failure was blamed on other colonies for lack of support.[13]

When news of the affair arrived in London, the British government decided to secure British interests in North America once and for all. Plans were drawn up, and Major General Edward Braddock was ordered to sail with the 44th and 48th Regiments of Foot. The general would be commander-in-chief in North America and, brimming with self confidence in appearance at least, he prepared to teach the colonials how to fight. Years later an officer who had served with him recalled, with the advantage of hindsight, "The general was, I think, a brave man and might probably have made a figure as a good officer in some European war. But he had too much self-confidence, too high an opinion of the validity of regular troops, and too mean a one of both Americans and Indians."[14]

The troop ships arrived at Hampton Roads, Virginia, during February 1855, and plans were drawn up for a four-pronged attack against the French. Braddock would lead one column himself. Having recently turned 60, he may well have seen this as a chance to round off his career with a glorious victory over England's foremost and traditional enemy. Dealing with the various colonial governors however, turned out to be a trial. He required local troops, vehicles and provisions which were not forthcoming as officials haggled over money and details. He did find an ally, however, in that luminary of his age, Benjamin Franklin. A member of the Pennsylvania Assembly, Franklin traveled around the countryside using his influence to procure 150 additional wagons for Braddock's use. The grateful general wrote that Franklin provided "almost the only instance of ability and honesty I have known in these provinces."[15]

Braddock eventually marshaled a force of 1,400 redcoats and 700 colonial militia at the most westerly British military outpost in North America: Fort Cumberland, Maryland. On the site of a former trading station on the upper Potomac River, colonial militia had hewn oaks and chestnuts from the surrounding forest to build a sturdy stockade of vertical logs protecting powder magazines and barracks. One officer described the fort as "situated within 200 yards of Will's Creek, on a hill, and about 400 from the Potomack; its length from east to west is about 200 yards, and breadth 46 yards, and is built by logs driven into the ground, and about 12 feet above it, with embrasures for 12 guns, and 10 mounted, 4 pounders, besides stocks for swivels, and loop holes for small arms."[16] Despite the hard work, Braddock was not impressed with the militia. "Their slothful and languid disposition," he wrote, "renders them very unfit for military service." The frustrated general assigned Ensign Allen to the task of drilling and "making them as much like soldiers as possible."

There was an attempt to enlist Indians to serve and about 50 warriors and their families arrived. They were objects of great curiosity to the English troops. "In the day," wrote one officer, "they are in our camp, and in the night they go into their own, where they dance and make the most horrible noise." Braddock attempted to impress the Indians with a military band and a feast was given in their honor. The general, however, could not conceal his contempt for the natives, and all but eight warriors departed. "He looked upon us as dogs," recalled one chief, "and would never hear anything that we said to him."[17]

On June 10, 1755, the ponderous expedition of troops, wagons, artillery and pack horses finally set out from Fort Cumberland. Three hundred leading axemen cut a swath through the wilderness of the Allegheny Mountains towards their target, Fort Duquesne. Scouts ranged through the woods on either side to guard against ambush, but their advance was carefully watched by furtive Indian allies of the French. Any careless straggler was killed and scalped. The departure of the militia left frontier settlements exposed and they were soon under Indian attack. About 30 settlers, mainly women and children, died by hatchet and knife, and others were taken prisoner to be borne away to remote Indian camps.

The column's tardy progress frustrated Braddock. Heavy wagons and guns were left to plod on behind under the command of Colonel Thomas Dunbar, while Braddock pressed ahead with about 1200 men, pack horses, 30 wagons and a few light cannon. But George Washington, a volunteer officer with the advance troops, was still displeased: "instead of pushing on with vigor without regarding a little rough road, they were halting to level every mole-hill, and to erect bridges over every brook, by which means we were four days in getting twelve miles."

Near Fort Duquesne, meanwhile, 18-year-old Pennsylvanian James Smith had been taken prisoner by Indians. He was forced to "run the gauntlet," clubbed by a row of warriors on either side. Surviving the ordeal, he was treated by French surgeons at the fort and, walking with the aid of a staff, began to recover. He heard news of an approaching British force and left his quarters to see "the Indians in a huddle before the gate, where were barrels of powder, bullets, flints &c. and everyone taking what suited; I saw the Indians also march off in rank—likewise the French Canadians, and some regulars.... I was then in high hopes that I would soon see them flying before the British troops, and that General Braddock would take the fort and rescue me."

On the morning of July 9 the advance guard of Braddock's forward column arrived at the Monongahela River. Only eight miles from Fort Duquesne, it was the ideal place for an ambush. Due to a loop in the river, the troops had to cross twice, but they splashed over under a cloudless blue sky without a shot being fired. Several mounted scouts led the way followed by a company of axemen protected by 300 redcoats under Lieutenant Colonel Thomas Gage. Behind them came more troops and gun crews with two brass six-pounders and caissons and then another 200 men. Marching not far behind was Braddock with the main body and more artillery, wagons, cattle, and pack horses. All crossed the river in safety.

At one o'clock the scouts suddenly fell back. An engineer marking out the path had seen a man dressed like an Indian warrior, but adorned with the gorget of a French officer, running towards them. Then, seeing the British force, the stranger suddenly stopped. He pulled off his hat and waved it. Behind him, hundreds of French, Canadians, Ottawas, Abenakis, Delawares, Caughnawagas and Potawatomis promptly dashed into the trees on either side. Muskets cracked and smoke billowed from the foliage and shadows as they opened fire on the axemen and their escort. The redcoats swung with parade ground precision into battle line, then, on Gage's order, a musket volley crashed out. Balls whined through the leaves and undergrowth hitting few men but, with the ear-splitting din, the volley took effect on the Canadian militia. As the redcoats fired a second time the militiamen turned and scrambled through undergrowth as they fled to the rear. Another volley erupted and musket balls ripped through the trees. Commander Captain Liénard de Beaujeu fell dead and Captain Jean-Daniel Dumas took command. The two British six-pounders came into play belching grapeshot towards the enemy ranks. The Indians, unused to artillery fire, scrambled for shelter, but did not run, and the French regulars held their ground. Dumas, stripped to the waist and fighting like an Indian, rallied his remaining men.[18] The redcoat line advanced, the troops shouting, "God save the King!" Dumas felt he was fighting a lost battle, but "I advanced with the assurance that comes from despair, exciting by voice and gesture the few soldiers that remained." His men rallied and "the fire of my platoon was so sharp that the enemy seemed astonished."

While Dumas and the French regulars held the front, the Indians spread out and moved through the trees along both flanks of the exposed British lines. The redcoats made fine targets against the shadowy green. Crouching behind fallen tree trunks and tangled foliage, the Indians shot back, then reloaded as they dashed from place to place, fleeting targets impossible to hit. The British received a withering fire from an unseen enemy, the discipline crumbling as both officers and men fell. "The Indians," recalled one officer, "kept an incessant fire on the Guns and killed the Men very fast. These Indians from their irregular method of fighting by running from one place to another obliged us to wheel from right to left, to Desert the Guns and then hastily to return and cover them."[19]

Braddock, some distance to the rear, could hear the battle raging and, leaving 400 men to guard the baggage train, advanced rapidly with the main body of troops. He saw with dismay his advance guard falling back, their two cannon abandoned, dead and wounded littering the road. The beaten, retreating troops clashed and mingled with Braddock's men, and the entire force came under fire as gunsmoke belched from the surrounding hills. Bloodcurdling war whoops echoed through the trees as the Virginian militia took cover and returned fire from behind logs and bushes. This held the French and Indians at bay till some semblance of order was restored in the British ranks. But Braddock was furious with such tactics. He considered firing from cover cowardly behavior. Eighty Virginians in advance, obscured by gunsmoke while shooting from behind a fallen tree trunk, were mistaken for Indians and fired on from behind, the survivors forced to fall back. As bullets rained down, some soldiers attempted to take cover, but Braddock beat at them with the flat of his sword cursing them as cowards until they stood once more on open ground. "On the right," recalled one British officer, the enemy "had possession of a hill, which we could never get possession of, though our Officers made many attempts to do it: but if the Officers dropped, which was generally the case, or that the enemy gave a platoon of ours advancing up the hill a smart fire, they immediately retreated back down again … it struck a panic through our men to see numbers daily falling by them, and even their comrades scalped in their sight."[20]

More British cannon swing into action and boomed with little effect. Terrified redcoats hastily reloaded and shot without aim, often hitting comrades milling about amidst the confusion and smoke. Frightened and wounded horses thrashed about. Braddock's horse went down, one of four to be shot from under him during the battle.

"The yell of the Indians is fresh in my ear, and the terrific sound will haunt me until the hour of my dissolution," recalled Captain Leslie. "I cannot describe the horrors of that scene. No pencil could do it, or no painter delineate it so as to convey to you with accuracy our unhappy situation."[21] Rather than order a retreat to regroup, Braddock rode about demanding the troops stand and fight. Captain Robert Orme, badly wounded, recalled, "The officers were absolutely sacrificed by their unparalleled good behaviour, advancing before the men sometimes in bodies, and sometimes separately, hoping by such example to engage the soldiers to follow them; but to no purpose.... Poor Shirley (Braddock's secretary) was shot through the head, Captain Morris was very much wounded. Mr. Washington had two horses shot under him, and his clothes shot through in several places; behaving the whole time with the greatest courage and resolution."[22]

Finally Braddock realized the situation could not be saved. With a heavy heart he ordered the retreat. Bugles blared and drums rattled as the embattled troops began to fall back. Then, as a final blow, the general dropped from his horse, a musket ball through one arm and into his lungs. Gasping for breath, he asked to be left where he lay, but was borne to the rear by two officers. With Braddock down the rout set in as panic-stricken soldiers bolted for safety, all semblance of order lost, "artillery, ammunition, provisions and baggage" all left behind. "Despite all the efforts of the officers to the contrary," recalled Washington, "they ran as sheep pursued by dogs, and it was impossible to rally them."[23] Of 86 officers in the battle, 63 were killed or wounded. Of the 1,373 enlisted men, only 459 escaped unhurt.

Stragglers were pursued and cut down by the fleet-footed warriors as they crossed the Monongahela. Prisoners were taken but others escaped as the Indians paused to scalp and loot the dead. They wasted no time in sampling barrels of rum among the debris strewn about. The gasping Braddock, meanwhile, ordered Washington to ride for Colonel Dunbar's column to arrange stores and hospital supplies for survivors who could make it back.

That night the fleeing troops did not dare stop, fear of howling Indians urging them on. But the victorious enemy, content with their day's work, made no pursuit. The following morning Braddock attempted to ride, but was soon moved to a litter, the carriers bribed by Captain Orme with the promise of a guinea and bottle of rum each.

At noon the first fugitives straggled in Dunbar's camp and then a wounded officer was carried in on a sheet. The news of defeat at the hands of howling, scalping savages spread like wildfire and, thinking the horde close behind, many soldiers and teamsters took to their heels rather than answer the drum roll to arms. The following day the ailing Braddock arrived along with the limping, demoralized remnants of his army. With retreat the only thing in mind, orders were issued for the destruction of all wagons and stores that could not be easily moved back to Fort Cumberland. Black smoke billowed into the summer sky as over 100 wagons went up in flames, the ground shaking to the concussion of exploding shells. Gunpowder barrels were smashed open, their contents thrown into a stream, and provisions were dumped amidst the thickets and trees.

Captain Orme, though wounded himself, had stayed with the ailing Braddock through the retreat. The lethal bullet was deep in the general's lungs and the surgeons could do nothing to help. "Who would have thought it?" Braddock muttered, images of the chaos pervading his mind. The following day, Sunday, July 13, "we shall know how to deal with them another time," he murmured. At 8 o'clock that evening he took his last breath, his name forever linked with inglorious defeat. The following day Dunbar ordered Braddock buried in the roadway. All signs of the grave were obliterated by passing men, horses and wagons to avoid his body being dug up and scalped.

This melancholy scene was a sharp contrast to the proceedings at Fort Duquesne. Behind the timber walls, and in the surrounding camps, the celebrations continued on.

American captive James Smith had heard "great noise and commotion in the fort, and, though at that time I could not understand French, I found it was the voice of joy and triumph." The victors had returned to the fort and "I observed that they had a great many bloody scalps, grenadiers' caps, British canteens, bayonets, &c. with them.... Those that were coming in, and those that had arrived, kept a constant firing of small arms, and also the great guns in the fort, which were accompanied with the most hideous shouts and yells from all quarters; so it appeared to me as if the infernal regions had broken loose.... About sundown I beheld a small party coming in with about a dozen prisoners, stripped naked, with their hands tied behind their backs ... these prisoners they burned to death on the banks of the Allegheny River opposite the fort ... the Indians in the mean time yelling like infernal spirits. As this scene appeared too shocking for me to behold, I retired to my lodging both sore and sorry."[24]

British pride was also sore and sorry after this debacle. Governor Dinwiddie chose not to believe such bad tidings when they first arrived. "I am willing to think that account was from a deserter who, in a great panic, represented what his fears suggested," he wrote to Lord Halifax. "I wait with impatience for another express from Fort Cumberland which I expect will greatly contradict the former." As he penned these words Fort Cumberland was being turned into a hospital for the droves of wounded. Dinwiddie finally excepted the horrible truth when letters from Captain Orme and George Washington arrived. He read Orme's letter with "tears in my eyes," but from Washington's letter he learned more alarming news: Colonel Dunbar was intending to continue his retreat all the way to Philadelphia, abandoning the frontier. Dinwiddie wrote to Dunbar at Fort Cumberland, "Dear Colonel, is there no method left to retrieve the dishonor done to British arms? As you now command all the forces that remain, are you not able, after a proper refreshment of your men, to make a second attempt? You have four months now to make of the best weather of the year for such an expedition. What a fine field of honor will Colonel Dunbar have to confirm and establish his character as a brave officer." Dunbar's response was to march for Philadelphia, the opposite direction to Fort Duquesne. He left a handful of Virginian militia and the wounded to defend Fort Cumberland should the French advance along the road Braddock had cut for their use. "The whole conduct of Colonel Dunbar appears to me monstrous," Dinwiddie wrote to Orme, "To march off all the regulars and leave the fort and frontiers to be defended by four hundred sick and wounded, and the poor remains of our provincial forces, appears to me absurd."

But the French did not have the troops on hand for an all-out invasion as feared. Canadian and Indian war parties, however, made use of Braddock's road to make raids on settlements in the Susquehanna Valley, Pennsylvania, during the fall of 1755. They burned homes and barns, killed civilians, slaughtered livestock and took prisoners. Two Frenchmen with a war party of Delawares and Shawnees raided Great Cove, and Sheriff Potter later testified that "twenty-seven plantations were burnt and a great quantity of cattle killed; that a woman ninety-three years of age was found lying killed, with her breast torn off and a stake run through her body; that of ninety-three families which were settled in the two coves and the Conolloways, forty-seven were either killed or taken and the rest deserted."[25] One settler, Charles Stuart, was taken during this raid, but spared because of his previous kind treatment of Indians. After his release in a prisoner exchange he told of a speech given by Delaware King Shingas, who claimed that he regretted going to war against the English, but when they had approached Braddock for a guarantee of Indian lands if they fought alongside him, he "said that no Savage should Inherit the Land." Despite this, the Delawares had remained neutral until after Braddock's defeat when the French threatened to "cut them off. On which the Indians joined the French for their own safety."[26]

With Braddock's death Governor William Shirley of Massachusetts became commander in chief of British forces in North America. He ordered Colonel Dunbar to resume offensive operations, but should this be impractical, he was to march his troops to Albany and join the expedition against Fort Niagara on Lake Ontario. Dunbar eventually marched north at a snail's pace that ensured his troops would be of no use in the Niagara campaign. It would seem that fighting savages in the American wilderness was not to the colonel's taste.

The French and Indian War had begun badly for the British. But another less significant action had occurred far to the northeast in Nova Scotia. A British force under Lieutenant Colonel Robert Monckton had marched on Fort Beausejour, a strategic post controlling the Isthmus of Chignecto, the only passage between the fortress of Louisbourg and Québec during the icy winter months. As Braddock marched towards destruction on June 16, the French commander at Beausejour had run up the white flag after a two week siege. A British shell killing six officers and one prisoner in a "bomb-proof" shelter had been the last straw.[27] Although this small victory did little to offset the Braddock disaster, it was a glimmer of light for the British and a portent of things to come.

3

Revenge at Lake George

News of Braddock's expedition sailing for North America had sent a wave of apprehension through the French government in Paris. Possession of the Ohio valley region had been the previous concern, but the dispatch of British regulars meant the whole of New France was now under threat. As Braddock marched towards Fort Duquesne, two regular French battalions came ashore from troop ships at Louisbourg, and soon after another four battalions debarked at Québec.[1] Not all had arrived, however, eight companies having been captured in a troop ship by the British on the high seas. Those that did arrive were under the command of General Baron Jean-Armand Dieskau, formerly the military governor at Brest, the chief French naval base on the Atlantic.[2] Dieskau would have to cooperate with the Canadian militia who his second-in-command, Pierre-Andre Gophin, Comte de Montreuil, described as "independent, wicked, lying" braggarts who were "well adapted for skirmishing, very brave behind a tree and very timid when not covered."[3] But the militia were necessary to make up for a shortage of regular troops, both French and Canadian. They provided their own weapons and clothing and received government provisions and munitions when on campaign.

But even with these militia and Indian allies Dieskau's troops would not be able to defend the whole frontier, thus the territory between Lake Ontario and the coast became the prime concern. British control of this strategic region could thwart communications between Québec and French territory to the southwest and the city itself could come under threat.[4]

On the upper Hudson River, about 50 miles north of Albany, was what the Mohawk called the "Great Carrying Place." From this point on rapids made the river unnavigable, thus it was strategically important as the overland crossing between the Hudson River and South Bay, the lower section of Lake Champlain. With the exception of the Great Carrying Place, travel was possible by water all the way between New York in the south and Montréal in the north (a canal would be opened in 1819). Lac du St. Sacrement (Lake George) was closer, but her waters to the north descended through the turbulent rapids of the La Chute River before flowing into Lake Champlain. In 1709 the British had built Fort Nicholson, a basic wooden stockade, at the Great Carrying Place, but it had been abandoned in 1713 at the conclusion of Queen Anne's War. Two decades later a Dutch trader and smuggler, John Henry Lydias, built a trading post called Fort Lydias on the site. Profiting from the passage of contraband between Albany and Montréal, Lydias was a colorful but dubious character, being called "an English agent by the French, a forked-tongued serpent by the Indians, a traitor by provincial authorities, and a swindler by embarrassed title holders from several colonies…. The subject of frequent romanticized and antiquarian profiles during the two centuries that followed."[5] Fort Lydias prospered until it went up in flames at the hands of

French and Indian raiders in 1745, but the smuggler was residing in Albany at the time and lived on to die in England in 1791 at the ripe old age of 87.

As part of the new British offensive, Connecticut-born General Phineas Lyman ordered the construction of a new fort on the site. During mid–1755 British engineer Captain William Eyre commenced construction of a substantial post which would have timber and earth walls with ditches protecting three sides, while the fourth was considered impregnable, protected by two bastions hard against the waters of the Hudson River. A V-shaped ravelin protruded from the north wall and two other bastions provided cross fire along the base of walls enclosing a parade ground, twin double-story barracks, guardhouse, blacksmith's shop, and officers' quarters. The powder magazine lay within one bastion to supply the 35 guns mounted on the walls. The adjacent island became the training camp for provincials and the famed rangers led by Robert Rogers.

Fort Lyman (later Fort Edward) quickly became a hub of activity for redcoats, provincial troops, civilian employees, and women who provided services other than washing and cooking. General Lyman heartily disapproved of such unseemly activities, feeling they would lead to the "sacrifice of all our character."[6]

But an even bigger threat to British character was Fort St. Frédéric. Built at Crown Point on the western banks of Lake Champlain, the formidable stronghold lay about 60 miles to the north. Constructed by the French in 1734, it was their southern-most military post on the New York to Montréal corridor. Colonel William Johnson had been appointed as a major general by Braddock and tasked with St. Frédéric's capture as part of the British offensive of 1755. Johnson had moved to the New World from his native Ireland in 1738 to manage the estate of his uncle, Vice-Admiral Sir Peter Warren, and acquired his own large land holdings while prospering through a variety of business ventures. Johnson also had the foresight to befriend the native Mohawk. He welcomed them into his home, learned their language, spoke on their behalf, and in 1755 became agent to the Mohawk and the Iroquois Confederacy.[7]

Moving from Fort Lyman on August 26, Johnson marched with 1,500 provincial troops and 40 Mohawk towards what the French called Lac du St. Sacrement. Phineas Lyman rode as second-in-command. Lieutenant Colonel Seth Pomeroy, one of the best gunsmiths in Massachusetts, wrote to a friend requesting he pray that "the Lord God of Hosts would go forth with us and give us victory over our unreasonable, encroaching, barbarous enemies."[8]

Cutting a wagon track through the woods, they arrived two days later at the lake's southern end in what Johnson described as "all thick wood, not a foot of land cleared." Lac du St. Sacrement was renamed Lake George "not only to honour his Majesty but to ascertain his Dominion here."[9] The Lake was one to three miles wide and about 32 miles long. The French held the northern end. Johnson's immediate task was to build a fort. Most officers wanted only a simple stockade to be garrisoned by about 100 men as a base for operations against Fort St. Frédéric, but Johnson seemed in no hurry to proceed. He wanted a stronger post that could resist French artillery if the need arose. Orders were issued and the men went to work. As axes swung and trees fell, an additional 200 warriors arrived with Johnson's ally, Mohawk King Hendrick.

A British fort on Lake George was a British threat. Baron Dieskau marched from Montréal with 3,000 French reinforcements for Fort St. Frédéric. With him were 700 Indians, 300 of them Iroquois. New of Braddock's defeat had caused a split among the Iroquois Confederation. While the Mohawk remained loyal to the British, many others now marched with their old enemies, the Algonquin, to the beat of a French drum.

William Johnson influenced the Mohawk to fight for the British and gained glory by beating the French at the Battle of Lake George (Wikimedia Commons).

Even before Braddock's defeat the Iroquois had found themselves in a perplexing situation. "We don't know what you Christians, English and French, intend," said one chief at a meeting in New York. "We are so hemmed in by you both that we hardly have a hunting place left. In a little while, if we find a bear in a tree, there will immediately appear an owner of the land to claim the property and hinder us from killing it, by which we live. We are so perplexed between you that we hardly know what to say or think."[10]

Once at Fort St. Frédéric, however, Dieskau was not happy with any Indian, regardless of tribe. He accused them of "mischievous intrigues" and the Algonquin "were spoiled by the Iroquois.... Never was I able to obtain from them a faithful scout; at one time they refused to make any; at another time, seeming to obey me, they set forth, but when a few leagues from the camp, they sent back the Frenchmen I had associated with them, and returned in a few days without bringing me any intelligence."[11]

On September 3 Johnson ordered up more men and guns from Fort Lyman, still under construction under Colonel Joseph Blanchard of the New Hampshire Regiment.[12] Dieskau learned from scouts that Fort Lyman now held a garrison of only 500 men encamped outside the walls, the barracks not complete. He planned to march south with part of his force. "My detachment was composed of 600 Indians, 600 Canadians and 200 regulars belonging to the La Reine and Languedec Regiments," he recalled.[13] The expedition traveled by boat down Lake Champlain before disembarking at South Bay. They trekked on foot across the Great Carrying Place towards Fort Lyman, but when only three miles away, his Indians scouts took a wrong path. An enemy dispatch and two British deserters were captured, however, and from them Dieskau learned that Johnson had about 3,000 men in his unfortified camp on Lake George. That night Dieskau held a council of war with his Indian allies and gave them a choice: to attack Fort Lyman or Johnson's camp. They chose the camp.

Johnson, meanwhile, "received Intelligence from some Indian scouts, I had sent out, that they had discovered three large roads about the South Bay, and were Confident a very Considerable number of the enemy were Marched or on their March Towards our encampment at the Carrying Place."[14] But where exactly would they strike? On the morning of September 8 Johnson announced a plan to divide his force. Five hundred men would march to South Bay to secure the French boats and another 500 would reinforce Fort Lyman. With a shake of his head, King Hendrick held up a bundle of sticks. He snapped one, then showed Johnson how, held together, the bundle would not break. A force unified was far stronger than one divided (a similar story is told in Aesop's Fables and also about Genghis Khan and a bundle of arrows). If such a plan were to proceed, the chief would withdraw his Mohawk. Johnson saw the wisdom of Hendrick's words and ordered the two forces to be combined under the command of Colonel Ephraim Williams. A thousand men would march for Fort Lyman. The Mohawk went with them, but Hendrick was still not happy. "If they are to be killed," he said, "they are too many. If they are to fight, they are too few."[15]

Williams' detachment, however, marched out a little after 8 a.m. Assuming there would be no danger till nearing Fort Lyman, no flanking scouts were deployed as a precaution against ambush. The column quickly became fragmented and two miles on they halted to regroup near a large pond. But "the scouts reported to me that they had seen a large body of troops on their way to the fort," recalled Dieskau. "I immediately made my arrangements, ordered the Indians to throw themselves into the woods, to allow the enemy to pass, so as to attack them in the rear, while the Canadians took them in the flank, and I should wait for them in front with the regular troops."[16]

The oblivious British column, with King Hedrick and his Mohawk in the lead, moved into a steep sided ravine. The scene was set for their annihilation. But "this was the moment of treachery," Dieskau claimed. "The Iroquois, who were on the left, showed themselves before the time and did not fire. The Abenakis, who occupied the right, seeing themselves discovered, alone with a few Canadians attacked the enemy in front and put them to flight." It is possible that the Iroquois were thwarted by difficult, steep terrain, and Johnson later stated that a gun had accidentally discharged. But regardless of what transpired, at least one side of the ravine erupted in fire and smoke and the British column was hit with a fusillade of musket balls. The Mohawk rapidly retreated on foot, losing 40 braves along the way, and Hendrick had his horse shot from under him. At 63 he was unable to outrun his younger pursuers and, stabbed in the back, was killed and scalped. And Colonel Williams, attempting to rally his men, also fell, a ball through his head. Men dropped amidst an ear-splitting crescendo that echoed amidst the rocky, smoke shrouded slopes as bullets rained down, and seven other officers also died. The regular French infantry moved swiftly forward to join the assault and the British fell back, but some were rallied by Colonel Nathan Whiting and conducted a fighting retreat.

The troops at Lake George "heard a heavy firing, and all the Marks of a Warm Engagement, which we Judged was about 3 or 4 Miles from us," recalled Johnson. "We beat to arms, and got our men in all readiness; the fire Approached nearer, upon which I judged our People were Retreating."[17] Johnson ordered Lieutenant Colonel Cole out with 300 men to support the beleaguered detachment. As they marched, wagons were rolled into position around the camp, until now only protected by a fragmented walls of knee-high logs. Before long dozens of frightened men, some with bloody wounds, straggled back into camp. It looked as though another Braddock's defeat was in the air. A wave of anguish swept through the camp and many hastily grabbed their belongings, preparing to bolt. But Johnson and other officers drew their swords and, with a threat to impale any who ran, order was restored. Cannon were wheeled into place and boats were dragged from Lake George to be overturned along the line of defense. Then the scurrying, fighting rear guard appeared, the enemy close behind. The survivors scrambled over the improvised breastworks and back into camp.

At about 11:30 "the Enemy appeared in sight, And Marched along the road in very regular order, directly upon our Center," recalled Johnson. The regulars "with bright and fix't Bayonets made the Center Attack; The Canadians and Indians Squatted, and Dispersed on our Flancks."[18] But according to Dieskau, "the Iroquois collected on a hill, unwilling to advance. Some of them even wanted the Abernakis to release three Mohawks whom they had captured." It would appear that many of Dieskau's Indian allies were reluctant to fight the Mohawk, fellow Iroquois. "The Abernakis," continued Dieskau, "seeing the Iroquois immovable, halted also, and the Canadians, seeing the retreat of one and the other, were thereby intimidated."[19] While some may have tarried, Canadian and Indians did move forward on the flanks, taking cover behind logs and scrub, while the regulars, Braddock style, marched in the center towards the fortified camp. Braddock had only faced musket fire, but now British artillery opened up, lethal grapeshot and canister hitting the French ranks. The disciplined soldiers, however, held their ground, firing volleys. "To give them due credit they fought like brave fellows," recalled medic Thomas Williams, "disputing every inch of ground, in the whole time of which there seemed to be nothing but thunder 'lightning' (and) perpetual pillars of smoke."[20] The gunsmith Colonel Seth Pomeroy and other officers had to keep a tight reign on their men, urging them to return fire and not keep under cover. "The hailstones of heaven have not been much thicker than their bullets come," he recalled.[21] One of the hailstones found its mark when Johnson was hit in the buttock. While he sought medical aid, General Lyman took command. In an attempt to get a better shot Colonel Moses Titcomb and Lieutenant Barron dashed from behind the breastworks and fired from behind a large tree about six yards to their front. But if they had hoped to set an example to the men, it went terribly wrong when both were shot dead.

The British artillery took its toll on the Canadians and Indians to the left of the enemy line. Many, dodging grapeshot, shells and bullets, moved across to join those fighting on the right. As Dieskau also moved across a ball tore into his leg. His second-in-command, Montreuil, also wounded in the arm, attempted to help move him to cover, but the fallen commander refused to budge. Another ball smashed through Dieskau's right knee and into his left thigh.[22] Montreuil ordered two Canadians to move him to safety, but one of them fell, hit by a musket ball. Dieskau, now with his back to a tree, refused to be moved once more. The regulars had fallen back and he urged Montreuil to leave him and inspire them to renew their attack. Then Montreuil's cartridge box was shattered by a musket ball. He left Dieskau as ordered, but once again instructed two men to remove him.

By now, the British could see the tide of battle had turned their way. As the French fire slackened, the defenders began to cross the breastworks, reloading and firing as they slowly advanced, moving to cut off the enemy's retreat to their boats on South Cove. Those French regulars still in the fight, with Indian support, opened up a heavy fire that drove them back. But Canadian militia and Indians, feeling the day lost, had been leaving the field to collect scalps and plunder from the dead of Williams' detachment, ambushed earlier that day. By the time Montreuil reached the French regulars, they had formed ranks to join the retreat.

Late that afternoon about 300 dispirited Indians and Canadians rested around the pond where Williams' command had paused earlier that day. Suddenly the adjacent woods erupted with gunfire. A morning patrol had heard gunfire from the "Bloody Morning Scout" and 200 reinforcements had marched from Fort Lyman. The ambush was brief. "Our brave party fought nobly, put the enemy to flight, and made a considerable slaughter," stated the British report.[23] Many of the dead were thrown into the pond, their blood spreading till the water was quite red, thus arose the story of the "Bloody Pond."

Back at Lake George, as the victorious British moved across the battlefield, one man saw a desolate and wounded figure leaning against a tree. The soldier raised his musket and took aim. The wounded and bleeding Dieskau signaled not to fire, but the trigger was pulled. A ball ripped through the French commander's hips from one side to the other, perforating his bladder. The soldier, a Frenchman fighting on the British side, demanded Dieskau's surrender. The agonized general looked into the man's eyes. "You rascal, why did you fire? You see a man lying in his blood on the ground and you shoot him?" The man stared at him. "How did I know that you had not got a pistol? I had rather kill the devil than have the devil kill me."

Dieskau was carried by several men to General Johnson's tent. "On learning who I was, he sent for surgeons," recalled Dieskau, "and, though wounded himself, refused all assistance till my wounds were dressed."[24] But the Mohawk had lost King Hendrick and many others, and an angry dispute took place with Johnson in the native tongue. The Indians glared with hatred at Dieskau, then moved angrily outside. The Frenchman asked what they wanted. "To burn you, to eat you, and smoke you in their pipes," Johnson replied, "but never fear; you shall be safe with me or they shall kill us both." Dieskau was removed to another tent with a guard of 50 soldiers, but even there one determined Mohawk was seized with a sword concealed beneath his robe.

The surviving French made it back to their boats at South Bay. Montreuil reported French losses as 98 killed and 124 wounded, mostly regulars. Johnson had won the day, but reported 160 killed, 103 wounded and 67 missing. Most British casualties had occurred during the Bloody Morning Scout.[25] Dieskau was sent on a litter to Fort Lyman and eventually sailed to England where he remained until the conclusion of the Seven Years' War in 1763.[26] Never fully recovering from his wounds, he died in 1767.

William Johnson was hailed as a hero for the victory. He received a baronetcy from King George II and 5,000 pounds—all of which became a bone of contention. The British thrust against Fort St. Frédéric had, in fact, been halted, and who had actually commanded during the battle? Some said Phineas Lyman, who had taken command after Johnson was wounded. But he received no mention in Johnson's report, and the following year Johnson changed the name of Fort Lyman to Fort Edward in honor of the king's grandson.

4

The French Strike Back

Johnson had sent the French back north, severely damaged, but he expected "a More Formidable Attack. And that the enemy will then come with Artilliry." And that was not his only concern; his wound was described as "very Painfull, the ball is lodged and cannot be got out." Perhaps Lyman took comfort in the fact that Johnson carried the musket ball for the rest of his life.

Although the French had been repulsed, their Indian scouts still lurked in the woods and would take a scalp if possible. Johnson felt his "men are so harras'd, And Obliged to be so Constantly on Watchfull Duty, That I think it wou'd be both Unreasonable, and, I fear in Vain, to set them at Work upon the Design'd Fort." He ordered up the New Hampshire regiment as reinforcements. "When these fresh Troops arrive I shall Immediately set About Building a Fort."[1] Johnson was determined to build a strong post—despite continued opposition from those who felt a basic stockade to protect stores would do the job. Fort St. Frédéric was the target, was it not?

To add to Johnson's problems, his Mohawk allies, with victory, booty and scalps in hand, felt their job was done. They moved off to rejoin their squaws and papooses waiting at home. Johnson's refusal to hand Dieskau over to their tender mercies probably helped them along the way.

The reinforcements arrived and more trees fell. But fort building was not relished by colonial troops who wanted to fight. They were part-time soldiers, mostly farmers who had grasped their trusty flintlock from above the hearth to do battle with the French. These guns were not designed to carry bayonets as were the muskets of regular troops, but they carried hunting knives and hatchets in their belts. Their homes were rustic, unpainted homesteads with large barns surrounded by fields of corn, pumpkin and other crops.[2] The need to harvest the basic essentials sometimes clashed with military service and, as with the French, some officers had little time for the militia they led. "We are a wicked, profane army, more especially New York troops & Rhode Island, nothing to be heard among a great part of them but the language of Hell," Colonel Williams had written before being killed in the Bloody Morning Scout. "I assure you Sir that if ever the place is taken it will not be for our sakes but for those good people left behind."[3] But perhaps the rustic militiamen had other qualities. Private William Smith, camped near Albany, recalled that basically they were an honest lot. "Not a chicken has been stolen," he wrote. Other problems arose, however. One man was given 100 lashes and imprisoned till the campaign's conclusion for "Profane Swaring & a Sodomittical atempt."[4]

Governor William Shirley of Massachusetts, commander-in-chief since Braddock's death, questioned the delays and the location of the new fort. Had not Dieskau threatened British territory via South Bay on Lake Champlain?[5] A fort at the southern end of Lake

George did not directly impede this line of attack. Then news arrived of the French building their own stronghold at the northern end of Lake George. On a rocky outcrop called Ticonderoga by the Mohawk, Fort Carillon overlooked the junction of Lake George and Lake Champlain through the rapid-strewn La Chute River. The British would have to reduce this new threat before any assault on Fort St. Frédéric could be made. Johnson needed reinforcements, supplies, and repairs carried out to the battered boats used as breastworks at the Battle of Lake George. He traveled to Fort Lyman to organize men and munitions and returned on September 29. Here he was chagrined to find men "who were sitting down and no work going forward." His own officers were no help, having little enthusiasm for the project. He vented his fury and they quickly agreed to construct "a place of strength with magazines and store houses and barracks … with all possible despatch."[6] The new post would be called Fort William Henry after a grandson of King George.

Engineer William Eyre had been promoted to major for his skillful command of the three British cannon during the Battle of Lake George.[7] He designed the new post and was given the task of supervising its construction. Eyre followed the basic principles devised by the Frenchman Sebastian Le Prestre, Marquis de Vauban. Despite Vauban having been deceased for nearly 50 years, his influence was still in vogue. The arrival of gunpowder had radically altered fort construction. The high stone walls of medieval castles were easily destroyed once artillery came into play. Fort William Henry was built low, the emphasis on thick rather than high walls, the better to absorb cannon balls and repel exploding shells. The walls went up first, consisting of horizontal pine log sections filled with hard-

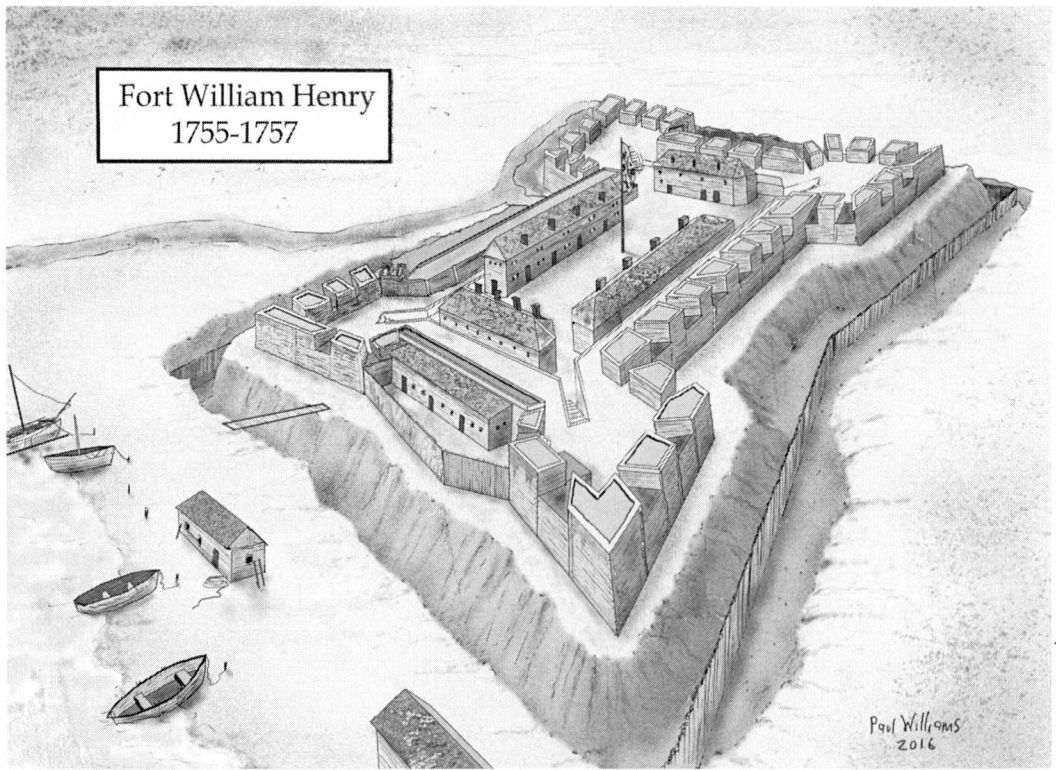

Author's rendition.

4. The French Strike Back

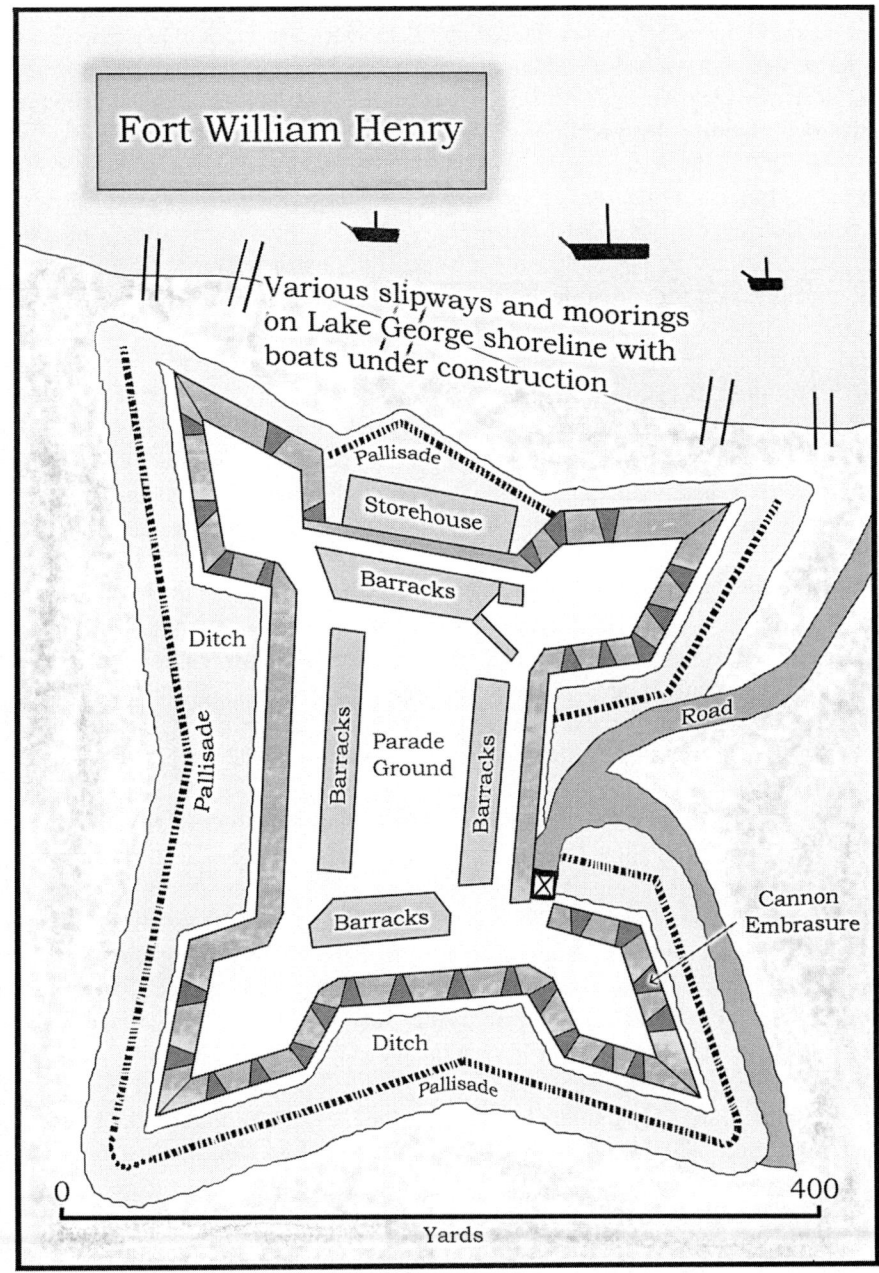

Author's rendition.

packed earth, the height averaging about 15 feet. Diamond-shaped bastions protruding from each corner would enable the defenders to cross-fire on attacking troops who managed to cross, on three sides, a picket wall at the base of a ditch eight feet deep and 30 wide. The fourth wall was protected by the lake. Embrasures allowed for artillery and musket fire through the walls. On November 13, 1755, the flagstaff was raised.[8] Various buildings went up around the parade ground, including two double-story barracks with bunks for 500 men, a hospital and storehouses. Under the barracks were brick-lined casemates which held the powder magazine and what was called "the laboratory." Here shells were loaded and explosives were prepared. Outside, a dirt road, 35 yards long, led from the main gate to a wharf protruding 160 feet into Lake George where numerous vessels were moored along with other boats along the shoreline. Small buildings with a variety of uses, including barracks for rangers, appeared outside the walls, and gardens were established to grow fresh food.

But those venturing beyond the outer works still took their lives in their hands. Lurking in the forest, leveled for one mile around, were Canadians and Indians waiting to strike. Winding through these dangerous woods was the 12-mile road providing the link with Fort Edward, where the garrison was also under threat. The surrounding forest, meanwhile, blushed into tones of yellow and gold as winter approached. As construction continued, there was no thought of an advance on French territory till the following spring.

The provincial troops slung muskets, doffed tricornes, and headed for home. Colonel Jonathan Bagley was left with a garrison of 400 men of the 3rd Massachusetts Regiment to hold the fort against any French incursions amidst the ice and snow of the coming frigid months.

As the year 1756 dawned, the British government took a fresh look at the American scene. The capture of Fort Beausejour and the Battle of Lake George had been glimmers of light amidst darker events. Braddock's army had been slaughtered, an expedition against Fort Niagara commanded by William Shirley had stalled due to lack of supplies, and Johnson's expedition against Fort St. Frédéric, despite his victory, had ground to a halt. On March 27, 1756, Fort Bull was stormed and captured by the French, the small garrison wiped out.

In early 1756 a new commander-in-chief for British troops in North America was announced: 50-year-old John Campbell, the 4th Earl of Loudoun. But Loudoun would appear to be a surprising choice. He had no record of victories, and his performance during Bonny Prince Charlie's Jacobite rebellion ten years earlier left something to be desired. Clan Campbell was a traditional supporter of the British Crown. Loudoun and 1,500 soldiers marched from Inverness one night to capture Prince Charles, rumored to be in the village of Moy. But as they approached, the war cries of various clans and the clatter of claymores being beaten against rocks echoed through the hills. Then shots rang out. Loudoun's piper fell dead. Convinced they were about to be slaughtered by hordes of rebels, the troops panicked. Loudoun "concluded that the best thing for me to do, was march back to town, which I accordingly did."[9] They tramped back to Inverness before abandoning the town to the Jacobite forces.

No doubt the *five* clansmen who caused the racket and fired the shots, responsible for what became known as the "Rout of Moy," were well satisfied with a good night's work.

Lord Loudoun arrived in New York at the end of July 1756, with an impressive entourage including his mistress and 17 secretaries. He was described as hot-tempered and irritable, the result, no doubt, of having to contend with various colonial governments to procure funds, supplies and provincial troops. Braddock had experienced similar trials. New France, on the other hand, was an autocracy with ultimate power in the hands of one governor, the Marquis de Vaudreuil.[10] This however, did not prevent vexing disagreements with the French military commander who replaced the captured Dieskau. Louis-Joseph, the Marquis de Montcalm, 44, arrived at Québec with fresh troops just five days before King George's formal declaration of war on France, May 17, 1756. Perhaps the close scrapes with icebergs and stormy seas during the voyage from France had been a harbinger of events to come. "Our campaign will soon begin," Montcalm wrote to his wife upon arrival. "Everything is in motion ... the savages have made great havoc in Pennsylvania and Virginia, and carried off, according their custom, men, women and children."[11] Governor de Vaudreuil was not happy to see the new general. Paris had overruled his desire to command the army himself. Unlike Lord Loudoun, however, Montcalm had a distinguished war record from the Wars of Austrian and Polish Succession. During 11 campaigns over 31 years he had been wounded five times. He had been living the peaceful life of a provincial nobleman for seven years before being recalled to active duty in New France.[12]

The British held a cluster of three forts at Oswego on Lake Ontario. One was an old fortified trading post, the second a poorly designed stockade called Fort Ontario, and, across the river, Fort Oswego, still under construction. These became Montcalm's first major objective. On August 11, 1756, an advance force of Canadian militia and Indian allies arrived and opened fire on Fort Ontario. The following day Montcalm and the French regulars arrived with artillery and set about digging entrenchments. The British kept up a constant fire with their own guns, but could plainly see their inadequate walls would be reduced to matchwood once Montcalm opened fire. That evening Fort Ontario was abandoned and the garrison retreated across the river to join their comrades in Fort Oswego. Indians and Canadians were sent over the river to deliver musket fire from the opposite flank, and on August 14, with a few cannon finally in position, Montcalm opened fire. The British guns replied, but the British commander, Lieutenant Colonel James Mercer, was killed by a well-placed French cannon ball.[13]

With Montcalm was his 26-year-old aide-de-camp, Captain Louis Antoine de Bougainville. The former musketeer was destined to become a famous explorer, the first Frenchman to circumnavigate the globe and, with the French Navy, would help the Americans win their Revolution. "An hour later the enemy hoisted a white flag and two officers came to make proposals for surrender," Bougainville recalled. He was sent to propose the articles and remain as a hostage. "The articles are that the garrison will be prisoners of war, that the officers and soldiers take away their baggage and will be taken to Montréal to be exchanged. The place to be evacuated at once and the garrison placed inside Fort Ontario."[14] The British agreed to these terms, but the French Indian allies had other ideas. Most captives were moved from Fort Oswego to Fort Ontario, but not all made it. One prisoner recalled that the Indians rushed in where "they went searching for Rum; which they found, and began to Drink, when they soon became like so many hell hounds; and after Murdering, and Scalping all they could find on that side, Come over the River with a Design, to do the same to all the rest; and on them coming near the fort where we was, and Hearing the Confused noyes of those within United in their Hideous yells and rushed the Guards Exceeding hard, to git in among us, with their Tomehawks; and it was with Great difficulty that the French could prevent them."[15] The Indians took prisoners and Montcalm, appalled with these proceedings, paid ransom money for their return to the tune of "eight to ten thousand livres."

Brigadier General Daniel Webb had arrived in North America a little before Lord Loudoun and was now under his command. Marching from Albany to reinforce Oswego, he arrived at Fort Bull, rebuilt after being destroyed by the French, where friendly Indians told him of Oswego's fall. Webb was reputed to be "cautious" and, fearing a repeat of the Braddock disaster, beat a hasty retreat leaving Fort Bull and nearby Fort Williams in flames.

Montcalm, however, was marching back to Montréal. His destruction of Oswego had left the French as undisputed masters of Lake Ontario, their communications to the south and west safe, and the area able to be held by garrisons at Fort Niagara and Fort Frontenac. When news of this debacle reached Loudoun, he realized that Montcalm could concentrate his forces at Fort Carillon, and the Lake Champlain-Albany corridor was once again under threat.

William Johnson left the army to become Superintendent of Indian Affairs and the task of capturing Forts Carillon and St. Frédéric fell to Massachusetts born Major General John Winslow. He wrote to Loudoun complaining of bad conditions at Fort William Henry, garrisoned by British regulars and two companies of Rogers' Rangers. "The Camp Disorder Prevelent near a Third Part not Fitt for Duty," he reported, and he was angered to hear that officers had "stripped the Hospital of Bed, Sacks and Sheets, provided for the Sick."[16] Loudoun dispatched Lieutenant Colonel Ralph Burton to report on the state of both the fort and the encampment outside the walls. He reported, "about 2,500 men, 500 of them sick, the greatest part of them what they call poorly. They bury from five to eight daily, and officers in proportion. Extremely indolent and dirty to a degree."[17] In a day when bacteria were not known to cause disease, bad air was considered the culprit, thus Burton wrote, "the fort stinks enough to cause an infection." Burton was also concerned with certain aspects of construction. "The fort itself is not finished, one side being so low that the interior is seen into from the rising ground on the South East side, also the East Bastion has the same defect from the grounds from the West, both of them considerably higher than the Fort, the Ditches being dug in loose sand crumbles away so that they are at present almost without form."[18]

Burton's report included, among other problems, polluted well water, damp casemates and powder magazine, rotting timbers, and the poor state of the fort's big guns. Recommendations included raising the walls, building a palisaded storehouse outside the north wall, and re-digging the outer trenches, the crumbling slopes to be reinforced with fascines (bundles of light wood bound together used in strengthening earthworks).

During the fall of 1756, the enlistment of many provincial troops expired and they returned home as cold north winds brought the first falls of sleet and snow and the surface of Lake George froze to glassy ice. But Rogers' Rangers, trained to fight hit-and-run like Indians, remained on duty. They had their own base camp on Rogers' Island in the Hudson where a blockhouse, barracks and hospital stood. Fort Edward stood on the opposite bank.

On January 17, 1757, Rogers received orders to march with his men the 12 miles to Fort William Henry, now commanded by Major Eyre. It was garrisoned by 400 men of the 44th regiment and 100 rangers under Captain John Stark. Here "we were employed in providing provisions, snowshoes, &c. till the 17th," recalled Rogers.[19] Joined by Stark and men from two other companies, the command of 84 men set out across the ice of Lake George. Their task was to reconnoiter French movements from Fort Carillon and, if possible, take prisoners for interrogation. The first night they camped on the east bank of the narrows, but already 11 men, having "hurt themselves in the march the day before," were sent back.

The remaining 74 officers and men continued on across the ice until, on the 19th, they climbed the shore into the rugged woods, wearing snowshoes. On the 21st they arrived at Lake Champlain "about midway between Crown Point and Ticonderoga" (Fort St. Frédéric and Fort Carillon). Here they saw a French sled making its way northwards, from one fort to the other. Rogers deployed his men to intercept, but they were spotted by a convoy of about nine sleds following the first. The Frenchmen about faced and made a dash back towards Fort Carillon, but not all made it. Pursued by the rangers, three sleds, six horses and seven men found themselves the unwilling guests of Captain Rogers. Under questioning, the captives revealed Carillon was garrisoned by 300 French regulars, 200 Canadian militia and 45 Indians. They were to be reinforced by another 50 Indians from St. Frédéric, which was garrisoned by 600 regulars. A spring offensive against Fort William Henry was being planned and many more troops were to arrive.

Rogers' command was now in a tight situation. Those enemy who had escaped would report their position. The rangers set out with all due haste and returned to their former campsite. There they rekindled their fires, dried their muskets, and prepared for a stiff fight. Next day they set out, single file, retracing their steps, a mistake as it transpired. Captain Rogers and Lieutenant Kennedy led the way—straight into an enemy ambush. "The enemy saluted us with a volley of about 200 shot at a distance of about five yards from the nearest, or front, and thirty from the rear of their party," recalled Rogers.[20] Lieutenant Kennedy died where he fell and a ball grazed Rogers' head. Another man was killed and several others wounded but, according to the French account, "after one discharge of musketry, which did not have

Robert Rogers led his famous Rangers in numerous forays against the French and their Indian allies (Library of Congress).

the desired effect that one would expect, the rain which had been falling all day having wet the guns, our troops pounced on the enemy with the bayonet and overwhelmed them."[21] But Private Thomas Brown recalled that Rogers "ordered us to advance. I receiv'd a Wound from the Enemy (the first Shot they made on us) thro' the Body, upon which I retir'd into the Rear, to the prisoner I had taken on the Lake, knock'd him on the Head and killed him, lest he should Escape and give Information to the Enemy."

The rangers regrouped on a hill and returned fire. Rogers stated that this "gave us an opportunity to ascend and post ourselves to advantage." Bullets flew as the two sides maneuvered, ducking and weaving through the snow, from tree to tree, from rock to rock. Men fell on both sides amidst a haze of gunsmoke as the French attempted to outflank the rangers on their right. "One Indian threw his Tomahawk at me, and another was just upon seizing me," recalled Private Brown, "but I happily escaped and got to the Centre of our Men, and fix'd myself behind a large Pine, where I loaded and fir'd every Opportunity: after had discharged 6 or 7 Times, there came a Ball and cut off my gun just at the lock."[22] Rogers was hit, a ball slicing through his hand and wrist.

The French called out for Rogers to surrender. Reinforcements were on their way, they said, who would cut them "to pieces without mercy." It was a pity that so many brave men should be lost. If the rangers surrendered now they would be "treated with the greatest compassion and kindness, all of which fell on deaf ears."[23]

The sun sank in a frosty sky, and the muskets fell silent as night came on. Badly outnumbered, Rogers ordered his men to withdraw under cover of dark. Those too badly wounded were left behind, and Private Brown saw Captain Spikeman come into the tender care of one Indian who "sripp'd and scalp'd him alive." Brown evaded capture till the next day and lived to tell the tale of his imprisonment and eventual release.

Rogers' bruised and bleeding command made it back to Lake George the following morning and sent word to Fort William Henry to send sleds for the wounded. Next day, the 23rd, a most welcome relief force appeared across the ice, and the rangers trudged back behind the sheltering walls of the fort that same evening. Rogers had lost 14 killed, six wounded and six missing. The French loss was 11 killed and 30 wounded, three of whom later died.[24]

5

Fire and Ice
The Winter Raid

Lord Loudoun was not happy. He examined the map once more and refined his tactical priorities. The vast French fortress of Louisbourg in Nova Scotia controlled the strategic waters approaching the St. Lawrence River, the gateway to Canada. Captured in 1745 during King George's War, it had been returned to the French. Now the time had come to do it all over again.

Despite this priority, the capture of Carillon and St. Frédéric was still on the table. The Fort William Henry shoreline rang to the thud of hammers and the rasp of saws as boats were built for the expedition. The largest craft on the slipways, the *Lord Loudoun*, had ports cut to carry 16 guns. Another smaller sloop could mount 12 guns and two others were armed with four swivel guns. Over 200 smaller craft including whaleboats and bateaux were either complete or under way.

But Montcalm had no intention of allowing Fort Carillon to fall and laid plans to thwart the British designs. He submitted to Vaudreuil a plan of "surprising Fort George (William Henry), and burning at least the outer part of the fort with 800 men" to be led by a regular army officer. But the Canadian-born governor, in a growing rift with Montcalm, had ideas of his own. Following Baron Dieskau's defeat he had little confidence in officers sent out from France. They had no knowledge of local terrain and how warfare must be waged on the American frontier. To him, Montcalm was another Dieskau. And Montcalm had little time for the governor and Canadians in general. They had no concept of civilized warfare as practiced in Europe. They were little better than their savage Indian allies.

Vaudreuil decided the raid should be commanded by a Canadian officer. His younger brother, François-Pierre de Rigaud de Vaudreuil (called Rigaud), had proved himself a worthy campaigner. He had destroyed Fort Massachusetts in 1746 and led Montcalm's advance guard in the campaign against Fort Oswego.[1] And Vaudreuil felt a larger force of 1,500 men carrying scaling ladders could actually capture Fort William Henry, not merely damage it.

Bougainville recalled that Montcalm "has several times made in writing all the remonstrations that his office and the King's orders to him allow him to make." Montcalm's aide-de-camp poured out his own thoughts on what he considered a folly: "The object of this expedition is still uncertain. What is certain is that it will use up the few eatables we have been able to get together, that it will prevent us from starting an early campaign, and this motion will perhaps get the English in motion a month earlier than otherwise." He felt it was impossible to take Fort William Henry by surprise, "lacking one of those miracles which only happen in Canada."[2]

The expedition consisted of 250 French regulars, 650 Canadian militia, 300 Abenaki and Caughnawaga Indians, and 300 *Campagnes Franches de la Marine* (independent companies of the Marines). Canadian regulars took this title as the governance of overseas colonies came under the Ministry of the Marine in Paris.[3]

In late February each man was supplied with overcoat, blanket, wool cap, mittens, tomahawk, needle and thread, snow shoes, deerskin shoes, drag rope, breechclout (for the Indians), tinderbox, etc., etc. and, to make sure they all looked spruce—a comb.[4] They set out from Fort St. Jean and marched 100 miles south to Fort Carillon, arriving on March 9.[5] Here 300 scaling ladders were assembled and rations for 12 days were issued: bread, salt pork and peas. It paid to be an officer, for he also received three pints of brandy and two pounds of chocolate. On March 15 the expedition set out south with sleds across the frozen surface of Lake George. All artillery was left behind as it could not be taken across the fragile ice. They carried musket, bayonet, tomahawk and knife—and incendiaries. Engineering officer Captain François le Mercier had prepared these for use against the timber boats and walls of the enemy fort.

On the dark and moonless night of March 19 a sentry walked his chilly beat on the ramparts of Fort William Henry. He suddenly paused and peered across the gloomy ice. A strange sound had reached his ears—nothing one would expect—like the howling of a distant wolf. It sounded like some metallic object chipping ice. Then a dim, distant, light appeared. The officer of the day was warned, and the garrison was quietly called to arms.

Major Eyre had under his command 474 men: 402 redcoats of the 44th Regiment and 72 rangers under Captain John Stark. But 128 of these lay in hospital bunks, mainly suffering from scurvy and smallpox.[6] The men of the 44th were survivors from Braddock's defeat and well knew the fighting prowess of the enemy. As they hastily lined the ramparts, the artillerymen cleared their guns for action, and Stark's rangers bustled in from their fortified barracks outside the walls. All remained quiet for two hours. A false alarm, perhaps? Then straining ears heard the faint sound of many feet approaching across the ice.

"Fire!" A blaze of musket balls, grape and canister shot into the night. Despite few hits, chaos reigned among the French as they ran in disorder, dropping scaling ladders and weapons in their wake. The fort on full alert, there was to be no Canadian miracle this night.

All went quiet once more. From the ramparts, it was as though the dark night had swallowed the enemy force. But at 4:30 a.m. a sharp-eyed sentry on the shoreline saw more movement on the ice. A party of Canadians and Indians were moving stealthily towards the boats, incendiary sticks and tinderboxes in hand. French commander Rigaud realized with the element of surprise lost, the only hope now was to destroy the timber vessels and outer works, as originally proposed by Montcalm. The sentry fired, and in the next instant the 32-pounder behind him roared. Once more, the shadowy figures scattered into the night.

Before dawn's first glimmer, a scouting party emerged from the fort and cautiously made their way out onto the ice. "The enemy wee put into confusion," recalled one soldier, "as you may judge by their leaving behind a great number of Scaling Ladders, Tommihawks, Scalping Knives &ca &ca."[7] The presence of scaling ladders meant the enemy were numerous enough to storm the walls. Eyre realized this was a serious threat, no mere raiding party.

At first light the garrison saw the daunting vision of Rigaud's 1,500 men assembled on the ice at the base of Sloop Island, about three miles to the south.[8] No doubt Eyre felt relieved to see no sign of enemy artillery. Without heavy cannon to splinter the walls he had every hope of holding out. He ordered signal guns fired. The booming carried across 12 miles, alerting Fort Edward, and their cannon boomed a reply. "About Six o' Clock the French divided themselves in Small parties each side of the Lake," recorded one defender, "those on the East Side came to the hill where Genl Johnson fought them last Year, & as they came in Parties, the Major saluted them with Some Sower Grapes from a 32 pounder which made them Hoop and Yelp."[9]

Throughout the day the French regulars kept up a constant, long range fire, as militia and Indians made their way towards the fort, crouching and firing from behind the numerous tree stumps dotting no-man's-land. No defenders were killed, but half a dozen received wounds. Rigaud dispatched regular troops from the Royal Roussillon and Languedoc Regiments to head off any reinforcements coming up the road from Fort Edward.[10] This was seen from the ramparts and Eyre fired a 32-pounder in their direction. The ball crashed through the trees and one ill-fated man lost his leg.[11]

No reinforcements appeared, and the firing died out as night came on. All remained quite for some hours. Suddenly the shoreline lit up as several bateaux burst into flames. Learning from previous mistakes, the French had managed to get amidst the craft unseen. And then the 12-gunner sloop erupted in a "blaze & gave such light as we could see for about half a Mile round the Fort," recalled one soldier. "The wind turn'd the Force of the Fire from us, And the Fire gave us an opportunity to Discover where the enemy intended to Storm, or Scale the Fort, that our Cannon Scatter'd them from their Quarters and killed some, which we could see by their Draggin the Dead away to the ice [in] which they broke holes, and put them in."[12]

The following morning, March 20, the French were again seen formed up in one body some distance away, Rigaud displaying his strength. Five men walked out and approached the fort, one waving a red flag, used by the French to signal a parley to prevent confusion with the white background of their national flag.[13] Major Eyre dispatched Lieutenant Drummond with four officers, and he spoke to Captain le Mercier, the French officer who had prepared the incendiaries. Following an exchange of letters with Major Eyre, le Mercier was led through the gates, blindfolded, to prevent observation of the British defenses. The blindfold removed, he spoke with Eyre in his quarters and proposed that the fort be "delivered up in a peaceable manner," the garrison to be treated with the full honors of war.[14] Realizing Eyre would be aware of the murders at Oswego, he gave assurances that the garrison would be protected from "Mischief from the Savages," but advised leaving considerable booty behind to keep them happy. If no surrender was forthcoming, however, "the Cruelties of the Savages cou'd not altogether be prevented."[15]

The wily major told the Frenchman he would discuss the situation with his officers and stepped outside. He gave orders to remove the highly flammable roofs from the storehouses and assured the men he had no intention of entrusting their safety to the Indians. This was greeted with hurrahs and shouts of "Monongahela and Revenge."[16] Le Mercier must have realized things were not going his way by the time the major returned. Eyre told the captain that he believed there were 1,000 Indians out there and "they expected to be Equally ill Treated" should the fort be taken either by storm or surrender. "I desired him to take my compliments to his General," Eyre recalled, "and tell him that my fixt resolution was, to defend His Majesty's Garrison to the last Extremity."

Le Mercier reminded Eyre of his garrison's danger from the Indians, then left the fort. At about 2 p.m. "The Major came out on the bastions," recalled one soldier, "Order'd Sand

Baggs to be fill'd and to be laid round on the Ramparts & Swivies (swivel guns) to be Erected on the same in order to make ourselves as Strong as possible, expecting to be Attacked more fierce than ever. Accordingly he was Surrounded on every side by the French, who began to Fire upon us like hail."[17]

As the redcoats and rangers returned fire, Eyre moved around the ramparts encouraging the men. He told them that the French would give no quarter; they would be murdered by the "savages" if the fort be taken. His men, their morale high, the months of tedious garrison duty relieved by a good fight, laughed among themselves and mocked the marksmanship of the French. And many of those in the infirmary now found the will and energy to grasp their muskets and join the fight.

The firing died away as night came on. All was quiet, but then shadowy figures moved in from the darkness again. Despite fire from the ramparts, the determined raiders scrambled aboard craft along the shore and dozens of vessels ignited as a flurry of glowing cinders spread flames from one vessel to another. Other raiders gained entry to the outer storehouses and pillaged "clothing of all sorts, guns, tents, a quantity of kettles, boxes, medicine chests, and barrels of various kinds of liquor." Then they set fire to the storehouses, sawmill and huts. But many "got so drunk that they would have remained around the fort, wrapped in the sleep of drunkenness, had they not been removed before day."[18]

By dawn the next day, March 21, the assailants had withdrawn across the ice once more. They took satisfaction, no doubt, from the charred and smoking boats behind them. But the blaze had not spread to the vulnerable, pine walls of the fort. Rigaud, in camp on land to the west of Lake George, was plotting his next move when a damp snow began to fall at about 9:30 a.m. and the air turned icy cold. Gunpowder dampened along with morale, and the provisions were running low, consumed much faster than planned. One packhorse was slaughtered for food,[19] and the useless scaling ladders were put to the torch. Men crowded around the flames, the warmth providing some relief. Return to Fort Carillon seemed the only option now, but the weather was so bad Rigaud could not order a retreat till conditions improved. The troops stayed sheltering from the snow and cold till the following day, March 22.

Lieutenant Wolff of the Bentheum Regiment was serving as a volunteer with the French regulars. He felt there was little to be gained remaining inactive while the well-fed enemy sat behind their walls—better to do something destructive while there was still a chance. The last of the four enemy sloops, the *Lord Loudoun*, sat unscathed on the stocks, her bowsprit a mere 15 yards from the fort. Being able to mount 16 guns, she would be a serious menace on Lake George once the ice thawed. Wolff proposed a burning party against this vessel and the palisaded, unburned storehouse on the north wall. Rigaud approved the scheme and Wolff called for volunteers from the regulars. He selected 20 men and they spent the daylight hours cutting and drying wood. As night closed in, they set out across the ice once more. But their approach was seen and the British opened fire. "Our Men from the East Bastion play'd so well with their small Arms that the French turn'd tail," recalled one defender.[20] The determined assailants came forward again and attempted to torch the palisaded storehouse, hard against the vulnerable, timber north wall, but were driven back by musket fire.

But the determined defense had an "Achilles heel." The redcoats had failed to clear away a large woodpile which became a refuge from British sight. From here Wolff made a dash for the *Lord Loudoun* and a tinderbox was struck. The flames took hold and quickly spread along the hull, illuminating the fort and the cold night sky. The bright glare exposed more enemy approaching and "we fired among them very Smartly, and killed some but as their custom is to take as good Care of their Dead as the Living, we can't tell what number we had killed but their loss must be considerable," recalled one optimistic soldier. The French casualties were actually light. With the *Lord Loudoun* burning brightly, the sortie a success, the French drew back and disappeared into the night once more. The British had sustained no casualties and stayed on the alert. Outside the fort all went quite apart from hearing "one Miserable Fellow who was Mortally wounded groan all Night."

With dawn's first light there was no sign of the French. But the cloud of smoke from the still burning sloop, and the blackened, charred remains of numerous craft along the shore, bore testimony to their work. Eyre sent out a patrol under Lieutenant Brewer, and in the course of the morning three live enemy soldiers were found, one still skulking behind the woodpile.[21] He had not retreated with the others because "the blaze had given off so much light, that he was afraid of being seen and shot down." The other two were wounded, one dying shortly after being taken into the hospital.

Rigaud, meanwhile, was leading his men back towards Fort Carillon. But the temperatures that had delayed their departure now rose and the icy surface of Lake George began to thaw. The heavy sleds, sinking in the slush, had to be abandoned, and the wounded, supported by comrades, were obliged to walk. A trail of abandoned equipment and booty marked the expedition's path back north as the dispirited column fragmented and men fell behind. On March 24 the first, dejected men straggled back into Fort Carillon.

Despite the damage done, Fort William Henry had not been taken, the raid not as successful as hoped. Montcalm recalled, "a singular accident, namely, total loss of sight from the reflection of the sun on the ice. One third of the detachment has returned blind. Canadians, Indians and our men to the number of fifteen score, had to be led by their comrades, but at the end of twenty-four hours, sight was restored with simple remedies."[22]

Back at Fort William Henry, Major Eyre could take comfort in having repelled an attempt to destroy his post with no British killed and only seven wounded. The French claimed seven killed and nine wounded of their own force. If accurate, these casualties were light considering the length of the fight and the amount of lead thrown. Eyre noted that a few "Whaleboats, Scows, or Gundales & Bayboats escaped the Conflagration," and two of the torched sloops were not beyond repair.[23] But most of the British flotilla and outbuildings were charred, smoking ruins. Any plans of a redcoat advance against Fort Carillon in the short term had been shattered—and the French had not finished with Fort William Henry yet.

6

Fort William Henry Aware

As Major Eyre had been defending British colors at Fort William Henry, the redcoats of the 35th Regiment of Foot had been tramping northward from Albany. It would be the job of six companies, supported by provincials, to relieve the fort's garrison. As they marched, the regiment's commander, Lieutenant Colonel George Monro, received word of the French attack. He gave orders for a forced march and rode with all due haste to Fort Edward. Here he learned that the danger had passed, the French, having done their worst, were on their way back to Fort Carillon.[1]

But Monro pressed forward. Having little idea of French strength and movements, there was always the chance the enemy would return in strength. When Loudoun wrote to William Pitt, Leader of the House of Commons, he commended the fort's men for their "alertness and Activity with which each behaved in their different Stations ... and those in the Reinforcements, marched through deep Snow, and lay in it without Tents, with the greatest cheerfulness."[2]

On March 27, five days after Rigaud's withdrawal, the comforting rattle of British drums was heard at Fort William Henry and the colors of the 35th came into view. The men of the 44th regaled the new arrivals with stories of the siege and valiant defense. It was a far happier tale than Braddock's defeat. Monro assumed command and the 44th marched out, their colors held high. Outside they found, in passing, one dead Frenchmen in a burnt woodpile, others stuffed into ice holes (the ground too frozen to dig), and one dead Indian, scalped, possibly by a Canadian who cared little about who provided his trophies of war.[3]

Now 56-year-old Lieutenant Colonel Monro was in command, the charred remains of the boats a sobering sight. He would not only have to hold the fort, but also build a new fleet. Born in Ireland in 1700 to a Scots military family, Monro had joined the 35th in 1718 as a lieutenant. Over the years, he worked and purchased his way up through the officer corps. The policy of eligible army officers having to buy their commissions ensured only the wealthy could command power, thus maintaining the status quo. During this time the 35th policed unruly Irish elements, some bordering on minor revolts, but saw no genuine combat.

The regiment, ordered to North America, departed from Gravesend on April 15, 1756. They sailed on the troop transports, *Essex*, *Sydenham* and *Fortrose*, escorted by the 70-gun HMS *Grafton*.[4] A booming salute from shore batteries welcomed the ships when they arrived at New York on June 16, 1756. The redcoats made a fine sight as they came ashore, but there were chinks in the 35th's armor. A British regiment's normal complement was 1,000 soldiers, but the 35th had only 464 officers and men. Monro's second-in-command, Major Henry Fletcher, would arrive three months later with another 471 soldiers—of a sort.

They were mainly dregs who had been pressed into service, and convicts were offered a pardon if they agreed to serve. It would take much hard work and a cat-o'-nine-tails to whip them into shape.[5]

The trees around Lake George turned green as the snow melted and spring arrived. To the south, Lord Loudoun assembled redcoat infantry in New York to be shipped by the Royal Navy to Halifax, Nova Scotia, for his thrust against Louisbourg. The task of protecting the Lake Champlain corridor, meanwhile, was given to Brigadier General Daniel Webb, the man who had promptly called a retreat when hearing of Oswego's fall. Webb commanded from Fort Edward with a mixed force of regulars, provincials, militia, rangers, and a handful of Mohawk.

At Fort William Henry, Monro's garrison of six companies of the 35th and two ranger companies were reinforced with 895 provincials from New York, New Jersey and New Hampshire. Barracks within the walls could only accommodate about 500 men, so a fortified camp was established on ground to the southwest. With the dispiriting, charred remains of the burned boats cleared away, work was started on a new fleet, but progress was hampered by experienced boat builders being frightened off by Indians who roamed freely through the woods between Fort Carillon and Fort William Henry. They were only to happy to lift the scalp of any unwary worker who did not watch his back. The stealthy warriors informed the French about troop numbers at Forts Edward and William Henry, the cannon they had, the boats under construction, and an outbreak of disease within the garrisons. On June 22 Richard Rogers, one of Monro's best officers and brother of the famed Robert, died of smallpox at Fort William Henry.[6]

The British only had a small number of Mohawk scouts. Lord Loudoun had little faith in Indian loyalty and, despite William Johnson's influence, did not encourage their use. Perhaps this is why he believed false reports of the French withdrawing most troops from their Lake Champlain forts to reinforce Québec. In June he wrote to Webb, urging a thrust to the north. "You will have nothing to oppose you at Ticonderoga and Crown Point, but the Garrisons, and, I imagine, very few more for scouting."[7]

But Webb wasn't so sure. He learned from a French prisoner that there were many boats and cannon at Fort Carillon, and these were intended for an attack on Fort William Henry. On July 2 four French deserters said the same, and one week later Mohawk scouts brought in a prisoner who claimed reinforcements were arriving, and Montcalm himself was due to arrive with the main body at any time. "Canoe loads of Indians arrive every day" recalled Bougainville. "The number from the Far West now passes a thousand. Some are from a nation so far away that no Canadian interpreter understands their language."[8]

British rangers scouting the woods to the north found themselves under attack from roving bands of Indians, and on July 6 Lieutenant Adam Williamson received a sobering report. A British party crossing Lake George had been hailed from the shore by a lone man, starving and in a state of near collapse. Unable to relate his story till after return to Fort William Henry, he explained how he had been sent out with a scouting party of 30 men. Two were detailed to guard the boats while the other 28 moved into the woods where they soon found themselves under savage attack. The survivor thought the rest had been killed, but Williamson noted that "two more came in by night and gave a bad account of the affair."[9]

But with Louisbourg threatened, Loudoun was convinced that the French were withdrawing from the Lake George area to defend Québec. While he advised Webb to take the offensive and move north, Vaudreuil advised Paris that Loudoun was awaiting the arrival of a British fleet to transport assault troops to Louisbourg, therefore, "it appears the English are nowise active in following up their project of attack on Carillon and St. Frédéric."[10] In late June Bougainville recorded that Vaudreuil, "in order to take advantage of the absence of Lord Loudoun, who has led away the best troops … has determined to lay siege to Fort George, called by the English William Henry."[11]

General Webb wanted his troops to stay put and prepare for defense, not move north.[12] Colonel Monro, however, on his own initiative, decided to send out a reconnaissance in force. Colonel John Parker, a reliable veteran who had fought the French in King George's War over a decade earlier, was selected to lead the expedition. He would command 350 men, five companies of his own New Jersey Blues and volunteers from the New York militia.[13] Parker was ordered to move up Lake George with a flotilla of 27 whaleboats and, to give the French a taste of their own medicine, burn the sawmill and boats at Fort Carillon—and also take prisoners for interrogation.

The disastrous slaughter of the British at Sabbath Day Point was the result.

The following night, July 24, a dispatch rider galloped through the torch-lit gates of Fort Edward with the bad news. General Webb, appalled, was already rattled by a fierce firefight that had taken place less than half a mile from Fort Edward only the day before. A party of 80 carpenters and their soldier escort had been attacked by Indians. Reinforcements from the fort came to their rescue and the Indians retreated after "having killed & scalped one Serj, one corporal & 10 men & wounded a few others."[14] Rangers followed them up and discovered a camp of about 500 hostiles camped at the ruins of old Fort Anne on Wood Creek. It seemed the French were everywhere, closing in.

The garrison at Fort Edward was directed: "No Soldier on any Pretence Whatsoever to Strool from ye Camp or Be Seen in ye River from Under ye Cover of ye Muskatery of ye Line or Fort."[15]

The morning after hearing of Sabbath Day Point, Webb set out for Fort William Henry. His report to Loudoun stated that the sortie had gone ahead "without my knowing any thing of the matter till too late to prevent it."[16] He took along several officers to assess the situation, along with an escort of two companies of redcoats and 156 rangers. Despite having been at Fort Edward for one month, he had never visited Fort William Henry before. They arrived that afternoon to meet a chagrined Colonel Monro. Sabbath Day Point was a bad result for a middle-aged officer with his first combat command. It appeared that the French were in strength to the north, and his post may have to withstand a much more formidable assault than Rigaud's winter raid.

But the enemy were not the only danger at a frontier army post. "There was a man shot off his gun accidently," recalled Captain Israel Putnam, "& shot a man in the next Tent through the body; who never spoke more words than these: I am a dead Man; the Lord have mercy on me."[17]

Webb had his officers survey the fort and surrounds. The camp to the southwest, beyond the fort's vegetable gardens, sheltered 300 men of Parker's New Jersey Blues and 231 New Hampshire provincials. Deemed vulnerable to attack from nearby dense woods, the officers recommended that it be dismantled and moved to a new, fortified position on the high ground previously occupied by William Johnson's men at the Battle of Lake George. Over the next few days engineer officer Major James Montresor[18] laid out plans for the new camp, and on July 27 Webb held a "Sort of Council of War" to discuss tactics and plans for the post's defense. After some discussion it was agreed that at least 2,000 troops would be required. As the fort could only hold 500 men, most troops would be quartered in the new, entrenched camp. Monro asked Webb which post he felt was the most likely to be attacked first, William Henry or Edward. "Fort William Henry for sure," replied Webb, as there would be little possibility of the French bringing artillery overland to attack Fort Edward. "If it is so," replied Monro, "I should think Fort William Henry ought to have as Great a number of men as can possibly be spared. As if Fort William Henry holds, so will Fort Edward, but if Fort William Henry is taken, Fort Edward will surely fall."[19] Webb agreed, but said he could only spare 1,000 men. He would have them march from Fort Edward the following Saturday, July 30. Monro requested that the reinforcement include four companies of his own 35th regiment, but Webb would not agree, saying he could not spare so many regular troops.

Smoke was seen to the north. The camp fires of an approaching enemy, perhaps? Webb ordered Israel Putnam and his rangers to scout up Lake George. Three whaleboats were available and the following morning the rangers launched off. Major Montresor, meanwhile, inspected the fort. His journal noted that he "ordered that the store house should be taken down & the Communication stopt with the embrasure made up for musquetry. The place of Arms to be stockaded properly. The top of the Magazine to be pared off, & sand put over it, also the funnells or air holes stop' with sand & bags. The Banquetts made up & several Embrasures to be made for Musquetry. The advance work to be taken down & the earth sloped down. The East Bastion raised one Log, agreed also for proper Signals between this fort and Fort Edward."[20] The garrison would fire a 32-pounder if the enemy were seen to approach. Fort Edward would fire guns every 15 minutes to indicate "message understood."[21] Monro asked Montresor how well the fort would withstand an enemy assault. "In my opinion," replied the major, "it could not hold out twenty four hours if the French brought cannons against it." But work commenced and entrenchments appeared as picks and shovels were put to good use. At the same time forest trees came crashing to earth. The trunks would be used as timber breastworks to help fortify the new, entrenched camp.

Captain Putnam and his rangers, meanwhile, moved warily up Lake George, tales of horror about Sabbath Day Point fresh in their minds. As they rowed towards the first narrows the forward lookout saw something moving ahead, white flags being waved from three Indian canoes. It was just possible they could be friendly Mohawk, but as they approached the canoes turned and moved swiftly north. Despite this, Putnam followed with caution, the eyes of his men scanning the banks. If the French were moving south, it must be reported to Webb. A number of islands forced the boats close to shore, an ideal place for ambush. Furtive figures were seen moving amidst the foliage on both sides of the lake. This was enough for Putnam. He ordered the boats back and they rowed with all due haste back towards Fort William Henry.

Montcalm, meanwhile, encouraged by Sabbath Day Point, continuing gathering his forces for the assault on Fort William Henry. Six battalions of regular infantry marched in and set up camp outside Fort Carillon, and these were joined by Canadian militia, the *Compagnies Franches de la Marine* and about 1,800 Indians, in all, a force of about 8,000 men. "An English corpse came floating by the Indians' camp," recalled Louis de Bougainville. "They crowded around it with loud cries, drank its blood, and put its pieces in the kettle. However, it was only the western Indians who committed these cruelties. Our domesticated ones took no part in it; they spent all day in confession."[22]

The following morning, July 29, Webb issued orders for boat patrols to be sent up Lake George every evening "to watch the Enemy motions."[23] Then he and his entourage departed for Fort Edward. Lieutenant Adam Williamson took charge of constructing the new camp's defense and issued instructions based on Major Montresor's plans. Over the next three days a horizontally-laid log breastwork arose to chest height around the camp with bastions protruding every 100 yards to allow crossfire onto the main wall base. Six bronze guns were hauled uphill from the fort to the camp and placed at strategic points around the breastworks.

Webb, meanwhile, delayed sending the promised 1,000 reinforcements. Once they marched, he would have only 1,600 troops to defend Fort Edward. He sent out urgent pleas for the New York militia to muster at Albany and for other state governors to send militia to his assistance. Needing every man, he also asked William Johnson to rally as many Iroquois as possible at Fort Edward. But it would take considerable time for these troops to assemble, and one thing Colonel Monro did not have was time. Monro's reinforcements finally set out from Fort Edward on August 2, three days late, under the command of American-born Lieutenant Colonel John Young. The command consisted of 122 redcoats of Young's 60th Regiment, 812 men of Colonel Joseph Frye's Massachusetts militia, and 57 men of the New York militia. They hauled along with them six cannon and also six whaleboats to replace some of those lost at Sabbath Day Point.[24]

No doubt Monro was relieved to see the reinforcements arrive as they trudged in after dark that same night. The slow moving artillery and whaleboats were still some distance behind, one boat having been abandoned when its carriage broke down. The new arrivals brought Monro's command up to 2,351 men. It was just hoped that these would be sufficient to repel any French assault, but the British had no idea of how many men Montcalm had. If Fort William Henry fell, Fort Edward could soon follow, leaving Albany and the British colonies open to invasion. Monro was faced with the daunting possibility of losing North America to the French.

7

Montcalm Arrives

On August 2 the evening patrol cast off from Fort William Henry, two boats carrying 14 men. Moving steadily up Lake George in the dark they initially heard and saw nothing to raise suspicion. Four miles up, however, a strange shape, possibly a tent, was sighted on the water's edge. They moved closer to investigate.

"Fortunately for them," recalled Father Roubaud, "a sheep belonging to our people began to bleat; at this cry, which disclosed the ambush, the enemy faced about, steered for the opposite shore, and plied their oars that they might escape under the cover of the darkness and the woods."[1]

Hundreds of Indians leapt into their canoes "with yells as terrifying by their duration as by their number" and paddled furiously in pursuit. As the swift craft closed in for the kill, the British opened fire. Most balls went wide, but one warrior was wounded and a Nipissing chief fell dead in his canoe. One British boat made it to shore but the other was not so fortunate. The Indians came alongside and scrambled on board. The struggle was brief and desperate. Four of the seven soldiers fell beneath tomahawk blows while the other three were taken captive. Of the seven men who made it into the woods, five staggered back into Fort William Henry the same night and two turned up at Fort Edward the following day.[2] The flashes and sounds of gunfire had alerted the British and they now realized that swarms of Indians were camped just four miles to the north. Monro, quartered in the entrenched camp, realized that this could only mean one thing: the feared French assault was on his very doorstep.

Eight days earlier the Marquis de Montcalm, at Fort Carillon, had issued orders for the advance on Fort William Henry. The expedition was to proceed by both land and water. A Great Council took place the following day where Montcalm presented a belt of 6,000 beads to bond the 33 different tribes who had come to fight alongside the French troops. The renowned Nipissing chief, Kisensik, wearing a medal presented to his father by King Louis XIV, thanked the tribes from the high country for having joined "we domesticated Indians" in defense of "our lands against the English who wish to usurp them. Out cause is good and the Master of Life favors it." He delivered praise for Sabbath Day Point and turned to Montcalm, "thou who hast passed over the great ocean, not for thine own interest, for it is not thy cause that thou hast come to defend, it is that of the great King who said, 'Go, cross the great ocean and go and defend my children.'" His words were translated to the tribes and received with applause.

Montcalm responded, "The great King has without doubt sent me to protect and defend you, but above all charged me to see that you are made happy and invincible by establishing among you this friendship, this unity, this joining together to carry on the good work, which should exist among brothers, children of the same father, of the great

Onontio (King of France). I give you this belt as a sacred pledge of his word, symbol of good understanding and strength through the conjunction of the different beads which compose it. I bind you together so that nothing can separate you before the defeat of the English at Fort George (William Henry)."[3]

Once various tribal leaders had spoken, the belt was handed to the Iroquois. They were the most numerous, having 363 delegates at the council. But their spokesman offered it to the "savage" tribes of the West who had traveled so far. Their spokesman accepted the offering, thus maintaining diplomatic stability between the tribes.

Montcalm's second-in-command, François de Gaston, the Chevalier de Lévis, had the formidable task of leading the land force across the rugged terrain to the west of Lake George. "His march had none of those facilities that are furnished in Europe by those great roads, made with a Royal magnificence, for the convenience of the troops," recalled Roubaud. "Here were dense forest to pierce, steep mountains to climb, miry swamps to traverse."[4] But Lévis was the right man for the job. Like Montcalm, he was a member of France's social elite and a professional soldier to the core. He had fought in both the Austrian and Polish Wars of Succession and would not ask any man to do what he would not do himself. He would sleep under the stars and led on foot rather than horseback, earning the admiration of his men whose privations he shared. But Lévis was equally at home in exquisite mansions and charming gracious ladies in the ballrooms of the elite. Diplomatically astute, he took care to sidestep the conflict between Montcalm and Vaudreuil.[5]

Lévis' wing would consist of about 2,500 men: 670 regulars, 1,300 Canadian militia and 500 Indians, mainly Iroquois led by Kanectagon, a renowned warrior and hunter. Also under Lévis' command was Captain Luc de la Corne. From a prominent Canadian family, la Corne had lived among the tribes and spoke several native languages. Perhaps being considered "a great villain and as cunning as the devil," by some who knew him well, was another good reason for appointing him "general" of the Indian tribes.[6]

Lieutenant Wolff, the German officer who had burned the *Lord Loudoun*, also marched with Lévis. A volunteer unit of 300 German volunteers was led by Louis Coulon de Villiers, who had taken George Washington's Fort Necessity in 1754. Many other Germans, however, had been recruited with false promises of commissions as officers or doctors and promptly deserted to the British when told they would be just footsloggers with the troops.

Montcalm would command the main waterborne force of 4,142 men. With an additional 1500 Indians and Canadians in an advance guard in canoes, he had a total force of a little over 8,000 men.[7] His artillery included 45 cannons, mortars and one howitzer. They would sail on 245 bateaux, 21 of which were pontoons created by joining two craft to transport the artillery. But the boats and most troops were at Fort Carillon on Lake Champlain. The falls and rapids of the La Chute River made it impossible to enter Lake George by water, so "five hundred men ordered to work all night portaging over the carry," recalled Bougainville. "One has no idea of the difficulty involved in moving a considerable amount of artillery, 250 bateaux, food for six weeks for one thousand men, all this without horses or oxen, by men's arms alone. Also, they cannot appreciate in Europe the merit of the operations carried out in America. The hardships cannot be imagined, and it is impossible to give a fair idea of it."[8]

Combined with a shortage of various supplies, some more Indians decided that the victory at Sabbath Day Point had been enough. A handful of Miami and about 200 Ottawa and Mississauga carried their canoes to Lake Champlain and cast off, paddling north. "There was no way of holding them," recalled Bougainville, "they had made a coup," and, having not been supplied with adequate clothing and blankets, set out for home. This, he felt, "results from the poor condition of the government and is the result of the greed of the leeches of the colony."[9] There was no shortage of corruption among senior officials, an unfortunate fact for the French that retarded their operations throughout the war.

Lévis' land force marched at 4:00 a.m. on July 30. They were to make their way through the woods to Ganaouske Bay and await the arrival of Montcalm's main force. The Indians under Kanectagon insisted on taking the lead and cut a cracking pace through the tangle of tree roots, low hanging branches, ditches and ravines. The French were no match and quickly fell behind as the Indians cut inland to avoid the sheer rock face of Bald Mountain, towering 1,000 feet above Lake George. Once back at the water's edge, Lévis halted the advance to allow his troops to catch up and rest, before pushing on. By 4 o'clock that afternoon 20 miles had been covered and camp was set up by a stream flowing from the woods into Lake George.

Chevalier de Lévis, Montcalm's second-in-command, fought hard while sidestepping the fractious Canadian politics of his time (Library of Congress).

At Montcalm's main camp, the following day, 150 birchbark canoes and two bateaux cast off. "The sight was singular," recalled Bougainville, "who could imagine the sight of fifteen hundred naked Indians in their canoes."[10] Unlike Lévis' command on the west bank, they were to land nine miles south on the east shore to await Montcalm's arrival. Father Pierre Roubaud was with them and saw that evidence of Sabbath Day Point was still visible. "Abandoned English barges, which, after having floated a long time at the will of the winds and waves, had at last run aground on the beach. But the most striking spectacle was a somewhat large number of English bodies stretched out on the shore, or scattered here and there in the woods. Some were cut to pieces, and nearly all were mutilated in the most frightful manner. What a terrible scourge war appeared to me!"[11]

Lévis, meanwhile, sent Lieutenant Wolff back with a dispatch and an escort of 19 Canadians for two exhausted officers who could not continue the arduous trek. The rest of the command pressed on over terrain less torturous than the day before and camped for the night in a convenient ravine. The following morning the Indians led them inland, along the ravine, before reaching open ground. Here they turned south and followed another stream to Ganaouske Bay. Camp was set up and Lévis ordered three huge bonfires to be prepared, the signal for Montcalm's command.

At 2 p.m. the same day, August 1, Montcalm's vast flotilla cast off. At about 5 o'clock that afternoon they rendezvoused on the east bank with the Indians and Canadians who had gone in advance. Then a storm blew up and the normally placid waters of Lake George whipped up into waves which crashed over the sides of the bateaux, rain soaking the men. The blow passed and the troops cast off once more, the Indians in advance. At 10 p.m. the welcoming sight of the three signal fires "placed triangularly on the top of a mountain" shone through the night.[12] The flotilla dropped anchor off Lévis camp and the army was reunited for the final thrust against Fort William Henry.

The following morning, August 2, Lévis' men set out once more across the rugged terrain and selected a suitable bay for Montcalm's next camp, about four and a half miles from the British post. Moving on, Lévis set up a camp of his own at about 5 p.m. from where scouts were dispatched. Night came on and "about eleven o'clock two barges, which had left the fort, appeared on the lake," recalled Roubaud. "All the missionaries were together on a somewhat large boat. A tent had been put up on this in order to protect us from the injurious effects of the air during the nights … this awning, thus set up, made in the air a sort of shadow that was easily discovered by the light of the stars. Eager to inquire into it, the English steered directly towards us." It was then the bleating sheep revealed the French camp and the howling Indians set out in pursuit. Three prisoners were brought in from the captured boat to endure a hideous death at the hands of relatives of the Nipissing chief killed in the pursuit. The escapees from the second boat, meanwhile, "were wandering at random in the woods," recalled Roubaud. "Monsieur de Montcalm delighted with these details retired, that he might, with his accustomed prudence, consider the operations of the next day."[13]

One prudent move was to keep his men under arms during the night. There was always the chance those Englishman "wandering at random in the woods" would, in fact, guide a sortie from Fort William Henry to attack the French camp. But Montcalm had nothing to fear. Following Sabbath Day Point Colonel Monro had determined upon defense, not attack. At 3 a.m., August 3, "the army got under way," recalled Bougainville, "the Chevalier de Lévis forming the advance guard with his detachment and all the Indians, in case they came out against us, or to invest the place if they did not … the brigades followed in column by battalions, the Marquis de Montcalm at their head."[14] As the sky brightened on the eastern horizon, French vessels carrying the artillery and supplies rounded Diamond Point.[15] In the distance they saw the low silhouette of Fort William Henry.

On the ramparts "we were alarmed by the sight of a great number of boats, bateaux, canoes, &c. coming up the lake," recalled Colonel Joseph Frye of the Massachusetts Regiment.[16] Orders were shouted and smoke boomed out across the water as the 32-pounders erupted, warning distant Fort Edward that the enemy had arrived. "The French fired at the fort from their boats lying at the point but their Shot did not reach half way."[17]

"We took care to salute the fort by firing a volley," recalled Roubaud, "which was, to begin with, mere ceremony, but which announced more serious volleys to come." At Fort Edward, "we were alarmed before 5 o'clock in the morning with the report of a Cannon from Fort Wm. Henry," recalled Colonel Montresor, "two or three shots sometimes within a minute or two of one another and sometimes above a quarter of an hour & more till 10 o'clock."[18]

As the French approached Roubaud was surprised at the enemy's lack of preparation. Several barracks were still standing outside the walls, "well fitted to favour the besiegers." These buildings would provide cover for the French, and the British tents in the entrenched camp had not been collapsed to provide a clear line of fire. The British soldiers were now obliged to burn the barracks and drop their tents while "exposed to many volleys on the part of the Savages, who are always ready to avail themselves of advantages that are given to them."[19] The British did manage to herd cattle and horses grazing on the flats into "the Picquet Store yard,"[20] but as the enemy closed in the animals became panicked by the rattle of gunfire and flying lead. They broke down the restraining pickets and spread out across the flats where the Indians could not resist the chance for booty. The Indian fire trailed off as they went after the livestock, capturing 50 horses and dozens of oxen, "the first fruits of this little war; but this was only one of the precursors and preparations of the siege," recalled Roubaud.[21]

At the first appearance of the enemy, Monro had ordered two Massachusetts companies and a detachment of redcoats under the command of Captain John Ormsby from the entrenched camp to the fort. Ormsby took command upon arrival and had under him 55 redcoats, 91 New Hampshire and 308 Massachusetts troops, a total of 455 men.[22] About 2,000 men were with Monro in the camp, along with women and children. Monro wrote to General Webb at Fort Edward: "the enemy are in sight upon the lake, and we know that they have cannon. They cut off our boats between two and three this morning that were towards the first Island. As yet we know nothing of their numbers."[23] The colonel sent a detachment of 100 rangers and provincials under Captain Richard Saltonstall along the road to keep communication with Fort Edward open. But Lévis' Indians had landed to the northwest and were swarming through the woods, circling around the fort, intent on heading off any reinforcements from Fort Edward. "Charged with going from the road to Lydius (Fort Edward) to report to the Marquis de Montcalm that the advance guard was in position," recalled Bougainville, "I was hard put to find him, seeing that he was on the move amidst mountains heavy with timber, where everything is road because there is no road at all." Saltonstall's detachment came face to face with Lévis' Indians and a blaze of musketry broke out.

Colonel Monro, meanwhile, was busily writing another dispatch to Webb: "I send this by three Rangers and shall send you three more in half an hour and will continue to do so. We have a few Men wounded by their Random Shott, but their body has not yet appeared. I believe you will think it proper to send a reinforcement as soon as possible. I can tell you nothing at present." Shortly the main body did appear marching to the southwest of the fort. They were about 1,000 yards off and the fort's chief artillery officer, Lieutenant Thomas Collins, gave orders to fire on them, white-uniformed French regular infantry.[24] Collins commanded 17 cannon, 13 swivel guns, three mortars and one howitzer in the fort. The entrenched camp mounted six cannons and four swivel guns.[25]

The rumble of distant guns could be heard at Fort Edward; a battle was under way. But how many men did Montcalm have? Webb sent out two ranger parties to gather intelligence and report back.

Saltonstall's men fighting to hold the Fort Edward road, meanwhile, were getting the worst of it. Amidst the flanking woods and haze of gunsmoke Ensign Samuel Williams was killed along with 18 others as the Indians, in overwhelming force, drove them back towards the camp. One Mahican warrior fighting with the British was taken prisoner along with three provincials. Saltonstall's troops clambered back behind the camp's fortifications, but the Indians pressed the attack and dashed up to the breastworks where hand-to-hand combat took place. One corporal had his arm severed clean off with a single, vicious blow from a tomahawk. Captain William McCloud brought his 12-pounders into play and the Indians were driven off as grapeshot ripped across the clearing.

Montcalm assessed the situation. The best outcome for him would, of course, be an early capitulation by Monro, saving much hard work in moving artillery and digging entrenchments. One of his aids, Captain Fontbrune, under a flag of truce, advanced with a small party towards the enemy carrying a letter from Montcalm to Monro: "I have this morning invested your place with a numerous army, a superior artillery and all the savages from the higher

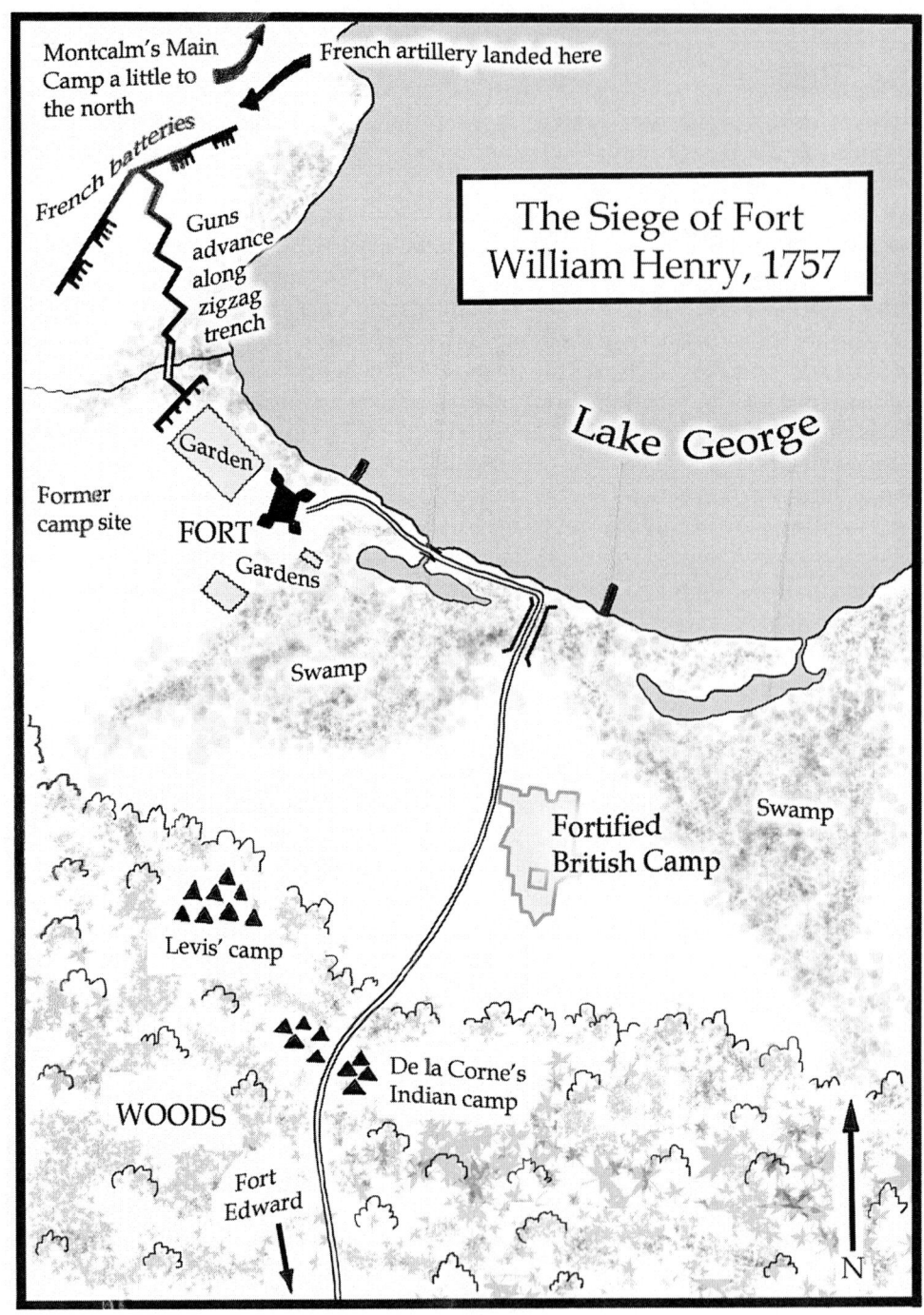

Map by the author.

parts of the country; the cruelty of which, a detachment of your garrison have lately too much experienced. I am obliged, in humanity, to desire you to surrender your fort. I have it yet in my Power to restrain the Savages, and oblige them to observe the Capitulation, as hitherto none of them have been killed, which will not be in my Power in other circumstances: and your insisting on defending your Fort, can only retard the Loss of it a few days, and must, of necessity, expose an unlucky Garrison; who can receive no Success considering the Precautions I have taken. I demand decisive answer immediately, for which purpose I have sent you Sieur Fontbrune, one of my Aids de Camp: you may credit that he will inform you as from me. I am, with Respect, Sir, your most humble, most Obedient Servant Montcalm."[26] "During the parley," recalled Bougainville, "the Indians appeared in a great crowd in the space around the fort and an Abnaki speaking bad French but very clearly shouted, 'Ah, you won't surrender; well, fire first; my father (Montcalm) will then fire his great guns; then take care to defend yourself, for if I capture you, you will get no quarter.'"[27]

But Monro had no intention of being captured—just yet. According to Roubaud the colonel told Fontbrune that he was "little afraid of barbarity; besides, I have under my orders Soldiers who are determined, like myself, to die or to conquer." "The haughtiness of this answer," recalled Roubaud, "was very soon proclaimed by the noise of a volley from the enemy's artillery."[28] Monro trusted Webb to be on the road with reinforcements to help even the odds, whatever they were. He still had little idea of Montcalm's numbers.

"All day long the Indians in the cleared area around the fort fired their guns from the shelter of tree trunks," recalled Bougainville. "They were answered by a few discharges of musketry and cannon. There were seven killed or wounded."[29] Montcalm and Lévis met, made plans, and issued commands. Lieutenant Colonel Marc-Antoine Privat would continue to guard the boats with 500 men, while the remaining regulars were placed in three divisions under Montcalm. While troops moved to the west of the fort, a ravine running from Lake George was occupied by the Royal Roussillon Regiment under Lieutenant Colonel Chevalier de Bernetz. The Indians and Canadian were to keep up their harassing fire on the fort for the moment, but Montcalm had other plans for them in mind. He dispatched Colonel François Bourlamaque and Captain Jean-Nicolas Desandrouins on a reconnaissance ride around the fort and entrenched camp. Was it possible to take the British positions by storm? After scouting through the surrounding woods and analyzing the defenses, they returned with the conclusion that they were "too strong to be attacked sword in hand."[30] The simple fact was Montcalm did not have enough men to properly invest both fort and camp. "The chief defence of this intrenchment was its position, which overlooked the surrounding country which was accessible to artillery only on the side of the fort, as Mountains and swamps skirted the different avenues leading to it," recalled Roubaud, "it was not possible to invest it and entirely block all the ways to it. Six thousand Frenchmen or Canadians and seventeen hundred Savages, who formed our whole force, were not sufficient ... hardly would twenty thousand men have been able to do it."[31]

As twilight approached, Lieutenant Jacques Vaudry de la Chesnaye of the Canadian militia cut a meal from a bullock shot earlier in the day. He made the mistake of acting alone and found himself under the muskets of three scouts from Putnam's rangers, sent out by Webb. They bundled their captive back through the woods to Fort Edward. But, as it turned out, Chesnaye's bad luck would be good luck for Montcalm.

Colonel Monro, meanwhile, dashed off another dispatch to Webb: "Genl. Montcalm sent his aid de camp with a letter to me to surrender the Fort &ct. My answer was, 'That we were determined to defend both the fort and the camp to the last,' they have not yet erected their batteries but the Indians have been firing upon us from the wood all day: Capt Cunningham of the 35th Regt is wounded in the arm, and a corp(oral) of the same Regt has had his arm cut off, and a few men wounded. I forgot to tell you, Genl Montcalm says in his letter 'he has a numerous and superior artillery to ours.' I make no doubt that you will soon send us a reinforcement. The men all seem to be in good spirits."[32]

Webb sent urgent requests to Albany for the colonial militia to "make forc'd Marches" to Fort Edward. He had received Monro's earlier plea and had Captain George Bartman write a reply: "Sir, we have just fir'd the two minute Guns repeated each quarter of an hour to shew you we knew your situation; but as for determining any further the General cannot till he has more particular intelligence from you.... The General doubts not but everything will be done for the best on yours and Colonel Young's part, and is determin'd to assist you as soon as possible with the whole army if requir'd.... This goes by three of Putnam's Rangers with orders to destroy it if it is likely to be taken. I am, Sir, with most sincere wishes for your safety till we can come to your assistance, your humble servant G. Bartman, aide de camp."[33] As night came on, the Indians and Canadians withdrew to light their camp fires, eat and rest. But a handful did remain to fire the odd shot towards the fort's walls and the entrenched camp. This would keep the enemy on edge and deprived of sleep. Kanectogen led other warriors into the forest to keep watch for rangers carrying dispatches between the enemy posts. Most French artillery and supplies had yet to be landed and signal fires were lit to guide the barges in. The unloading took place in a cove a little to the south of the French main camp. Montcalm spent this first night with the La Reine Regiment on the old British camp site to the west of the fort. From there he could see the glow of enemy bonfires illuminating the night, a precaution against surprise attack. The besieged soldiers peered cautiously back over the walls at the enemy campfires flickering through the woods. Their spirits were high, expecting the tables to be turned very soon. The French would be attacked by Webb's troops marching to Fort William Henry's relief.

8

The Siege Tightens
Webb Nowhere in Sight

The following morning, August 4, Montcalm began to reorganize his troops for the fight to come. The regulars who had marched with Lévis' Canadians and Indians during the trek from Fort Carillon were returned to their battalions, but Lévis retained under his immediate command four militia brigades, de Villiers' volunteers and the Indians, about 3,600 men in total.[1] They were to "cover the right of the army," recalled Bougainville, "to send scouts on the road to Lydius (Fort Edward), to watch the enemy on this side, and to make them believe, by continuous movements in this area, that we occupied all this line of communication, for it was quite impossible to invest the whole place."[2] But the Indians had ideas of their own. Scouting to the south was not to their taste. A law unto themselves, most wished to continue their musket fire against the fort.

The regulars were positioned in accordance with Montcalm's orders by 11 a.m. and, with Colonel Bourlamaque and Captain Desandrouins, he studied the ground for the coming attack. If the British positions could not be taken by storm, it meant a siege which could go on till one side or the other ran out of food, munitions, morale, or a combination of all three. Montcalm simply did not have the resources for a protracted siege and Webb may march with reinforcements. The job would have to be done quickly, the British battered into submission with artillery. But this could not be done from a distance. An ever-encroaching zigzag trench would have to be dug towards the fort, the angles providing cover for diggers, troops and guns moved to a new battery site much closer to the fort. The terrain to the south and east, being either mountainous or swampy, did not favor the installation of batteries, thus the fort's northwest bastion became the focus of attack. To protect French troops from enemy fire and reinforce the trenches, the preparation of gabions (earth and stone filled wicker frames) and fascines (tightly bundled packs of wooden sticks) was got under way.

Orders were issued for a road to be leveled from the artillery landing cove to the proposed position of the first battery entrenchment. Troops manning the fort's walls saw the enemy's picks and shovels go to work at 1 p.m. British guns boomed and a barrage of shot and shell flew towards the enemy works. Under Lieutenant Collins was a detachment of Royal Artillerymen and also seasoned gunners from the Royal Navy, sailors only too happy to apply the traditions of Drake and Hawkins to the defense of Fort William Henry. Collins' three mortars and one howitzer were designed to arc projectiles high into the air and land amidst enemy positions, unlike conventional cannon designed to fire straight into the ranks of enemy troops or fortifications. The two biggest cannon, 32-pounders, were mounted on the fort's northwest bastion. Before their artillery was installed, the French could only reply with musket fire, but stumps and fallen trees provided some cover and "during the day the Indians peppered away at the fort," recalled Bougainville.[3] Montcalm, however, was not happy with this. He wanted them ranging to the south to block any move from Fort Edward. He placed little value on musket fire against stout timber and earth ramparts which could only be reduced by artillery.

"This day we had several Skirmishes from all quarters in which our people behaved with great Bravery," recalled one defender, "a mortar being pointed towards another Indian Hutt fell on it and killed several."[4] But then one of the fort's three mortars burst, sending hot lumps of metal flying. Such failures could kill gun crews, but in this case the injuries were minor. It was a bad omen for things to come, however, as most of the British artillery were cast from fragile iron. Collins' four small six-pounders were made from robust bronze, far less likely to fail under the stress of heat fatigue and constant firing.[5] The howitzer was pulled into place to replace the burst mortar. The firing continued, but then the stressed iron muzzle of the 18-pounder split after becoming "extremely Honeycomb'd." The damaged cannon was pulled to one side and a nine-pounder wheeled into place.

Monro ordered a second defensive line constructed in the already fortified camp and Bougainville recalled that he removed a fire threat by taking "the roofs off their barracks and storehouses, and to throw into the lake their firewood and useless planks. The Indians, who, seeing this from a distance, believed that they were throwing away valuable things,

The Indians "peppered away at the fort" despite Montcalm's wanting them on scouting duties to the south (author's rendition).

came to complain to the Marquis de Montcalm of what the enemy was doing and asked him for troops to make them stop."⁶

The French saw water being carried into the entrenched camp and a large detachment of la Corne's Indians and Canadians moved to the base of a hill to cut off the supply. Captain Ralph Waldo was sent out with 100 Massachusetts provincials to remove the threat and they took position on high ground. A hectic exchange of gunfire broke out and the French were driven back. But then whooping Indian reinforcements burst from the woods. The two sides blazed away at each other, but the outnumbered British could not hold their ground, despite reinforcements, and men fell as they beat a hasty retreat. Captain Waldo was mortally wounded and some British fell from "friendly fire" as they retreated. The enemy pressed the attack and came right up to the earth and log walls before being driven back by a blaze of grapeshot from the camp's guns.⁷

To the northwest French troops were busy hacking the road from the landing cove to a site 700 yards from the fort's northeast bastion. This was the intended site for the first French battery. Here picks, spades and axes flew as 800 men, protected by six companies of regulars, dug a long trench, the earth and rock thrown up to form a protective bank. Digging up roots and stumps and clearing away fallen trees was heavy work, but "they took full advantage of the terrain and overcame the difficulties," recalled Bougainville.⁸ And Roubaud was impressed with how they "bore themselves in the difficult and dangerous labor to which they had been assigned. On seeing the joyous manner with which they carried to the trenches the fascines and the gabions, you would have taken them for men invulnerable to the rapid and continual fire of the enemy. Such conduct indicates much bravery and much love of country; but then that is characteristic of the Nation."⁹

The British lobbed shell and ball at the earthworks and, expecting Webb to arrive at any time, their morale remained high. The "frogs" would no more take Fort William Henry now than they had during Rigaud's raid six months earlier.

At Fort Edward, however, Webb was in no hurry to rush to Monro's relief. The Canadian prisoner taken by Putnam's rangers, Lieutenant de la Chesnaye, was questioned and claimed that Montcalm had a well-equipped force of 11,000 men—and Webb believed him.¹⁰ Although Webb had dispatched a plea for reinforcements, Fort Edward now had a garrison of only 1,600 troops and Monro had a total of about 2,500 men in both fort and camp. Even if Webb had known that Montcalm had only 8,000, to lead his garrison to Monro's aid could well end up as a repeat of the Braddock disaster. And an undefended Fort Edward would leave the British colonies open to invasion. Perhaps Montcalm had other troops poised to do just that? The rumble of distant cannon fire could be heard, so British colors still flew over Fort William Henry. But for how long? The first colonial militia would soon arrive at Fort Edward, but far too few to pose any threat to Montcalm. It could be a week before sufficient numbers arrived.

Webb weighed his options, sent for Captain Bartman, then dictated another letter to Colonel Monro. He did not think it prudent to march to his assistance, he said, "till reinforced by the Militia of the Colonies," and: "One of our scouts brought in a Canadian prisoner last night, from the investing Party, which is very large, and have possess'd all the Grounds five miles on this side of Fort William Henry. The number of the Enemy is very considerable, the prisoner says eleven thousand and have a large Train of Artillery with Mortars and were to open their batteries this day. The General thought it proper to give you this intelligence, that in case he should be so unfortunate from the delays of the Militia not to have it in his power to give you timely Assistance, you might be able to make the best Terms were left in your power. The bearer is a Serjeant of the Connecticut Forces and if is happy enough to get in will bring advices from you. We keep continual Scouts going to endevour to get in, or bring intelligence from you. I am sir, with the heartiest and most anxious wishes for your welfare, your most obedient humble servant, G. Bartman, aid de camp."[11]

In other words, don't count on Webb—best to get the most favorable surrender terms possible.

The oblivious Monro, meanwhile, wrote another dispatch to Webb: "We are continually harrass'd by the Indians all around us…. We have both officers and men wounded by them, we have seen off their regulars but not within shott of us; we believe they are employed in erecting their Batteries, and as we are very certain that part of the Enemy have got between you and us upon the high road, would therefore be glad (if it meets with your approbation) the whole army march'd. You may depend upon Colonel Young and me doing our part as far as his and our power."[12]

At Fort Edward the sergeant entrusted with Webb's dispatch slipped out with two other rangers and set off through the woods towards Fort William Henry. After nightfall 450 French soldiers continued digging beneath the moon and stars while, in Artillery Cove, over a dozen guns and mortars were landed along with ammunition, provisions and supplies. At dawn's first light, August 5, the exhausted work parties retired to be replaced by fresh hands. Fearing sorties from the fort against the workers, Montcalm had camped the La Sarre and Royal Roussillon brigades close enough to support the diggers in case of attack. But he had underestimated the British guns, the French tents being ripped by cannon balls and exploding shells. With dead and wounded strewn about, Montcalm ordered the camps struck and moved to safer ground.[13]

This minor success, however, came at a price for the British. The two 32-pounders went the way of the mortar, the barrels bursting amidst fire and smoke. And then the 18-pounder went the same way. Three of their most effective weapons were out of action before the enemy's big guns had even opened fire. The fort being the focus of attack, Monro had two of his 12-pounders manhandled down the hill from the entrenched camp to be mounted on the walls.

Musket fire erupted in the distant woods. The three messengers dispatched by Webb had been detected amidst the foliage and shadows by Kanectogen and his keen-eyed braves. The sergeant was killed and another man taken prisoner while the third escaped through the trees. Kanectogen "brought back here the prisoner and the jacket of the dead man," recalled Bougainville. "In the lining we found a letter dated the fourth at midnight." Thus Montcalm learned that Webb had no intention of reinforcing Fort William Henry and was advising Monro to get the best terms possible. Despite this success, Montcalm was displeased with his Indian allies because, "instead of remaining camped with the Chevalier de Lévis and of making continual reconnaissances, spent all day at our camp, showing a great impatience to see the big guns fired and going to fire some shots from the gardens which are around the fort."[14]

One English woman let her desire for fresh vegetables overcome common sense. Perhaps she had a misplaced faith in the chivalry of the French and their Indian friends. The lady ventured out into the fort garden but "her boldness cost her dear," recalled Roubaud, "a Savage concealed in a bed of cabbages perceived her, and with his gun killed her on the spot. The enemy had no opportunity of coming to take her away her body; the victor, still concealed, kept guard all day long, and took off her scalp."[15]

But Montcalm's faith in Webb's letter was shattered when an Indian scout brought news of 2,000 British on the road from Fort Edward. Perhaps that dispatch had been a ploy to throw him off guard? In the fort "a party of Indians were seen advancing with great Speed towards the road that leads to Fort Edward which Confirmed us in our Belief of a Relief," noted one officer.[16] The Indians, meanwhile, fanned out towards Fort Edward—but there was not a redcoat to be seen.[17] Montcalm was relieved to hear it was a false alarm. But this diversion could have been avoided had more reliable scouts been to the south. What if Monro had carried out a sortie while many Frenchmen were miles away chasing shadows?

Montcalm called a council of the chiefs. They assembled at 5 p.m. and the general vented his displeasure, saying that that they neglected scouting duties, lacked spirit, and "instead of carrying out his wishes they went into the cleared land around the fort and exposed themselves unnecessarily," recalled Bougainville, and "the loss of several Indians killed in these shootings had been extremely painful to him."[18] While the Indians' fire did inconvenience the English, it was not their prime task, Montcalm said. They were to "keep him informed of all the moves of the enemy, and at all times to keep on the line of communication scouting parties." He advised them to return to Lévis' camp for food and ammunition, and, "in order to restore their spirit, to get them back again on the right path, to wipe out the past and brighten the future with the light of good fortune, he would give them two belts and ten strings of wampum." He then disclosed the contents of Webb's letter to Monro and "the measures that he planned in consequence."

The Indians accepted Montcalm's gifts and said they would follow his wishes in future—but they had a few complaints of their own. They were not kept informed and were not listened to and their advice was ignored. It was as though they were slaves. "My Father," their spokesman said, "thou hast brought into these places the art of war of this world which lies beyond the great ocean. We know that in this art thou are a great master, but for the science of the craft of scouting, we know more than thee. Consult us and thou will derive benefit from it." Montcalm replied that mistakes occur "in the tumult of such important happenings," and they must know from the past the value he placed on their talents and "he was going to take the very best measures so that in the future there would be no more similar mistakes, and that nothing should interfere with the happy conduct of affairs." Montcalm then told them "that tomorrow the cannon would start to fire. This news produced great joy in the assembly, which broke up very contentedly."[19]

That night the sentries at Fort William Henry saw something, a vessel, gliding across the water towards British sloops moored at the jetties. It appeared that the French were going to attempt a repeat of Rigaud's success by burning the vessels. A hail of lead was unleashed from the ramparts sending up shards of water about the craft and musket balls thumped her timbers. The boat quickly turned and vanished back into the night.[20] Shortly, "it was noted that the English vessels showed much activity," recalled Bougainville. Fearing a return raid by the enemy, "the bateaux guard this night was reinforced with three companies of grenadiers."

The Indians, meanwhile, were "very weary of the silence of our 'great muskets,'" recalled Roubaud. They "were anxious no longer alone to bear the brunt of the war." It was necessary to "hasten the work on the intrenchments, and plant our first battery."[21] During the night Montcalm had 1,000 men hard at work to complete the first entrenchment and make repairs to earthworks damaged by enemy shells. The work done, a battery of eight guns, including one mortar, was hauled into place,[22] and work progressed on earthworks for another battery to the right along with a "communication trench."[23]

The troops manning the moonlit walls of Fort William Henry had seen French cannon coming ashore and, despite their bombardment of the enemy positions, the relentless digging had gone ahead. The British well realized that dawn's first light would bring a storm of shot and shell from Montcalm's new battery, and the fight would enter a new phase, not to their advantage.

What had become of the reinforcements? Where was General Webb?

9

A Demand for Surrender

At six the following morning, August 6, "there were cries of joy," recalled Father Roubaud, "and all the mountains resounded with the uproar."[1] The big French guns had opened fire. But sprouts and cabbages in the fort's west garden were the only casualties, as the French gunners had yet to find the range. And the Royal Artillery, not to be outdone, "fired two shells & one thirty two pounder before the enemy fired," recalled Lieutenant Williamson.[2] Colonel Frye of the Massachusetts Regiment wrote that the French "gave us two guns and soon after seven more, very quick, one after the other, which hot fire they continued all day."[3]

The French gunners targeted the fort's west and north walls and the boats moored at the jetties. Their aim improved and "towards the afternoon they got their distance very well," recalled one British soldier. Several French mortar shells lobbed over the northwest bastion to explode on the parade ground. Men ran for cover as smoke and shrapnel flew.[4] Although not a prime artillery target on day one, the entrenched camp, about 1,300 yards away, came under fire. Balls hit home, but not in a direct line, the skillful gunners delivering cannon balls by "ricochet"—or bounce—across the intervening ground. One sentry "had his thigh shot off by an 18-pounder," recalled Colonel Frye. The ball continued on and ripped through Frye's tent.[5] To add insult to injury, it was found that the French were firing shot embossed with "his majesty's mark, which we imagined they took at Oswego."

The French gunners scored another success when one of the fort's brass six-pounders was blown off its carriage, "ruined" beyond repair. And "when a shott would strike any Timbers of the Fort," recalled Lieutenant Collins, "or a shell burst within twenty or thirty yards, it would shake like an earthquake."[6] And then the British gun problem reared its head again. Soldiers winced as one iron 18-pounder burst under the strain, to be followed by a 12-pounder a short time later.

Then a cry of joy went up from the French batteries. The perplexed British looked around to see their colors fluttering to the ground. A lucky shot had blown the flagstaff pulley away, a bad omen for the besieged garrison. The only way to get the flag flying once more was for someone to scale the staff and nail it back in place. "It was soon hoisted," noted one observer, but at a cost. One of the brave climbers "had his head shot off with a ball, and the other wounded."[7]

Back at Fort Edward, meanwhile, the gates were thrown open as the hero of the Battle of Lake George arrived to the huzzahs of the troops. Sir William Johnson rode in "all in war paint like his troop, tomahawk at his side, halberd in hand." Behind him were 180 Mohawk braves followed by 1,500 militiamen. A welcome sight for General Webb, no doubt. But Bougainville later heard that the meeting did not go smoothly. Johnson told Webb that his whole force should march at once, but the general refused. He would not expose himself to complete defeat in woods still red with the blood of Englishmen (killed under Johnson at the Battle of Lake George). Johnson replied that the shores would be as fatal to Montcalm as they had been to Dieskau, that French bones would cover the battlefield, and he swore by his halberd and tomahawk that he would conquer or die. But Webb remained unmoved. Johnson then "tore off one of his leggings at hurled it at Webb's feet. 'You won't do it?' said he—'No.' Tore off the other legging. 'You won't?' Hurled a garter. 'You won't?' Hurled shirt, tomahawk, and halberd down, and galloped off with his troop who had imitated his actions entirely."[8]

Very soon another 46 Mohawk came in, to be followed by a constant flow of colonial militia. A forest of tents sprang up around Fort Edward's walls and the troops paraded to the music of drums and flutes. Webb wrote to the militia commanders still on the road urging "no unnecessary halts or delays.... The firing still continues very heavy at Fort Wm. Henry. Pray God they may hold out till we can march to their assistance, but am afraid the delays of the Militia, will put it out of their or our power."[9] That day Webb also wrote to Monro that he had "three Armies of five thousand Men in different parts of the woods. We shall set out in the night with the whole join'd together and make no doubt of cutting the enemy entirely off.... P.S. We shall bring a field train."[10] The vacillating general appeared to swing between despair and hope.

A false rumor spent through the troops that a heartening message had been received from Monro. "I hear that our people hold their ground good," wrote Sergeant Jabez Fitch of the Connecticut Regiment, "and Colonel Monro said he was as well pleased as if he was in his own country among ye potatoes."[11] But, the following day, "we are impatient of waiting," Fitch wrote, "not yet strong enough to engage the enemy."[12] The hand-wringing Webb had still not marched. He was in a quandary. What hope would his poorly trained tradesmen, shopkeepers and farmers have against those vicious Canadians and Indians who had slaughtered Braddock's command—now backed up by French regulars with artillery. And how hard would his handful of Mohawk fight against their Iroquois cousins who had sided with the French?

Best to stay put till more troops arrived.

Later that day, August 6, two exhausted rangers from Fort Edward scrambled into the entrenched camp. Having made their way through woods swarming with Indians, they were the first messengers to get through since Montcalm's arrival. But, having come close to capture, they had destroyed the letter written by Webb the previous night. Better at woodcraft than dialogue, "they delivered it in so confused a manner," recalled Monro, "I could not rightly understand it."[13] But he did get the impression reinforcements were mustering at Fort Edward. There was still hope, but how soon would Webb march? Monro had no idea of Webb's letter recommending he get "the best terms were left in your power."

Outside, more French bateaux arrived with supplies from Fort Carillon and work continued on the earthworks and communication trench for the right hand battery.[14] Through this, the fort shook and splinters flew as shells and cannon balls crashed against the walls. The remaining British cannon were sponged between shots to keep cool and boomed out a reply. Despite the pledge to Montcalm, many warriors could not bring themselves to leave the fight, so much more appealing to be on the firing line than scout to the south. Before the big guns boomed, "they had shot at the fort and entrenched camp from out of reach, behind a tree or stump," recalled Captain Desandrouins. But now he saw the inspired braves "slip like snakes through the undergrowth to the little marsh that was between the fort and the French camp, and there, lying flat, they opened so well directed a fire into the embrasures, that the enemy could barely use their artillery."[15]

As the first day of the French bombardment drew to a close, Monro wrote to Webb once more:

"I beg pardon for saying that if the reinforcements we had reason to expect from your letter, the only one I have received from you, which bears the date August 3, had arrived in time, our situation probably would have been better. I have frequently as possible acquainted you with every circumstance that has passed since the enemy's appearance and therefore submit the whole to your better judgment."[16]

That night soldiers manning the fort's ramparts could hear the relentless clank of pick and shovel as 500 French workers completed the second trench and repaired damaged earthworks. Then 11 more guns were hauled into place: two 18-pounders, five 12s, one 8, two seven-inch howitzers and one six-inch mortar. Next morning the beleaguered garrison saw that the planned zigzag trench was being dug towards their west wall. Moving slowly forward like an encroaching, lethal snake, it could only mean one thing: yet another battery was be installed much closer to the fort, guns that could actually breach the walls.

At six that morning, August 7, the new battery in the original position opened fire, "a little obliquely" on the fort "and by ricochet on the entrenched camp."[17] The British guns erupted in reply and once again the duel was on. Every time a French shot hit home, "the shouts of the savages brought news of it to our ears," recalled Roubaud.[18] The Indians, fascinated by the artillery, aspired to become gunners themselves. One warrior pointed a field piece and hit the mark with his first shot. Not wishing to risk a perfect score, he refused to try his luck again.

The Indians were particularly intrigued with the zigzag trench. Small arms fire could also be used from "those several zigzags which, forming the different branches of a tree, are so many covered ways," recalled Roubaud, "very useful for protecting the besiegers against the guns of the besieged." The Indians "armed with shovels and pickaxes were seen making a covered way to the fortified rock, (entrenched camp) the attack on which had fallen to their lot."[19]

At 9 a.m., after a double salvo from both French batteries, a red flag was seen waving from the French lines. They wished to parley and the guns fell silent. As the smoke cleared Captain de Bougainville, escorted by 15 grenadiers, marched ceremoniously forward to a drummer's beat. As they reached the gates an order to halt was heard and an officer marched out leading 15 redcoat grenadiers. Bougainville had letters from his general to deliver to the English commander. Two other British officers emerged. One stayed with the French grenadiers while the other blindfolded Bougainville, then led him through the fort and up the road to Monro's quarters in the entrenched camp. He handed the colonel a letter from Montcalm and the intercepted dispatch from Webb advising "make the best Terms" possible. Monro graciously received the letters and gave "much thanks for French politeness, expressions of pleasure at dealing with so generous an enemy," recalled Bougainville. Monro must have been mortified to read Webb's letter, but this did not change a thing. He said he had no intention of surrendering. The French officer was led back the way he had come, "eyes blindfolded all the time." He arrived back at the French trenches and "our batteries started firing again when they judged the English grenadiers had had time to get back into the fort." Despite Monro's response, he hoped that Webb's letter would persuade "the English to surrender the sooner."[20]

Colonel Monro may not have given such thanks for "dealing with so generous an enemy" had he realized that "during the time *the flag of truce was in our camp*," recalled Colonel Frye, "the Canadians and Indians had, with some regulars, got round to the back of our encampment, under the cover of a small knoll." Troops were supposed to hold position while a truce was in force. Captain Jonathon Taplin was already stationed on the knoll's opposite flank with 80 Massachusetts men sheltering behind fallen tree trunks. Two hundred British provincials were sent out as reinforcements when the enemy, about 300, were seen to move in. As Bougainville returned to the French lines, the new arrivals, commanded by Louis de Villiers, opened fire on Taplin's position. Musket balls flew back and forth through a haze of gunsmoke for three hours, neither side gaining an advantage. Then war whoops were heard as Indians rushed from the woods to reinforce the French. The British were forced back as men fell and the remainder scrambled back behind the breastworks protecting the camp. The French did not press home the attack because the British "were accordingly prepared, having both officers and men at their posts with fixed bayonets," wrote Colonel Frye.[21] Pierre Roubaud thought this action, having driven the enemy "from their first position" was a "splendid act on the part of the French, the Canadians, and the Savages."[22] But Bougainville took a different view: "We had twenty-one Indians and Canadians killed or wounded in this useless affair. The English, they say, lost an even greater number."[23]

The fort walls shook as shot and shell struck home, and one enemy mortar round exploded inside the barracks. Fort commander Captain John Ormsby was badly burned and handed command to Captain William Arbuthnot of the Massachusetts Regiment. But this officer lacked faith in his own abilities, apparently, and "considering the importance of the trust, desired some officer might be appointed to command the fort," recalled Colonel Frye, "accordingly Captain Giles Collins was appointed to that command."[24] British woes were heightened when another 12-pounder and one six-pounder cannon burst. Then men were sent flying on the battered, northwest bastion. A shell from a French nine-inch mortar had struck amidst the ammunition. Sixteen men were either killed or wounded as the gunpowder exploded in a ball of fire, and pieces of ragged coat were all that remained of one officer.

Despite being some distance from the French batteries, the entrenched camp remained under fire by "ricochet" from the French artillery. "It appeared that the enemy could throw their shells 1300 yards," recalled one defender. That evening a group of officers at dinner were thrown to the ground as an exploding shell landed alongside. They survived the blast, but their food was spoiled by "the dirt it tore up."[25]

As the ruffled and chagrined officers plucked gravel from their dinners, Montcalm received more palatable news. King Louis had bestowed upon him the coveted "Red Ribbon" (*Ordre Royal et Militaire de St.-Louis*, predecessor of the *Légion de Honneur*). The general received hearty congratulations from all including his Indian allies who "were delighted at the distinction with which the Grand Onontio had just decorated him, as they knew how highly he appreciated it," wrote Bougainville to the minister of war. Montcalm, despite his dislike of Indian methods, "has known how to win their affections. They themselves observed that he was acquainted with their customs and manners as if he had been reared in the midst of their cabins, and what is almost unprecedented, he has succeeded in managing them, throughout this entire expedition, without recourse to either brandy or wine."[26] The British, on the other hand, according to Roubaud, "were now retained as soldiers only by means of a liberal supply of rum."[27]

Despite enemy fire, the digging continued and the zigzag trench moved ever closer to the walls of Fort William Henry. As night fell, three companies of grenadiers and seven companies of light troops were assigned to protect the workers from any direct assault by troops from the fort. And the ever present Indians and Canadians seemed to hover everywhere, like a swarm of bees ready to strike.

Around 11 p.m. shots were heard outside the fort and two redcoats were taken prisoner, one "having his shoulder broken by several gunshots." They claimed to be deserters coming over to the French, but Bougainville doubted this story. He believed they had actually come out to observe French movements, but then fell into an Indian ambush. When the shots echoed around the hills, "all the mountains around the fort resounded with the cries of the Indians whose chiefs named themselves and answered. This little adventure perhaps discouraged the enemy from a sortie they were about to make."[28] Deserters or not, Monro was well aware that the former high morale was in rapid decline. "We now began to believe we were much slighted," recalled one officer, "having received no reinforcements from Fort Edward as was long expected." With despondent rumblings among the garrison, Monro issued a decree that "if any person proved cowardly or offered to advise giving up the Fort that he should immediately be hanged over the walls of the fort." And, furthermore, "he did not doubt but the officers in the Garrison would stand by him to the last."[29]

Despite burst guns and fading morale, a brisk fire from the ramparts was sustained, and the French diggers had to make progress under fire. "This night we could hear the enemy at work in our Garden," recalled one defender, "on which some Grape Shott was sent in among them, which had good effect as it drove them off." At least those wielding pickaxe and spade throughout the night would keep relatively warm. "The cold is as sharp during the night as the heat is extreme during the day," recalled Bougainville. "The forests and the proximity of the lake doubtless occasion this unpleasant temperature."[30]

10

We Must Fall into the Hands of Our Enemies

Morning's first light on August 8 saw the zigzag trench uncomfortably close. Despite musket and cannon fire from the fort, the French kept digging, and their artillery kept up a pounding fire on the splintered fort walls. At midday the sappers reached a stretch of marshy bogland. This called for a different approach, especially if heavy guns were to be hauled across. Fascines were laid in the marsh, topped by stones and earth, till a solid base appeared above the bog.[1] This gave support for a "corduroy" log roadway laid across the top, a ancient method used by the legions of Rome. Although men now worked without a sheltering trench, a gabion parapet provided protection from British fire on the exposed flank.

Inside fort and camp the disciplined redcoats continued to perform with "coolness and resolution." Many provincials, however, had given up hope of reinforcements and could see the post's inevitable collapse. They refused to expose themselves on the firing lines, merely shooting at the clouds to create the sound of a vigorous defense.

Perhaps the sight of a few rabble-rousers dangling from the fort walls would inspire others to do their duty? But Frye refused Monro's request to select a few men. How could he select anybody when the decision not to fight "was the declaration of the whole Body in General." Then Colonel Young was disabled, hit in the ankle by flying shrapnel from a French shell.

The desperate Monro, meanwhile, wrote yet another letter to Webb: "The fort and the camp will hold out in the hopes of the speedy relief from you which we hourly expect, and if that does not happen, we must fall into the hands of our enemies. Your letter dated the 4th instant was delivered to me by an Aide de Camp of General Montcalm's. That letter falling into his hands was a very unhappy thing and has to be sure elevated him greatly. As to the number of the enemy, the Canadian prisoner mentioned to you, every body here is of opinion that was greatly magnified. If they really had those numbers, they might have demolished us at once, with out loss of time. The enemy are constantly playing upon us from two batteries of nine pieces of cannon. Relief is greatly wanted."[2]

William Johnson, meanwhile, led his Mohawk and militia from Fort Edward northwest on the road to Fort William Henry. He was going to help Monro, come what may. Indian scouts swiftly relayed the news back to Montcalm. The reinforcements "were more numerous than the leaves on the trees"—or so the general was told. "I perceived a general commotion in all the quarters of our camp," recalled Roubaud. "Every corps was in motion,—French, Canadians, and savages; all were running to arms, all were preparing to fight."[3] Lévis and most of his Indian force rushed to occupy the Fort Edward road while the regulars checked their bayonets and prepared to fight. Montcalm marched to reinforce Lévis with the La Reine Battalion and three companies of grenadiers, leaving the St. Ours, Roussillon and La Salle Brigades to support the trenches and defend the camp.[4] The general joined Lévis at 5:30 and the regulars advanced down the road to confront Johnson head on, while the Indians and Canadians spread through the woods on either side. From there they could give Johnson a taste of Braddock's Defeat. But as Montcalm advanced, no enemy troops materialized—yet again. "Unfortunately the news of the march of the enemy was false," recalled Bougainville. "An Indian took fright and thought that he saw it."[5]

But the Indian "took fright" because he *did* see it. So what had become of Johnson's heroic advance? Three miles down the road a galloper had arrived with orders from Webb. The advance was to halt. A frustrated Johnson led his men back down the road to Fort Edward, where Webb had Captain Bartman write to Monro once more: "I am directed by General Webb to acquaint you, that it is entirely owing to the delay of the Militia that he has not yet mov'd up to your Assistance, but as he has now got a party of them and expects a thousand more tomorrow, you may depend, upon their arrival, that he will not fail to march to your Assistance: you will upon hearing him engag'd consult with Col. Young how you can by making a vigorous sally from the camp best support his attack. We have sent repeated Letters but are sorry only one has got in, tho we hope none have fallen into the Enemy's hands, as most of the parties have returned but were all closely pursued. We shall have about one hundred and fifty Indians with Sir Wm. Johnson, but shall keep them nigh as to prevent any mistake. We wish most heartily that you may be able to hold out a little longer, and hope soon to have it in our power to relieve you from your present disagreeable situation."[6]

Encouraging words, words that would never make it through. Webb's troops at Fort Edward were not at all impressed with the lack of action. Many were prepared to march regardless of the odds and felt Webb "a thoroughly frightened man."[7]

At Fort William Henry that night Lieutenants Collins and Williamson provided Monro with a damage report. "The timbers of ye East Bastion were knocked over two or three foot," reported Collins, and considerable damage had also been inflicted on "ye North West Bastion." And an enemy shell had "knocked in the passage of the magazine under the North Bastion" and had damaged the roof "of the casement where the Laboratory was." Williamson was even less encouraging. Based on "the state of the Artillery, Ammunition and other Stores" he was convinced that Fort William Henry "was no Longer Tenable."[8]

The following morning, August 9, it became apparent that the situation had deteriorated even further. Along the opposite side of what remained of the shell-pocked fort garden, French infantry were seen to occupy a new trench. "We prepared to plant our third and last battery," recalled Roubaud. "The proximity of the fort led us to hope that in three or four days we should be able to make a general assault, by means of a suitable breach."[9] Every defender shuddered at the thought of scalping knives and tomahawks in the hands of those "savages" who would show no mercy. And what if taken prisoner? Would, or could, the French prevent torture by fire and knife?

An exchange of shot and shell continued as the sun rose. Then, predictably, the barrel of another British mortar burst—and still no sign of Webb.

Senior officers requested that "a council of war should be called," recalled Colonel Frye. They assembled in the camp, discussed the situation and came up with a written resolution. Those officers present "were unanimously of opinion that considering the near approaches of the enemy and the batteries they have erected ... the excessive bad condition

Montcalm made a belated attempt to stop the massacre following the surrender of Fort William Henry (Library of Congress).

of the remaining artillery … all communication between us and Fort Edward cut off … there was not the least expectation either of relief or succours from him (Webb) without which it was impossible to continue the defence of the fort and camp longer than has been done; they therefore have requested colonel Munroe (whose behaviour on this occasion they are all thoroughly satisfied with, and take this public opportunity to return him their thanks for) to send a deputation to the enemy, and to obtain of general Montcalm honourable terms for the troops in camp, and garrison in the fort, upon delivering it up into his hands."[10] Monro was in no position to hang his senior officers from the fort wall, and this resolution mitigated blame, if any, for a capitulation.

"At seven in the morning the fort raised a white flag," recalled Bougainville.[11] The guns fell silent and Captain Rudolph Faesch of the Royal Americans walked from the fort across a no-mans-land of shell holes, spent cannon balls and scattered shrapnel. Born in Switzerland and speaking fluent French, the unenviable task of requesting a parley to discuss the fort's surrender had fallen to his lot. Faesch's appearance reflected the garrison's ordeal of the previous six days, unshaven and unwashed, his uniform stained with sweat and grime. He walked up to the enemy trenches and spoke to Captain Desandrouins, who was happy to see him arrive. "Some of us told him of the extreme fatigue we had suffered," recalled Desandrouins, "and of how glad we were that the thing had finally finished." The officers chatted amicably and Faesch explained his unkempt hair: "Not knowing to which tribe of savages I will be allotted, I have not known which hair style to wear."[12] Faesch was taken to Montcalm and an agreeable meeting took place, the general charmed by the captain's good humor. Following initial discussions, Colonel Young, unable to walk due to his ankle wound, rode out on horseback. He "came to propose articles of capitulation to the Marquis de Montcalm," recalled Bougainville. "I was sent to draw them up and take the first steps in putting them in operation."[13]

But before signing, Montcalm called for a meeting with the "chiefs of all the nations" to explain the proposed terms and his reasons for advocating their acceptance. In essence, the British "shall march out with their arms, drums beating, colours flying, and the other honours of war," but no ammunition. They would be conducted to Fort Edward with an escort of French troops and "some of the officers or interpreters attached to the savages early to-morrow morning." One English officer would remain as hostage until the safe return of the escort. The paroled troops would not serve against the French for a period of 18 months, and all French "officers, soldiers, Canadians, women, or savages" taken during the war would be released.[14] The British vessels, munitions and artillery would be surrendered, "except one six pounder cannon which the Marquis de Montcalm granted Colonel Monro and the garrison to witness his esteem for the fine defence they had made," recalled Bougainville. These were far more generous terms than those given at Oswego, the feeble defense there having not impressed Montcalm. But as Bougainville noted, it was in the general's interest to be generous because "in the first case there would have been two thousand more men to feed, and in the second one could not have restrained the barbarity of the Indians, and it is never permitted to sacrifice humanity to what is only the shadow of glory."[15]

Having read out the proposed terms, Montcalm requested the chiefs' consent and, remembering Oswego, a promise that the braves would abide by the terms. "One sees by this action of the Marquis de Montcalm to what point one is a slave to Indians in this country," recalled Bougainville. "They are a necessary evil." Father Roubaud recalled that "all these articles were universally approved: stamped with the seal of general approbation, the treaty was signed by the Generals of the two Crowns."[16]

But "had Monsieur Montcalm been a Man of Honor," recalled one British officer, "he would have performed his part; but instead of that such a scene of barbarity ensued as is scarce to be credited."[17]

The terms required the garrison of Fort William Henry to join their comrades in the entrenched camp till all British troops marched the following day. French soldiers under Colonel Bourlamaque would occupy the fort. Bougainville went to the camp to "advise the officers and soldiers to throw away all wine, brandy and intoxicating liquors." But Monro well knew the effect of alcohol on Indians, and "they themselves had realized of what consequence it was to take this precaution."[18]

The garrison packed its bags to march at midday. But even before then the Indians and Canadians had driven off horses grazing outside. Once the surrender was announced, the garrison formed up on the parade ground and formally handed the post to Bourlamaque. But as they did so the Indians swarmed in. Bent on pilfering anything of value, they scaled the battered walls and climbed through the gun embrasures. Unfortunately for the 30 sick and 40 wounded, they were left behind as stipulated in the terms: "All the sick and wounded ... shall remain with the marquis de Montcalm, who will take all possible care of them, and return them as soon as they are recovered."[19] As the garrison marched away, however, screams of agony could be heard from behind the walls. Those marching could do nothing, menaced by Indians who lined each side of the road. They "laugh'd and made considerable fun of us as we marched along," one soldier recalled, "well knowing, the property of our packs, would not remain with us, but a very short time."[20] In the fort "only with the greatest trouble could the provisions and munitions be saved," recalled Bougainville, who made no mention of the disabled being murdered. Father Roubaud recalled that the "sick soldiers had remained in the casemates" and "these were the victims upon whom they pitilessly rushed, and whom they sacrificed to their cruelty." He saw "one of these barbarians come out of the casemates into which nothing less than an insatiable avidity for blood could make any one enter, so insupportable was the stench which exhaled from them. He carried in his hand a human head, from which trickled streams of blood, and which he displayed as the most Splendid prize that he could ever have secured."[21]

But Father Roubaud, appalled with this sight, would die in Paris sometime after 1789—the year the Bastille was stormed, the onset of the French Revolution. Thousands of men, women and children would meet the same fate as the English prisoner, decapitated by Roubaud's "civilized" countrymen with the guillotine.

Bourlamaque's grenadiers finally entered the casemates and forced the Indians out. One of those saved was Captain John Ormsby, the wounded former fort commander. Others had been scalped, castrated, mutilated and killed.[22]

The garrison marched into the entrenched camp but the Indians followed. Only 200 French soldiers had been detailed to guard the camp, and the Indians scaled the breastworks and stalked through the tents. They became bolder, their reputation for ferocity discouraging opposition, and began to pillage the officers' baggage and other supplies. Frightened children clung to their mothers for protection as the menacing intruders ransacked the tents. Bougainville wrote that the French attempted to stop the theft by "consultation with the chiefs, wheedling on our part," but the situation remained grim, tensions rising and tempers on edge. "We will be most fortunate if we can prevent a massacre," Bougainville wrote. He found the French in a "detestable position," one which "makes the victory painful to the conquers." Montcalm went to the entrenched camp where he "made the greatest efforts to prevent the greed of the Indians and, I will say it here, of certain people attached to them from being the cause of misfortunes far greater than pillage."[23] Some Canadians encouraged the Indians to ignore the surrender terms. This included Luc de la Corne, the "general" in charge of the Indians.[24]

At least one of the provincials could see what was likely to happen and, upon seeing "that the French flag was hoisted in Fort William Henry," bolted over the breastwork and took his chances in the woods. He made it through to Fort Edward at 8 o'clock that evening, bringing first news of the fort's fall.[25] "This seems to Be the Most Unfortunate Day that Ever I knew," wrote Sergeant Jabez Finch. General Webb knew it would be an especially unfortunate day for him, his credibility at stake, and perhaps Fort Edward itself. Would Montcalm's guns soon arrive? The road built to Fort William Henry provided easy means. That night muskets blazed as the nervous militia camped outside opened fire on shadows in the woods. A sentry, seeing what he believed to be Indians, had fired the first shot.

Webb dictated more letters to the quartermaster in Albany. "The General desires you will forward all the Militia," wrote Captain Bartman, "and send up what Pork and bread you can possibly spare with the greatest Expedition."[26]

Back at the occupied camp, meanwhile, Montcalm was reluctant to have his Indian allies threatened with French bayonets to enforce the capitulation terms. This was noticed by those Indians dissatisfied with a lack of scalps, pillage and prisoners to ransom. But grenadiers did eventually manage to move the Indians out. Montcalm arranged for two chiefs from each nation to accompany the prisoner escort to Fort Edward. No doubt he felt this would make them feel included and obliged to honor the capitulation terms. But, despite a semblance of order by 9 p.m.,[27] Indians still loitered near the camp. French and British officers mingled, however, exchanging pleasantries and information. According to "several French officers" they had 3,000 French regulars, 6,000 Canadians and 2,500 Indians, "11,500 in all," recalled Colonel Frye.[28] With the victory won, there was no need for French officers to provide false figures, so the Canadian questioned by Webb had, most likely, repeated what he honestly believed. With the French troops spread out, it would be impossible for most to know only 8,000 were actually there. It would appear Montcalm had deliberately spread a false rumor to intimidate the enemy, and, in Webb's case, it had worked to perfection. Father Roubaud, however, denied that Montcalm would resort to such subterfuge. He admitted that the 11,000 mentioned by Webb in his letter to Monro "were exaggerated far beyond the truth. This error ought not, however, to be attributed to fraud and deceit—which, although useful to the Country, cannot be justified to the conscience of an honest man."[29] But all's fair in love and war. And while Roubaud may have been an honest man at the time, in later life he would spy for the English and forge letters supposedly written by Montcalm predicting the loss of Canada and the coming American Revolution.[30]

Monro decided to move out under cover of dark, the best way to avoid the Indian menace. The troops assembled as quietly as clinking guns, bayonets and buckles allowed and marched from the camp at midnight. They halted on the road to Fort Edward and waited for the promised escort, but the only Frenchman to emerge was a messenger from Montcalm. Six hundred Indians were missing from their camps, he said. There could be little doubt that they were poised with muskets and scalping knives on the road to Fort Edward. The British had muskets, but no powder and ball. Best to wait till morning. The troops about faced and marched back into camp where they huddled against the cold and, if possible, got some sleep. "All the remainder of this night the Indians were in great numbers around our lines," recalled Frye, "and seemed to show more than usual malice in their looks which made us suspect they intended us mischief."[31]

11

Massacre

"A great misfortune which we dreaded has happened," wrote Bougainville. "Apparently the capitulation is violated and all Europe will oblige us to justify ourselves." Bougainville had been dispatched by Montcalm to "carry to the Marquis de Vaudreuil the news of the surrender of Fort William Henry."[1] Good news. But then the bad news arrived within a few days.

At dawn on August 10 Indians had been seen in large numbers around the entrenched camp, "in a worse temper, if possible, than last night," recalled Frye, "every one having a tomahawk, hatchet, or some other instrument of death." The terms called for the British to depart that morning, and Monro gave orders to march. But the Indians invaded the camp once more. "They began by asking for goods, provisions,—in a word all the riches their greedy eyes could see," recalled Roubaud, "but these demands were made in a tone that foretold a blow with a spear as the price of a refusal."[2] The Indians commenced pillaging, seizing the troops' baggage and pulling packs from the soldiers' backs. The horses intended to pull the six-pounder granted by Montcalm were seized and driven off.[3] Monro complained to French officers only to be told their best hope of being spared was to surrender the baggage without complaint. One told him "that if any resistance was made by which a single Indian should be killed it would not be in the power of Mr. de Montcalm to save a man from butchery." With no sign of the promised escort, Monro reluctantly complied, "but this was no sooner done than they began to take the officers' hats, swords, guns, and clothes, stripping them all to their shirts, and on some officers left no shirt at all," recalled Frye.[4]

The French surgeon and soldiers detailed to care for the disabled had disappeared during the night, and "the Indian doctors began with their tomahawks to cure the sick and wounded," recalled one officer.[5] Sergeant Jonathan Carver watched as the Indians "began to attack the sick and wounded, when such were not able to crawl into the ranks, notwithstanding they attempted to avert the fury of their enemies by their shrieks and groans, were soon dispatched." Surgeon Miles Whitworth later testified, "the French Troops posted around the lines were not further than forty feet from the Hutts where the said wounded men lay, that several Canadian Officers particularly one La Corne were present and that none, either Officer or Soldier, protected the said wounded men."[6]

Mohawk serving with the British and black slaves were either taken prisoner or "unmercifully draged over the breast work and scalped," according to one witness.[7] Frye claimed that one slave was later "burned alive." And the French officers assured the British they would be scalped once the stripping was through. This "thru them in a panick" and one company of redcoats led a brisk movement from the camp down the road towards Fort Edward. "Our little army began to move," recalled Sergeant Carver—over 2,000 troops, woman and children. The redcoat regulars were in the van while the New Hampshire provincials came up at the rear. The menacing horde of Indians followed. Carver was one of the last to leave and got the impression "the entire column was encircled by the savages," but Frye recalled that it was the rear that came under attack, "which Occasioned an order for a halt, was at last was done in Great Confusion but as soon as those in the front knew what was doing in the rear they again pressed forward … till we came to the Advanc'd guard of the French."

But the 400 French escorts had no hope of protecting so large a column, and few had any inclination to do so, according to British survivors. Carver found himself being stripped "of my coat, waist-coat, hat, and buckles, omitting not to take from me what money I had in my pocket." He ran to a French sentinel for protection "but he only called me an English dog, and thrust me with violence back again into the midst of the Indians."[8] Colonel Frye recalled being stripped down to his "Briches Stockings Shoes & Shirt, the Indians round me with their Tomehawks and Spears &c threatening Death I flew to the Officers of the French Guards for Protection but they would afford me none."[9] Frye then ran for his life into the woods.

But many others got no such chance. And according to Bougainville it was not the wild Indians from the west who first "shouted the death cry and hurled themselves on the tail of the column," but the Abenakis from the Christian missions.[10] The others followed their example. "Woe to all those who brought up to the rear, or stragglers whom indisposition or any other cause separated however little from the troop," recalled Roubaud. The "ferocious beasts … struck, right and left, heavy blows of the hatchet on those who fell into their hands…. The son torn from the arms of the father, the daughter snatched from the bosom of the mother, the husband separated from the wife."[11] Roubaud claimed the Chevalier de Lévis and other French soldiers risked their lives to save people who fled, "some towards the woods, some towards the French tents; these towards the fort, others to every place that seemed to offer an asylum." Roubaud claimed that the "main part of out troops, occupied in guarding our batteries and the fort, was, on account of the distance, unable to give them aid." Sergeant Carver, however, felt that an "unprejudiced observer" would conclude that a body of 10,000 Christian troops "had it in their power to prevent the massacre from becoming so general."[12]

Montcalm was guilty of gross negligence to say the least. Was this due to a fear of Indian tomahawks being turned against the French? Or sheer exhaustion after the nine-day siege? But "one of our Sergeants," claimed Roubaud, "who had strongly opposed their violence, was thrown to the ground by a blow from a spear. One of our French Officers, in reward for the same zeal, received a severe wound which brought him to the gate of death."[13] Those British who had "been able to preserve their arms carried them clubed" recalled one officer.[14] "Clubbed" arms were muskets swung by the barrel, used as a club.[15] Carver ran towards a large party who held the enemy at bay, "but innumerable were the blows that were made at me with different weapons as I passed on; luckily however the savages were so close together, that they could not strike at me without endangering each other." But then a spear thrust grazed his side to be followed by another in his ankle. He ran into the midst of the troops with his shirt in tatters and his "flesh was scratched and torn in many places by their savage gripes." His eyes scanned the "horrid scene that now ensued; men, women, and children were dispatched in the most wanton and cruel manner, and immediately scalped. Many of these savages drank the blood of their victims, as it flowed warm from the fatal wound."[16]

Colonel Monro, meanwhile, managed to ride into the French lines where he demanded a halt to the slaughter. "Monsieur de Montcalm," recalled Roubaud, "who was not apprised of the affair for some time, on account of the distance to his tent—came at the first notice to the place of uproar, with a celerity which showed the goodness and nobility of his heart." Montcalm's noble heart must have been remarkably detached if he had no knowledge of proceedings. If, in fact, he had simply turned a blind eye to appease his allies, Monro's plea finally jolted him to action. Montcalm "seemed to be in several places at once," claimed Roubaud, "he would reappear, he was everywhere; he used prayers, menaces, promises; he tried everything, and at last resorted to force." Bougainville was not present, but stated that "the Marquis de Montcalm rushed up at the noise; M. de Bourlamaque and several French officers risked their lives in tearing the English from the hands of the Indians." But Bougainville claimed the victims had brought it on themselves, "a great number of English soldiers, hoping to put them in a good humor, had given them rum which, despite all our warnings, they had kept in their flasks."[17] This was hotly refuted by Monro later on.

Montcalm "with authority and with violence" recalled Roubaud, managed to save the life of Colonel Young's nephew "from the hands of a Savage; but alas! his deliverance cost the life of some prisoners, whom their tyrants immediately massacred, through fear of a vigorous act."[18]

Sergeant Carver, meanwhile, was acting with "one vigorous effort" in an attempt to save his own life. The cluster of troops around him were "much thinned" as soldiers were either killed or taken prisoner and "death seemed to be approaching with hasty strides." Twenty men decided not to die where they stood and charge the enemy. We "sprung at once into the midst of them," Carver recalled, but he quickly found himself alone, his compatriots killed or dispersed through the struggling throng. He later found that only six or seven had survived. "I endeavoured to make my way through my savage enemies in the best manner possible," he recalled, "dextrously avoiding their weapons; till at last two very stout chiefs, of the most savage tribes, as I could distinguish by their dress, whose strength I could not resist, laid hold of me by each arm, and began to force me through the crowd." Carver assumed he was about to die as he was dragged towards a swamp, but fate intervened in the form of an "English gentleman of some distinction" running by. His breeches of "fine scarlet velvet," his only clothing, revealed him to be a finer catch than a mere sergeant. One of the Indians released Carver and "endevoured to seize him as prey," but the gent was a fine specimen, and the chief found himself flung to the ground. Carver was released as the other Indian went to "assist his brother" and "I seized the opportunity and hastened away to join another party of English troops that were as yet unbroken, and stood in a body at some distance." He glanced back to see a tomahawk "gash" into the gentleman's back "and heard him utter his last groan." A few moments later a boy of about 12 ran up to Carver begging for help "so that he might stand some chance of getting out of the hands of the savages." Carver agreed, and the boy took hold of the sergeant as they ran amidst the bloodshed and screams. But "in a few moments he was torn from my side" and the boy's shrieks were heard as he was killed. "I could not help forgetting my own cares for a minute, to lament the fate of so young a sufferer."

Carver made it through to "the division that had advanced the furtherest from the fort," but having little faith in their survival, decided to take his chances in the woods. "Suffice it to say, that I reached the wood; but by the time I had penetrated a little way into it, my breath was so exhausted that I threw myself into the brake, and lay for some minutes apparently at the last gasp." He regained his breath to see "several savages" stalking through the woods searching for victims. They passed out of sight. Should he lay concealed or attempt to get away? Afraid they would retrace their steps, "I thought it most prudent to get farther away from the dreadful scene of my past distresses ... as fast as the briars and the loss of one of my shoes would permit me."

Sergeant Carver was not alone in his quest for safety amidst the swamps and trees. Others, including Colonel Frye and Captain Hitchcock of the Massachusetts Regiment, were struggling through the foliage in the general direction of Fort Edward. The two officers saw several Indians approaching and, expecting to fall victim to tomahawk and scalping knife, dropped to the ground. But the warriors had not seen them and stalked by. The two men smeared themselves with dirt as camouflage and pressed on.

Ordnance officer James Furnis was pursued through the woods for three miles by two braves who finally caught and overpowered him. But fortunately they were more interested in ransom money than taking a scalp, and Furnis was taken back to Fort William Henry. With the fury of the assault having abated, the French were finally restoring some semblance of order, and the guards demanded Furnis be handed over. He soon found himself being held amidst other British officers including Monro and Young. Some had gained French protection following the attack, and others had been retrieved from resentful Indians who considered prisoners taken as rightful spoils of war, regardless of any surrender terms.

About 50 bodies lay on the blood-spattered roadway, and dozens of others lay amidst the tree stumps and woods. About 100 survivors had taken refuge with the French, while the Indians held about 900 prisoners.[19] Many survivors were still making their way to Fort Edward in fractured groups, or were dispersed through the woods. This was a far cry from the promised march to a drummer's beat with colors held high, a six-pounder drawn by horses, the dignity of the regiment intact.

Of the 900 prisoners, "the Marquis de Montcalm at once took away from the Indians four hundred of these unfortunate men and had them clothed," recalled Bougainville. "The French officers divided with the English officers the few spare clothes they had and the Indians, loaded with booty, disappeared that same day. Only a few domesticated ones remained."[20]

Pierre Roubaud walked into Fort William Henry where "a crowd of women came &d, with tears and groans surrounding me, threw themselves at my feet; they kissed the hem of my robe, uttering from time to time lamentable cries that pierced my heart. it was not in my power to dry up the sauce of their tears; they asked for the return of their sons, their daughters, their husbands, whose capture they were deploring." Then he heard of a 6-month-old infant in the hands of a Huron warrior. He approached the man and attempted to purchase the boy's release, but to no avail. After further haggling, the Huron finally agreed to hand over the child in exchange for "an enemy's scalp." Fortunately for the child—though not for the victims—scalps were plentiful that day. Roubaud set out for the camp of the Abenakis and asked "the first one I met if he was the possessor of any scalp, and if he would do me the favor of giving it to me." Much to Roubaud's delight, "he untied his bag and gave me my choice." Roubaud returned with the "barbarous trophy" and presented it to the Huron. "Here, here is thy payment." The Huron was happy to keep his part of the bargain. "Thou are right," he replied, "it is indeed an English scalp, for it is red. Well then! here is the infant, take it away; it belongs to thee." The priest took the child and arranged for his care by an English woman, but then located the father, a wounded man, and soon the mother. "It is easy to imagine the transports of joy to which she abandoned herself, especially when she was assured of the life and liberty of her husband, to whom she thought she had spoken her last farewells."[21]

Captain Desandrouins made his way towards the fort and after walking only 400 yards came across an Indian attempting to conceal a prisoner. He grasped the Indian by the wrists and, with the assistance of another officer, the cowering prisoner was set free. Desandrouins then tracked down and liberated three other officers he had shared a meal with the preceding day and, with the help of the Jesuit priest, Abbe Picquet, managed to locate Lieutenant Adam Williamson. The terrified and stripped officer was reunited with other survivors at the fort and Desandrouins had the Indians return his uniform.[22] In the casemates, the prisoners soon discovered the dead and mutilated bodies of their comrades.

Many Indians, unhappy with captives being retrieved, said they would not fight for the French again—but about 500 prisoners were still in their hands. It was impossible for the Indians to hide such a large number if a proper search was made. It must be assumed that the French simply decided to turn a blind eye to avoid further conflict with their allies. The captives would be retrieved, if possible, at a later date. There was still, however, an untapped supply of trophies for those Indians who felt deprived. The graves of British and American dead outside the walls, including Richard Rogers, were dug up and scalped.[23]

Colonel Monro wasted no time informing Montcalm that the surrender terms had been violated. There was no obligation on the part of the British to honor their side of the agreement. The 18 month parole was null and void; the troops making it through to Fort Edward could resume arms immediately. Lieutenant William Hamilton of the 35th made the same point and Montcalm said "he was heartily sorry for what had happened, but protested that it was not in his power to prevent it." And, despite the massacre, he insisted "he would certainly hang up any officer or soldier included in the capitulation that should be taken in arms before the time of not serving was expired."[24]

Most Indians cast off and paddled their canoes up Lake George towards home during the afternoon. They took plunder and prisoners, some disguised as Indians, along with them. Only about 500 Abenaki and Nipissings remained. The Abenakis, having initiated the savage attack, must have cast grievous doubts in the minds of the priests as to just how successful their efforts had been. "Such was the circumstances of the unfortunate expedition which dishonoured the bravery that the Savages had displayed throughout the course of the siege," recalled Roubaud. And he hoped God "will some day enlighten these unfortunate creatures on the dangers of their strange manners of life and Will restrain them from their instability and their wanderings; but although it is an event which a Missionary is indeed permitted to desire, it is not in his power to bring it about."[25]

12

Outrage

At about 10 a.m. the colors of the 35th were seen from the walls Fort Edward. About 30 disheveled soldiers minus their coats and other trappings were seen running as though the devil was after them. Astonished soldiers flocked about as they staggered breathlessly in "extreamely confused at the Indians behaviour after the Capitulation," recalled Colonel Montresor, "murdering every one that they could lay their hands on, tearing the clothes off their backs and not prevented by the French, who were lookers on." Listeners hung on their every word, and wild stories spread like wildfire, inflamed with each repeat. Soon other survivors came into view, a bigger batch this time, including Lieutenant Collins of the Royal Artillery and Captain Cunningham of the 35th.[1] But, surprisingly, not only soldiers British arrived. "This morning early 2 French officers deserted from their Camp & Came into the Line," noted Montresor.[2] Perhaps some Frenchmen had disowned their own countrymen following that morning's proceedings.

Orders were given for a cannon to be fired every two hours as a guide to those lost in the woods, and drums rattled as 500 men under Swiss-born Major Augustine Prevost of the Royal Americans formed ranks. They marched one mile up the road towards Fort William Henry to meet other survivors. One of the many to emerge from the woods was Edward White, the servant of James Furnis. Colonel Montresor asked White about his friend's fate, only to be told that Furnis had been left in the rear, "but did not see him afterwards."[3]

Furnis was fortunate to be among the prisoners at Fort William Henry where Montcalm, despite the massacre, could take satisfaction in having achieved his aim, removal of the British fort from lands claimed by France. But, despite Webb's fears, he did not have the resources for a push against Fort Edward. Most of the Indians, his eyes and ears, had departed, and the French knew they were essential for any drive further south. Fort William Henry, however, would be demolished. The ruins would be a warning to the British or any others who considered violating French territory. As preparations were made, an inventory of captured provisions and arms was got under way. A total of 44 guns, some burst, had been taken. This included 23 cannon, 17 swivels, three mortars and one howitzer. There were also 2,522 solid shot, 542 shells, 1400 pounds of bullets, "some grapeshot," one chest of grenades and six chests of "fireworks," possibly rockets, best for unnerving the enemy, although one landing in an ammunition store could take many lives. Provisions captured included 1237 barrels of salt pork. The French were known for fine cuisine, and this extended to army rations, apparently. "There is a great difference between the English salt pork and ours," noted Bougainville. "The latter is infinitely better ... in the English colonies the pigs live in the woods, while in Canada they are fed domestically."[4]

Montcalm had allowed the enemy to keep their colors, but he did have other symbols of success. The captured guns and provisions were loaded aboard barges for transport to

Fort Carillon. With so much material to move however, it was decided to bury some of the ammunition in Artillery Cove.[5] Like some mythical pirate's treasure, the shells and cannonballs could be retrieved at a later date.

Late the following day, August 11, Bougainville arrived back in Montréal. "The news I brought caused a sensation," he recalled, only knowing of Monro's surrender. A traveller had arrived a mere three hours earlier with the unsettling report of Fort William Henry holding out. But even with news of victory, Montcalm's political enemies sharpened their knives. Some complained that he had not kept the garrison as prisoners and not marched against Fort Edward. "These same people had always advised against taking prisoners," recalled Bougainville, "the colony not being in condition to feed them." As regards an advance on Fort Edward, "invincible obstacles prevented us from thinking of it, the lack of munitions and provisions, the difficulty of a portage of six leagues without oxen or horses, with an army worn out by fatigue and bad food, the departure of all of the Indians of the Far West who have five hundred leagues to go over lakes and rivers which freeze and prevent them remaining longer, the flight of all almost all the domesticated Indians, the necessity of sending back Canadians for the harvests already ripe, sixteen hundred men assembled at the fort whose capture they think so easy, these then are the reasons which stopped the further advance of the King's army."[6] Bougainville claimed Fort Edward could have been taken as well if the campaign had commenced six weeks earlier and "the enemy would not had time to render his defence so strong." He blamed the delay on the incompetence of the Commissary of Stores for not ordering a wheat survey early enough "as the welfare of the colony demanded." But "this Commissary of Stores is only the dummy of the great society to which the Governor General (Vaudreuil) himself belongs. It is thus that they serve the King in the colonies."[7]

Next day news of the massacre arrived. This was a sensation the French could well do without.

With most of his Indians gone, and the Canadians eager to return to their homes, Montcalm wasted no time in commencing the demolition of both the fort and entrenched camp. Over 1,000 men went to work and plumes of smoke billowed into the summer sky as the timber barracks and other buildings were set ablaze. The wooden ramparts were torn down, piled up, and set on fire.[8] "It was only during the burning that we comprehended the greatness of the enemy's loss," recalled Roubaud. "Casemates and secret underground passages were found filled with dead bodies, which for several days furnished fresh fuel for the activity of the flames." Some of the remaining Indians found barrels of spirits and Roubaud found himself obliged to protect "some French officers whose lives were threatened by savage drunkenness."[9] One soldier was forced to "run the gauntlet" for selling brandy to the Indians, and the same day another was executed for "wanting in respect for the Sieur de Langlis, officer of the colony troops."[10]

As the timbers burned and the earthworks were leveled, the French army began to embark and head north back to Fort Carillon, taking their artillery with them. "Hardly a handful of men remained to cope with the enemy, if they had assumed the offensive," recalled Roubaud. But the British "tranquillity gave us the opportunity of accomplishing our work."[11]

British action may have been tranquil, but their emotions were not. At midday on August 11 the plumes of distant smoke were seen from the walls of Fort Edward as distressed survivors continued to arrive. A few French deserters informed Webb that Montcalm had "put fire to the fort & that the Indians were going off displeased."[12] The Indians dispersing rather than moving towards Fort Edward was welcome news for an indecisive general who had shown little inclination to fight.

Webb's decision to stay put while the siege was in progress was not shared by William Johnson and others present at the time. Johnson's brief move towards Fort William Henry had caused a split in the French force. It would appear that Webb could have at least sent out large detachments in force to intimidate and harass the French. This would have relieved the pressure on Fort William Henry and eased the frustration of his own troops. Those provincials in the beleaguered fort who had given up hope may well have taken heart from the sound of gunfire in the enemy's rear and returned to the fight.

Webb wasted no time in writing an account to Lord Loudoun, delayed at Halifax, his assault on Louisbourg thwarted by fog. It comes as no surprise that Webb appeared innocent of any neglect. "The enemy are 11–12,000 strong," he wrote, "confirmed by two Lieuts. and two soldiers who deserted," while Webb supposedly now had only "4,500 men fit for duty," less than previously claimed. Webb praised the regulars for their performance at Fort William Henry while the provincials "were rather backward. I suppose owing to their being so little accustomed to that type of war."[13] Webb could well have been writing about himself.

Arrivals during the evening included Colonel Frye and Captains McCloud and Hitchcock. Guided in by signal guns, they were just happy to be alive despite being scratched and battered during their flight through the woods. Major John Gilman of the New York Regiment also turned up. Among Gilman's losses was his young black slave captured by Indians. Pursued through the woods, the major had been "obliged to swim the Hudson River three times." A famished Sergeant Carver did not make it to safety till August 13 after "enduring the severity of the cold dews for three nights." Once at Fort Edward, "with proper care my body soon recovered its wonted strength, and my mind, as far as the recollection of the late melancholy events would permit, its usual composure."[14] The following day, the "melancholy events" were topped off with both rain and a solar eclipse. But it "was So Clouded we could Scaircely Perseve it," recalled Jabez Fitch. And Private Luke Gridley recorded "day 14 which was ye Sabath two frinchmen Came In hear & one frinch ofesser with ye flags truce ye time of ye Sun Cleps."[15]

The French officer to arrive during "ye Sun Cleps" was Lieutenant Savournin of the La Sarre Regiment. He had been dispatched by Montcalm with a 30-man escort to parley in regard to the British prisoners still held at Fort William Henry. Savournin, blindfolded, was taken through the gates to the general's quarters. He handed over two letters from Montcalm, one for Lord Loudoun and the other for Webb. In these Montcalm apologized for the massacre, but claimed he was not responsible and had done all in his power to prevent it.

Details for the transfer of prisoners were discussed and agreed upon. They would all be returned except Captain Faesch who would remain hostage with the French until certain prisoners were released, and Captain Ormsby, who was too badly wounded to travel. Montcalm insisted that the surrender terms were still valid and "added that the least infraction on the part of the English," recalled Bougainville, "would bring unpleasant consequences."[16]

The following morning, August 15, two companies of redcoats and 200 volunteers marched from Fort Edward under a cold rain. At Half Way Brook they met the prisoners with an escort commanded by Luc de La Corne, one of those who had encouraged the Indians to violate the surrender terms. Colonel Monro and about 500 others were handed over along with the six-pounder cannon previously promised. As they marched back towards Fort Edward they counted about 30 dead bodies "and from the frequent stench" it was assumed many more lay in the woods. At 3 o'clock Jabez Fitch saw Monro ride in on horseback, flanked by James Furnis and Adam Williamson, both on foot. Colonel Young, due to his foot wound, was borne on a stretcher, and behind them plodded the wet survivors from the massacre at Fort William Henry.[17] But even they were not the last to arrive. "Came in one of the Regulars who had been out in the woods ever since Fort Wm. Henry was taken," noted Captain Putnam four days later.[18] Exactly how many had been killed in the massacre is not known, estimates varying from 70 to 200 men, women and children.

Bougainville claimed French losses during the siege, including Indians, as a mere 17 killed and 40 wounded. This included one officer wounded and none killed.[19] If correct, these were remarkably light casualties based on the reported clashes and British cannon fire throughout the siege. The British claimed 45 of their own killed and 70 wounded, before the massacre took place.[20]

Lord Loudoun, meanwhile, was aboard ship off Nova Scotia. A dispatch boat from Massachusetts came alongside with the startling news that Fort William Henry was under siege. A few days later he learned of the surrender and the terms "inhumanly and villainously broken." "I am on the way," he wrote to Webb, "with a force sufficient to turn the scale, with God's assistance; and then I hope we shall teach the French to comply with the laws of nature and humanity ... the murders committed at Oswego and now at Fort William Henry, will oblige me to make those gentlemen sick of such inhuman villainy whenever it is in my power."[21]

Colonel Frye and his regiment left Fort Edward for Albany on August 13 and three days later Colonel Monro and the survivors from the 35th followed. But Webb, still fearing a French advance, kept the recently arrived militia on station. Fed up with poor living conditions, no tents, blankets and cooking utensils, many were far from happy. They had come to fight under a redcoat general who did not fight and Fort William Henry had fallen. It comes as little surprise that morale was low. The New York provincials packed up to go home and threatened death to any officers who stood in the way. But the mutiny was forcefully quelled and court martials followed. A sergeant was shot, but not only rank and file were found guilty of mutiny. Captain Samuel Knowles was cashiered after having his sword ritually broken over his head.[22]

But Webb was not the only one with mutiny concerns. "Madness and indecent folly on the part of the Canadians," recalled Bougainville on August 17. "Officers and men leave without permission. It was necessary to fire over their heads to stop them." The demolition of Fort William Henry was not yet complete. But, with order restored, things quieted down, and two days later, "all the army sang a *Te Deum*."[23]

Many of the Indians, meanwhile, had arrived in Montréal. They sold plundered goods to the locals, including Colonel Young's silver mounted pistols, and over 200 prisoners were put up for sale. Vaudreuil took them to task for having violated the capitulation. They placed the blame on the domesticated Indians for having led the attack, but the governor was not impressed. The prisoners were proof of their own betrayal, and they must be returned. He offered two kegs of brandy for each prisoner, but the Indians felt their prizes were worth more than that. On August 15, "in the presence of the entire town," recalled Bougainville, the Indians assembled the prisoners and "killed one of them, put him a kettle, and forced his unfortunate compatriots to eat him"[24]—a warning to Vaudreuil to raise his price. The news of this going abroad would cause further condemnation of the French. Far better to pay up before any more prisoners went the same way. Vaudreuil "let them do what they pleased," recalled one resident, "they were seen roaming about Montréal, knife in hand, threatening everybody, and often insulting those who they met. When complaint was made, he said nothing. Far from it; instead of reproaching them, he loaded them up with gifts, in the belief that their cruelty would relent."[25]

"I believe that if immediately upon their arrival," recalled Bougainville, "the Governor had stated to them that until all the English were given up, there would be no presents, or even any food, that under the most severe penalties he had forbidden the citizens either to sell or to give them brandy, that he himself could have gone to their cabins and snatched the English away from them."[26]

But Vaudreuil handled things his own way and by the end of August had managed to retrieve virtually all the prisoners held in Montréal. The price had been 30 bottles of brandy and 130 livres worth of goods per captive. The Indians, their canoes loaded up with clothing, tobacco, vermilion, lace and liquor, paddled away to a final, wild gathering at Lachine, the place for departure. Here "they were swimming in this liquor, drinking it by the kegfulls," recalled Bougainville, "and not leaving the keg until they fell down dead drunk." In early September the prisoners freed in Montréal were taken downriver to Québec where they put behind bars while vessels were prepared for their voyage back to British territory. They included survivors from Sabbath Day Point, several women and children, and Captain Faesch, previously held by Montcalm as a hostage. The men were required to work in the city magazine during the day and, combined with scant rations and smallpox, several did not live to board the three vessels prepared for their departure.

The ships sailed in late September and dropped anchor at Louisburg on October 11 for a brief stopover before continuing to Halifax, but smallpox was on board and several more died. At Halifax 304 survivors were placed aboard British ships which sailed south and they debarked in Boston Harbor during early November, nearly four months after the massacre had occurred.[27] They were now safe, but several hundred more prisoners remained spread throughout numerous Indian villages and the work of recovering them went on. Precise figures will can never be confirmed, but it would appear that 308 soldiers and an unknown number of civilians remained missing by the end of 1757, their bodies not found or identified following the massacre, or still held captive. More were recovered, and by the end of the Seven Years' War in 1763, about 174 soldiers remained on the missing list.[28] Some would have assimilated into the tribes to live out their days, assuming they did not die of the smallpox epidemic which ravaged the Indian communities, the result of infected scalps and prisoners having been brought back to their villages. One drummer boy managed to escape and rejoin the 35th three years after the massacre, but had to relearn his native tongue.[29]

On August 15, Colonel Frye and the survivors of the 35th arrived in Albany. News of the capitulation and subsequent massacre spread like wildfire through the British colonies, the numbers of dead and scalped exaggerated with each retelling. Here was more proof of French inhumanity after the killing of the disabled at Oswego. But a letter to Loudoun from Vaudreuil, later published in American papers, claimed the British had brought the massacre on themselves by supplying liquor to the Indians and not putting up a vigorous defense. But Monro insisted in an official report that he had personally supervised the destruction of all liquor following the capitulation. According to Monro the French had stood by as the attack took place, but Montcalm claimed he had paid 2,000 livres of his own money to secure the release of prisoners, proof of his own innocence in the affair.

It comes as little surprise, however, that mere words from the French could not stem the moral indignation that swept through the colonies. Captain Israel Putnam had reconnoitered the battlefield and, despite apparently seeing a "spectacle" that was "too diabolical and awful either to be endured or described," he gave a concise description. The fort "was entirely demolished; the barracks, out-houses, and buildings, were a heap of ruins; the cannon, stores and boats were all carried away. The fires were still burning; the smoke and stench offensive and suffocating. Innumerable fragments, human skulls and bones, and carcasses half consumed, were still frying and broiling in the decaying fires. Dead bodies, mangled with knives and tomahawks, in all the wantonness of Indian fierceness and barbarity, were everywhere to be seen. More than one hundred women, butchered and shockingly mangled, lay upon the ground, still weltering in their gore."[30]

The following appeared in the *London Magazine*: "It is certain that the Growth of the English Colonies has long been the grand Object of the French Envy, and it is said that their Officers have orders from their superiors to check it at all events, and to that end, make the present War as bloody and destructive as can be possible! It is evident, that all their Measures tend this Way.... To what a Pitch of Perfidy and Cruelty is the French Nation arrived? Would not an ancient Heathen shudder with Horror, on hearing so hideous a Tale.... It is hard for an Englishman to kill his enemy that lies at his feet begging his life."[31]

Or was it?

Perhaps the writer was ignorant of another hideous tale that cut close to the British bone. Only 11 years earlier, the English had bayoneted the Scots wounded after the Battle of Culloden. The redcoats had then indulged in an orgy of rapine and pillage through the Scottish Highlands, burning the village of friend and foe alike. The English commander was Prince William, the Duke of Cumberland. "Butcher Cumberland," as many called him, was commander-in-chief of the British Army when Fort William Henry fell. Perhaps the British had memories of "Perfidy and Cruelty" best swept under the carpet when remonstrating about the inhumanity of the French.[32]

13

Carnage at Fort Carillon

On August 31 Lord Loudoun dropped anchor in New York harbor to learn that the French had retreated back to Fort Carillon. Montcalm had destroyed Britain's northernmost post, but the southern end of Lake George had merely become a no-man's-land, not actually occupied by the French. Loudoun marched his soldiers to Fort Edward and claimed he might yet wreak revenge by capturing Fort Carillon. But by then the British militia had dispersed and no such move transpired. It was time for the British to lick their wounds and reassess the situation.

Lieutenant Colonel George Monro was distraught with the fall of his post and the massacre that followed. Despite recognition of a valiant defense, his first combat command had seen defeat, and the terms he signed had not been honored. He wrote to Loudoun denouncing his superior's lack of action, but, despite whisperings and rumblings, no official blame was attributed to Webb. The ailing, 57-year-old Monro never recovered, and on November 3 he collapsed and died in a frosty Albany street. His death was attributed to apoplexy, but many felt the memory of scalped bodies of men, women and children was the real reason. The day after his death, Monro was buried at St. Peter's Church, Albany.[1] Built in 1715, the stone building had been the first Anglican church north of New York, and the first west of the Hudson,[2] a fitting, last resting place for one who, through defeat, had played his role in an ultimate British victory. "Remember Fort William Henry" would be the battle cry of the British troops.

Wishing everyone would, in fact, forget Fort William Henry, Loudoun and Webb were recalled to England. The failure to take Louisbourg and the William Henry disaster made it apparent a fresh approach was required. These gentlemen were ultimately rewarded for their shortcomings, however. Lord Loudoun was promoted to lieutenant general and served against the Spanish in 1762 without fighting any major battles. Upon return at the war's end in 1763 he was appointed governor of Edinburgh Castle and was promoted to full general in 1770.

In 1759 Webb was promoted to major general and then lieutenant general in 1761. But he never regained the respect of his fellow officers. "I have been treated like a dog," he complained in a letter from Germany to General Amherst, and "have room for complaint against some of your friends."[3] The year 1757 also saw the end of "Butcher" Cumberland's military career. After a bundled campaign against the French in Germany he returned to England where his father, King George, greeted him at court with "Here is my son who has ruined me and disgraced himself."[4] Cumberland promptly resigned all military appointments and turned his attention to fast horses and politics.

But British commanders were not the only ones derided. The Marquis de Vaudreuil was "a timid man and one who knows neither how to make a resolution, or keep one once

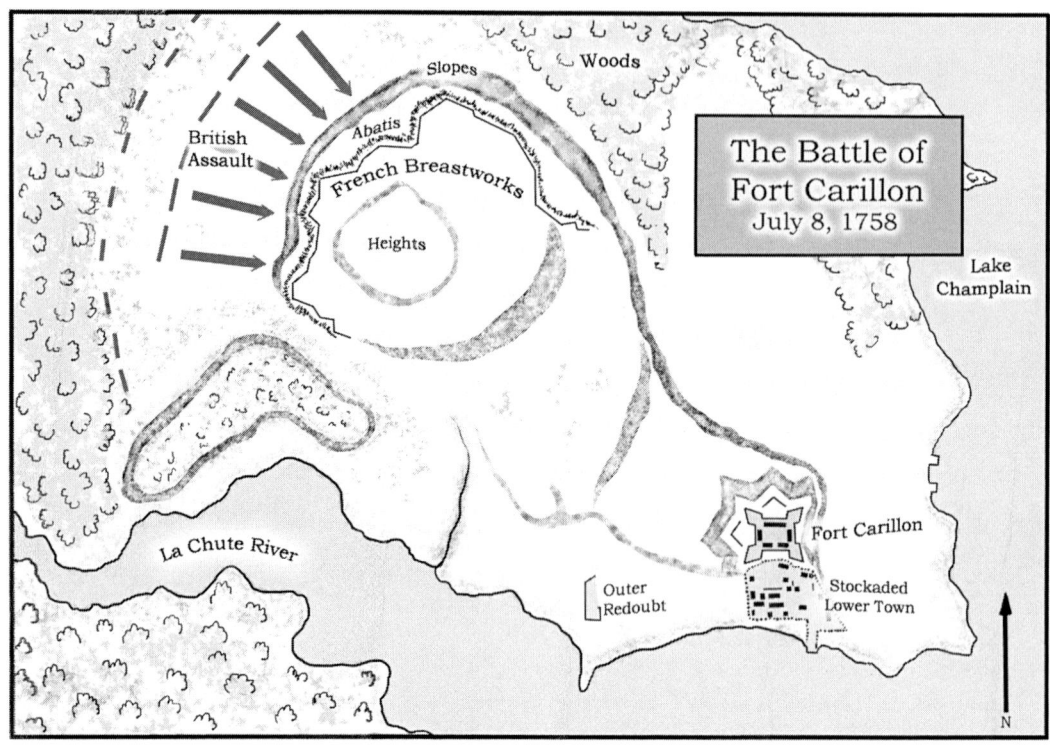

Map by the author.

made," claimed Bougainville."⁵ But "I have ruined the plans of the English," claimed Vaudreuil in a letter to Paris in February of 1758. "I have disposed the Five Nations (Iroquois) to attack them; I have carried consternation and terror into all those parts." His main achievement would appear to have been ordering an attack on the settlement of German Flatts, New York, in November of 1757. This occurred as Bougainville penned his "timid man" lines. The village, located on the Mohawk River, was populated by industrious settlers from the Palatinate region in Germany who had little time for their English neighbors. Vaudreuil had hoped they would join the French cause along with the Oneida Indians who resided nearby. But when their cooperation was not forthcoming, he took the "you're with us or against us" attitude and ordered that German Flatts be annihilated. At 3 a.m. on November 12 French shells burst in the settlement and a force of 300 Canadians and whooping Indians swept in. The occupants fled into five blockhouses built for such an occasion, but brisk enemy gunfire saw them surrender one after the another, and the structures went up in flames. Sixty homes along with their outbuildings were put to the torch, and between 50 and 60 settlers were killed, while three times that number, mainly women and children, were taken prisoner. Refugees crossed the Mohawk and alerted the British garrison of 200 soldiers at Fort Herkimer. Commanding officer Captain Townsend, however, sent only 50 men to counterattack.⁶ Shots were exchanged, but to no great effect. The Canadians and Indians killed the village livestock, then disappeared back into the woods. When British troops arrived in force, where once a thriving settlement had been, they found nothing but dead bodies and smoldering ruins.⁷ "The Indians pillaged and burned everything," recalled Bougainville. "They brought back 150 prisoners among whom was the mayor of the village.

We had only three men slightly wounded."⁸ These settlers had only been guilty of attempting to remain neutral in a vicious war.

General James Abercrombie, Loudoun's second, was appointed as the new commander-in-chief in North America, backed up by Generals Jeffery Amherst and John Forbes. In 1758 redcoat reinforcements were shipped to America, and Secretary of State William Pitt asked the colonies to supply 20,000 men, most costs to be borne by the British crown. Glad to see the back of Loudoun, they readily agreed.⁹ By the year's end 50,000 regular and provincial troops would be under arms, the French badly outnumbered. Pitt also introduced changes regarding the equality of regular and provincial officers. Beforehand, the general rule existed where a regular officer outranked a provincial officer, regardless of the rank held by either. The American officers "know no more of what is to be done than a sergeant, till the orders come out," wrote Massachusetts army chaplain John Cleveland. Most British officers had seen little active service and were from class-ridden, gentrified families. Not happy with the changes, they had a sneering contempt for the locals. "A farmer is not to be taken from the plough and made an officer in a day," wrote one in the *London Chronicle*.¹⁰ The provincials did lack the discipline of regulars kept in line with the lash, but perhaps a farmer who had fought Indians in the wilderness was more use than a young gent from London. The Americans bridled at an attitude which persisted throughout the war and, no doubt, helped prepare them to take up arms against the British in 1775.

Despite the usual logistical frustrations, General Amherst launched a fresh campaign against Louisbourg while Forbes did the same against that old thorn in British pride: Fort Duquesne. And then, of course, there was Fort William Henry to avenge. Fort Carillon still stood unscathed while the ashes of British defeat lay at the opposite end of Lake George. Built along similar lines to William Henry, Fort Carillon stood on a rocky plateau with water on three sides. On the Southern slope stood a stockaded village of taverns, shops, and bakeries fronting the junction of the La Chute River and Lake Champlain. British rangers kept an eye on the fort, and on November 19, 1757, 300 "showed themselves at the edge of the woods," recalled Bougainville. "A sergeant and fifteen men, who were covering the wood choppers and charcoal burners, showed good spirit and fell back without loss." A detachment of 60 men moved quickly from Fort Carillon, opened fire, and "the enemy disappeared after having set fire to a charcoal kiln."¹¹ But such minor harassment was a mere prelude to coming events.

The campaign to take Fort Carillon came under the personal wing of the overall British commander, General Abercrombie. But this gentleman had achieved his position at the behest of King George's patronage rather than a flair for military skill. The expedition's guiding light was Brigadier Lord George Howe. Considered by many the best officer in the British army, Howe spent nights in the woods roughing it with Rogers' Rangers and introduced reforms for frontier fighting. He unified the regulars and provincials, becoming the idol of those under his command.

The largest army seen on the American continent assembled around the scorched remains of Fort William Henry. As the mist rose on the morning of July 5 the British force of over 6,000 regulars and 9,000 provincials cast off aboard a massive fleet and headed north.¹² The provincials in blue uniforms, and the regulars in red, were buoyed with optimism. How could the French withstand such a mighty host? Beneath the summer sky, various craft with colorful banners waving, moved steadily across the waters of Lake George. At the rear came the flatboats and bateaux carrying artillery and stores.

Counted among the troops were the Scottish Highlanders of the 42nd Regiment.

Following the Battle of Culloden the wearing of kilts, bearing of arms and playing of bagpipes had all been banned in Scotland—unless you joined His Majesty's armed forces. The warrior-minded young Highlanders enlisted in droves.

At 5 p.m. the flotilla paused at Sabbath Day Point—an ill omen, perhaps. At 11 that night the expedition cast off once more after the slower artillery and baggage arrived.[13] At dawn the advance boats arrived at the northern end of Lake George. By noon all the troops, but not the artillery, were ashore, and the ranger companies of Robert Rogers and Israel Putnam moved into the woods to scout ahead. The plan was to move towards Fort Carillon by a circuitous route to the west of the river, not using the original road as the bridges crossing the La Chute River had been destroyed by the French. The army formed and marched in four columns, but soon became scattered and confused amidst the undergrowth, fallen tree trunks, and low hanging boughs of dense woods.

A French force of about 350 men had watched the flotilla pass, but did not fall back towards Fort Carillon with sufficient speed and were cut off by the British advance. Lord Howe was moving in front of the main British force with 200 rangers under Major Putnam when they were challenged by a cry from the woods. Despite replying in French, the foliage erupted with a volley of musket fire. The rangers shot back and Major Rogers' force, some little distance off, moved quickly to the sound of battle. The French soon found themselves under fire from two fronts. They fought with desperation but, heavily outnumbered, spread out in a confused retreat through the woods. Some drowned attempting to swim the rapids of the La Chute, and only about 50 made it back to the French lines, the others either killed or captured.

The British had won the skirmish, but paid a horrendous price. When the smoke cleared Lord Howe lay dead, shot through the chest. "The fall of this noble and brave officer," recalled Rogers, "seemed to produce an almost general languor and consternation through the whole army."[14] Abercrombie, although an exceptional organizer, did not have the charisma or track record to inspire the troops. The British "were only a body without a head since the death of Milord Howe," recalled Bougainville.[15]

Following a bewildering night in the woods, Abercrombie ordered a withdrawal to the original landing place. A major reassessment was in order. Late the following morning, July 7, Lieutenant Colonel John Bradstreet was ordered forward to repair the bridges destroyed by the French, with hindsight, the logical choice. The repairs were speedily completed without coming under enemy fire. The army advanced once more along the portage road and in the late afternoon arrived at the now deserted French sawmill at the Falls. Montcalm, meanwhile, hastily prepared timber fortifications atop a rise about three quarters of a mile to the northeast of Fort Carillon. The officers, axes in hand, worked alongside the men before planting their colors on tree trunks piled high to form a zigzag breastwork along the crest of a ridge. Before this an abatis of sharpened, interlocked tree branches was constructed. To take the position, the enemy would have to advance uphill over stumps and fallen trees. Behind these defenses Montcalm would have only 3,526 men, mainly French regulars and Canadian militia. A mere 250 Indians were on hand. Many had become disenchanted with the French alliance. "What is the cause of it?" asked Bougainville. "The great loss they have suffered from the smallpox, the bad medicine the French have thrown to them, the great greed of the commanders of the posts and their ignorance of Indian customs? They are merchants that favour and intrigue while charged with a business most important to the safety of the colony. Besides the English have sent a wampum belt to all the nations and make them the finest offers."[16]

On the morning of July 8 Sir William Johnson joined the British with 300 Choctaw, Delaware and Iroquois warriors, then another 150 arrived, more Indians with the British than the French for the first time. From over the river, they "let off a great fusillade" from the slopes of Rattlesnake Mountain, but at that distance scored no hits. Unlike earlier battles, the presence of Indians would have no effect on the final outcome.[17]

Normal tactics required an artillery barrage of the enemy's fortifications before making any massed infantry assault. Montcalm had taken Fort William Henry by bombardment alone. At Fort Carillon the British artillery were yet to arrive, however, and Abercrombie believed from prisoners that enemy reinforcements were on the way. An engineer assessed the French fortifications, and concluded they could be taken by storm, thus Abercrombie played right into Montcalm's hands.

At 12:30 the first gunfire was heard. A French skirmish line beyond the breastworks had fired a volley as British rangers and provincials moved from the woods. The skirmishers fell back behind the breastworks, and the Americans opened musket fire on the heights. Redcoats emerged from the woods behind them, and the provincials opened ranks to allow the four columns to begin their advance.[18] They would have to advance over ground prepared by the French for their own advantage, but the sight of the vast red tide with glinting bayonets was too much for "a large number" of the Canadian militia who turned and fled. Making for the boats on Lake Champlain they had to pass Fort Carillon, and found themselves under French fire. One deserter was wounded and the others turned back to take refuge behind their original fortifications, or shelter behind stumps. "These were not Canadians of the best sort," recalled Bougainville.[19]

Order was restored as the redcoats advanced, keeping the best line they could while scrambling over felled trees and ragged stumps. Behind them the provincials delivered a steady fire on the French line, but then the wooden rampart erupted with a blast of billowing smoke. The French infantry fired through loopholes while grapeshot from Montcalm's cannon swept the slope. The advancing redcoats were "cut down like grass," recalled provincial Private Joseph Nichols.[20]

Meanwhile, "a few of the enemy's barges and pontoons advanced down the River of the Falls," recalled Bougainville. The boats received musket volleys from volunteers and two companies of regulars along the shore, and then the fort's cannon opened fire. Fountains of water splashed about the craft and splinters flew as balls struck home. Two smashed boats went down, the survivors left floundering in the water. Oars were hastily put to work as the remaining boats turned back. They stayed securely anchored for the remainder of the fight.[21]

The redcoats on the slope reached the sharp prongs of the abatis and, stalled in their advance, returned musket fire, reloading their Brown Bess flintlocks as fast as possible. A soldier could get off four shots per minute, assuming there were no misfires. After an hour the ragged redcoat line, with many officers either killed or wounded, finally fell back to the sheltering woods. Behind them lay dead and groaning men slumped across blood-splattered stumps and logs. Abercrombie and his aides, back at the sawmill, could not see the carnage. When the bad news arrived orders were sent to renew the assault.[22] Again the redcoat lined surged forward, and again the French guns spoke. Montcalm dashed along the firing line through a grey haze of gunsmoke shouting encouragement. "*Vive notre General!*" his men yelled.

Hit by another barrage of grapeshot and musket balls, the redcoats retreated, but yet again they were ordered forward. Men cursed and fell amidst the stumps and bodies of their comrades, and the provincials moved forward to lend support. "A man could not stand erect without being hit, any more than he could stand in a shower without having rain fall upon him," recalled David Perry, a 17-year-old from Massachusetts.[23] Despite this, some managed to cut their way through the abatis and actually arrive at the base of the wooden breastworks. One Rhode Island man, William Smith, though wounded, managed to scale the wall and tomahawk a French soldier, then drop back to the ground. His bravery seen by a British officer, two redcoats were ordered to bring him back which, through a haze of gunsmoke and covering fire, was bravely achieved.

Throughout the afternoon the redcoat lines surged back and forth, losing men with each futile charge. Behind the barricades, Colonel Bourlamaque received a severe wound and Bougainville's head was grazed by a musket ball. Some Canadian officers were well prepared for defeat, an escape bateaux being kept in readiness "under the pretext that the Marquis de Montcalm wished to send dispatches to Montréal," recalled Bougainville. "Can one think ill of Sieurs Mercier and de Lotbiniere for thus having taken precaution to save for the colony their talents so precious to it?"[24]

Canadian reserves on the low ground to the French right, not under attack, were ordered out by de Lévis to make two sorties beyond the breastworks and fire into the enemy flank. But the enemy column, recalled Bougainville, "composed of English grenadiers and Scottish Highlanders, returned unceasingly to the attack, without becoming discouraged or broken, and several got themselves killed within fifteen paces of our abatis."[25] The Highland warriors in particular fought with relentless courage, half of them cut down including Major Duncan Campbell, carried from the field with a mortal wound. Captain John Campbell and a handful of followers actually scaled the log wall, plunged into the French and fought with fury, only to die by bayonet thrust.

More than once French cannon fire set fire to their own abatis, the flames and smoke adding to the confusion. Men scrambled over the walls and managed to extinguish the flames before they spread along the line. Behind the bulwarks a constant supply of powder and ball arrived along with casks of water to quench raging thirsts.[26]

At six o'clock another charge against the French line was made, against the center and the left, only to have more men die in a pointless, suicidal attack. Demoralized, and knowing the day was lost, the British fell back, carrying wounded, as rangers and provincials kept up a brisk covering fire. By 7:30 the field fell silent as the despondent British force trudged back to the Falls. The French made no attempt to pursue. Despite the British casualties, Montcalm knew he was still vastly outnumbered and, expecting a renewed assault the following day, ordered the fortifications to be strengthened during the night.

Despite his overwhelming numbers, however, his artillery cold and untried, Abercrombie gave the order to move out. "Wherever I went, I found people, officers and soldiers, astonished that we left the French ground," recalled the Rev. John Cleveland.[27] Boats were hastily boarded and the once grand expedition sailed sadly south. Over the next two days the French reconnoitered to find "Wounded, provisions, abandoned equipment," recalled Bougainville, and "shoes left in miry places, remains of barges and burned pontoons; incontestable proof of the great loss our enemy had suffered." The British loss on July 8 was 547 killed, 1,356 wounded and 77 missing. Montcalm's force lost 104 killed and 273 wounded.[28]

Bougainville observed that, had the British portaged barges into Lake Champlain, they could have cut off the French supply line from the north and, with only five days provisions on hand, the French would have been obliged to abandon Fort Carillon.[29] History has placed the British defeat squarely on Abercrombie's shoulders. But at least one surgeon serving with the troops felt there was another reason: "Sad, sad it is to see how the Sabbath is profaned in the camp," wrote Dr. Caleb Rae, especially by "the horrid custom of swearing, more especially among the regulars; and I can't but charge our defeat on this sin."[30]

The redcoats would score similar losses 57 years later when they repeated history at New Orleans, despite their artillery barrage before the charge. Some lessons are slowly learned, as seen with Pickett's Charge at Gettysburg in 1863, and troops assaulting barbed wire and machine guns at the Somme in 1916. These were far greater disasters than Fort Carillon. This would become another obscure battle largely lost to the mists of time.

14

The Death Throes of Fort Duquesne

Montcalm's success at Fort Carillon was the outstanding French triumph of the French and Indian War. But even that was a defensive battle, a territorial retreat from their success at Fort William Henry.

The great French fortress of Louisbourg at Nova Scotia, meanwhile, was under attack by an expedition under General Jeffery Amherst. It surrendered after a six-week siege on July 26. News traveled slowly and Bougainville, at Fort Carillon, did not hear until September 2, and then it was from the enemy. As arrangements were being made for an exchange of prisoners, Captain Abercrombie, nephew of the British general, sent Bougainville an article about the capitulation cut from the *New York Gazette*. But "I believe the news false," wrote Bougainville. He already had a bet with Abercrombie that Louisbourg would not be taken before August 15. Bougainville preferred to believe the falsehood was "published in their colony to encourage the citizens and the soldiers." According to last letters from the fortress, it was only being fired on by two batteries from a distance of 600 yards, too distant to do great damage to the massive stone walls. The defenders "had made entrenchments to resist the assault, all the streets were barricaded, the houses loopholed, the wharves fortified, everything, then, proclaimed the resolution to conquer or perish."[1]

But the horrible truth was confirmed from French sources on September 6. And that was not all. Fort Frontenac had fallen on August 28. While Louisbourg held much control over the gateway to the St. Lawrence, Fort Frontenac, located at the source of the same river on Lake Ontario, controlled the major supply and communication line from Québec to the southwesterly posts. At Frontenac they had lost, in addition to boats and artillery, "many munitions and provisions destined for supplying the Far West," recalled Bougainville, "an irreparable loss under the present circumstances."[2]

About 100 Indians at Carillon were most displeased to hear confirmation that their French allies were in decline. What retribution might the British take? They expressed a desire to head for home, but Montcalm was not prepared to let his best scouts go just yet. Wampum belts, brandy, and a roast pig feast were offered. And, best of all, "a war song sung by the Marquis de Montcalm." The general had, no doubt, not envisioned this when he joined the army at the very tender age of nine.[3] Given these inducements the warriors agreed to stay—but only for another week.

The French, however, may have taken solace from a minor victory at the Great Carrying Place between Abercrombie's camp on Lake George and Fort Edward. The day following Louisburg's fall a British convoy was ambushed at Half Way Brook by Canadians and Indians under La Corne. They killed 116 men and butchered 35 teams of oxen. When news arrived at Fort Edward, Robert Rogers led 700 men out to hunt the culprits down, but after an extensive sweep through wooded terrain had no success. On August 8, as they

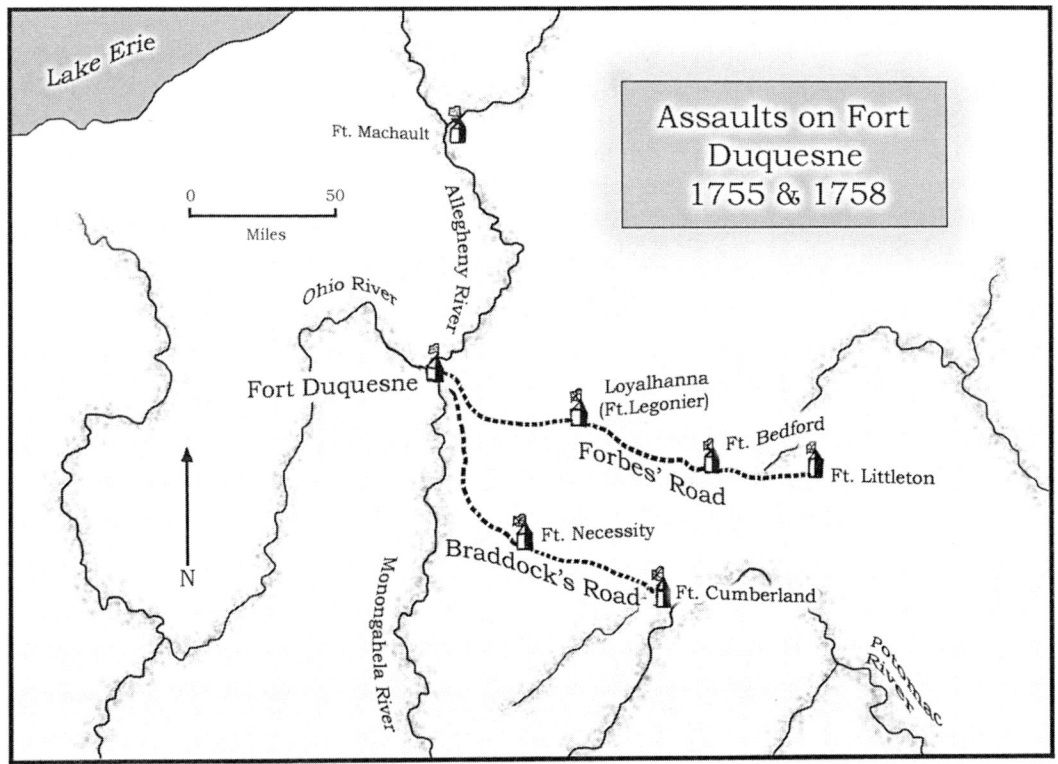

Map by the author.

marched back towards Fort Edward, the advance guard under Israel Putnam walked straight into another ambush by 450 French, Canadians and Indians under Joseph Marin. Abenaki warriors bolted from the undergrowth and Putnam and three others found themselves in hand-to-hand combat. The major was taken captive as a brisk gunfight followed. He was pulled through the woods with a leather thong around his neck as the French, finding themselves outnumbered, withdrew. Once clear of the enemy, Putnam was tied to an elm tree by the Indians who gleefully placed branches about his feet and set them alight. But Joseph Marin bolted onto the scene and demanded his immediate release. The Abenakis begrudgingly complied, and Putnam leapt clear of the flames. Marin took his captive back to Fort Carillon where he was kept under guard until being exchanged.[4]

Fort Duquesne, that elusive French stronghold in Ohio territory, was still in French hands. It was commanded by Captain François-Marie Le Marchand de Lignery who had received the *Ordre Royal et Militaire de St.-Louis* for his role in Braddock's defeat. Brigadier John Forbes was given the task of leading another expedition to take the post and, having no wish to emulate Braddock, decided to cut a new road through the wilderness and apply new tactics. It was his plan to march from Philadelphia, move slowly, and establish forts with munitions and supplies as he progressed. This would prevent the need for a heavy baggage train when nearing Duquesne. He also hoped the enemy Indians "little accustomed to remain long in the same place," recalled Bougainville, "would have left a permanent camp, and at the same time, their long sojourn there in the continual waiting for a nearby invasion, would have resulted in a great consumption of things of all sorts."[5]

Forbes wrote to William Pitt of "the new road across the Allegheny Mountains, and over Laurell Hill, (leaving the Rivers Yohiegany and Monongahola to my left hand) straight to the Ohio, by which I have saved a great deal of way, and prevented the misfortunes that the overflowing of those rivers might occasion."[6] Forbes was in favor of "equipping numbers of our men like the savages…. In this country we must learn the art of war from enemy Indians, or any one else who has seen it carried on here."[7] But he, like many other British officers, was not impressed with the colonial militia. He felt many of their lower-ranking officers were "an extremely bad collection of broken innkeepers, horse-jockeys, and Indian traders." Naturally he didn't think much of the rank and file either, but like Braddock before him, would find cause to modify his views.[8]

Colonel George Washington firmly believed they should be following Braddock's shorter road from Fort Cumberland rather than trying to carve a new one across rugged, wooded terrain. And some Indians were of the same view. Sixty warriors officered to go along with Colonel Byrd's Virginians if the troops followed Braddock's road. This was "a new system of military discipline, truly," replied Forbes, "and shows that my good friend Burd is either made a cat's-foot of himself, or knows little of me if he imagines sixty scoundrels are to direct me in my measures." The army's quartermaster-general, Sir John Sinclair, found dealing with "friendly" Indians and provincial commissioners "the greatest curse that our Lord can pronounce against sinners." Both Virginia and Pennsylvania claimed the Ohio country as their own and, to keep the Virginians happy, Forbes agreed that Braddock's Road be maintained and upgraded.

But Forbes should never have been burdened with command of such an arduous expedition. "I really cannot relate how much I have suffered in both body and mind of late," he wrote on September 2.[9] Suffering from an inflammation of vital organs and unable to ride, the ailing brigadier was carried on a litter slung between two horses. He was leading scarlet-clad Royal Americans, provincials from various colonies, and 1,200 Highlanders of Montgomery's Regiment. With wagon drivers and others, about 6,500 men in total.

The expedition moved at a snail's pace across the Appalachians. Lieutenant Colonel Henry Bouquet, a Swiss officer of the Royal Americans, led the advance and commenced construction of a post on Loyalhanna Creek (later named Fort Ligonier), about 50 miles from Fort Duquesne. Major James Grant saw an opportunity for independent action, and suggested he dash ahead with a small force to reconnoiter and take prisoners for interrogation. Without consulting Forbes who was with the main body to the rear, Bouquet agreed and Grant marched from the camp leading 900 Highlanders, Royal Americans and provincials.[10]

On September 14, 1758, under cover of darkness, they crested a rise about half a mile from the Fort Duquesne. Major Andrew Lewis was sent forward with 400 men to attack Indians supposedly in block houses outside the fort. Following a confused advance through the woods, Lewis became convinced they had been discovered, and trudged back with the bad news at dawn. Rather than falling back, Grant hastily came up with a second, ill conceived plan to bring on a fight. Glory be to him if he could actually capture Fort Duquesne.

Grant separated his men into various detachments who, under cover of morning fog, spread out, with no means of communication. Captain MacDonald was ordered forward with 100 Highlanders to an open field fronting the fort. Grant, with a reserve of 100 Highlanders and a company of Marylanders, remained in reserve on the hill. "In order to put on a good countenance, and convince our men they had no reason to be afraid," Grant reported, "I gave directions to our drums to beat the reveille." But MacDonald's men had much to fear as their rattling drums and wailing bagpipes had the French and Indians scrambling for muskets and ammunition. "Hardly had McDonald gone half the distance," reported Bouquet, "when he heard the whoop of the Indians, followed immediately by a sortie of nearly 300 French and Indians, who fell upon them."[11] The Highlanders opened fire and halted the enemy advance, but quickly found themselves surrounded. They broke through the cordon and reached the woods, despite Captain MacDonald and others having been shot and killed. The French, reinforced by troops moving from the fort, pursued them and the other British detachments back to Grant's hilltop position where a gunfight ensued for the best part of an hour, the yells and war whoops of the Indians shrill among the gunfire. Under a hail of bullets from an elusive enemy, "Fear got the better of every other passion," recalled Grant, "and I trust I shall never again see such panic among troops." As with Braddock, they bolted and fled. Captain Thomas Bullitt's 100 Virginians, however, fought a brave rear-guard action while many others managed to escape back to Loyalhanna. The British lost 342 killed, wounded and captured, while the French had only 16 casualties. Grant and Lewis were among those taken prisoner. Once paroled, Grant would claim the provincials' lack of discipline was the cause of the defeat, not his own planning, underestimation of the enemy's strength, and a desire to reap glory by capturing the fort rather than reconnoiter, as was planned. Colonel Bouquet wrote that the retreating troops "would probably have been cut to pieces but for Captain Bullitt and his Virginians, who kept up the whole French force till two thirds of them were killed."[12] Perhaps Bullitt was one of those whom Forbes considered a "broken innkeeper, horse-jockey, or Indian trader."

The English prisoner James Smith held at Duquesne recalled that one Indian had his own explanation for Grant's defeat. "Grant, in the first place, acted like a wise and experienced officer, in artfully approaching in the night without being discovered; but ... in place of slipping up quietly, and falling upon them with their broad swords, they beat the drums and played upon the bag-pipes." The chief concluded that Grant "had made too free with spirituous liquors during the night, and became intoxicated about day-light."[13] General Forbes seemed to be thinking along the same lines when he wrote "my friend Grant most certainly lost his wits, and by his thirst for fame brought on his own perdition, and ran great risk of ours."[14]

Despite this victory, however, the French were in bad shape. On the day of Grant's repulse, many Indians "left to return to their villages without anything being able to stop them," recalled Bougainville. "One then is very worried over the fate of Fort Duquesne."[15] The capture of Fort Frontenac had seen vital supplies en route fall into British hands. Encouraged by Grant's defeat, however, fort commander Captain Lignery decided the best form of defense was attack. He sent out the bulk of his force, 440 Canadians and 150 Delaware braves, to attack the post at Loyalhanna, despite some 2,000 men being garrisoned there. The stockade was still under construction and many troops were camped outside. On October 12 pickets guarding grazing stock some distance from the post came under attack. Colonel Byrd, in temporary command, sent out 200 Maryland troops who, outnumbered and under heavy fire, were soon driven back. Pennsylvania provincials marched out to join the fight with three companies of North Carolina men, under Major Hugh Waddell (great-grandfather of Captain James Waddell of the Civil War commerce raider CSS *Shenandoah*). As the French and Indians advanced, the provincials put up a stiff resistance, as recalled by captive James Smith at Fort Duquesne, who heard first-hand: "They met his army near Fort Ligoneer, and attacked them, but were frustrated in their design. They said that Forbes's men were beginning to learn the art of war, and that there were a great number of American riflemen along with the redcoats, who scattered out, took trees, and were good marks-men."[16] Despite this, the provincials fell back, but then the British artillery came into play. Balls and shells reined down and the French were driven back into the woods. After dark the assailants began sniping and launched another attack but, driven off with artillery once more, they abandoned the assault and headed back for Fort Duquesne. The British could claim a victory, but much damage had been done, the outside camps pillaged and livestock driven off. Colonel Bouquet, when he returned, saw the carnage and felt his men had failed, regardless of what the French thought. "This enterprise, which should have cost the enemy dearly," he wrote to Forbes, "shows a great deal of contempt for us, and the behavior of our troops in the woods justifies their idea only too well."[17]

Two weeks later, on October 26, Sir William Johnson and other officials concluded a parley with 500 Indian chiefs at Easton, Pennsylvania. They made peace with certain Iroquois tribes, former allies who had gone over to the French, and the Delawares and Shawnees.[18] The wily Indians had not been receiving gifts from the French as in earlier times, due largely to corruption among officials who sold at a profit instead. Forbes wrote to "the Shawanese and Delawares on the Ohio" informing them of his move against the French and advising that they send word "to any of your people, who may be at the French fort, to return forthwith to your towns; where you may sit by your fires, with your wives and children, quiet and undisturbed, and smoke your pipes in safety."[19] Along with French defeats, the Indian leaders could see the tide had turned and their future lay with the British interests—for the time being at least.

Following the Battle of Fort Carillon, Montcalm had written to Paris asking to be relieved of his command, only to have the request refused, and he now received disturbing reports of conditions at Fort Duquesne. He wrote to his wife, "Mutiny among the Canadians, who want to come home, the officers busy with making money, and stealing like mandarins. Their commander sets the example, and will come back with three or four hundred thousand francs; the pettiest ensign, who does not gamble, will have ten, twelve or fifteen thousand. The Indians don't like Ligneris, who is drunk every day."

In early November French captives informed Forbes, now at Loyalhanna, that the garrison at Fort Duquesne had been reduced due to lack of supplies. The brigadier set out on November 18 with a force of 2,500 men. He had intended to wait till spring, but it seemed Duquesne was vulnerable now. They traveled light, taking only a few small cannon, and no tents or wagons. They advanced on the fort, and on the night of the 23rd the distant boom of explosions could be heard. Next morning the troops moved out in three columns commanded by Colonels Montgomery, Bouquet and Washington. Soon grisly remains of soldiers who had died during Grant's attack were seen scattered through the woods. The heads of dead Highlanders had been placed atop wooden poles, their kilts draped beneath them. The Scots troops ached for revenge, but this was not to be. They moved in to see smoke curling into the cold, wintery sky from the deserted remains of Fort Duquesne, the fortifications blown up, the barracks and storehouses put to the torch.

George Washington wrote to Governor Francis Fauquier of Virginia on Forbes' behalf, "the enemy, after letting us get within a day's march of the place, burned the fort and ran away by the light of it, at night, going down the Ohio by water, to the number of about five hundred men." This turn of events "has been a matter of surprise to the whole army, and we cannot attribute it to more probable causes, than the weakness of the enemy, want of provisions, and the defection of their Indians."[20]

14. The Death Throes of Fort Duquesne

There had been no final grand battle, the fort taken by siege or storm, but the expedition was a success. Braddock's defeat had been avenged, and Fort Duquesne could be added to the British victory list. A stockade was constructed and garrisoned by 200 provincials which, with time, would grow to a post of importance, Fort Pitt, from which the city of Pittsburgh would emerge.

During December, the British expedition, "destitute of every comfort of life," marched back towards civilization, John Forbes still carried by litter. He made it back to Philadelphia, but did not recover from his illness and the grueling trek, dying there on March 11, 1759.

As the British had marched towards Fort Duquesne, Louis de Bougainville, having survived his bullet wound at Fort Carillon, almost lost his life by other means. "I passed the night stranded on a rock raised more than six feet above the low tide mark," he recalled. He had swum to shore through icy waters after being shipwrecked 26 miles above Québec. "I had been forced to abandon the bateau which the high seas had smashed." He made it back to Québec, but it was not long till he was on the water once more. On November 15 he sailed on board the 18-gun privateer *Victoire*, one of a small fleet bound for France. He had been dispatched by Montcalm to procure arms and reinforcements from a government now engaged in virtual global war. It was a stormy crossing and Bougainville came close to being shipwrecked again while being pursued close to land by enemy privateers. Once in Paris his service was recognized with a brevet to colonel and, from Louis XV himself, he received the coveted *Ordre Royal et Militaire de St.-Louis*.

But, when requesting reinforcements, "one does not try to save the stables when the house was on fire," he was informed by Monsieur de Berryer, the minister of Marine. Despite this, a plan to save Canada was presented to Madame de Pompadour, the king's valued friend, advisor, and former mistress. The scheme called for an invasion of British Carolina by 4,000 French troops who would arm German settlers and Cherokees, forcing the redcoats to withdraw from their moves against Canada. Pompadour presented the plan to a committee of ministers who agreed—it might just work. But where was the money to come from? the "King's coffers were empty," recalled Bougainville, and despite Pompadour's attempt to raise two million francs, the plan was shelved for lack of funds.

The despondent brevet colonel sailed for Canada with "only four hundred recruits and a few munitions," a token reinforcement which could make no difference to a tide of war that was now in full flow against the outnumbered French.[21]

15

Québec

While the masses went hungry due to failed harvests, the Canadian elite ate and drank to their heart's content. "Let them eat cake," Vaudreuil could well have declared, when told the peasants had no bread.

With Louisbourg occupied by the British, French vessels entering the St. Lawrence were forced to run a gauntlet of enemy ships. Not all made it, and the price of a barrel of flour soared to 200 franks.[1] Even more Indian tribes could see times had changed and they sent emissaries to William Johnson's conferences on the Mohawk River. "They understand very well the advantage of adhering to the stronger side," noted Captain Pierre Pouchot, commander of Fort Niagara, "for, although some of them are genuinely fond of us, they only like Europeans in relation to their own interests."[2]

Despite Frontenac and Duquesne having fallen, Fort Carillon was still held by the French in early 1759. The British launched campaigns to remedy that, and take Québec as well. Forty-two-year-old General Jeffery Amherst had taken Louisbourg, and replaced Abercrombie as commander-in-chief. The disaster at Fort Carillon had cast a huge dent in British pride, and the new commander took personal charge to put the matter right. Construction of a new fort was commenced near the ashes of Fort William Henry, and on July 21, Amherst's expedition of 11,000 men sailed north up Lake George. They arrived that evening, driving off a small French force, and took shelter along the deserted fortifications previously defended by Montcalm. Cannon were hauled into place and opened fire while Colonel Bourlamaque, commanding the fort, had most of his troops board boats and retreat northwards up Lake Champlain. Four hundred men were left behind to hold the fort as long as possible, and stall the enemy advance. They returned cannon fire, and several British, including Colonel Townsend, were killed by grapeshot and exploding shells.

On the evening of the 26th Bourlamaque ordered the remaining garrison to withdraw, but they had no intention of leaving the fort as a gift to Amherst. Three French deserters arrived in the British camp with news that a slow burning match had been left in the powder magazine. Amherst offered 100 guineas to any brave soul who would enter the fort and extinguish the flame. There were no takers. At 11 p.m. there was a shattering roar as the bastion holding the magazine exploded. Burning fragments were sent hurtling into the night sky and other structures caught fire. Despite the blast, the French flag still flew above the walls, and a British sergeant volunteered to rectify the problem. He braved the burning ruins and a cheer went up as the enemy colors fell.

The retreating French also destroyed Fort St. Frédéric as Amherst approached, then, at the end of July, they continued north to Isle aux Noix. Here Vaudreuil had ordered them to dig in and hold out at all costs. Amherst had assured William Pitt he would "make an eruption into Canada with the utmost vigor and despatch,"[3] but halted his advance at St.

Frédéric to build ships capable of challenging French vessels further north.[4] He commenced construction of a new fort, Crown Point, alongside the ruins of Fort St. Frédéric. It would be a massive structure, designed to mount over 100 cannon and hold 4,000 men. Fort Carillon was also repaired, strengthened, and renamed Fort Ticonderoga.

Fort Niagara, meanwhile, had also come under attack. It was a strong, strategically important post built where the waters of the Niagara River flow into Lake Ontario. Brigadier John Prideaux had arrived on July 6 with 2,000 regulars, 1,000 provincials and 1,000 Iroquois under William Johnson.[5] Having slipped past French guard boats on the lake, they landed in a marsh, taking the French by surprise. A smaller timber fort, Little Niagara, over one mile upriver, was abandoned and put to the torch. The garrison joined their comrades behind Fort Niagara's walls commanded by Captain Pierre Pouchot. The Indians had previously called Pouchot "Gategayogen," meaning the "Center of Good Fortune,"[6] but many, after making contact with Johnson's Iroquois, now deserted the post.[7] The worthy captain, however, with a garrison of 600, was determined to hold out. He counted on reinforcements ordered into the area by Vaudreuil to take Fort Pitt and restore the Ohio region to the French. One of those to receive Pouchot's plea for help was Captain de Lignery, the man who had abandoned Fort Duquesne to Brigadier Forbes.

Pouchot refused Prideaux's demand to surrender, and the British engineers went to work. Their hastily prepared trenches, however, were raked by enemy fire, and had to be

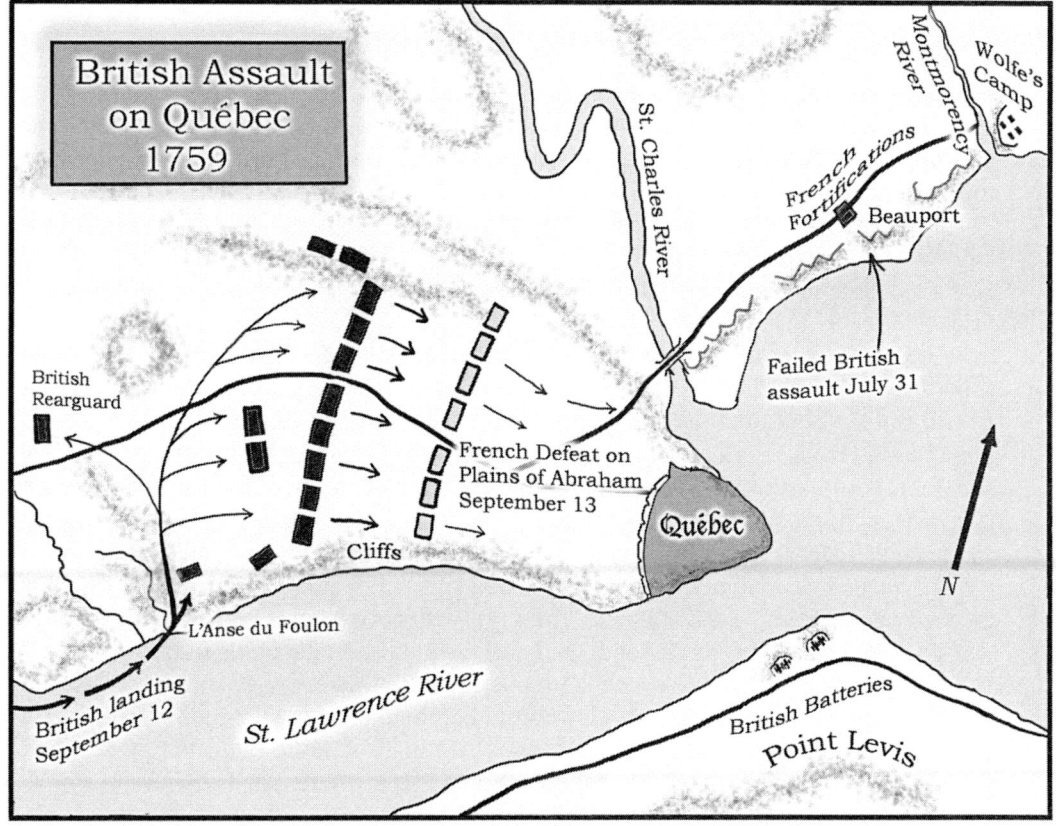

Map by the author.

abandoned. "Fools and blockheads, G—d d—n them," wrote Clan Chief Allan MacLeane.[8] New trenches were dug, guns were hauled in, and a fusillade of shot and shell was unleashed on the French walls. But this would be no nine day siege like Fort William Henry. Over the next few weeks, despite much damage and the garrison sustaining 100 casualties, Pouchot held out. The British batteries moved ever closer, but on July 19 Brigadier Prideaux was killed when a British shell exploded prematurely just after leaving the cannon barrel.[9] William Johnson took command and pressed the attack. By the 22nd a large breach had been formed, and the flag bastion rampart and battery had been destroyed. Volleys of musket fire were poured into the breach, and timber buildings caught fire as hot fragments from exploding shells flew about. Bags filled with earth replaced shattered masonry but, despite many of his guns being disabled, Pouchot refused to lower his colors. Scouts had brought word that a relief column was on the way.

On the morning of July 24 Pouchot was heartened to hear gunfire from the south. A French relief force had arrived under de Lignery and Captain Philippe Aubry. They led 1,100 troops and 200 Indians. It was a motley force and the colony troops included many whites who lived as Indians, their faces painted black and red, wearing deer skins adorned with porcupine quills, and eagle feathers trailing from long hair or shaven, plastered heads.[10]

Johnson had been warned of their approach and dispatched Colonel Eyre Massey with a force of provincials, regulars and Indians to head them off. They formed a defensive line behind an abatis at a clearing called La Belle Famille, the Iroquois taking the flanks. A parley between opposing Indian factions broke down, and the apparently over-confident French moved into the open and opened fire. The redcoats, lying concealed, held their fire and then rose before delivering a withering volley at close range. Braddock-style, it was now the French who were mown down. The redcoats fired several volleys and then moved forward, firing at will, before making a bayonet charge into the faltering enemy line. The French broke and fled, and the Iroquois dashed to the pursuit. To Massey's fury they killed many wounded and others trying to surrender.[11] The surviving French and Indians beat a retreat to their canoes and boats in the Niagara River, and escaped to safety in Lake Erie.

From the fort walls Pouchot had heard the battle, and could see a flurry of activity along the distant shoreline. Delivery was at hand. But then the shooting petered out, and British colors were still to his front with no relief force in sight. Things were not going to plan. At two o'clock an Indian scout arrived and divulged news of the disaster, but Pouchot shook his head in disbelief. The cannon fire between fort and trenches continued until 4 p.m. when a bugle sounded from the British lines. A parley was required. The guns fell silent, and a redcoat officer approached. He carried a demand for surrender along with a list of French officers captured from the failed relief force. A still disbelieving Pouchot dispatched an officer into the British lines who saw with his own eyes commanders Philippe de Aubry, and a badly wounded de Lignery, who would soon die of his wounds.

Pouchot now realized that enough blood had already been shed in a futile defense. Upon surrender his garrison was allowed the honors of war in recognition of a valiant defense. They were to march out with colors held high—and be protected from Indian assault. There would be no revenge for Fort William Henry here. The French would, however, be held captive in New York. As the garrison departed the Indians swarmed in to pillage whatever remained of value in the battered fort. July 26 was a bad day for the French—the same day Fort Carillon was abandoned to Amherst's troops.

During the following month the French garrisons at Presque Isle, Le Boeuf and Machault burned their posts and retreated to Fort Detroit. Plans to take Fort Pitt were abandoned, leaving the upper Ohio region firmly in British hands.[12]

To the north, meanwhile, Québec was under assault. Built on a high promontory jutting into the St. Lawrence River, and protected by solid masonry walls, the capitol of New France was proving a hard nut to crack. One month before the fall of Forts Niagara and Carillon, 32 year-old Major General James Wolfe had arrived with a British fleet. Wolfe had seen much action in previous years, and had served with distinction as a brigadier under Amherst at the siege of Louisbourg. After the Battle of Culloden in 1746, he had refused to shoot a wounded Scot, one reason for his esteem among the Highland troops.

Thirty-year-old James Cook, the future famed navigator, was in one lead vessel taking depth soundings and mapping the river. The fleet carried 8,000 British troops including Major Fletcher's battalion of the 35th, and the 3rd Battalion of 60th Royal Americans.[13] Having been at Fort William Henry, they had a score to settle with the Marquis de Montcalm, and it was he who commanded Québec's defense.

As the British landed on Île d'Orleans to the east of the city, consternation broke out as seven French "fire ships" were seen to approach. Carried by the current, they were ablaze from stem to stern, and would cause havoc if they got amidst the fleet. English long boats splashed into the river, and grappling hooks were thrown. Pulling strongly on the oars, the sailors managed to pull the floating infernos clear.

The following day redcoats were landed on Point Lévis, directly opposite the city, and the installation of batteries began. Soon masonry crumbled and fires broke out as shot and shell reigned on Québec. French redoubts and batteries had been constructed under Bougainville's direction along the river bank eastwards to the Montmorency River, and the French had some 12,000 troops for the defense. They outnumbered the 8,000 British, but only 4,000 were regulars, whereas the enemy were better disciplined Royal American or British regulars, ideal troops for a long siege where patience was required.

"On July 31 the enemy anchored three vessels broadside in front of our camp on the left, one with sixty guns," recalled Bougainville. Over the next few hours, along with batteries on the opposite shore, they delivered "a fire of which there are few examples, for in this space of time there were nearly four thousand shot, bombs, or grenades thrown."[14] The guns fell silent, and landing craft arrived crammed with 3,500 troops under a darkening sky. They came ashore near the fortified village of Beaufort to be greeted with a hail of French lead. Thirteen companies of grenadiers and 200 Royal Americans were the first to approach. The French delivered a lethal volley, then fell back to a second position and, reloading, fired into the redcoats once more. Then the heavens opened up with a deluge of rain, the flintlock muskets on both sides falling silent, their powder wet. Wolfe could see there would be no victory this day, and ordered a withdrawal. The redcoats slipped back down the muddy slope and clambered back aboard their boats having lost 433 dead, wounded and missing. This included one colonel, eight captains, twenty-one lieutenants and three ensigns.[15] Indians descended the slope, scalping the dead and wounded. Montcalm had sustained only 60 casualties. "I have no more anxiety about Québec," Vaudreuil wrote to Bourlamaque. "M. Wolfe, I assure you, will make no progress. He contented himself with losing about five hundred of his best soldiers."[16]

The slightly built James Wolfe, however, was far from through. Having the tenacity of the British bulldog, he laid siege to Québec, and torched settlements and farms along the St. Lawrence from where much of the city's food was supplied. About 1,400 homes went up in flames, the inhabitants forced to flee.[17] But, while the French situation declined, not all went well in the redcoat camps. Disease spread, and Wolfe himself fell ill. "My antagonist has wisely shut himself up in inaccessible intrenchments, so that I can not get at him without spilling a torrent of blood," Wolfe wrote on August 31. "The Marquis de Montcalm is at the head of a great number of bad soldiers, and I am at the head of a small number of good ones, that wish for nothing so much as to fight him; but the wary old fellow avoids an action, doubtful of the behaviour of his army."[18] The British may have been good soldiers in Wolfe's eyes, but the brigadiers under Wolfe had little confidence in him. Brigadier George Townshend was a talented artist and took delight in drawing humorous cartoons of his commander. In the mess one night Wolfe asked to see what the officers were laughing at. He glared at the cartoon and promptly crumpled it up. Wolfe looked coldly at Townshend. "If we live, this shall be inquired into," he said.[19]

In early September the frustrated Wolfe decided he must bring things to a head. Ice would soon force the navy to depart. A plan to land troops far upstream devised by his officers was delayed by rain, and he decided on a more daring plan of his own. British ships had moved upstream beyond Québec and, fearing their intentions, Montcalm sent Bougainville with 3,000 men to oppose any landing. Wolfe, however, decided to launch his attack up the cliffs of L'Anse-au-Foulon, less than two miles upstream from the city. Lightly defended, he felt they could be scaled despite the steep 174-foot climb.

Considering the cliffs unassailable, Montcalm had only 100 men guarding the heights. And on the night of September 12 only 40 were present, the others having been released to help harvest desperately needed crops. Twenty-four men led by British Colonel William Howe, brother of the revered and fallen Lord Howe, scaled the heights. They overpowered the unwary French, wounding and capturing their commander, Captain Louis du Vergor. One Frenchman, however, did manage to escape. At the base, over 4,000 troops landed and began climbing the steep ascent, their muskets slung on their backs. A narrow, slanting path encumbered with abatis and trenches was cleared of obstruction, and troops filed up onto the plateau above.[20] The French escapee, meanwhile, dashed into Québec and gave a hysterical warning which fell on deaf ears. "We did not believe a word of the account of a man whose head, we thought, had been turned by fear," recalled one officer.[21]

At dawn's first light, an astonished Montcalm saw red uniforms and glinting bayonets as the British lined the opposite side of the Plains of Abraham. Word was sent to all French troops to ignore a diversionary British naval bombardment to the east, and hasten to Québec. And Bougainville, to the west, received orders to return, an action that would take some time. By 10 a.m. Montcalm had about 3,500 men on hand, and ordered an attack on the British line. Perhaps he could strike before all the enemy had scaled the heights. Montcalm mounted a black horse, and marched his men onto the plain in battle formation. More than half of these were militia, colonial regulars and Indians. They spread out on the flanks, while French regulars deployed in the center. Opposing them were well disciplined redcoats formed up, two deep, across the plain between cliffs overlooking the river on their left, and dense woods on their right.

The French line advanced, but lost form on the flanks as the militia knelt and opened fire before their shots could do any real damage. This was not the way they liked to fight, far more at home with hit and run, shooting from behind stumps and trees. Many, however, moved through the woods to the French right and fired into the British left flank. To avoid this, Wolfe ordered his men to lie in the grass.[22] Much had been learned since Braddock's day. Houses to the French right were torched by Montcalm's militia to avoid enemy occupation, and smoke from the fires obscured the British left as the white-uniformed, disciplined regulars in the French center moved steadily forward. As they approached the redcoats were ordered to their feet, and the French delivered two somewhat ragged volleys. At 40 yards, Wolfe gave the order to fire. The redcoats "gave them, with great calmness, as remarkable a close and heavy discharge as I ever saw," recalled Captain Knox of the 43rd Foot. The French line staggered, the second British line stepped forward through the smoke, and delivered another lethal volley. Musket balls ripped through the enemy ranks again, and the French fell back as men fell. The redcoats charged with a roar, the Highlanders drawing their broadswords as they ran. But bullets still flew from Canadians and Indians on the flanks. Wolf, already suffering a wrist wound, fell with musket balls to his groin and chest. Helping hands carried him to the rear where asked to be laid down. He refused a surgeon, saying, "It's all over with me." But then he heard "They run, see how they run." "Who run?" he asked. "The enemy, sir. Egad, they give way everywhere." The dying general gave a few last orders, then said, "Now, God be praised, I will die in peace."[23]

The men of the British 35th found themselves in pursuit of the Royal Roussillon Regiment, old adversaries from Fort William Henry. The discarded French plumes were plucked from the ground and quickly decorated the hats of the victorious redcoats.[24] The 78th Fraser Highlanders, in pursuit, were hit with cannon fire from floating batteries guarding the bridge over the St. Charles River, and Canadians fired on them from a cluster of buildings and woods on the flank. The 78th drove them out, but suffered the heaviest casualties of the British force. The French fell back behind the city walls, or streamed across the bridge to their fortifications east of the city. Near the bridge Vaudreuil was encountered, belatedly arriving with more militia. Some later claimed his arrival was timed to either claim a victory for himself, or a defeat for Montcalm. Whatever the truth, seeing the day lost, Vaudreuil about faced and joined the exodus to the east.[25]

With Wolfe dead and Brigadier Monckton wounded, the artistic Brigadier George Townshend took charge, and hastily organized a defensive line against Bougainville's approaching troops. "When I came within range of the battle," recalled Bougainville, "our army was beaten and in retreat. The entire English army advanced to attack me."[26] He gave the order to retreat. There was to be no reversal of fortune for the French this day.

Among the badly wounded to fall back behind the walls was the Marquis de Montcalm, hit in the abdomen and thigh. Québec itself was not stormed and remained in French hands—for the moment. Montcalm lived through the night, but when told his wounds were mortal: "So much the better," he said, "I am happy I will not live to see the surrender of Québec." He died early the following morning. Perhaps it was fitting that a British shell crater in the floor of the Ursuline Chapel provided Montcalm's burial place. He remained there until 2001 when his body was moved to the *Hôspital Général de Québec* cemetery alongside other fallen soldiers.

Although still in French hands, it was inevitable that Québec must fall. Vaudreuil stated the French had lost 640 killed, wounded and missing. But many militia deserted straight after the defeat, so the real loss is obscure. The British claimed 1,500 enemy casualties, and 644 of their own.

On September 18 Québec's garrison commander, Jean-Baptiste Nicolas Roch de Ramezay, signed the articles of capitulation. The capitol of New France was now in British hands. Although the war in North America would drag on for another 12 months, the decisive action had just been fought.

16

England, Mistress of Canada

As the dust settled the day of Montcalm's defeat, Major Robert Rogers led an expedition from Crown Point. Their object was to strike the Indian mission of St. Francis near the southern shore of the St. Lawrence River, the home of the Abenakis. This tribe had initiated the Fort William Henry Massacre. Such a raid would teach those Indians still loyal to the French that they were not beyond English grasp. Ten days later, after dodging French patrol boats, the expedition landed at Missisquoi Bay at the north end of Lake Champlain. They set out through the woods to the northeast, but two days later were overtaken by allied Indian scouts with bad news: their boats had been discovered by the French. Rogers could not turn back and would be pursued. He could still strike the Abenakis, but the only way back to British territory was an arduous, overland trek hampered by wooded mountains and fast-flowing streams.

Shortly before sunrise on October 4, Rogers struck St. Francis with a force of 142 men. Taken by surprise, the Indians were cut down and the village set ablaze. Many braves were away fighting for the French, and exactly how many died is obscure. According to Rogers, "The fire consumed many of the Indians who had concealed themselves in the cellars and lofts of their houses. About 7 o'clock in the morning, the affair was completely over, in which time we had killed at least two hundred Indians and taken twenty of their women and children prisoners, fifteen of whom I let go their own way, and five I brought with me, namely, two Indian boys and three Indian girls. I likewise retook five English captives which I also took under my care."[1] Rogers claimed he lost one killed and seven wounded, a number disputed by the Abenakis. Leaving the burning village behind, the rangers struck out through the woods to endure an epic fight for survival. They soon ran out of food and the command split into smaller groups in the hope of killing game. One captive was a plump squaw with more flesh than any other five, according to Robert Kirkwood of Montgomery's Highlanders. He claimed that Rogers "followed the squaw who was gone out to gather roots, and there he kill'd and cut her up … we then broiled and eat the most of her, and received great strength thereby."[2] Rogers made it back to Crown Point, and the remains of the command, about 90 men, eventually made it back in various groups. The others had been either killed or captured by pursuers, or simply vanished in the woods.

The raid was considered a great success by the British, Rogers hailed as a hero. General Amherst received the major's report in early November and wrote, "every step you inform me you had taken has been very well Judged and Deserves my full approbation."[3]

The Canadian winter of 1759–60 was especially harsh. British ships cut off supplies, and food was scarce. But the corrupt French administrator, Monsieur François Bigot, still wined and dined extravagantly with his like-minded friends. The peasants, meanwhile, scraped for survival with what morsels they managed to procure.

Despite the fall of Québec, Montréal was still in French hands, and Vaudreuil was still on the loose. Chevalier de Lévis gathered French regulars and militia for a spring offensive. The plan was to retake the capitol from British hands, and on April 20, 1760, Lévis sailed up the St. Lawrence from Montréal with 7,000 men. On April 26 they landed at St. Augustin, and next day Brigadier James Murray, despite being outnumbered two to one, marched his troops from Québec to confront Lévis. Near the village of St. Foye he attacked the French as they advanced up a road with dense woods on either side. Murray drove the enemy back during an intense and bloody fight, but Lévis soon realized he was confronting a far smaller force. The French went on the offensive and, after two hours combat and heavy losses on both sides, the redcoats were forced to fall back into Québec. Now it was the British who found themselves besieged behind the city walls. Lévis hoped to receive additional supplies from the French Navy while he starved the garrison out.

On May 16 ships were seen to approach. Were the vessels British or French? The fate of Canada hung in the balance. To Lévis' disgust it was the British naval ensign that fluttered to the masthead. HMS *Lowestoffe* was followed by HMS *Diana* and HMS *Vanguard* under the command of Commodore Swanton. Québec's fate was sealed. The British gunports opened, the guns were run out, and smoke bellowed across the St. Lawrence as round shot splintered Lévis' remaining supply ships. Some were deliberately run aground in the vain hope that Lévis could salvage the precious cargo and continue the siege. Captain Jean Vauquelin of the *Atalante* nailed his colors to the mast and fought it out with two enemy ships until he ran out of ammunition, then cast his sword overboard. Wounded, Vauquelin was taken prisoner and well treated by the British officers who honored his valiant defense.[4]

With his supplies destroyed, Lévis was in an impossible position. With a heavy heart, he ordered a withdrawal. That night his demoralized army retreated back south. They left stores, the sick and the wounded—and Québec, for the last time.

That summer three British armies, under Jeffrey Amherst, James Murray and William Haviland, converged on Montréal, the last major objective. In September, after pushing aside futile attempts at resistance, they arrived outside the walls of the island city. Vaudreuil called a council of advisors, capitulation heading the agenda, and a parley was arranged with General Amherst. He offered much harsher terms than those imposed when Québec fell. The capitulation of all New France was included, and the honors of war were denied because no defense had been fought. The Chevalier de Lévis wanted the negotiations terminated. He would withdraw his troops and fight on. The governor, however, seeing further bloodshed useless, overruled him. Lévis could not believe it had come to this, France being expelled from North America. He stormed from the meeting and burned his colors rather than surrender them to the despised British.

Montréal, along with New France, was surrendered on September 8, 1760. Overseas the Seven Years War continued, and there was always the chance that New France could be handed back once a final peace treaty was signed, as had happened with Louisburg in 1748. The French colonists were given the choice of sailing for France should the colony remain in British hands, but private property, civil law and Catholicism were guaranteed protection, along with Indian allies and their missionaries.[5]

Vaudreuil, however, a native Canadian, was expelled, along with François Bigot and other senior officials. They sailed for France where the cold stone walls of the Bastille prison were provided for their comfort. An enquiry into the loss of New France saw Vaudreuil exonerated, but the corrupt Bigot had all property confiscated, and he was exiled from France. Lévis, paroled by the British, was promoted to lieutenant general once back home.

Upon release from parole, he fought again in Germany in 1762, and was created a duke before dying in 1783.

Lévis' service to his country was forgotten in 1794 when French revolutionaries sent his widow and two of his three daughters to the guillotine. His son had inherited the duke's title, but escaped the same fate by flight across the Channel where his father's former foes, the English, provided protection.[6]

The surrender of Montréal brought serious conflict in North America to a close. A French expedition did occupy Newfoundland in June of 1762, only to surrender to a British force dispatched by Amherst on September 18. But overseas the war raged on till the Treaty of Paris in February of 1763. Various territories were exchanged, and from this, Britain emerged as the world's foremost colonial power. "England," recalled Bougainville, "mistress of Canada by the peace treaty, of the sea by a navy incomparably stronger than those of all the powers of Europe combined."[7] France handed Britain all of mainland North America east of the Mississippi, excluding New Orleans and the immediate territory. This would become part of the United States with the Louisiana Purchase in 1803.[8]

17

Dakota Territory, 1866

"Presently the escort fell in line and we moved towards the stockade, but just before entering a halt was made, and I looked eagerly for the occasion of the delay. It almost took my breath away, for a strange feeling of apprehension came over me. We had halted to give passage to a wagon, escorted by a guard from the wood train, coming from the opposite direction. In that wagon was the scalped and naked body of one of their comrades, scarcely cold.... My whole being seemed to be absorbed in one desire,—an agonized but un-uttered cry, 'Let me get within the gate.'"[1]

Such was the arrival at Fort Philip Kearny, Dakota Territory, for Mrs. Frances Grummond during the fall of 1866.

Over 100 years had passed since the Fort William Henry Massacre. But the relationship between white man and red was still contentious, and the scene was being set for another event which would see dead and mutilated bodies strewn about not far from the wooden walls of an American fort.

Only 15 years after American and British troops had fought side by side to expel the French from North America, the two former allies turned their guns and bayonets on each other. With an ironic twist of fate, the French were only too happy to join forces with their former enemies, the Americans, to expel the British from North America—sweet revenge. And so the United States of America was born. This set an example of how an authoritarian government could be overthrown if the will and determination was there, and the involvement of the French government soon came back to haunt them. The French peasants were most displeased with their lot in life and, using the American Revolution as a model, staged one of their own. Heads rolled as the First French Republic was born, and a Corsican named Napoleon Bonaparte soon set Europe on fire.

The tricorne was replaced by the top hat, and an English dandy called Beau Brummell revolutionized men's fashion. Powered wigs, ruffles and frills disappeared as the modern male suit was born. In 1803 the Louisiana Purchase brought vast tracts of wilderness into American hands. The United States fought another war with the British and, despite numerous reverses including the burning of Washington, D.C., the last big battle was a crushing American victory at New Orleans. This triumph strengthened America's belief in her own invincibility and self esteem. Immigrants flocked from the Old World to the New, more space was required, and the battle for Indian lands continued. The eastern tribes fought the white invaders under great leaders like Pontiac, Little Turtle and Tecumseh. The Greatest Indian victory did not occur at the Little Bighorn, but in 1791 when an American army under General Arthur St. Clair was routed, suffering nearly 900 casualties.[2] Andrew Jackson evened the score at Horseshoe Bend in 1814, and the eastern tribes were eventually overwhelmed, placed on eastern reservations or sent west across the Mississippi to a huge area called Indian Territory. In the 1840s a war with Mexico saw vast news tracts, including Texas and California, came under American control. The United States now spanned North America from coast to coast.

The country, theoretically, was at peace. But beneath the surface there was a festering disunity; black people in the southern states were held in bondage, sold like so many cattle on auction blocks. Fighting broke out between pro-slavery and abolitionist settlers in what became known as "Bleeding Kansas," and in 1861 the Americans states, North and South, turned their guns on each other. The prewar army lost many of its of 18,000 men to the South, and a separate, massive Volunteer Army was raised by Abraham Lincoln to meet the crisis. When the South was crushed four years later, the Volunteer Army was disbanded. The decision was made to bolster the Regular Army to 54,000 men, and recruiting commenced.[3] It would be their job to police the former Confederate States, and protect the frontier where a post-war influx of settlers flowed west in search of a new life. Freight wagons carrying merchandise shared the busy trails with wagons and stage coaches carrying passengers and mail to the towns and cities that grew day by day on the Pacific slope, in the southwest and the Great Basin. Miners flocked to California, Idaho, Colorado and Arizona.[4] A transcontinental railway was under construction, and the iron horse moved westward across the plains from the Missouri River in Nebraska, and eastwards from California, tunneling and bridging the hostile slopes of the Sierra Nevada.

The goldfields of Montana were difficult to reach. The usual path was by steamboat from St. Louis up the Missouri to Fort Benton, or along the overland trail to Fort Hall, Idaho, before turning north across mountainous terrain. Georgian-born John Merin Bozeman was one of thousands who traveled to Montana in 1862. But rather than wield a pick and shovel, he felt a more lucrative trade would be guiding immigrants along a faster, more direct route—the Powder River country, the unsettled prime hunting grounds of the Lakota Sioux, Cheyenne and Arapahoe Indian tribes.

The Powder River rises from three forks in what is now Wyoming, and winds its way northeast for 375 miles before becoming a tributary of the Yellowstone River. This area had been visited by whites going back to the early 19th century, and frontier scout Jim Bridger had led Lord George Gore on a hunting expedition through the area from 1855 to 1857. Upon return to Ireland Gore claimed to have killed 105 bears, 1,600 deer, and 2,000 buffalo—a hint of things to come.[5]

John Bozeman and mountain man John Jacobs set out from the gold town of Bannack, Montana. They crossed the divide at what would become known as Bozeman Pass, then southeast through the Powder River country to Bridger's Ferry on the North Platte River. It was here that the new route would intersect with the existing Oregon Trail, about 55 miles northwest of Fort Laramie. The following year Bozeman and Jacobs led a train of 46 wagons with 89 men, ten women and several children north, only to be confronted by hostile Lakota and Cheyenne 150 miles up the trail. All except Bozeman and nine others, fearing for their scalps, took the Indians' advice and turned back. The remaining ten pressed on, riding after dark and resting by day. After arrival in Virginia City Bozeman was hailed as a hero, and the new route took his name.

The following year, 1864, four wagon trains carrying 1,500 people traveled up the Bozeman Trail. Most passed without incident, but not all. One civilian train, led by Captain Townsend, was attacked by Lakota and Cheyenne on July 7. The Indians set fire to the grass around the corralled wagons. Women and children helped dig a protective trench and carried water from the river while the men drove the hostiles off with gunfire. The train continued on without further incident. Five days later, however, a small train of five wagons was attacked, overwhelmed and looted. Fanny Kelly, Sarah Latimar and two children were taken captive, while three wounded men escaped and four others were killed—an ill omen for events to come.[6]

Sporadic Indian raids continued along the Oregon, Overland and Bozeman Trails. Lieutenant Colonel William Collins of the 11th Ohio Volunteer Cavalry, stationed at Fort Laramie, reported in February of 1865, "the permanent cure for the hostilities of the Northern Indians is to go into the heart of their buffalo country and hold forts till the trouble is over. A hasty expedition, however successful, is only a temporary lesson, whereas the presence of troops in force in the country where the Indians are compelled to live and subsist would soon oblige them to sue for peace and accept such terms as the government may think proper to impose."[7]

General Patrick Connor had crushed a Shoshone village in 1863, and a few months after the Confederate surrender led troops from Fort Laramie to punish the hostile tribes in the immediate north. He established Fort Connor on the Powder River and, on August 29, 1865, surprised and burned an Arapahoe village on the Tongue River. This short-lived victory, however, merely ensured that the Arapahoe would fight alongside the Lakota and Cheyenne. Connor's troops found themselves on the defensive, harassed by an elusive foe who drove off stock and raided wagons carrying supplies. Troops were reduced to rags and living off horse meat. The press regarded the campaign as "a dismal failure" carried out with "large, ungainly columns filled with troops anxious to get home now that the Civil War was over." The troops withdrew, leaving a few companies to occupy a small collection of adobe buildings on the Powder River. Fort Conner, as it was called, was tolerated by the Indians as it posed no threat to their best hunting grounds further north.

On March 10, 1866, General John Pope, commander of the vast Department of the Missouri, issued General Order 33. This created the Mountain District, covering territory from the North Platte River in Nebraska to Virginia City, Montana.[8] Connor's campaign had demonstrated that mere military incursions into the Powder River region had no lasting effect. A permanent military presence was required, and Pope ordered the building of two new forts and the relocation of Fort Conner, to be renamed Fort Reno, further north to protect travelers on the Bozeman Trail. It was well realized that the Powder River tribes may well object, so plans were made for a new treaty to be arranged at Fort Laramie to supersede the previous treaty of 1851.

The Bozeman Trail forts, however, were to go ahead regardless of what piece of paper the Indians agreed, or did not agree, to sign. "The Indian, in truth, no longer has a country," Pope wrote on August 1, 1865. "His lands are everywhere pervaded by white men; his means of subsistence destroyed and the homes of his tribe violently taken from him, himself and his family reduced to starvation, or to the necessity of warring to the death upon the white man, whose inevitable and destructive progress threatens the total extermination of his race."[9]

Chosen to establish the new posts was 41-year-old Colonel Henry Beebee Carrington, commander of the 18th United States Infantry Regiment. In some ways Carrington was an odd choice, having seen no combat during the Civil War. But this was with the value of hindsight. Division commander General William Tecumseh Sherman did not expect armed troops to have the same Indian problems that civilians had encountered on the Bozeman Trail. The Indians out west were still reliant on hunting game with bow and arrow and a handful of muskets. And, in any case, the new treaty would guarantee safe passage through the Powder River country.

"While still waiting for recruits," recalled Colonel Carrington's wife, Margaret, "General Sherman visited the post, entering into the spirit and plans of the expedition with his usual energy and skill. At his suggestion some of the ladies began their daily journal of events."[10] And he assured the ladies "to take with them all needed comforts for a pleasant garrison life in the newly opened country, where all would be healthful, with pleasant service and absolute peace."[11]

But, despite the Indians' primitive weapons, such complacence seems out of place considering previous conflict. The army were not immune from Indian attack. In 1854, 11 years before Connor's failed campaign, the Lakota Sioux had wiped out Lieutenant John Grattan's party of 29 men near Fort Laramie; the result of an unwarranted military attack during a minor dispute over possession of a cow. And in 1865 Sergeant Amos Custard and 21 other soldiers were killed when their corralled wagons were overrun near the Platte Bridge Station on the Oregon Trail.[12] The Lakota and their allies could do much damage when required.

The conservative, scholarly Connecticut born Henry Carrington had, as a child, attended school in Torringford, and at that time heard the fiery John Brown vent his anti-slavery rhetoric. He also witnessed riots and demonstrations against those who, like himself, wanted slavery abolished. Lung problems negated his desire to enter West Point and pursue a military career, and in 1841 he entered Yale and studied law. In 1848 he moved to Columbus, Ohio, where he joined his cousin's law practice and established a reputation as a reliable, church-going pillar of the community. At this time he began courting Margaret Sullivant, seven years his junior. From an auspicious family, her grandfather had founded the settlement that became Columbus, and her father had established Ohio State University. She received an excellent education at Oakland Female Seminary in Hillsboro, Ohio and, at the age of 20, married Henry Carrington in 1851. Of their six children only two, Harry and Jimmy, would survive beyond infancy and travel with them to the west.[13]

In 1854 Carrington met and befriended Senator Salmon Chase, an invaluable connection as it transpired. Chase was elected governor of Ohio in 1855, and was re-elected as a Republican candidate two years later. Carrington became involved in the burgeoning Republican Party and Chase appointed him adjutant general for Ohio, tasked with reorganizing the state militia, thus Carrington's military ambitions began to bear fruit. In 1859 Chase returned to the senate and Carrington's law partner, William Dennison, was elected governor of Ohio. Carrington was retained as adjutant general, and acted as Abraham Lincoln's bodyguard when the newly elected president's disguised train steamed through Ohio on the way to Washington, D.C.[14]

The Civil War erupted in April of 1861, and Lincoln called for 75,000 volunteers. Militarism and volunteer units were in vogue, and war meant glory and promotion for young men with an adventurous spirit—so many thought. Three weeks following the call to arms the highly organized Carrington had filled Ohio's quota of 10,000 men with enough men to spare for more regiments. This fast work enabled General George McClellan to cross the border into West Virginia and secure that area for the Union, a separate free state from Confederate Virginia being the result.

Over 300 officers resigned their commissions to join the Confederate Army, and the

Opposite: **Colonel Henry B. Carrington, a lawyer turned soldier, was before his time in humane treatment of soldiers, but somewhat out of place with a frontier combat command (Library of Congress).**

government had no choice but to take suitable replacements from civilian life. In June 1861, Salmon Chase, now Lincoln's secretary of the treasury, secured for Carrington the colonelcy of the 18th Infantry Regiment of the Regular Army. On June 24, 1861, Carrington established the regimental headquarters in Columbus, where the citizens showed their esteem by presenting him with a fine house. Aware of Carrington's lung problems, Chase assured Carrington that he would be assigned posts and climates which "would most certainly preserve you in sound condition."[15] Thousands of other officers were anxious to fight the Johnny Rebs in any case. Carrington remained on recruiting and training duties while, In July of 1861, his wife's cousin, Irvin McDowell, led the first major advance by Union troops.[16] McDowell met the Confederates at Manassas Junction and suffered defeat at the First Battle of Bull Run. Bigger and better armies were needed to crush the rebels, recruiting and training of utmost importance. Carrington worked hard, and at Governor Morton's request moved to Indiana. In March of 1863 he was promoted to brigadier general in the Volunteer Army, commanding the District of Indiana, while retaining his rank of colonel in the Regulars. In the course of the war Carrington would be responsible for the training and dispatch of over 200,000 volunteers. His regiment, the 18th Regular Infantry, meanwhile, slogged it out earning laurels in various campaigns including the capture of Atlanta in September of 1864, the victory that finally ended any hope of Confederate success.[17]

When the last Rebel armies raised the white flag in 1865, demobilization of the huge Yankee Volunteer Army began. Brigadier General Carrington's rank reverted to that of colonel in the Regular Army, but he was luckier than most, retaining command of the 18th Infantry. The regiment was transferred to Fort Kearny, Nebraska, where Carrington was appointed commander of the Mountain District, protector of the Bozeman Trail.

"Few days on the plains are more bright and promising, notwithstanding such a cloud of dust as the plains only can supply, was the nineteenth day of May, A.D. 1866," recalled Margaret Carrington.[18] The 18th Infantry was on the move, but this "bright and promising" outlook offset an ill-omened event. The Carrington home in Fort Kearney, just a few days before, had burned to the ground, many personal possessions lost amidst the flames. "I recall the terror of the scene," recalled son Jimmy Carrington many years later, "the mad scramble to save a few things, but especially the rapid popping of several big army revolvers that the fire set off."[19] It seems an ominous coincidence that George Custer's home at Fort Abraham Lincoln would burn to the ground in 1874, the same year his Black Hills expedition invaded the lands of the Lakota and Cheyenne.

On May 19 "Carrington's Overland Circus," as it became known, marched from Fort Kearney alongside the "alkaline and muddy" Platte River towards Fort Laramie. This was the first leg of their march to the Bozeman Trail, an area "infested with bloodthirsty savages," recalled Private William Murphy. "There were nearly 2,000 troops in the command, but over 1,300 of these were intended to relieve volunteer troops who were guarding the telegraph and mail line in Wyoming."[20] There were also civilian employees, 226 mule-drawn wagons, and women and children were also present. This included Carrington's wife and their two sons, Harry and James. Coming up at the dusty rear was a huge herd of horses, mules, cattle and oxen.[21] Included in the command was the 30-piece regimental band. They carried not only brass instruments, drums and flutes, but also seven-shot Spencer carbines. The general infantry, however, were armed with Springfield rifles. These were a vast improvement over the muskets carried during the French and Indian War. The percussion cap had replaced the old flintlock mechanism so prone to misfire, and the rifled barrel fired a much more accurate bullet than the old smooth-bore. But they were still single-shot muzzle-loaders, an outmoded weapon compared to the magazine-loading repeaters that had seen action during the war, a clear sign of the army's complacence towards Indian fighting in 1866.

On May 30 the column arrived at Fort Sedgwick, "near the so-called city of Julesburg," recalled Mrs. Carrington. The settlement of nearly a dozen houses and stores had been rebuilt after being burned by Indians in February of 1865. The previous January the town had been looted and the garrison drawn out by decoys into an attempted ambush which saw 18 men killed as they fought their way back to the fort. The 15-foot-high walls made of sod saved the garrison, and this fight gave a hint of events about to unfold on the Bozeman Trail. The attacks on Julesburg were in retaliation for Colonel Chivington's infamous massacre of peaceful Cheyenne at Sand Creek, which had sparked a needless Indian War.[22]

Carrington's column paused at Fort Sedgwick for three days while they crossed "the quicksands, shoals and currents of the ubiquitous Platte." This was achieved by use of a flatboat and "the common sense of Captain Ten Eyck, an old surveyor and lumberman," recalled Margaret Carrington. Her son Jimmy recalled, "big skies stretching to the blue horizon, distant mountains, gorgeous sunsets, and in the heat of some days a shimmering mirage that looked like a great sea."

Not all troops were destined for the Bozeman trail, and the First Battalion took a different trail towards their assigned posts in Colorado, Utah and Kansas.

Carrington's command came in contact with Indians encamped along the trail. "'Old Little Dog,' whose son burned Julesburg, in 1864," recalled Mrs. Carrington, "came into camp and complained that some one of our soldiers had entered his lodge and stolen his rifle." Colonel Carrington soothed the old chief by having the regimental band play for him, and gave assurance that his gun would be returned. The aging Indian then "sprang upon the bare back of his pony with all the elasticity of youth and *more* than the skill of our mounted infantry, and galloped swiftly away."[23] The rifle was found and returned, and on June 13 Carrington issued Special Order No. 7: "The pending treaty between the United States and the Sioux Indians at Fort Laramie, renders it the duty of every soldier to treat all Indians with kindness. Every Indian who is wronged, will visit his vengeance upon *any* white man he may meet. As soldiers are sent to preserve the peace of the border, and prevent warfare, as much as to fight well, if warfare becomes indispensable, it will be considered a very gross offence for a soldier to wrong or insult an Indian ... all bargaining with Indians on the march, except with the approval of a commissioned Officer, is forbidden. Soldiers will attend to their own duties as soldiers, and all intercourse with Indian lodges or individual Indians while at Laramie, or on the march from Laramie Westward, will be through Head Quarters."[24] It would appear Henry Carrington intended to fulfill Sherman's prediction of a "pleasant garrison life in the newly opened country."

All remained peaceful with the Indians, but some other problems arose. Two sergeants were swept away and drowned while bathing in the river's swift current, and at Scott's Bluffs, "an eight-yoke bull team stampeded with two wagons loaded with parts and equipment for a sawmill and ran down a steep hill to the North Platte," recalled Private Murphy. "I do not believe any of the steers were alive when they got to the bottom of the hill."[25]

Fifty-five miles from Laramie, the column arrived at Fort Mitchell. "This is a sub-post of Laramie of peculiar style and compactness," recalled Margaret Carrington. "The walls of the quarters are also the outlines of the fort itself, and the four sides of the rectangle are respectively the quarters of officers, soldiers, and horses, and the warehouse of supplies. Windows open into the little court or parade-ground; and bed-rooms, as well as all other departments, are loop-holed for defense."²⁶ A period drawing by William H. Jackson also reveals a wooden stockade extension on one side. At this post Carrington detached more soldiers of the 18th under Captain Robert P. Hughes.

The existing garrison had seen some action the previous June. Captain William D. Fouts and a company of the 7th Iowa volunteers had "escorted" 185 lodges of Brule Lakota from Fort Laramie to Fort Kearney. Apparently the Indians were not happy with the arrangement, and turned on the escort. Captain Fouts and three soldiers were killed. The Fort Mitchell garrison rode out but the Indians escaped across the Platte. A message was sent clacking along the telegraph line to Fort Laramie, and Colonel Thomas Moonlight set out with a cavalry force in pursuit. But they were no match for a wily enemy who could live off the land and had little trouble outdistancing the troops.²⁷

In February of the same year the garrison had also taken part in two other fights. The 1865 report by Colonel Collins at Fort Laramie gives an insight into the duties performed by soldiers on frontier posts: "Co H has been stationed at Fort Mitchell 55 miles East of Laramie on the Platte River. The company participated in the celebrated Indian fights at Mud Springs and Rush Creek where 150 men under Command of Lt Col Wm O Collins fought from fifteen hundred to two thousand of the dusky warriors, since that time the Company has carried the Mail from Julesburg to Laramie. This has been heavy and laborious duty, yet they have never flinched but have had the Mail through in good time. Besides

Fort Mitchell was one of the many posts guarding the wagon trail to California and Oregon, and the garrison saw action against hostile Lakota and Cheyenne (author's rendition).

this company has built one Mail Station, near the Land Mark Chimney Rock, besides repairing the one at Mud Springs."[28]

On June 13 Carrington's command encamped four miles east of Fort Laramie. Built as a privately owned trading post called Fort William in 1834, at the confluence of the Laramie and North Platte Rivers, it was purchased by the U.S. government in 1849 to serve as military base to protect travelers to Oregon and California. The previous treaty had been signed near Fort Laramie in 1851, and when Carrington arrived huge numbers of Indians were present to hear the government's fresh proposal.

On June 16 Lakota Brule Chief Standing Elk rode into Carrington's camp. He was curious to know why so many soldiers had arrived, but was "thoroughly friendly," the colonel recalled. "There is a treaty being made at Laramie with the Sioux that are in the country where you are going," the chief said. "The fighting men in that country have not come to Laramie, and you will have to fight them. They will not give you the road unless you whip them."[29] He rode off, and news of troops' destination quickly spread.

Carrington rode to Fort Laramie with a detachment who were to replace the existing garrison. Hundreds of tepees were spread around the post and along the banks of the North Platte and Laramie Rivers. Swarthy braves tended their ponies as squaws worked about the camp, and the children played with bows and arrows. "We were shown examples of their marksmanship," recalled Private Murphy. "The young boys could hit a button, a pencil or a small article at about 30 yards."[30] Many of Carrington's new recruits had seen action during the Civil War, but had no Indian fighting experience. They were soon to learn that a blue uniform could make a fine target at a far greater distance than 30 yards.

Within the fort, Old Glory fluttered above timber platforms where the government commissioners sat with leading chiefs of the Lakota, Cheyenne and Arapaho nations.[31] Colonel Carrington was presented to them by E. B. Taylor, head of the Commission, as "the White Chief going up to occupy Powder river, the Big Horn country and the Yellow Stone." Many Indians were appalled. No treaty had been signed. Lakota chief Man-Afraid-of-His-Horses jumped to his feet and unleashed a tirade of abuse, saying the troops would be attacked and their stock driven off. "In two moons the command will not have a hoof left," he said. Chief Red Cloud then stood and accused the commissioners of treating the assembled chiefs like children. "The white men have crowded the Indians back year by year," he scolded, "until we are forced to live in a small country north of the Platte, and now our last hunting ground, the home of the People, is to be taken from us. Our women and children will starve, but for my part I prefer to die fighting rather than by starvation.... Great Father sends us presents and wants new road. But White Chief goes with soldiers to steal road before Indian says yes or no!"[32]

Fine print in the 1851 treaty had, in fact, allowed the government to establish post and roads. At that time, however, the Oregon Trail, used as part of the route to the Californian goldfields, was under discussion. The Bozeman Trail had not been envisioned.

Black Elk, a Lakota child at the time, was told years later, "up on the Madison Fork the Wasichus had found much of the yellow metal that they worship and that makes them crazy, and they wanted to have a road up through our country to the place where the yellow metal was; but my people did not want the road. It would scare the bison and make them go away."[33] Private Murphy recalled, "The great game trail along the Bozeman Trail was a myth. All the time we were in the country I do not believe I saw more the 100 buffalo. It was great grass country, however."[34] Murphy's words confirmed the Indian prediction.

The Indians "treated me coldly" Carrington reported to department headquarters in Omaha.[35] This was an understatement, and Mrs. Carrington provided a more candid recollection. Her husband was walking towards his horse, Grey Eagle, "and at his left were two Indians, one of them Red Cloud, who had his right hand on a large knife at his side and looking at Grey Eagle. I thought the Indian was going to stab Henry in the back, and perhaps jump on Grey Eagle and ride off. I called out in my fright, 'Oh! Henry.'" Carrington placed his hand on his revolver "then slowed his step, looking side-wise at the Indians and allowing them to pass."[36] Red Cloud "withdrew from all association with the treaty-makers, and in a very few days quite decidedly developed his hate and his schemes of mischief."[37]

The Powder River country was known by whites as "Absaroka," the name given to the Indians living in the region by their neighboring tribe, the Hidatsas, when Europeans first made contact during the 18th century. French explorers translated "Absaroka" as "children of the large beaked bird," thus they eventually became simply known as the Crow. By the 1860s the Crow

Margaret Carrington, described by one soldier as "the mother of the regiment, loved by every man, woman and child" correctly asserted that Fetterman disobeyed her husband's orders, as proven by testimony at the Sanborn Commission (author's collection).

had been forced from the area by the Lakota and their allies. While these tribes took a hostile stance towards European expansion, the Crow remained friendly towards the whites. In her book *Absaraka, Home of the Crows*, published two years later, Margaret Carrington stated that the white invasion was justified on behalf of their friends, the Crow. "Somebody had indeed ventured to style this country *Wyoming*," she wrote, "a name which might do very well for a county of Pennsylvania, but had the least application to the stolen land of the Crows." But the Lakota had originally been an eastern tribe. Their conquest of Crow lands was the result of them being forced westward by conflict with other tribes under pressure from ever expanding white settlement.

Those Indians hostile to Carrington's arrival packed their tepees and disappeared into the hills. Others, meanwhile, happy to receive gifts and accept future benefits, signed the dubious document. There were reputable chiefs among them, like Spotted Tail. Having taken part in the Grattan fight of 1854, he had been sent east under arrest to Fort Leavenworth, Kansas. It appeared hanging was to be the warrior's fate, but President Pierce wisely intervened and granted a pardon instead. Spotted Tail saw the numbers and the strength of the whites, and Indians in European clothing tending crops. He realized resistance was futile, and became an advocate of peace.[38] But other Indians were described by one seasoned scout as "the 'Laramie loafers' and 'road beggars'—a class of Indians who hang around Fort

Laramie and gain their living by begging and stealing."[39] On June 29 Taylor telegraphed Commissioner of Indian Affairs C.N. Cooley: "Satisfactory treaty concluded with the Sioux and Cheyennes. Large representations; Most cordial feeling prevails."[40]

To the northwest, however, those braves who had firearms garnered gunpowder while others crafted arrows and sharpened spears. And all prayed to Wakan Tanka for victory over the white invaders.

18

On the Bozeman Trail

While at Laramie Carrington employed two new guides, James Brannan and James Beckwourth. Both had an intimate knowledge of the country and tribes. Brannan had scouted for Connor's expedition and Beckwourth, of white/African American blood, had married into the Crow tribe. Born as a slave, he had been freed by his white father in 1824 and become a prominent mountain man and explorer. His *Life and Adventures* had been published in New York and London in 1856 and Paris in 1860.

Carrington also met the prominent Philadelphia photographer Ridgeway Glover. The affluent, blond, long-haired Quaker had traveled west for *Frank Leslie's Illustrated Newspaper* to draw and take photographs as best he could with the awkward camera equipment of the day. He declined Carrington's invitation to accompany the expedition as his work around Fort Laramie was not yet complete, but he did plan to travel up the Bozeman Trail to Virginia City, and do some fur trapping on the side.[1] They would meet again, but the ill-fated Glover would get no further north than Fort Phil Kearny.

The ladies visited the post, and shopped at the bustling, overcrowded sutler's store where "Indians, dressed and half-dressed" recalled Mrs. Carrington, "mingled with soldiers of the garrison, teamsters, emigrants, speculators, half-breeds, and interpreters…. Bright shawls, red squaw cloth, brilliant calicos, and flashing ribbons passed over the same counter with knives and tobacco, brass nails and glass bead." While trade goods were abundant, the War Department seemed to be taking only perfunctory interest in Carrington's command. "I find at this post a supply of hard bread for only four days for my command, and in poor condition," he complained to department headquarters at Omaha on June 16, "not a single utensil for baking flour, only one thousand rounds of ammunition, Cal. 58. I brought what I could, and shall find 36,000 rounds at Fort Reno, giving me a total of 60,000 rounds, obviously very inadequate. I find myself greatly in need of Officers, but must wait the arrival of new appointments, or until others are relieved from recruiting Service."

"Major Bridger told us that he had seen kegs of powder distributed to the Indians and carried away on their ponies," recalled Mrs. Carrington, "but this gave no concern, as there was none for *us*." But despite the handicaps, and a request to stay till the treaty negotiations were complete, Carrington received orders to march. "I move tomorrow," he telegraphed back.[2]

Accordingly, Carrington departed Fort Laramie on June 17, and continued northwest along the Oregon Trail alongside the south bank of the North Platte. The command now consisted of eight companies, about 700 men, of the Second Battalion of the 18th Infantry, also numerous wagons, artillery, civilian contractors, live stock, and a handful of wives and children. Carrington only had 12 commissioned officers on hand, including himself. According to the book, each company should have had a captain assisted by a first and second

18. On the Bozeman Trail

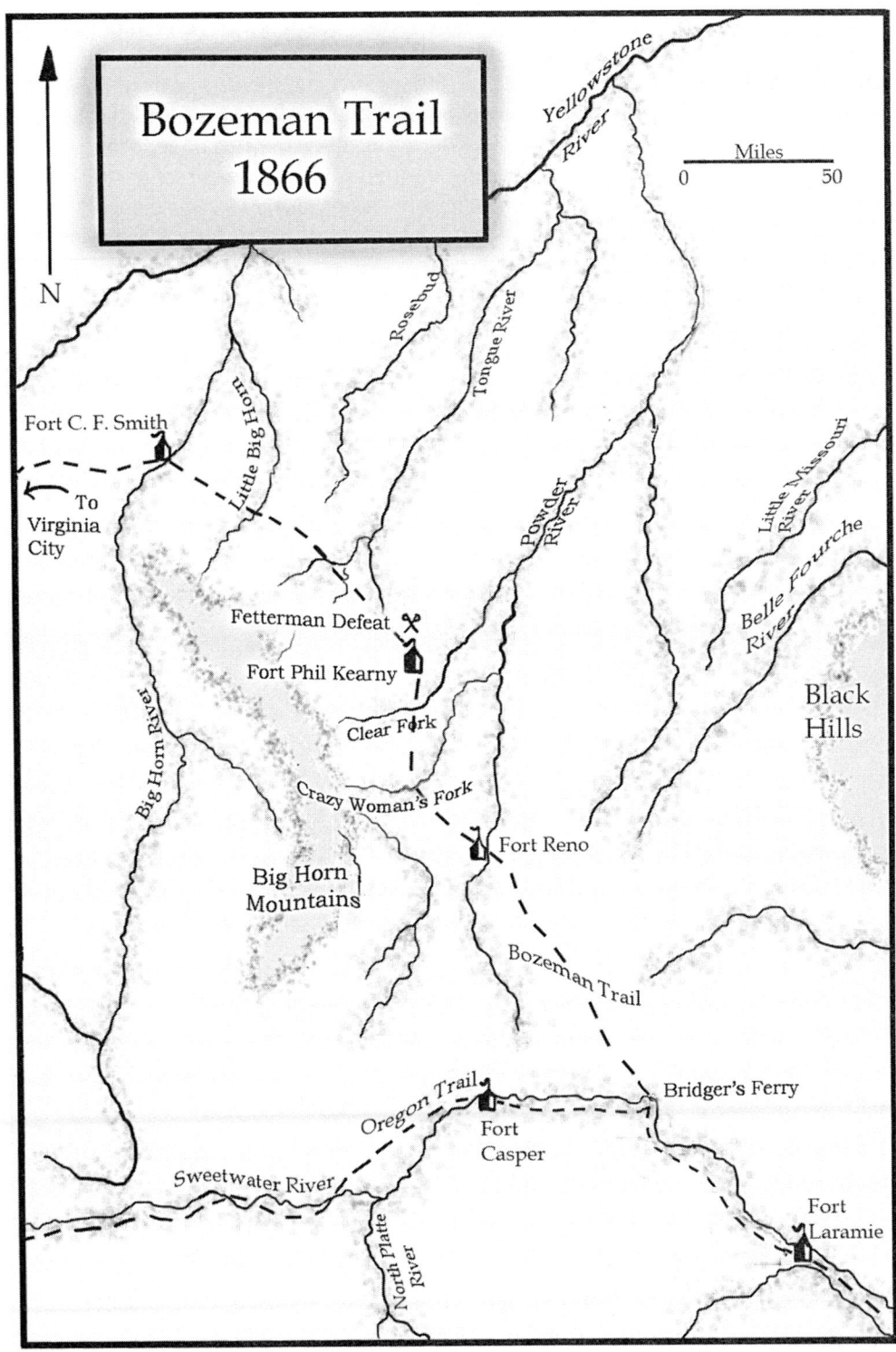

Map by the author

lieutenant.³ This meant 24 officers in addition to headquarters staff. Although basically a foot regiment, mounted infantry were riding what horses Carrington had managed to procure, essential for the job at hand. "We bade farewell to Laramie with great composure and no regrets," recalled Margaret Carrington. Despite the bustling sutler's store, she had found the fort "neglected, as were all frontier stations, during the war; being occupied by changing garrisons, whose jack-knives and bayonets, so useful in their proper sphere, had pretty much used up all the pine and plaster wherever those appendages were ornamental or useful; while the parade-ground was as barren and ignorant of sod as the great highway to Salt Lake City itself."⁴

As the column marched, a dust cloud appeared. Numerous horsemen were riding their way. The order was given to halt and prepare for action. As the riders approached, they were seen to be armed Indians, but of the friendly Winnebago tribe. They had been in government service at Fort Reno, and discharged a few days earlier. They now asked to be included in Carrington's command. Being deadly enemies of the Lakota, however, Carrington was informed that some chiefs in favor of signing the treaty had demanded their removal from Lakota lands. "If this be true," recalled Mrs. Carrington, "it was sharp in the Sioux, for the service lost its best scouts, and no depredations had taken place about Reno while it was known they were there. Upon first alarm these Winnebagoes would spring to their ponies, with rifle and lariat, regardless of rations or clothing, and, with one good whoop, disappear in pursuit."⁵ Carrington told the Winnebagoes that it was not in his power to offer them employment, and they rode on.

On June 19 they passed the final telegraph station at Horseshoe Creek before entering the remote Mountain District which, despite its name, was comprised mostly of plains, hills and valleys. The following day the command arrived at Bridger's Ferry where the Bozeman Trail began its 545- mile journey to Virginia City, Montana. Carrington's foremost guide was the man the ferry had been named for: trail blazer and explorer Jim Bridger. The 62-year-old Virginian had moved west with his family in 1812 and ten years later, after training as a blacksmith, joined a party who went up the Missouri River to trap beaver in the Rocky Mountains. In 1824 he sighted the Great Salt Lake in what would become Utah, and became the first white man to report its existence. He trapped for different fur companies, and in 1830 went into business with four partners in the Rocky Mountain Fur Company. As the beaver numbers declined he established, with partner Louis Vasquez, Fort Bridger in 1842. This became an important trading post on the Oregon and California Trails, then a military post, and Pony Express station. Bridger had departed due to conflict with Mormon settlers who accused him of aiding Indians. In earlier days he had lived among the tribes, and his third native wife was the daughter of a Shoshone chief.⁶ He had purchased the North Platte ferry and improved the crossing a decade earlier but, in search of wider horizons, had sold out and moved on.

"Better not go *fur*," Bridger advised the pale face ladies. "There is *Injuns* enough lying under wolf skins, or skulking on them cliffs, I warrant! They follow ye always. They've seen ye, every day, and when ye don't see any of 'em about, is just the time to look out for their devilment."⁷

The frontier teemed with individuals of colorful character like Jim Bridger, Bill Cody, Kit Carson and California Joe. But not all were men. The formidable Annie Sokalski, widow of a deceased army officer, was later described by Frances Grummond who encountered her at Fort Sedgwick. Not only did Annie carry two revolvers dangling from her belt, but she had 13 dogs for company and "was a noted and dexterous horse woman. During General

Sherman's visit at the Post she dashed into the parade-ground one day clad in a wolf-skin riding habit, with wolf-tails at the bottom of the skirt almost sweeping the ground, and a fur hat from which floated another bunch of wolf-tails. As she galloped swiftly past headquarters where the General was standing, he raised his hands in astonishment and with this ejaculation addressed his host: 'What the devil of a creature is that? Is she a wild woman, a Pawnee, or a Sioux, or what?'"[8]

Once ferried over the river, the column was on the Bozeman Trail, what could be deemed "hostile" territory. Mills, the current owner of Bridger's Ferry, being married to a Lakota woman, had previously lived without threat, but Carrington's arrival changed all that. Lakota warriors had swooped and driven off his stock.[9] On June 21 the colonel issued lengthy instructions regarding "the doubtful attitude of certain Indian tribes which lie in advance of the command." Precise orders were given regarding the corralling of wagons, deployment of pickets and just about every other aspect that entered Carrington's well-organized mind. This included Special Order No. 8: "No firing will be permitted on the march, even upon Indians showing hostile intent, except under immediate orders of a Commissioned Officer, and not then, without reference to Head Quarters, unless an attack be so sudden as to require instant repulse."[10]

As the column neared Fort Reno the ladies bought goods from "French Pete" as Pierre Gazeau was known. He lived with his Lakota wife and several children, and sold supplies from wagons to travelers including "canned fruits, liquors, tobacco, beads, cutlery, crackers, and cheese." Dr. Horton's wife received from Pete the gift of a spotted fawn, a welcome diversion and playmate for children accompanying the trek. The pet would come to an unfortunate end at Fort Phil Kearny when it drank paint instead of the usual treat of sweet milk.

On June 27 the troops got their first glimpse of the distant Big Horn Mountains, gleaming in the sunshine, and next day they reached their first destination on the Bozeman Trail. The collection of derelict buildings, formerly Fort Connor, now Fort Reno, was hardly worthy of the name. The warehouses and stables were the only buildings protected by a rough stockade. The barracks, powder magazine and guard house lay exposed on the open plain. The existing garrison, commanded by Captain George Bailey, consisted of companies of C and D of the 5th "U.S. Volunteers"—actually "Galvanized Yankees"—Confederate soldiers given the choice of donning blue uniforms and serving on the frontier, or rotting in prison back east. Now their only desire was to get back to family and friends still living in the defeated South.[11]

"The warerooms were built of cottonwood logs," recalled Private Murphy, "chinked and daubed with mud, and having dirt roofs. Some of the daubing had dropped out and snow had drifted in. The dirt roofs also leaked and added to the dirty mess." From here supplies including flour and bacon were loaded into Carrington's wagons, but the bacon was so old that "the fat had commenced to fluff from the lean," and as regards the flour, "the mice had tunneled through it."[12] The crumbling post was located on a bluff overlooking the Powder River from where water was brought up by wagon, but on the second day a fresh water spring was found beneath the bluff. This provided far more palatable refreshment than the river water, "muddy and so strongly alkaline as to be prejudicial to both man and beast," recalled Mrs. Carrington.[13] Her husband's original orders had called for Fort Reno to be moved "on the new emigrant line towards Virginia City, about 40 miles."[14] The discovery of the fresh water supply, however, meant that "it was decided to retain the post as part of the district command."

The "new Fort Reno," as Margaret called the future Fort Phil Kearny,[15] would be built further along the trail. Carrington himself used "new Fort Reno" prior to Fort Phil Kearny being named. (This has caused confusion. Some writers are under the impression that another Fort Reno was constructed somewhere near the first. Carrington himself clarified this in a later communication: "Being instructed to look to existing supplies at Fort Reno for the Commisariat at New Fort Reno, (now Fort Philip Kearney,) I was obliged to send at once to Reno for provisions.")[16]

William Henry Bisbee, travelling with his wife Lucy and 14 month-old son, Eugene, recalled Fort Reno as "presenting sufficient ugliness and barrenness to warrant gladness that we were not to remain there long."[17] The 26 year-old first lieutenant was a seasoned campaigner who had joined as a private in 1861. He was wounded during the Civil War at Hoover's Gap and Atlanta, and for bravery at Stone's River was promoted from sergeant major to lieutenant. Bisbee was destined to have a fractious relationship with Carrington, but a long and successful military career, rising to the rank of brigadier general.[18]

Three wagon trains were camped on the river bottom awaiting the colonel's instructions. "These immigrants were impatient to proceed," reported Carrington, "but so mixed with mule and ox trains, that they had no concert of purpose." Accordingly, he issued detailed instructions as to how emigrant trains were to conduct themselves. They would be required to have at least 30 men before proceeding, keep closely grouped and, mirroring instructions to his own troops, "all citizens are cautioned against any unnecessary dealings with Indians; against giving or selling them ardent spirits; against personal quarrels with them, or any acts having a tendency to irritate them, or develop hostile acts or plans."[19]

The military wives were surprised to hear from the émigré ladies that they had no apprehension of danger. No doubt they realized their mistake when the cry "*Indians!*" was heard. The sutler's horses and mules were seen galloping into the distance with an Indian war party driving them on. A bugle blared, 80 men scrambled into saddles and rode in pursuit. The troops disappeared into the distance "but as the night was dark and cloudy," reported Carrington, "the trail was lost."[20] The following day the dejected soldiers returned without the stolen stock—strike one to the Indians.

The fact was, the average mounted infantryman was no match for an Indian brave raised to fight and ride a fleet-footed pony from childhood. "The little boys would gather," recalled Lakota warrior Black Elk, "and fight each other with mud balls that they threw with willow sticks." And older boys played "Throwing-Them-Off-Their-Horses, which is a battle all but the killing; and sometimes they got hurt." The boys "would line up and charge upon each other, yelling; and when the ponies came together on the run, they would rear and flounder and scream in a big dust, and the riders would seize each other, wrestling till one side had lost all its men, for those who fell upon the ground were counted dead."[21]

The troops' one compensation was a single captured Indian pony. Weighed down with gifts of food and clothing from Fort Laramie, it had not been able to keep the pace. Having accepted the gifts, Mrs. Carrington felt that the Indians had "violated their obligations and commenced a new career of robbery and war."[22] Carrington sent a dispatch back to Omaha giving news of his progress, and "I am of the opinion that I should have a larger force, and from conversation with General Sherman at Kearney, thought it not unlikely that he would obtain the 2nd Infantry, now at Louisville, and I then receive the support of another Battalion of the 18th Infantry."[23]

July 3 brought smiles to the troops faces—pay day. Four months wages were forthcoming which meant the purchase of a variety of goods including tobacco and alcohol. But the wise soldier kept his thirst under control if Private Murphy is to be believed: "At the guard tent four stakes were driven into the ground and the drunken soldier was stretched at full length and tied to them. This was called the 'Spread Eagle.' The sun was beating down on him and I thought he was dead. Flies were eating him up and running in and out of his mouth, ears and nose."[24] If correct, it seems more than likely this was done without Carrington's permission. He would later come into conflict with his own officers regarding extreme disciplinary measures. And "the Commander gave the soldier his discharge as a compromise," Murphy recalled.

The following day the boom of big guns echoed across the plains. The Indians would hear and feel the heat of Carrington's artillery soon enough, but they were not the target on July 4. Paymaster Major Henry Almstedt, "an old artillery officer" supervised the Independence Day salute.

Following a ten-day stay, Carrington led the command from Fort Reno northwest along the hot and dusty Bozeman Trail, also known as the Montana, or Virginia City Road. Captain Joshua Proctor was left with Lieutenant Kirtland and Company B to reconstruct and fortify Fort Reno, and 22 horses were allocated for courier and escort duties. Once headquarters endorsed the plan to maintain Fort Reno at its present location, the post would be reinforced with an additional company from Carrington's command, and "new buildings were erected," recalled Margaret, "the parade was enclosed, suitable bastions and block-houses were built, and a substantial stone magazine was completed."[25]

Carrington marched with seven companies of the Second Battalion, 18th Infantry, all suffering from a temperature that climbed to 113 degrees. "Many of the soldiers had bad feet owing to being forced to wear woolen socks in hot weather, but no other kind was issued," recalled Private Murphy. "Add to this the fact that there was only one ambulance available for sick soldiers, as the women and children had all the others in use, and you have a picture of what it meant for a soldier to be sick." The heat affected not only men but their transport as well. "Wagon tires began to break or fall off," recalled Mrs. Carrington, and there was no charcoal for blacksmiths to carry out repairs. Twenty-six miles up the trail the command pitched their tents, after dark, at Crazy Woman's Fork, a tributary of the Powder. Old timers told two stories of how the sluggish creek got its name. One was that a squaw once lived there alone in a tepee, and died after becoming insane, and the other was of a white women who became demented after seeing her husband killed and mutilated in an Indian raid.

The morning light revealed "half of our transportation was disabled, although inspected daily and repaired to all the means at hand," recalled Mrs. Carrington." Timber was cut, a charcoal pit was fashioned and fired, and every available blacksmith was put to work."[26]

On the morning of July 12 "headquarters" (Carrington) with companies A, C and H marched out to scout locations for "new Fort Reno" (future Fort Phil Kearny) while the remaining four companies, under Captain Henry Haymond, continued repairs at Crazy Woman's Fork. They were to follow Carrington "as soon as possible," Margaret recalled. As they marched, the countryside changed as a divide was crossed. Cactus and sage brush gave way to grassy flats and shadowy, green forests on the hills. The area teamed with game, the best hunting grounds of the Lakota, Cheyenne and Arapahoe, now being invaded by the bluecoats yet again. It was from these hills and streams that Connor's troops had been harried the previous year.

Shortly after midday they pitched camp at Clear Fork, a stream flowing from the nearby Big Horn Mountains, "so swift that horses and mules have difficulty in crossing; so clear that every fish and pebble is well defined," recalled Mrs. Carrington, "natural charms that have endeared the country to the savage, and will in the future have equal beauty for those who seek homes in a new and hitherto undeveloped land."[27] While enjoying the sunset perched in chairs the ladies discovered heat and Indians were not the only menace, "we were sitting just over three valuable rattlesnakes, which an orderly was kind enough to find and mangle to death. We sat no more by the brink of Clear Fork, but dreamed of rattlesnakes until the bugle sounded the reveille the next day." Apparently there was no shortage of rattlers along the trail. "Killing the reptiles with whips and revolvers was one of our daily amusements," recalled Lieutenant Bisbee.[28]

On July 13 the march continued, and before long two cracker boxes were found by the roadside with warning messages written on their sides. Two civilian trains had been attacked and stock driven off. Indians were seen on the hilltops at some distance, and word went down the line to have every gun ready. Later that day the command arrived at Big Piney Fork, just east of the Bozeman Trail, where camp was set up. The Big Horn Mountains were about four miles to the west, and "at last we had the prospect of finding a home," recalled Mrs. Carrington, "and Cloud Peak seemed to look down upon us with a cheerful face as the sunlight made his features glow and glisten."[29]

The "beautiful plateau" upon which Fort Phil Kearny was built, as it appeared in the 1980s before partial reconstruction of the stockade (author's collection).

For nine soldiers, however, the "glow and glisten" of the distant Montana goldfields was the attraction. Having made a large part of the journey compliments of Uncle Sam, now was the time to press on under their own steam. Their desertion was discovered on the following morning, and a detachment rode out in pursuit. Seven miles up the trail, however, their path was blocked by a party of Cheyenne. The warriors were trading with the traveling merchant "French Pete" and sent a young teamster, Joe Donaldson, back with the soldiers. He carried a message from Chief Black Horse: "We wish to know does the White Chief want peace or war?" The chief wanted to parley with Carrington through the "Black White Man," interpreter Jack Stead.[30] Married to a Cheyenne, Stead was not of African descent, but had dark hair, eyes and complexion. The colonel, however, was not in camp. Jim Bridger had recommended the Tongue River valley or Goose Creek as a likely place for the new fort, and Carrington had ridden out at 5 a.m. with several officers to inspect the terrain. During a ride of 70 miles they saw no Indians but did come across two brush lodges which showed signs of recent occupation. Upon return Carrington heard Black Horse's message. He drafted a reply to "the Great Chief of the Cheyennes" saying that the Great Father in Washington and his soldiers wished to be his friend. "I will not let white men do hurt to the Indians who wish peace." But he also wanted to know who had been responsible for stock previously stolen. He offered to have Black Horse come in along with "two other Chiefs and two of your big fighting men, when the sun is over head, after two sleeps." They could talk, and "when you wish to go, you may go in peace and no one shall hurt you."[31]

Jack Stead rode out with Joe Donaldson, but the Cheyenne camp site was found to be deserted. Stead followed their trail for 30 miles before spotting their tepees along the banks of the Tongue River. He delivered Carrington's message and found they had moved from fear of attack. This tribe was well aware of Connor's assault on the Arapahoe village the previous August. Stead assured Black Horse of Carrington's peaceful intentions, and the chief agreed for the meeting to take place.

Although remote, the region had been previously mapped, and even before arrival Carrington had favored the forks of the Big and Little Piney streams to be the best location for the new post. "A beautiful plateau had been passed just before the command halted, which seemed particularly inviting," recalled Mrs. Carrington. The inspection of the Tongue River region had not changed the colonel's mind, and the "beautiful plateau" was chosen. But Private Murphy had other ideas: "For some reason they picked out a location about seven miles from the timber and five to eight miles from any hay bottom."[32] Frank Fessenden of the regimental band, however, was more in tune with Carrington: "A more ideal spot for a fort could not be imagined."[33] Carrington reasoned that a fort in the Tongue River valley, further north, would have been too far distant from Fort Reno, suitable pine building timber even further remote, and the Bozeman Trail in the Piney forks region would have been under Indian control. The inviting plateau had an ample supply of fresh water from Little Piney Creek, and not far away was a convenient rise. "This shapely conical summit was the real watch-tower from which the faithful picket guard would signal danger as his watchful eye caught glimpses and his waving flag announced an approaching foe," recalled Frances Grummond, who would arrive with her husband at a later date.[34] All things taken into account, the Piney forks seemed the logical place for the new post to be built. "It occupies the very heart of their hunting grounds," Carrington reported. Shortly after arrival he had scouted the immediate area and observed "bear, buffalo, elk, deer, antelope, rabbits and sage hens."[35]

19

Fort Phil Kearny Takes Shape

The year 1862 had seen a major Indian uprising in Minnesota. Late annuity payments and hunger among the Santee Lakota had seen them bolt from their reservation and kill hundreds of settlers in a vicious war. This would lead to the largest mass execution in American history when 38 Indians were hanged by the neck till dead. During this uprising, Fort Ridgely had been attacked, and during a two-day battle nearly overrun. The post was only saved by Sergeant Jones' artillery fire.[1] But the Indians may well have never attacked if the fort had been protected by defensive walls. The decision was made for the Bozeman Trail forts to be protected by timber stockades. But they would not be the heavy earth and horizontal log fortifications used on Fort William Henry, designed to retard the cannon fire of a European army. For defense against tribesmen wielding muskets, bows and arrows, a traditional, single layer, vertical picket timber stockade was deemed sufficient. Fort Philip Kearny would be named after Major General "Fighting Phil" Kearny. Despite having lost one arm during the Mexican War, he had proved himself again during the Civil War, only to be killed at the Battle of Chantilly in 1862. Kearny had won the admiration of all, and Robert E. Lee arranged for his body to be returned to Union lines under a flag of truce.[2]

Early on the morning of July 15 Carrington and Captain Tenadore Ten Eyck staked out the new fort based on plans previously drawn up. Ten Eyck would be the fort's nominal commander while Carrington would supervise construction and command the Mountain District. Ten Eyck's father, Conrad, had been a signer of the Constitution of the State of Michigan and appointed as the state's first marshal by President Andrew Jackson. Tenadore had enlisted as a private in the Wisconsin Volunteers, but was quickly promoted to Captain commanding Company H of the 18th Infantry. He was captured in 1863 and spent over one year in a prison camp where he nearly died from dysentery. His wife interceded with President Lincoln who managed to arrange his release and, under Carrington's command, he spent the remainder of the war on administrative duties.[3] Leaving his wife to care for their five children back east, he accompanied the Bozeman Trail expedition as Carrington's second in command. But Ten Eyck's fondness for alcohol would lead to trouble further down the track.

Carrington and Ten Eyck supervised as teamsters flicked their reins and drove wagons around, repeating the process until the parade ground perimeter was clearly defined. A mowing machine was brought in and grass fell beneath the swishing blades. It was determined to have tents replaced with sturdy timber structures before the icy winter winds blew in from the north. Perhaps some superstitious soldiers may have seen the grasshopper swarm that descended on the troops that first day as a bad omen, but "a kind wind came along in the afternoon, and they left us as suddenly as they arrived," recalled Margaret Carrington. A "horse-power saw-mill" was prepared for action, but modern steam-driven

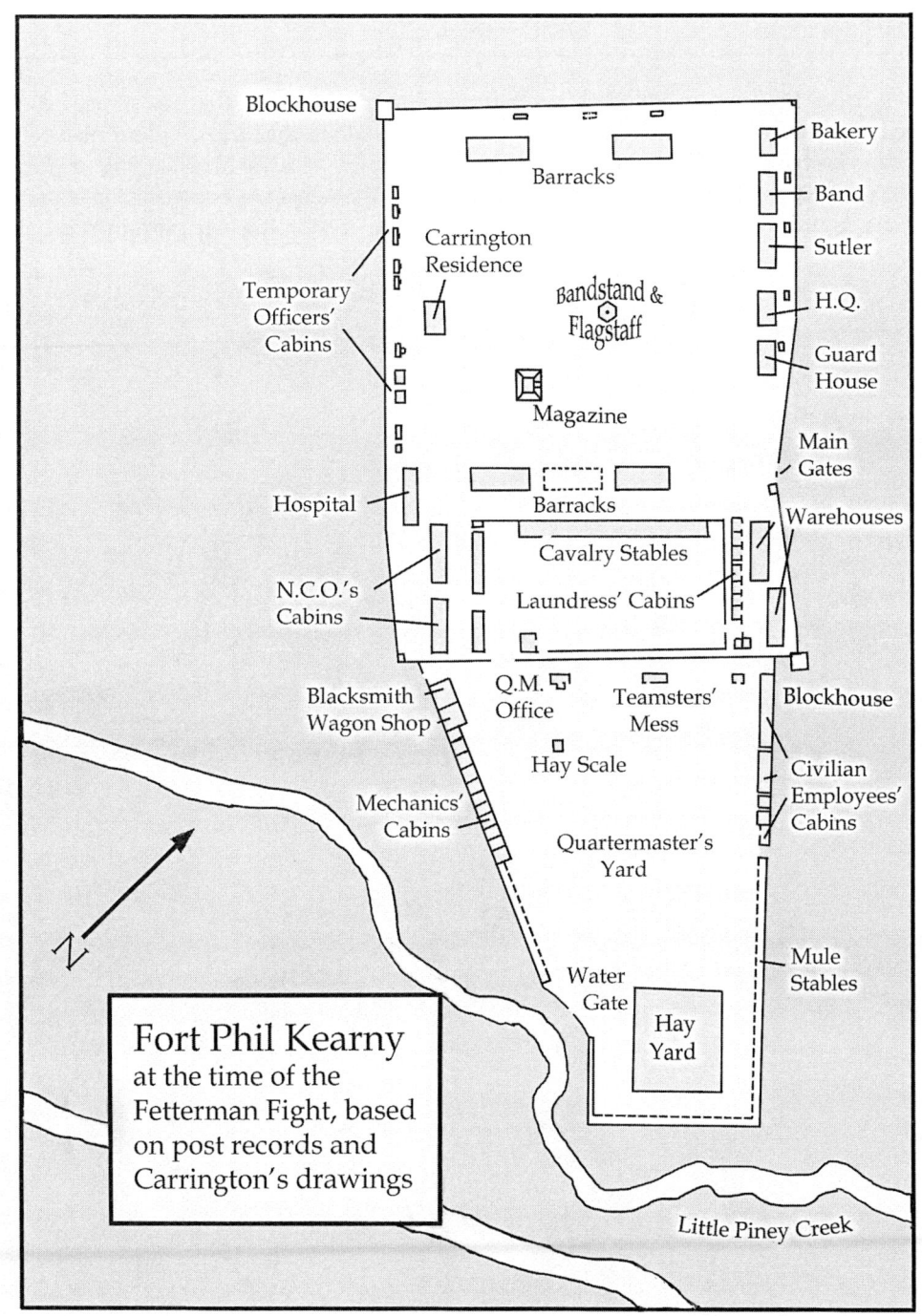

Author's rendition.

saw mills were on the way, a luxury not available when Fort William Henry had been hacked from the wilderness.[4] Work details scurried about, the previously quiet grassland about the Little Piney now a hive of activity. Black Horse and his people were expected, and Carrington was determined to leave them in no doubt that the troops were here to stay. Any demands for departure would fall on deaf ears.

When Black Horse and his followers arrived the following day, they saw spread beneath them an impressive sight. "The tents were pitched along the streets appropriate to the respective building sites of officers' and soldiers quarters," recalled Mrs. Carrington, "warehouses, sutler's store, band-quarters, and guard house; while the established general and picket guards, with the artillery parked on the parade, soon imparted form, comeliness,

Fort Phil Kearny under construction as seen from Pilot Hill. This drawing is based on a contemporary sketch which shows the "blockhouses"—roofless artillery bastions—protruding from the corners of the "stockade proper" (author's rendition).

and system to the whole." The Indians wisely waved a white flag. Once assured of safe passage, about 40 Cheyenne, both braves and squaws, set up camp outside the army lines. Drums rattled and brass played as the chiefs were ceremoniously welcomed by Carrington and his officers resplendent with "epaulettes and dress hats." The Indians themselves were in their finest garb with elaborate necklaces, beads, leggings, medals and earrings. At least one stood out in Margaret Carrington's eyes, a "very tall warrior, with richly-wrought moccasins and a fancy breech-cloth, had no other covering for his person than a large gay umbrella, which as his pony galloped briskly up, had far more of the grotesque and ludicrous in its associations than it had of the warlike and fearful."[5]

To give the visitors a display of the white man's power, Carrington ordered a howitzer fired. The shell shot onto a distant hill and a red flash and smoke were seen, to be followed by a loud boom. "It shoots twice," Black Horse observed. "White Chief shoot once. Then White Chief's Great Spirit fires it once more, for his white children."

Margaret Carrington and other ladies watched from the headquarters tent as a red sandstone pipe was passed around a conference table adorned with the Stars and Stripes. Jim Bridger "sat, or crouched, as watchful as though old times had come again, and he was once more to mingle in the fight, or renew the ordeal of his many hair-breadth escapes and spirited adventures."

Then the parley began. "The whole interview with this band of Cheyennes was frank," reported Carrington. "I long entertained some doubts as to their good faith, yet events confirmed the information they furnished me, and proved them sincere."[6] To Mrs.

Author's rendition.

Carrington, "the scene seemed just about as intelligible as a rapidly-acted pantomime would be to a perfect stranger to the stage."[7] The Cheyenne said that Lakota Chief Red Cloud, backed by 500 warriors, was pressuring them to go on the warpath and prevent this fort being built. They were distressed at the military occupation of their country while the Fort Laramie conference was still in session. "The Cheyenne chief stood there to represent his people," recalled Mrs. Carrington, "to question the plans of the white chief, and solemnly advise him of the issue that was forced upon the red man. It was an occasion when all idea of the red man as a mere wild beast to be slaughtered, quickly vanished in prompt sympathy with his condition."[8] Many young Cheyenne braves were now off on a hunting expedition, Black Horse said, and the old folk and women remaining felt threatened by the Lakota. Once the hunting party returned, 100 Cheyenne braves would help the bluecoats fight Red Cloud. "I had enough men to fight the Sioux," Carrington replied, "but if they kept good faith with the white men, and had trouble with the Sioux nearby, I would help them."[9] Perhaps Black Horse's desire for peace was reinforced when more troops and wagons arrived, Major Haymond's four companies. They had completed repaired on the broken metal tires at Crazy Woman's Fork. Haymond set up camp between the forks of the Piney streams not far from where the conference was under way. The Cheyenne agreed to stay at peace and not to attack immigrant trains. Carrington handed out a certificate which read: "Black Horse, a Cheyenne Chief, having come in and shaken hands and agreed to a lasting peace with the whites, and all travelers on the road, it is my direction that he be treated kindly, and in no way be molested in hunting, while he remains at peace. When any Indian is seen who holds up this paper, he must be treated kindly."[10]

The Cheyenne were given gifts of food and clothing, then rode back to their village. They packed their tepees and prepared to move further south to avoid the brewing storm. "There is no evidence of any of these Indians having violated their pledges," recalled Mrs. Carrington. But Chief Red Cloud's Lakota and those other Cheyenne who wished to fight, along with their Arapaho allies, would not be so easily pacified.

A little before dawn the following day, July 17, the troops in Haymond's camp were startled to hear a war whoop and the tinkling bell of the lead mare as it galloped away. Daring young Lakota braves had slipped past the sentries and infiltrated the herd.[11] More than 170 horses and mules took off in a stampede as mounted Indians closed in and drove the stock towards the distant hills. "They ran across the Pineys and we could scarcely see them for the cloud of dust they raised," recalled William Murphy.[12] Haymond hastily mounted and galloped in pursuit with only his orderly alongside. He left in such haste that he neglected to send word to Carrington of what had taken place, but did leave orders for those of his command who had horses to follow at the double.

Two hours later a breathless messenger galloped into the main camp with news that Haymond's party were surrounded by several hundred hostiles. Two foot companies and 50 mounted men commanded by William Bisbee set out with all due haste.[13] The reinforcements arrived and a running fight of 15 miles took place, but the Indians, fighting on their own terrain against soldiers with no experience against their will-o'-the-wisp tactics, had little hope of success. "The odds were against us," Bisbee recalled, "and we lost the mules as Red Cloud had promised."[14] Carrington's report, however, claimed that "all but seventy head were recovered."[15] The soldiers fell back towards the camp. "Three men were wounded and two killed," recalled Private Murphy. "One man, John Donovan, of my company was wounded twice, once with a poisoned arrow. One of the men received an arrow wound and another a bullet wound."[16]

But worse was to come. In the valley of Peno Creek they came across the grisly sight of the merchant "French Pete" Gazeau and his party. "It was terrible sight," recalled Private John Ryan. "The victims had been mutilated in the most horrible manner and it gave us all a most convincing lesson on what our fate should be should we fall into the hands of the Indians."[17] But the bodies, strangely enough, had not been scalped. It was most unusual for Indians not to take these prized trophies. Carrington reported six men killed. One was Joe Donaldson, who had brought the message from Black Horse to the army camp. Four were buried on site and two others brought back to camp. "The cattle and wagon loads of goods belonging to Gazeau, and which the Indians had not had time to destroy, were also brought to camp."[18] Along with the unscalped bodies it would appear that the Indians had been disturbed by the arrival of the troops. But also brought back to camp was Pete's Lakota wife and five children, found unharmed in the bushes. She told Carrington that the Cheyenne party of Black Horse, after leaving the army camp, had encountered Pete's party and commenced trading. Then Lakota arrived and asked Black Horse if the troops were going to turn back. "He told them the white chief was *not* going *back* but was going *on*." Black horse had been told to tell the Lakota and Arapahoe that presents awaited them at Fort Laramie "and they could get them whenever they went there and signed the treaty which was all ready there for them to sign. The Lakota, then unstrung their bows and whipped 'Black Horse' and the other Cheyenne chiefs, saying 'Coo'; which by the indians is deemed a matter of prowess."[19] The disgruntled Lakota rode off, and Black Horse warned French Pete to waste no time in moving to the army post, otherwise he would be killed. He set out only to be overtaken by the hostiles who had been fighting Haymond. In no mood for trading or small talk, they set upon the traders with hatchet and lance, but spared his Lakota wife and children who fled into the brush. "On the same day Major Haymond's four companies were ordered to change their position and encamp just below the fort," recalled Mrs. Carrington.[20]

Chief Red Cloud swore that he would fight the white invader, and he kept his word to a shocking degree (Library of Congress).

Perhaps this opening attack reinforced the vigor of men anxious to put themselves behind defensive walls. Once complete, the "fort proper" was to be 600 by 800 feet, built upon the gently sloping "beautiful plateau." The stockade was to be constructed from pointed pine vertical pickets eight feet high, sawn to provide a four-inch tight surface against the picket alongside. There was a "banquette" three feet above ground level from which a soldier could fire through an embrasure (often referred to as "loop-holes") cut into every fifth picket join. They flared from six inches on the inner opening to 12 inches on the outer.[21] Sentries would be stationed on platforms six feet square and four feet above ground level.[22]

Within Fort Phil Kearney's walls, offset to one side, was the parade ground flanked by quarters for officers and men, guard house, band building, sutler's store, warehouses and general office. Behind these at various points were the chapel, bakery and hospital. A flag staff enclosed by an octagonal band platform graced the parade ground center from which four 12-feet-wide walkways diverged towards each wall, creating four squares. Within one square was the powder magazine, and in the adjacent square the artillery park. Offset to the other side within the "fort proper" was a rectangular cavalry yard 600 by 200 flanked by stables, NCO's quarters and "Suds Row," the laundry. From this area a gate opened through the main stockade wall to another large enclosure, the quartermaster's yard. Built of rough cottonwood, this stockade enclosed those activities essential for the post's function, but not strictly military: wood yard, teamster's quarters, mule stables, blacksmith, carpenters, etc. One gate from this enclosure opened onto a bend in the Little Piney which provided the post's water supply. The entire post enclosed about 17 acres. "No rifle can reach the garrison," Carrington reported, "but hills and slopes are commanded by artillery, which I brought from Reno for each post."[23]

The words "bock-houses are at two diagonal corners" (of the main fort) appear in both Margaret Carrington's and Frances Grummond's accounts,[24] and Carrington mentions them a number of times. The blockhouses were constructed on September 6, 1866, based on General Order No. 14.[25] They were planned as gun platforms with embrasures for mountain howitzers commanding "all approaches, with enfilading ranges along the flanks," according to Carrington.[26] Such blockhouses would be prominent, standing out from the stockade wall, as shown on Carrington's plans.[27]

Three period drawings by different artists, however, drawn in 1867 show no blockhouses at these points. One does appear at the water gate corner on the quartermaster's yard, which is missing on Carrington's plans, but does receive mention in Frances Grummond's account.

A fourth drawing, however, does show protruding, roofless bastions on the relevant corners. It would appear that these were the "blockhouses," simply omitted from the other drawings.

Two soldiers had been killed and three wounded in the skirmish of July 17, and Carrington was about to lose more men, but not at the hands of hostile Indians. A courier arrived from Fort Laramie with orders for Captain Haymond and Lieutenant Phisterer, involved with the expedition's planning from the start, to report back east for recruiting duties. With his officer staff already well under strength, Carrington was most displeased with this turn of events.

With Jim Bridger acting as scout, Captain Thomas Burrowes led a train and escort out on July 18 to collect provisions from Fort Reno. On the night of July 24 a courier rode in from Burrowes at Clear Fork with the following dispatch: "There is a train engaged three miles from here. I cannot send them any help. The Sioux are very numerous. Send a force at once."[28] In short order Captain Nathaniel Kinney was leading 60 mounted men towards Clear Fork, 16 miles down the trail. They also had a mountain howitzer, designed for work in rough terrain. This could be broken into three sections: barrel, wheels and carriage, and carried on pack mules.

19. Fort Phil Kearny Takes Shape

Burrowes had arrived at Fort Reno, loaded supplies, and marched back towards Fort Phil Kearny on July 20 with 37 wagons escorted by 47 men. When approaching Crazy Woman's Fork he saw a corralled wagon train "with Indians around it. Presuming the train was attacked I pushed forward with my infantry to relieve them." Along the trail Burrowes discovered the body of Terrence Callery, killed by Indians. The corporal had left the column earlier in pursuit of a buffalo.[29] The Indians dispersed as the troops approached, and Burrowes arrived to find the besieged wagons were a military train under the command of Lieutenant George Templeton.

Templeton had left Fort Reno on July 19 bound for Fort Phil Kearny. Lieutenants Henry Link, Napoleon Daniels, Prescott Skinner, James Bradley and Alexander Wands were also present. James Bradley would have the dubious distinction of discovering Custer's dead at the Little Bighorn a decade later.

"We had a detachment of twenty-one men and officers," recalled band member Frank Fessenden, "seven wagons, two ambulances, three women, five children and one colored woman, a servant for the wife of Lieutenant Wands."[30] Chaplain David White was on his way to Fort Phil Kearny to tend the garrison's pastoral needs, and Dr. C.M. Hines was to join two other surgeons. Also with the train was Ridgeway Glover, his paper, pencils, camera and chemicals brought along to capture images of the western frontier.

At noon the following day the travelers approached Crazy Woman's Fork. This would provide water, but all grass along the track had been consumed by earlier trains. Templeton and Daniels rode ahead to search for a campsite with fresh grass. As the train arrived at the stream, the travelers were startled to see Daniels' riderless mount, arrows in its flank and neck, at the gallop back towards them. Alongside the panic stricken horse Templeton was riding for his life, hotly pursued by several whooping Indians. "One of them was so close that he had his spear drawn," recalled Lieutenant Wands, "ready to thrust as he passed my ambulance, which was at the head of the train."[31] Soldiers scrambled from the wagons as Wands ordered the train corralled. Whips cracked and rifles banged as the Indians veered away. Templeton, although wounded, was safe, but "the Indians attacked us fiercely," recalled Fessenden. "We had formed the wagons into a hollow square, placing the women and children inside for protection." About 100 hostiles surrounded the wagons, and a haze of gunsmoke filled the air as a furious fight took place, "for about three quarters of an hour," recalled Wands, "during which time they approached so near that the wagon covers were filled with arrows as well as bullets." All knew Daniels' fate when one Indian "put on his clothes and danced within view of the party."[32]

Unfortunately for the defenders, not all the soldiers were armed. Eleven had Springfield muzzle-loaders, but Wands and Lieutenant Henry Link both had Henry 16-shot repeaters, which may well have saved the command. One chief appeared to be directing fire with flag signals from a hill. Fessenden and Link, armed with his Henry, crept along a ravine. The officer, "with a well-directed shot," hit the chief. "As he started to fall from his horse, two Indians rode up, one on each side of him, and led him away," recalled Fessenden.[33] The Indians then fell back to a stand of timber, and the order was given for the train to make a dash for a nearby hilltop. But "the Indians came out of the timber, with loud yells, and again attacked us." The troops stopped at the base of a nearer hill to make a stand, but it was realized that a grove of woods offered protection to the Indians while the train remained exposed. The defenders made a dash for the hilltop where the troops "formed a more compact corral, with a much better position," recalled Wands.[34] But the Indians kept their fire up. Some soldiers dug rifle pits, but for Fessenden, "it looked for awhile that it were all off for our brave little party." Ridgeway Glover had to be dissuaded from needlessly exposing himself while setting up his camera to photograph the attack. The Indians, Glover wrote, "looked very wild and savage-like while galloping around us; and I desired to make some instantaneous views."[35] Glover was optimistic to say the least. In a day of head clamps and rigid, serious poses, anything that moved appeared blurred when the image was developed. But Private Samuel Peters did describe Glover as "an eccentric and peculiar being," and Chaplain White later wrote that "he behaved with great bravery and coolness for a non-combatant."[36]

Chaplain White "only prayed *internally*, while putting his time physically into the best exercise of self-defense," recalled Mrs. Carrington. "He thinks he did his duty; and the officers say that he thought it was just about the right thing to kill as many of the varmint as possible."[37] Chaplain White did more than his duty. As dusk approached it was decided to send for help, and "Chaplain White and Private William Wallace volunteered to make the heroic attempt," recalled Peters. Perhaps Private Wallace felt this would be his one chance in life to emulate his famous Scottish namesake. "They were properly mounted and furnished with a revolver each, and heroically rode from the corral amid the prayers and God speeds of the little band." Pursued by Indians, "their ride was a magnificent one."[38] But their bravery was unnecessary as it turned out. At about 7:30 the Indians gave up the fight and rode off. A dust cloud had revealed wagons and troops approaching so the odds were about to change. Jim Bridger rode in, and soon Captain Burrowes' infantry arrived.

The last light faded in the western sky, and all fell quiet after dark. Then horsemen were heard approaching. Lieutenant Kirkland had arrived with 13 mounted infantrymen and a mountain howitzer from Fort Reno in response to the chaplain's plea.

At the crack of dawn a party of infantry with an ambulance, under Lieutenant Link, set out to search for Daniels, presumed dead.[39] He was found about a mile from the point of first attack, "scalped, horribly mutilated, and twenty two arrows sticking in his body," recalled Wands. Fessenden also saw three bullet wounds. The bandsman kept one of the arrows taken from Daniels' body as well as "an arrow which was shot at me, and which narrowly missed me." Travelling with Fessenden was his wife and baby daughter who "went through all the sufferings and privations of that frontier life, on the march and at Fort Phil Kearny." Had the party been overrun, chances were the baby would have survived. At their first campsite after leaving Fort Laramie a group of Indians arrived who appeared very friendly. "We soon discovered the reason," recalled Fessenden. "The squaws wanted to buy our baby, offering beads, furs and trinkets of all kinds in exchange. When we refused they acted very sullen, and told us plainly that they would steal her if they got the chance."

"No other loss occurred to our force in that fight," Wands testified. "Indian loss was not known—several were dismounted and blood, robes, and moccasins, were found in the morning showing they must have suffered some." Captain Burrowes ordered the train to return to Fort Reno. They encountered an outward bound supply train of 39 wagons escorted by only nine soldiers, and Burrowes also ordered them to return. They arrived at Reno during the afternoon of July 21, and the following day, a Sunday, Chaplain White presided as Daniels' body was laid to rest with full military honors. Wands was not happy with this state of affairs. Before setting out, "the commanding officer at Fort Laramie was well aware of the strength of our party, and stated to us there was no danger on the road, as a satisfactory treaty had just been concluded."[40]

On July 23 Burrowes and Templeton resumed their march to Fort Phil Kearny. A civilian train traveled with them for protection. They overtook two other trains and camped for the night at Crazy Woman's Fork where more violence broke out, one civilian teamster wounding another with a knife during a fight. The following morning all moved out. The troops traveled at a faster pace and the civilian trains fell some distance behind. That evening the troops camped at Clear Fork where Indians approached, friendly Cheyenne brandishing Carrington's guarantee of safe conduct. They asked for food, and Burrowes agreed to supply hard bread, flour, sugar and coffee providing they leave the camp. The soldiers, however, were not inclined to believe anything an Indian said. "Some of them, pretending to be friendly," recalled Fessenden, "came into our camp, but we could see that they meant mischief. One buck offered me five dollars for my Colt revolver. When I told Lieutenant Wands about this, he ordered the Indians out of our camp."

Then word arrived that the trains were under attack by hostiles three miles back, and one man, Dillon, was wounded. Burrowes sent word to Carrington for reinforcements, and dispatched an ambulance with ten soldiers to pick up the wounded man. They returned in the early hours of the next day, the 25th, but Dillon had died along the way. At 5:30 more riders approached and men prepared for action, but the new arrivals turned out to be Captain Kinney with his 60 mounted reinforcements and the howitzer. They resumed the march and, without incident, finally arrived at Fort Phil Kearny at 2 o'clock that afternoon, the supply wagons and a batch of fresh officers more than welcome.[41] But news of Lieutenant Daniels' death was a severe blow, the first officer to die at the hands of Red Cloud's warriors.

20

A Summons to Duty

At this time a spate of what Carrington called "small action hostilities" commenced.[1] On July 22 one man was killed and another wounded when a train came under attack on the road between Fort Laramie and Fort Reno. The following day two men died at Dry Fork when Indians swooped on another train. Becoming bolder, hostiles "attempted to surround Fort Reno." An effort to drive off army stock failed, but they did manage to drive off a herd of privately owned cattle. Troops galloped in pursuit and managed to recapture the stock—a rare event. On July 29 Indians professing friendship approached another train near Fort Reno, but then turned on the travelers. Despite being armed with Henry repeaters, eight men were killed.

"While the garrison were in tents few ladies slept soundly," recalled Mrs. Carrington, "and officers and men alike threw themselves down for repose as if expecting each moment a summons to duty. Beyond the general guard lines, the pickets were thrown out in several directions to watch for the approach of Indians; so that enemies who knew the former position of the detail could not know its place two hours afterward. Scarcely had the post been located when these nightly visitation became frequent."[2]

On July 29 a frustrated Carrington wrote directly to the adjutant General in Washington: "I have to give sergeants important duties, having, for a line of one hundred miles, active Indian hostilities. Lieutenant Daniels en route to join me, with escort of fifteen men, was scalped and horribly mutilated. I have lost three men killed and wounded besides Lieutenant Daniels. I need officers, and either Indian auxiliaries, or men of my regiment, to build my posts, prepare for Winter, and clear out the Indians. I can resist all attacks, and do much active fighting, but I have a long line to watch and cover. The Indians are aggressive to stop the new route."

But by July of 1866 only 30,000 of the proposed 54,000 men for the restructured Regular Army had been recruited.[3] The army brass were besieged with requests for more troops.

"My infantry make poor riders," Carrington wrote on July 30, "and as I can only fight Indians successfully on foot, my horses suffer in pursuit and in fight." And to make matters worse, "there is at Laramie and elsewhere, a false security which results in emigrant trains scattering between posts, and involving danger to themselves and others." This report was dispatched to department commander Brigadier General Philip St. George Cooke in Omaha, who telegraphed it to Commander-in-Chief General Ulysses S. Grant in Washington, D.C. Cooke mentioned the "energy, industry, and activity of Colonel Carrington," and called special attention "to his want of ammunition and officers."[4]

Cooke, 57, although born in Virginia, had remained loyal to the Union after the Confederates opened fire on Fort Sumter. He had graduated from West Point in 1827, fought in the Mexican War, played a prominent part in suppressing rebellious Mormons, and saw duty in "Bleeding Kansas." A cavalryman, Cooke saw action against western tribes, and eventually wrote an influential book on cavalry tactics. When the war erupted, Cooke's son John resigned his commission in the U.S. Army and went South. He became a Confederate general who was wounded seven times, and Cooke's son-in-law, Jeb Stuart, became the south's most dashing cavalryman. They were not happy with Cooke's decision to defend the Union. "He will regret it but once, and that will be continuously," said Stuart. In 1862 Cooke's own command was one of those richly embarrassed when Stuart led a daring raid right around the Army of the Potomac. But it was Stuart who died by a Yankee bullet, while Cooke survived. Following the war he was placed in overall command of the 11 military posts in the Department of the Platte, a vast territory comprising parts of Montana, Dakota, Utah and Nebraska territories. He opened his headquarters in Omaha on May 2 1866, when organization for Carrington's expedition was already well under way.[5]

General Philip St. George Cooke wanted Carrington to attack the hostile camps, but he could not provide the weapons and men required (Wikimedia Commons).

Cooke appeared to be supportive of Carrington initially but, deprived of troops himself, took a more abrasive tone as time went on. But in some ways Carrington brought this on himself. A constant pattern was to plead for reinforcements to carry out the job, but at the same time send reassurances that he had the situation under control. On July 30 he wrote, "I do not, as you will see, consider every post in danger, neither do I, at present, apprehend any general outbreak." On August 29 he wrote, " Their demonstrations upon my post have cost me nothing, but have cost them men and horses." But, in the same dispatch, Carrington desired "five more companies" to establish additional posts along the Bozeman Trail, but then, "Be assured the public need not fear to follow this line of travel, using proper care and being well armed."[6] On one hand he wanted troops for "the present emergency" but, on the other hand had everything under control. It would appear that Carrington wanted to protest at a shortage of troops, but at the same time seem capable for the job at hand.

The decision to retain Fort Reno meant plans for a fort on the upper Yellowstone had to be abandoned. Carrington received orders to station two companies at Reno, four companies at Phil Kearny, and two at the fort yet to be built on the Big Horn River. In compliance, on July 31 he ordered company F to march south to reinforce Captain Proctor's single Company B at Fort Reno, and on August 3 Jim Bridger acted as guide for Captain Kinney and Captain Burrowes as they marched north with companies D and G. They were to select a suitable site and commence construction of Fort C.F. Smith.[7] Companies A, C, E and H comprised the garrison at Fort Phil Kearny for the time being, 343 soldiers, backed up by civilian quartermaster employees.

Lieutenant Phisterer and Captain Haymond left for their recruiting duties in the East on August 1. "I sent two officers on recruiting duty," Carrington complained to Cooke, "leaving me crippled and obliged to entrust too much to non-commissioned officers."[8] The death of Daniels en route was another blow. The five officers who survived the fight at Crazy Woman's Creek had arrived, but of these Lieutenant Templeton was also destined for Fort C. F. Smith, and Carrington would soon lose Lieutenant Bradley for two months, dispatched on escort duty.

Brevet Brigadier General William Hazen was on a tour of inspection. During August Cooke had informed Carrington that a regiment was being sent from St. Louis, and two companies of cavalry were to arrive. But Hazen arrived on August 27 with no reinforcements. The mounted troops escorting him returned to Fort Reno, and Lieutenant Bradley and 25 men were required as escorts for Hazen's trek to Fort C. F. Smith. This would take one third of the horses with Carrington's command, and they would be gone for two months. This gave Carrington eight officers, too few for the job at hand. But Hazen felt that Carrington had no real problems. Despite the death of Lieutenant Daniels and others, "Indian depredations, so far, have been of a desultory, thieving nature," he reported. "With care, nothing should have occurred, and the whole character of affairs here have been greatly exaggerated.... Col. Carrington appears to only think of building his post."[9] He was complimentary regarding the quality of the stockade's construction,[10] but felt it unnecessary for a garrison of this size. The effort could cause other buildings to have crude, temporary construction.[11] But not all others felt the same way. "My constant fear was that the Indians would work their way over the stockade under the cover of the darkness at night," recalled Francis Grummond.[12] At least the stockade provided some protection.

Hazen departed on August 30, and soon after vented his feelings: "The ideal Indian of the popular mind is found only in poetry and Cooper's novels. The Indian who now inhabits the plains is a dirty beggar and thief, who murders the weak and unprotected but never attacks an armed foe."

Perhaps Hazen changed his mind after December 21.

But he was not totally biased: "The fact that one in a thousand have been civilized proves nothing, neither does it that our people can sometimes be so low and deceitful as the Indian." Perhaps Hazen had Colonel Chivington's massacre of peaceful Cheyenne at Sand Creek in mind. "The Indian department has pampered these rascals, armed them, equipped them, and yielded to their demands, till many of them neither fear the government nor believe it has the ability to defend itself.... In 1859 I had the misfortune to be seriously wounded by Indians, and among our captures were two Lancaster rifles, not long before issued by the Indian bureau." The Bureau had handled Indian affairs since 1849, and were always at odds with the army regarding how best to handle the free roaming tribes of the west.[13]

On September 25 Carrington gave headquarters an update, detailing the progress of Fort Phil Kearny's construction: "Everything moves well. The men cheerfully come off guard, and go to work, and respond to alarm instantly, and eagerly by night and day. Sickness is almost unknown."[14] The first steam sawmill arrived during August, and another was cutting timber by October. They were located outside the stockade walls where civilian structures also appeared. On August 31 Ten Eyck gave permission to James Wheatley to built the first, an eating house run by his wife. During the fort's life, other enterprises were established outside the walls including a "ranche" and billiard room.[15]

"Colonel Carrington was a very busy man, and took great interest in the building of Fort Phil Kearny," recalled Fessenden. "He was always out early in the morning and saw that everyone was in charge of their departments, doing their duty. He took great interest especially in the construction of the magazine, so that it was built according to detail."[16] The magazine, a half dug-out, was constructed by special work details between September 24 and October 10.[17]

The best source of timber was the "Pinery," about seven miles to the southwest, and also Piney Island, about three miles away. Wood trains, usually 20 to 50 wagons, escorted by a non-commissioned officer and eight soldiers, made a daily trip. Other soldiers were detailed as wood cutters, and all were armed. In all there were 20 to 25 soldiers in addition to armed civilians driving the wagons.[18] The escort was increased as the Indians grew more numerous and bolder. Blockhouses were constructed at the logging sites to provide shelter when the wood cutters came under attack, or stayed overnight. But even this was no guarantee of safety, men a short distance from the blockhouses being killed and scalped.

"A train of over ninety wagons was employed at one period, and the timber would be cut, loaded and hauled the same day," recalled Mrs. Carrington, "which made a close framework or skeleton for support of a clay covering. Innumerable straight trees of from four to fifteen inches in diameter were found, which cut from thirty to forty feet in length, without a knot or branch, and these lay so closely in a wall as to need no chinking before the plaster was applied."[19]

"My eight companies of eighty effective men each, with quarters to build, and five hundred and sixty of them new recruits from general depot (although largely from old volunteers) do not give me a fixed, adequate command for the present emergency," Carrington wrote.[20] Those "old volunteers" who fought in the Civil War now had to learn the craft of frontier war while on the job. With a fort to build, there was no time to properly drill and train troops, and not enough ammunition on hand for target practice. The soldiers had to dodge bullets and arrows delivered by a furtive enemy who did not fight by the rules. During the Civil War some whites, like rebel guerrilla "Bloody" Bill Anderson proved themselves to be barbarous in the extreme, but for most prisoners, there was always the chance of being exchanged, or at least surviving in a prison camp till the end of the war. If captured by Indians, however, fire and torture would end the soldier's life. The frontier advice was "keep the last bullet for yourself." In her book Margaret Carrington made reference to the writings of James Fenimore Cooper, who immortalized the siege of Fort William Henry in his famous novel *The Last of the Mohicans*. She mirrored observations made by French officers fighting alongside Indian allies when she wrote, "In ambush and decoy, *splendid*; in horsemanship; *perfect*; in strategy; *cunning*; in battle, *wary* and careful of life; in victory, jubilant; and in vengeance, fiendish and terrible."[21]

In all Carrington had about 640 "effectives," less desertions and death, to protect the 545 miles of the Bozeman Trail. The muster rolls at Fort Phil Kearny for August 31 showed 343 men present to escort wagon trains and wood details, and complete the post before winter came on.[22] About 20 men from each of Carrington's four companies were mounted—providing the horses were healthy and had not been driven off.

"During the months of July, August and September, small bodies of Indians frequently appeared on the surrounding hills, and whenever opportunity offered, stampeded herds, and murdered soldiers," recalled Lieutenant Bisbee. "In the neighborhood of one hundred and fifty to two hundred horses and mules, and about fifty head of cattle were captured by the Indians during my stay."²³ Cattle that could not be driven off were shot, if possible, to deprive the troops of food. Captain James Powell recalled that "Indians who drive off stock seldom carry more fire arms than a pistol, relying mainly upon their arrow."²⁴

"At fifty yards a well-shaped, iron pointed arrow is dangerous and very sure," recalled Mrs. Carrington. "A handful drawn from the quiver and discharged successively will make a more rapid fire than that of the revolver, and at very short range will farther penetrate a piece of plank or timber than the ball of an ordinary Colt's navy pistol."²⁵ And much slower to fire than the Colt pistol was the muzzle-loading rifle issued to Carrington's infantry. While far more accurate at long range than either arrow or pistol, the soldier could only get off three aimed shots per minute. A percussion cap placed on an external nipple was ignited when struck by the hammer, which in turn ignited a paper cartridge containing powder and ball. As Carrington built Fort Phil Kearny, thousands of these Springfield muskets were being converted to breech-loaders which utilized the modern bullet, powder and ignition in a single metal casing which permitted vastly quicker loading and firing.²⁶ And the Spencer carbine, provided only to the 18th's band, utilized a magazine containing seven bullets in the stock. The issue of the muzzleloader when superior weapons were available can only be attributed to a complacent high command who grossly underestimated the Plains Indians, and a preoccupation with those troops policing the former Confederate states.

Hit and run attacks continued, with stock run off, civilians and soldiers killed. One week following Hazen's departure on August 30, the Indians struck during a severe storm, driving off 20 mules from a wagon train to the east of the fort, and two days later attacked government herders driving off 33 horses and 78 mules. A pursuit was promptly organized, "but night and broken-down horses rendered pursuit hopeless," Carrington informed Cooke. "I have sent twenty-five of my best mounted men with Gen. Hazen—have no corn, and with all pains to keep my stock can not pursue successfully till I have more cavalry ... if the single company of Indians, which were sent down for muster out on my way here, had been with me I could have punished the Indians and regained much stock."

"We would have our horses and mules out grazing, with men herding them," recalled Fessenden, "and the Indians would appear as suddenly as though they had sprung from the earth, like so many grasshoppers. They would run through the herd, yelling. whooping and waving blankets or buffalo hides, and stampede the animals, thus getting away with much stock."²⁷

Carrington kept a standing order for 15 horses to be kept saddled and bridled at all times. When Indians struck, one of three or four pickets on Pilot Hill would signal with a flag, while another galloped to the fort to give a verbal report. Soldiers would mount the 15 horses and, under the charge of an officer, ride out. "If the picket reported a large number of Indians approaching," recalled Lieutenant Wands, "and additional force was mounted on every available horse on the post, numbering from forty to fifty, and sent out. This occurred about one third of the number of times."²⁸

On September 13 a combined force of Lakota and Arapahoe swooped at two points, the fort's beef herd and a camp of 84 civilian hay cutters at Goose Creek. The hay cutters retreated, leaving their mowing machines behind, and corralled their wagons "on a hilltop, where we spent the evening and greater part of the night in digging rifle pits," recalled worker John Bratt. The contactor, Leviticus Carter, "paid our stuttering old blacksmith, Jose, five hundred dollars to go to the fort and get relief.... It must have been about nine o'clock in the evening when Jose mounted the best horse we had in camp and started for the fort," armed with two revolvers and a butcher's knife. "A few stars were out but the night was rather dark. Thin clouds of smoke from the prairie fire the Indians had started in the afternoon hung over our camp." Jose had only been gone ten minutes when "he came at breakneck speed into camp followed by a bunch of Indians, some of whom we tumbled off their horses before they escaped." Undaunted, Jose said that he was going to "try it another way." He "disappeared in the darkness in an opposite direction."[29]

"At one (1) A.M. I was called up by courier sent for aid, a hay party of eighty four (84) citizens near Tongue river, having been attacked, one straggler killed, and hay stacks fired, and six mowing machines broken with hatchets, hay heaped on them, and then fired," reported Carrington. "I sent Captain Adair with forty men to relieve them."

"Just about the peep of day we saw the Indians scattering to right and left of a large body of mounted men," recalled Bratt, "with old Joe in the lead."

The mowing machines were damaged by fire, and over 200 cattle were driven "into a herd of buffalo and they were irrecoverably lost," reported John Adair. The Indians, estimated at two to three hundred, must have been delighted to feast on fresh meat provided by Uncle Sam. All was not lost, however. "The machines were promptly repaired and put in motion," reported Carrington. "With the citizens who were well armed, I hope to have, in one week, a winter supply of hay for all contingencies." But the Indians were not through yet. That same evening they struck again, stampeding a government herd near the post. "One picket came in with arrow in his hip, another with a revolver ball in his side," Carrington recalled. They were pursued for 15 miles, but the Indians "took the red-buttes, where our horses could not pursue."[30] Carrington may have had adequate hay on hand, but the horses, becoming run down, needed corn. A shortage of ammunition and animal feed was relieved, however, with the arrival of a commissary train. He purchased "a few bushels of corn to restore horses," and received 60,0000 Springfield rounds, but "I ought to have if possible one hundred thousand rounds more, and from Laramie, more ammunition for my twelve pound field howitzer and mountain howitzer." General Hazen wrote in his report that the cavalry should be mounted on "half-breed horses, as they can subsist without forage on the native grasses of the country. The American horses are of no service without grain."[31]

On September 14 part of Private Gilchrist's uniform was discovered "without his body," and on the 16th Private Johnson, on hay detail, was cut off by Indians in a ravine, killed, scalped and his body carried off.

A few days later the pictorial history of Fort Phil Kearny received a mortal blow when Ridgeway Glover's body was found. He had been killed while walking alone to the fort from a woodcutter's cabin. "The head was found a few yards off, completely severed from the trunk, scalped," Samuel Peter's recalled.[32] He also mentioned other mutilations such as disembowelment and "a fire placed in the cavity." "He was very careless of life," wrote Chaplain White, "traveling frequently by himself—one time to the snow range of Big Horn mountains—with nothing but a butcher knife, though the country abounds with wolves, black, grizzly and cinnamon bears, and ferocious savages.... He was shot with a ball and instantly killed, the ball passing through his heart. I mention this fact so that his friends may be relieved of the horrors of savage torture."[33] "He had long yellow hair," recalled Fessenden, "and I had often told him that the Indians would delight to clip that hair for him some day. He said he was safe, as the Indians would take him a for a Mormon." Not only Glover's life was lost, his photos and drawings having never come to light.

On the day of Glover's death, September 17, 40 mounted men arrived at Fort Phil Kearny, but unlike most travelers, they were heading south. They were miners who had not struck it rich in the Montana goldfields, and had lost two men to Indians attack on the trail. Their leader, William Bailey, requested permission to camp outside the post. Carrington learned that the miners were all experienced frontiersmen, well armed and mounted, and seized an opportunity to reinforce his garrison by indirect means. He offered them jobs as quartermaster employees, which was put to a vote by the miners and accepted.[34]

The same day "a party of seven Indians dashed out from thick cottonwood at the confluence of the two Pineys and made boldly for the picket on Pilot Hill," recalled Margaret Carrington. "It seemed that almost instantly the relief of the mounted picket, always saddled and ready, were out of the east gate upon a run, and yet it was plain no riders or horses would be in time. The despised howitzers were brought into requisition, and a case shot was sent as a swifter messenger, with its relief of eighty bullets, and, as it hurtled through the air, the savages slackened speed a little to watch its advent. They found the 'gun that shoots twice' too much for their dodging, and its shell exploded over their heads, scattering its compliments and the earth in all directions, they turned their course and made for the brush as quickly as they had appeared. A second similar messenger dropped one Indian from the saddle, and then all took cover."[35] As this occurred about 50 Indians appeared near Piney Creek and made a dash for the miners' horses, but they opened fire with revolvers and rifles, driving them off as one Indian pony fell. The dismounted warrior deftly leapt up behind another and they galloped off without harm. Then yet more Indians appeared to the north on Lodge Trail Ridge. Carrington surmised that these assaults were decoys to keep the garrison contained while the timber train came under attack. A detachment tramped out the gate at the double to back the woodcutters up. They joined the timber train, and the Indians disappeared into the hills.[36] "Red Cloud is known to command the parties now immediately engaged," reported Jim Bridger. "White flags are used as signals between the different bands, thus covering a line of at least seven miles.... They are determined to burn the country, cut off supplies, and hamper every movement."

This conflict would appear to be purely that between white man and red, unlike the French and Indian War where Indians fought each other alongside European allies. But Carrington heard of a white man "with one thumb" named Bob North fighting with the Arapahoe, and Bridger reported, "There are men with them who dress and appear to be white men, and swear and talk in good English." On September 21 The hay cutters at Goose Creek were under attack once more, and when withdrawing were forced to corral the wagons about five miles from the fort. A detachment rode to their relief, and as the Indians withdrew, Lieutenant Matson found himself face to face with a white man dressed in Indian garb. He identified himself as "Captain Bob North," and was missing fingers on one hand. A scout galloped up and reported three men killed on a contractor's train returning from Fort C.F. Smith. As troops dashed along the road Bob North disappeared into the hills.

It comes as little surprise that the hay cutters were "demoralized and unwilling to work," recalled Carrington. Further south, more Indians "operated around Fort Reno" driving off stock. They killed one man and wounded two others. Fort C. F. Smith itself was in territory dominated by friendly Crows, and had nothing like the problems of Fort Phil Kearny, but even there the enemy sometimes struck a blow. "On one occasion a small party of Sioux visited," recalled Carrington, "claimed to be friendly, received some provisions, left the fort and killed and scalped one man, returning from where wood was being cut, within half a mile of the fort, and in sight of its garrison. They were promptly pursued but eluded punishment."[37]

On September 21 Carrington issued new orders which included "all soldiers, however detailed or attached, or in whatever capacity serving, will, upon a general alarm, take arms and be subject to immediate disposal with their companies or at the headquarters or department with which serving. All horses of mounted men will be saddled at reveille. It is also expressly enjoined that in no case shall there be needless running in haste upon an alarm. Tale-bearing, and gross perversion of facts by excited men does more mischief than Indians."[38]

The morning of September 23 saw a drizzling rain beneath a dark, somber sky. A civilian cattle herd as grazing outside the fort. With the speed of lightning a band of hostiles struck, whooping and waving blankets, and about 90 animals took off a in a wild stampede. But Lieutenant Frederick Brown was on the alert and led the first seven men saddled at a gallop through the fort gates. Fifteen miners grasped their guns and joined the pursuit. The chase went on over brook, gully and hill for 13 miles before the hostiles and the stolen herd were overtaken. A one-hour skirmish ensued. "Dismounting the infantry," Carrington reported, "Brown and a few men charged the Indians with revolvers, killing five Indians and one white man, I think Bob North, who has led them in every case, and wounding sixteen. One chief carried from the field by his men wore an elaborate feather head dress, and proper ornament of the same kind upon his person." The Indians retreated leaving all the stock to Brown's victorious band. No whites were killed, only one being grazed by an arrow, and six horses were wounded by gunfire. "It has inspired all my men with new courage," reported Carrington. "One week's feeding on corn has given new life also to my horses." Carrington later heard that the Indians "acknowledged five killed, eight wounded who died of their wounds, and many shot who would recover."[39] If Bob North was one of those, he lived to fight another day. He was hanged along with his Arapahoe wife by vigilantes in Kansas in 1869.

Frederick Brown was hero of the day as the stolen cattle were driven back to the fort. As quartermaster, Brown was responsible for the army stores, ammunition and livestock. A genial, popular man, he was well liked by the straight-laced Colonel and Mrs. Carrington, despite his considerable fondness for drink. He had served with the 18th as a quartermaster during the war, but unlike some others, had not received a brevet for gallantry in action, a possible reason for daring-do when the opportunity arose. Fighting Indians was his last chance to prove himself a combat man, and he kept a horse saddled at all times. When the enemy stampeded stock, Brown was first through the gates in pursuit. He would soon be promoted to captain, but was displeased to be ordered back to Fort Laramie. He would see no action there. Brown stalled the transfer, saying his paperwork and inventory were incomplete. Carrington had no wish to lose another officer, and backed him up.[40] Brown would see more action, staying on at Fort Phil Kearny till the ominous, chilly day of December 21.

On September 27 the wood party on Piney Island was at work, felling trees and trimming branches. Three soldiers labored their way through the pines till they were about 100 yards from the main party. Suddenly about 100 Indians appeared from between the trees. The main party dropped axes and made it safely back to the blockhouse, but the detached three men were left behind. Shortly afterwards, two of them arrived safely at the blockhouse, but Private Patrick Smith was still missing. Despite having been impaled with arrows and scalped, however, Smith was still alive. He managed to break the shafts, and crawl half a mile through thickets to the blockhouse. Word was sent to the fort for a surgeon, but Smith would not live 24 hours.

The Indians, meanwhile, moved back towards the fort for another attempt on the pickets on Pilot Hill. "The sudden repeated shriek of the steam-whistle," recalled Margaret Carrington, "and the equally hasty signal of the pickets, gave the alarm that the Indians were again close by."[41] Fifteen mounted braves dashed for the summit, but Private Rover, in charge of the pickets, slapped the army horses, sending them galloping down towards the Indians. Lieutenants Brown and Adair were leading 20 mounted men in pursuit, and the warriors shot arrows at the pickets' mounts as they thundered past. The pickets had their Springfields at the ready, and the Indians bypassed them, continuing across the summit. Brown and Adair led their men in pursuit, but the fleet footed Indian ponies soon disappeared into the hills.

Nine Cheyenne, including one squaw, arrived at the post that same evening. They were friends of the soldiers, they said. While approaching, however, they had been seen by Lieutenant Brown exchanging words with the hostiles who had carried out the attack on Pilot Hill. But these Cheyenne had been with Black Horse when he agreed to take no part in the war. Had they changed sides, however? They told Carrington they wanted "permission to hunt in the Tongue river valley and to trade at the Post." This would mean allowing them in through the gates. A lawyer residing at the fort, J. B. Weston, later recalled, "My own opinion at that time, and still is, that those Indians were hostile."[42]

Based on historic precedent caution was required when "friendly" Indians gained entry to a fort. Following the French and Indian War the British had been none too "friendly" in their treatment of France's former allies. Chief Pontiac's rebellion in 1763 was the result. Fort Michilimackinac stood alongside the Straits of Mackinac connecting Lake Michigan with Lake Huron. Like Fort Phil Kearny, it was not built to withstand cannon fire, only Indian attack. Formerly a French possession, it was garrisoned by 93 redcoats under Major Ethrington and, also being a trading post, housed several merchants and civilians, both British and French. For reasons best known to himself, the major refused to believe a warning that Indians planned to attack, and threatened to arrest anyone who repeated the rumor. Indians gathered around the fort in large numbers and traded furs for goods as usual. The Chippewas arranged a game of *le jeu de la crosse* to be played against the Sauks outside the stockade, and invited Major Etherington to witness the event. The game got under way, and the ball was flung about, edging closer to the fort.

British merchant Alexander Henry was in his quarters behind the walls, and later described what happened next: "I heard an Indian war cry, and a noise of general confusion. Going instantly to my window, I saw a crowd of Indians within the fort, furiously cutting down and scalping every Englishman they found." The Indians had flung the ball across the palisade and swarmed in through the open gate. Alexander Henry hid in the loft of a French neighbor's house before being taken prisoner. He survived an attempt to kill him and lived with the Indians for a year before being released.[43] An event with certain similarities occurred at Fort Mims, Alabama, in 1813. The Creeks were on the warpath, but Major Beasley refused to believe stories of imminent attack. The fort gates were left wide open and the Indians swarmed in. Over 400 soldiers and settlers died as a result, and the fort was burned to the ground.[44]

Such stories caused a distrust of all Indians when the hatchet was out, and the garrison had heard of the mortally wounded Private Smith's crawl to the Pinery blockhouse that very day. Despite unease at their arrival, Carrington provided the visitors with bacon and coffee, and they camped on the nearby island that divided the waters of Little Piney Creek. Night came on and the sentries cried, "All's well," but a little after nine, shadowy figures silently slipped over the stockade wall, or through the quartermaster's gate. Chaplain White was already in Carrington's quarters saying there was talk among the men of killing the Cheyenne, when a door flew open and a soldier sounded the alarm. Carrington reached for his revolver and dashed outside. The soldiers had "cocked their pieces, and were ready to deliver fire," when "two reliefs of the guard" arrived and ordered them to stop. The men held their fire and, disobeying Captain Ten Eyck, "rushed for the east gate." Here a furious Carrington confronted them, revolver in hand. He ordered them to halt twice, only to be ignored. He fired two shots in the air, and then they stopped. "So far as the light could determine, they were some of the best men of the garrison," recalled Mrs. Carrington. "They quickly realized the disgrace that would have fallen on the post and regiment had they perpetuated the massacre, and for many reasons were restored to their barracks with only admonition and caution as to future conduct."[45] One good reason was that there were so many of them, "nearly one hundred," reported Carrington. Fortunately he had not taken General Sherman at his word: "We must try and distinguish friendly from hostile, and kill the latter, but if you, or any other Commanding Officer strike a blow, I will approve, for it seems impossible to tell the true from the false."

The following morning, Carrington spoke with Chiefs White Mouth, Blackfoot, and Rotten Tail. Black Horse was not present due to illness. They "insisted that *they* were at peace," recalled Carrington, but some of their young men wished to join the hostiles. Red Cloud had visited their village urging them to war on the whites, but they had refused. Rotten Tail said he took half a day to ride through the vast village of the "war parties on Tongue River." The Lakota, Cheyenne and Arapaho gathering there would not attack Fort Reno, "but would destroy the two *new* forts in their hunting grounds, meaning Fort Phil Kearny and Fort C. F. Smith."[46]

Years later an Indian named Two Moons said that he was with the "friendly" Cheyenne and they had indeed been sent to see if the fort "could be taken by storm." They reported that the post was too strong, and the chiefs decided instead to "draw the garrison out, by detachments, and surprise them, a plan by which the recent recklessness of some of the troops in chasing Indians convinced them would succeed."[47] But Mrs. Carrington was convinced of the sincerity of the Cheyenne. When Brown saw them, she wrote, the Lakota had "contemptuously struck them and cried 'Coo!' as they did in July, when unable to induce the same party to engage in war against the whites."

"Other days were as full of changing adventures as this," she recalled. "Few were without their share of painful incidents. A game of croquet was planned, and while the ladies could neither ride nor walk beyond the gates, some amusement was attempted between Indian alarms; the evening found its recreation in the author's game, a quiet quadrille, good music, conversation, and other varieties, besides the needle and cook-book."[48]

21

A Forgotten Battalion

While Indians attacked unwary travelers and drove off stock around Fort Phil Kearny, Fort Reno had its share of problems too—but largely from within. "I fear Captain Proctor is too ill and nervous to command, but I have no one to succeed him," Carrington reported to Omaha on October 4. "He has lost all his stock, and has arrested his Adjutant Lieutenant Kirkland, without notifying me, or furnishing me, or the lieutenant with a copy of the charges.... General Hazen told me he found the same inefficiency. I hope to go there in a few days and judge for myself."[1] No doubt Carrington wanted to judge for himself, Kirkland being a cousin. Proctor would be relieved of command the following month, replaced by Lieutenant Colonel Henry Wessells.

On October 7, "I took charge of the system of police and discipline of the post," recalled Carrington, "entertaining the idea that the future policy might involve more formidable Indian aggression, and require more exact and careful watchfulness and defense."[2] Carrington's decision to reduce Ten Eyck's responsibilities may have also been influenced by the recent arrival of Lieutenant George Washington Grummond. It was time for reorganization of the fort's command. Lieutenant Adair was also replaced as post adjutant by Lieutenant Bisbee. Adair decided frontier life was not for him, and resigned his commission, but did agree to stay on till James Bradley returned from escort duties with General Hazen.[3] Lieutenant Wands was placed under Lieutenant Frederick Brown as assistant quartermaster.

The new Regular Army was still undergoing reorganization as more recruits enlisted, and on October 13 Carrington received word that the "Mountain District" had been abolished. This meant that the fort commanders were to report directly to Omaha, but Carrington remained as ranking officer on the Bozeman Trail.[4] And there were other changes in the wind. These would see the 18th Infantry split up, the 2nd Battalion which Carrington now commanded becoming the nucleus of the 27th, and the 1st Battalion staying as the 18th, of which he would retain command.[5] This would require his transfer from Fort Phil Kearny to the new headquarters of the 18th, Fort Casper on the Oregon Trail. This was not intended to take place till summer of the following year, but dramatic events would see a chilly advance of plans and an abrupt termination of Carrington's command of Fort Phil Kearny.

Accompanying George Grummond was his young wife Frances who was "in the family way." The scalped and mutilated man they saw being taken into the post was an ominous portent but "our arrival was hailed with manifestations of great pleasure," she recalled. "We had come through safely, were an addition, though a very small one, to their numbers, and we brought the mail!"[6]

The Grummonds arrived with "a mail party made up of an escort of six men, with two ambulances and one wagon for baggage!" recalled Frances.[7] She found the new post "excellently built," but at this stage the fort was still incomplete, and the their cabin would not be ready till November, "so that for the time tents were substituted for the ambulance, quite an advance for comfort, in comparison." Margaret Carrington told Frances of recent deaths at Indian hands. Little wonder "that strange feeling of apprehension never left me, enhanced as it was by my delicate condition."

Her husband, George Washington Grummond, was a former Great Lakes sailor. He had enlisted at the age of 26 as a sergeant in the First Michigan Infantry when the Civil War erupted, and at that time had a family, wife Delia, 23, and young son, George. He rose to the rank of captain and joined the 14th Michigan Infantry with the rank of major in March of 1863. Colonel Henry Mitzner procured horses for the regiment, thus they became mounted infantry, and Grummond saw action scattering Confederate guerrilla bands in East Tennessee. With the area under Federal control, the 14th garrisoned Fort Granger near Franklin, Tennessee, and it was here Grummond met Frances Courtney, ten years his junior. The attractive young lady was from an affluent family who, despite owning slaves, had remained loyal to the Union, and she became romantically involved with Grummond. She knew nothing of his wife and the birth of a second child back home. Promoted to Lieutenant Colonel, Grummond took part in Sherman's advance on Atlanta, but the former horsemen were now on foot again, despite having reenlisted on the understanding they would remain as mounted troops. Grummond, however, proved to be a tough campaigner, on horse or foot. But in August of 1864 junior officers petitioned the adjutant general to investigate his conduct and fitness to command. They sited drunkenness while on duty and needless physical abuse of his men. Court-martialed, he was found guilty of threatening to shoot one officer and shooting an unarmed civilian. The sentence, however, was a mere public reprimand. After all, Ulysses S. Grant was accused of being a drunk, and William T. Sherman of being insane. In time of war certain faults were overlooked.

Lieutenant George W. Grummond, an officer with a record and temperament for taking unnecessary risks (Library of Congress).

But one month following the court-martial Grummond was in trouble again. Ordered by General Robert Granger to advance his troops for a combined attack on rebels under

General Joseph Wheeler, the impetuous Grummond arrived three hours early. The enemy were put on the alert, and Grummond had to send for help to extricate his embattled command. Grummond's bundle "unquestionably hastened the movement of Wheeler from Lawrenceburg," reported Granger. Grummond was removed from the operation, and during 1865 received further reproach for "not even a semblance of company organization," "compelled to retire somewhat in confusion," and "pushing hastily forward."[8] On the other hand, he was commended for serving with distinction at the Battle of Bentonville in North Carolina during March of 1865.

His family, meanwhile, found themselves destitute, Grummond having failed to send money for their support. Following Lee's surrender, he returned to Tennessee and resumed his courtship of Frances and, behind the scenes, the wheels of divorce from wife Delia began to turn.

The war's end meant a big demotion in rank for those who stayed with the much smaller Regular Army. Officers such as Major General George Armstrong Custer found themselves as mere captains, for the short term at least. Grummond enlisted as second lieutenant in Carrington's regiment, the 18th United States Infantry, but told Frances that he had been recommended for a brevet of brigadier general; a fantasy, as it transpired. His wife was granted a divorce on September 23, 1865, on the grounds that Grummond "hath grossly, wantonly, and cruelly refused and neglected" to provide suitable maintenance for his family. But Grummond had already married Frances on September 3.[9] He has been soundly denounced for this bigamy—but was it an honest mistake? Andrew Jackson had accidently married Rachel Robards *two years* before her divorce had been finalized, not a mere 20 days, as in Grummond's case.[10] Despite the telegraph's arrival, mistakes were easily made in days of slow and uncertain communication, and Grummond's divorce occurred in distant Detroit. The judge awarded Delia $2,000 per month in quarterly installments over the following year. Where this was to come from is uncertain, as it was more than Grummond earned.[11]

Frances Courtney Grummond, from a genteel Southern family, found life on the frontier so harsh that, knife in hand, she "almost threatened then and there to end it all" (author's collection).

The newlyweds left Tennessee in December of 1865 and, after routine recruiting duties, set out for the western frontier. Along the way Frances met "the first Indian I had ever seen," a warrior known as "Wild Bill." This revealed how successfully whites had removed the tribes from Tennessee. "It was a complete wilderness, and full of Indians who were hunting," Tennessee pioneer David Crockett had recalled many years earlier.[12] Wild Bill warned the Grummonds that all the northwestern tribes were going on the warpath. But this was not taken seriously. "Fortunately for my peace of mind the facts were not then known to us," she recalled.[13] After a pause at Fort Laramie, the small Grummond party arrived to a warm reception at Fort Reno. Despite rumblings and rumors of Indian attacks, "my husband was a soldier reporting for duty, and had no hesitation in implicitly obeying orders."[14] It would seem these words were written to scotch rumors that her husband, God forbid, had anything to do with tragic future events.

The warm welcome the Grummond's received at Fort Phil Kearny was not backed up by the weather that first night. "The snow drifted in, covered my face, and there melting trickled down my cheeks," recalled Frances. A driving wind had forced unseasonal snow between the two tents set up, end to end, as their quarters. "Shaking out stockings and emptying shoes filled with fine snow was earthly and practical in the extreme." Their camp stove was lit by an orderly and the snow melted away. Frances, however, was not impressed. Being greeted with the sight of a mangled corpse as they arrived, then covered with snow during a freezing night was too much. "I had such a sensation of actual desperation come over me that with butcher-knife in hand for preparation of something for breakfast I almost threatened then and there to end it all." To make things worse, Frances had little knowledge of how to prepare breakfast or anything else. She had been brought up in a household where slaves did the cooking and housework. But she "resolved to 'take up arms against this sea of trouble' and master the situation." She cooked some bacon and "very hard biscuit from flour salt and water," but, while attempting to crack the biscuit, the butcher knife slipped and "almost severed my thumb, mingling both blood and tears."[15]

Within the next few weeks she was to learn that wild game was "juiceless," and the preparation of edible food "from canned fruits, meats, and vegetables taxed all ingenuity to evolve some product, independent of mere stewing, for successful results."[16]

But at least officers with families had stoves and quarters in which to eat. "At that time the Government did not furnish cooks or bakers," recalled Private William Murphy. "They simply furnished the rations and the soldier could cook them himself or eat them raw as he saw fit. They furnished no vegetables. We cooked soup, bacon and coffee, and dished it out to the men in their cups and plates. We had no dining room. We boiled everything. I believe the bacon would have killed the men if it had not been thoroughly boiled.... Ours was indeed a 'Forgotten Battalion.'"[17]

Sometimes food was procured from other sources. Chaplain White purchased a cow from travelers and shared the milk with Frank Fessenden provided he did the milking. But "I presume the Indians also wanted her," recalled Fessenden, "as they eventually got her."[18] One entrepreneurial laundress, "Colored Susan," found "a fortune was soon to be realized by selling villainous pies to soldiers for half a dollar or more," recalled Mrs. Carrington.[19] Not only did Susan sell at "exorbitant rates pies made of government flour and fruit," according to an internal report, "but also 'ardent spirits' to soldiers." Susan was, furthermore, "disorderly, breeding mischief in the garrison by inciting officers' servants to abandon their situations.... This woman, profane, abusive and of bad repute before her arrival, must observe better behavior or she will not be tolerated in the garrison."[20]

But Henry Carrington had more pressing problems than a liberated Susan. A telegram dated September 27 arrived via Fort Laramie from General Cooke: "Having one company of cavalry, you can probably dispense with your ninety-four horses, after mounting all the cavalrymen. They could be used for cavalry at Laramie. The same as to any useless horses at C.F. Smith and Reno."[21] It seemed apparent that Carrington's commanding officer was oblivious to conditions at Fort Phil Kearny. No cavalry had arrived, over half his horses had been run off by Indians, and 27 mounts were still absent with Hazen's escort. He was so short of good horses that only three mounts had gone with the two companies to establish Fort C.F. Smith, and those remaining were too weak to pursue hostiles due his grain orders not being fulfilled.

Then Carrington received a most unexpected dispatch. General Cooke was threatening to have him *court-martialed*! Carrington's reports for the previous three months had not been received at Omaha, which would explain Cooke's lack of knowledge of affairs at Fort Phil Kearny. But also included was an update from Cooke. The courier had been overtaken by a galloper 55 miles up the trail from Fort Laramie. He carried a telegram saying the reports had just come in. Annoyed with the delay, Cooke instructed Carrington to keep couriers on the move, covering 50 miles day, with weekly mail deliveries.[22] Carrington replied again explaining the condition of his horses. "By the 10th of October," recalled Mrs. Carrington, the horses "had been reduced to less than forty, were poorly adapted for a swift express of over two-hundred and thirty-five miles without a relay, and especially when they were almost daily required for active and outpost duty at the fort."[23]

But finally trains arrived carrying tons of oats and corn for the horses. With the long, cold winter coming on, however, even these supplies would fall short.

Carrington saw a chance to restock the garrison's beef supply when a herd of Texas longhorns arrived. They were being driven by 32-year-old Nelson Story and 24 cowboys, headed for the Montana goldfields where cattle could be sold for ten times their purchase price. Story had struck it rich in the goldfields, traveled to Texas, and invested $10,000 in the herd. The original intention was to drive the longhorns north to a railhead, but to avoid trouble with Kansas Jayhawkers he decided Montana via the Bozeman Trail would be a better bet. At Fort Laramie he was told to abandon the drive or face Red Cloud's warriors and quite possibly lose both his scalp and the herd. Story purchased Remington breechloaders for his men, and pushed on, but the Indians struck even before Fort Reno was reached. Two drovers received arrow wounds and a large slice of the herd was driven off. As night came on the cowboys followed the trail and found the cattle in the center of a ring of tepees. "We had to wipe out the entire group to recover our longhorns," Story told his son years later.[24]

The two wounded cowboys were left at Fort Reno, and the herd pushed on to Fort Phil Kearny, where Story encountered more trouble. They could not proceed, Carrington said, current regulations requiring at least 40 armed men to a party, while Story had only 25. He would have to wait till another train arrived so their numbers would bolster his own. With winter approaching, another train might not arrive till the following spring, Story replied, and in any case 25 men armed with Remington breechloaders were far more formidable than 40 men with muzzleloaders. But Carrington said rules were rules, and instructed Story to corral the herd three miles from the fort and await instructions. The cattleman protested. Being so far away would expose the herd to Indian attack, he said. Carrington replied that the grass around the fort was needed for government stock. Story herded his longhorns to the designated site, but may well have suspected Carrington stalling his advance till the snow hit, forcing him to sell to the army at a low, government price.

On the morning of October 22 Carrington was informed that Story and his herd had disappeared during the night. He was furious to have his orders violated, but ordered a sergeant and 14 men to catch them and provide escort, bringing the party to the required 40 men. Carrington was responsible for safety on the trail, and it would not be to his credit if the herd was taken by Indians and the cowboys killed.

The herd was driven through to Montana, travelling by night and grazing by day. Two Indian attacks were repulsed, but one cowhand was killed and scalped when he rode too far ahead. The longhorns arrived on December 9 to a joyous welcome from hungry miners who were prepared to pay handsomely for a good beef steak. Story made a huge profit, invested in various business ventures, became a millionaire, and in later life became a property developer in Los Angeles. He died there in 1926, aged 87, but was buried in the town he considered home, Bozeman, Montana.

On October 27, 1866, Lieutenant Bradley rode back into Fort Phil Kearny with the 25 mounted men of General Hazen's escort. On the return trip they had been "attacked by large party of Sioux," reported Carrington. Their civilian guide had been killed and scalped, and "Dr. McCleary had his horse shot and escaped." The skirmish "lasted for several hours, resulting in supposed loss to the Indians and their retreat." Private Brooks had been wounded, "but not fatally."[25] No doubt Bradley's men were pleased to see the fort's construction well advanced, the timber stockade, deemed by Hazen as unnecessary, a comforting sight.

"Two steam saw-mills just above the mill gate, and just a few rods distant, furnish constant supplies of post, plank, studding, rafters, lath and boards, and all lumber for every use," recalled Mrs. Carrington, and despite "constant skirmishing," "the stockade of two thousand eight hundred feet circuit was completed in October."[26] In honor of the occasion, a holiday was declared for October 29 and 30, and the following day a grand parade was held. The weather was bright and cheery, and the troops stood resplendent in new dress uniforms with "plumed hats." The band, their brass instruments glinting in the sunshine, graced an octagonal bandstand built around the new flagstaff in the center of a square. Troops formed three sides, and a platform for ladies, officers and auspicious civilians formed the fourth. "'Attention was sounded by the chief bugler," recalled Frances Grummond, "followed by the Colonel's 'Order arms! Parade rest.'"

Then Colonel Carrington addressed the command. He went through a rousing, patriotic history of the post which had survived all trials despite aggressive Indians who had "threatened to exterminate the command…. Stockade and block-house, embrasure and loop-hole, shell and bullet, have warned off danger, so that women and children now notice the savage as he appears, only to look for fresh occasion to punish him, and with righteous anger to avenge the dead…. The steam whistle and the rattle of the mower have followed your steps in this westward march to empire. You have built a central post that will bear comparison with any for security, completeness and adaptation to the end in view, wherever the other may be located or however long in erection … and for this day, its duties and its pleasures, we shall become better men and better soldiers of the great Republic."[27]

Judge John F. Kinney, post sutler, then stood and read a poem. Kinney "was a good diplomat," recalled Private Murphy, popular with "men, women and children."[28] Principal musician Sergeant Barnes then read a poem written by himself, "which at least did justice to his patriotic spirit," wrote Mrs. Carrington.[29] Chaplain White came next, standing to read a prayer, "then, in quick succession, an officer rang out the orders, 'Attention!' 'Present Arms!' 'Play!' 'Hoist!' 'Fire!'" recalled Frances. "With the simultaneous *snap* of presented arms in salute, the 'long role' of the combined drum-corps was followed by the full band playing 'The Star Spangled Banner,' the guns opened fire," and the large, magnificent flag "slowly rose to masthead and was broken out in one glorious flame of red, white, and blue!"

But even before the officers and ladies attended that evening's dance at the Carrington residence, Indians appeared on the surrounding hills. "Their flashing little mirror-signals were visible at many points for more than an hour before the sun went down," recalled Frances. "Dancing, singing and general merriment enlivened the evening until the chain of sentries, in quick succession, repeated 'Twelve o'clock at night and all's well.'"[30]

The very next night, however, a party of travelers were gathered beyond the stockade playing cards. Their camp fire provided excellent illumination for tempting targets. A volley of shots erupted from the darkness and three men were hit. Orders rapped out inside the fort, and a party of soldiers moved through the gate, but it came as little surprise that the wily enemy had vanished into the night. But then an Indian signal fire was seen on a hilltop to the west. Carrington ordered a howitzer swung round, and quickly a case shot flew across the dark sky. It exploded on target, and there was no more heard from the Indians that night.[31] "When night alarms are common," recalled Mrs. Carrington, "and three men are shot within thirty yards of the gates ... the stockade becomes a prison wall, and over its trunks are seen only the signs of precaution and active warfare." Of the three men wounded, one "has since died and one lost his leg," recorded Ten Eyck's diary,[32] "the other recovering."

22

Fetterman Arrives

November 3 saw new arrivals at Fort Phil Kearny, Company C of the 2nd Cavalry. Two companies had been promised, but the 65 men were more than welcome, despite the fact that "more than half this force were raw recruits joining for the first time," recalled Frances.[1] Some were armed with breech-loading Starr carbines which used the same ammunition as the Spencer, but most carried the same muzzle loading Springfields issued to the infantry. These were unsuitable for cavalry, their long barrels making them virtually impossible to reload on horseback. Carrington later complained that the new recruits were "uninstructed in the saber exercise, and even in mounting, until I had personally taken them in hand." These men, he wrote, and 45 infantrymen from general recruiting in New York, yet to arrive, were the only reinforcements he received during his tenure at Fort Phil Kearny.[2]

Three new officers arrived with Company C. This included Captain, Brevet Lieutenant Colonel, William Judd Fetterman, who would be second-in-command to Carrington over Ten Eyck. Fetterman's father had been a West Point graduate who died when he was nine, and he was raised by his uncle, also a West Point man. Fetterman's own attempt to enter West Point had failed, and he took up a career as a bank employee. As with Carrington, the war's outbreak provided an opportunity to fulfill his military ambitions, and at the age of 28 he was commissioned as first lieutenant of the 18th infantry.

Fetterman worked efficiently under Carrington with recruiting duties, was promoted to captain, and in November of 1861 took command of Company A. He fought at the siege of Corinth, Mississippi, and at Stones River, Tennessee, where the 18th lost nearly half its men, and was brevetted to major for "great gallantry and good conduct."[3] Following further recruiting duties, he resumed command of Company A, and through hard fighting was given command of the 800 men of the 18th's Second Battalion. He took part in Sherman's "March to the Sea," was given the important posting of acting assistant adjutant general of the 14th Corps, and was brevetted to lieutenant colonel. At the war's conclusion the volunteers were mustered out, and Fetterman remained a captain with the regular army. He recruited men for the 18th in the east, while Carrington marched west to garrison the Bozeman Trail. It was intended that Fetterman would take command of the newly formed 27th Infantry, formed from the 18th's Second Battalion, once the reorganization came into effect.[4]

According to Margaret Carrington, Fetterman boasted that "a company of regulars could whip a thousand, and a regiment could whip the whole array of hostile tribes."[5] Frances Grummond made the same claim in her own book.[6] Did Fetterman ever really make such a boast? It has been suggested in recent years that these claims were made by the two ladies to deflect any blame for subsequent events from Carrington to Fetterman, thus creating the "Fetterman was responsible" myth. But then Frances did state that both Brown and Grummond "warmly seconded" this opinion. If Frances wished to portray Fetterman as irresponsible, why did she spread the blame to her husband who would die in the same battle? And after a close fight with Indians on December 6, Margaret stated that Fetterman said "this Indian war has become a hand-to-hand fight, requiring utmost caution, and he wants no more such risks."[7] However, she later wrote in the same book that Indian attacks "drove Fetterman to hasty disobedience, and certain destruction." But, then again, wrote that the "impulses" of Quartermaster Brown led "Fetterman to disobey orders on the 21st of December, at the sacrifice of the whole detachment, is not questioned." Both ladies seem genuinely confused regarding Fetterman's motivations. Grummond's actions have been questioned. He had a reputation for reckless behavior. So who was to blame? Fetterman, Grummond, or Brown?

It appears from all sources that Fetterman was a gentlemanly, level headed officer. But he did have no Indian fighting experience. Would such a man make the "single company of Regulars could whip a thousand Indians" boast. With hindsight, probably not. But in November of 1866 the Fetterman and Little Bighorn battles lay in the future. It is quite possible that such a boast was made in a moment of bravado, perhaps with a few drinks under the belt.

Whatever was said, shortly after arrival Fetterman came up with plans to take action against their wily foe. The first was that he and Frederick Brown should take a force of 60 soldiers and 40 civilian volunteers to attack the Indian villages along the Tongue River. Feeling the venture too risky, Carrington refused—a wise decision as it transpired. History well records what happened to Custer's much larger force at the Little Bighorn. But Carrington agreed to a less ambitious idea Fetterman proposed.[8] That night a number of mules were hobbled along Big Piney Creek, a tempting target for hostiles who drove off stock whenever they could. Concealed in the adjacent cottonwoods soldiers waited in ambush. A bright moon was out, the mules in plain view. The soldiers waited—and waited. But no Indians showed. "But within three hours of the return of Fetterman they ran off a herd not a mile distant," recalled Frances. "The wonder was that Fetterman's own select party were not surprised and massacred through taking such a risk."[9] The stolen herd belonged to civilian James Wheatley,[10] who had already had two horses taken on September 21.[11] Wheatley had a score to settle.

A few days later Fetterman learned another lesson. Captain Ten Eyck and Lieutenant Bisbee "accompanied Fetterman and other fresh arrivals at the Post with the wood train to the Pinery," recalled Frances. "Venturing in advance of their escort they were fired upon from ambush and although unhurt were compelled to do some lively skirmishing down the Island, getting completely out of sight of the wood party guard." Seeing this, a bugler dashed back to the fort "with the exciting announcement that all were killed." Not surprisingly, Mrs. Bisbee "blanched" at the news. "The colonel with a relieving party dashed out at once at a fierce gallop but soon returned with the party, whom they met not far from the fort."

But, had the officers been killed, certain advantages would have been in store. Carrington "spoke in pathetic terms" that officers accompanying him "discussed the matter of promotion that would ensue in case the alarm proved to be correct." Carrington told them to desist and, changing tune, they "spoke very tenderly of their endangered brothers-in-arms and said, 'You are right, Colonel, this is not the time for such suggestions.'"[12]

Captain James Powell, 36, had arrived at Fort Phil Kearny with Fetterman on November 3. He took command of Company C to replace Lieutenant Adair, previously resigned. Powell had enlisted as a private in 1848, been promoted to second lieutenant at the outbreak of the Civil War, and fought under Fetterman in various campaigns.[13] He still carried two rebel musket balls received at the Battle of Jonesboro in 1864, and received a brevet to major on Fetterman's recommendation.[14] Unlike the erudite and cultured Carrington, Powell was a man of the working class and upon arrival "was a guest at his Colonel's table," Carrington recalled. "From that time he never entered the house upon invitation, or at his own prompting, socially."[15] Powell would later make damaging accusations against Carrington's ability to command. He claimed that while the officers maintained good discipline, "with the enlisted men it was chaotic," and men "performed their accustomed details in a very loose manner."[16] William Bisbee would also be a thorn in Carrington's side. They would clash over how best to maintain order, and regarding relationship between officers, Bisbee stated, "Almost without exception it was harmonious, except a general feeling of disgust towards Colonel Carrington," and discipline among the enlisted men was "very poor."[17]

Captain William J. Fetterman was a steadfast officer with a distinguished record. How did he come to disobey orders by crossing Lodge Trail Ridge? (author's collection)

Private George B. Mackay, on the other hand, testified that discipline was "very good as far as I could judge among the enlisted men" and "there was ill feeling among the Officers," but "the troops went out in a very loose manner, each man that chose to go, saddling up his horse and going without any ranks being formed." Carrington, however, "issued a very stringent order sometime in September, against the men going in this manner. The order was complied in some respects." Non-commissioned officers formed ranks "and two or three officers" rode with them.[18] Lieutenant Wands testified that the infantry behaved well except for wasting ammunition by firing at too long a range, and all troops not employed in details were "building the stockade, barracks, and store houses. No attention was paid to drill, and discipline under these circumstances could not be maintained."[19]

Times had changed since the days of the French and Indian War when the lash was freely used to keep soldiers in line. But other cruel methods were still employed. In 1869 "there had been four or five men drummed out of the Omaha Barracks," recalled Private Murphy. "In each instance the men were branded with a hot iron, their heads were shaved, they were marched around the fort with fife and drum playing 'Poor Old Soldier,' and then drummed out. The cruelty was not all practiced by the Indians."[20]

Colonel Carrington, however, was a reformist, and somewhat ahead of his time. He abhorred violence as a disciplinary measure, a sentiment not shared by all his officers and NCOs. The result was "Bully 38" (Bulletin 38) being posted on Sunday, November 11. "That perversion of authority on the part of non commissioned officers, which displays itself in profane swearing, verbal abuse, kicks and blows, and which violates every social, moral and military principle in the government of men, will be dealt with in the most decided manner." Carrington admitted that the troops, having volunteered additional construction working hours while under threat of Indian attack had "acquired a habit of discussing methods," and, to some extent, become lax, "but obedience must be complete and immediate. The case of Sergeant Garrett and Private Burke furnish a fit occasion to demand an immediate and thorough conformity to the spirit of this order."[21]

The "case of Sergeant Garrett and Private Burke" had occurred that very morning. As people walked to church, "the ladies of the garrison were horrified when the incident thus reprimanded occurred in their full view," recalled Frances Grummond.[22] John Burke of Company E arrived late for guard duty. Lieutenant Bisbee ordered the sergeant to reprimand him. Garrett verbally abused Bourke who gave an insolent reply.[23] Garrett then fractured his skull with his rifle butt. Frances stated that this action received "profane endorsement of the sergeant by his own lieutenant." But Bully 38 only made mention of non-commissioned officers as offenders, and Garrett was placed under arrest. Bisbee, however, received a personal rebuke from Carrington, and the order stated that officers will "carefully enforce this order, seeking to inspire among non-commissioned officers by precept and example, that calm and steady habit of command."[24] And as adjutant, it was Bisbee's job to prepare and distribute the rebuke of his own conduct. Carrington ordered Garrett's release on December 8 without any charges being laid.[25]

Lieutenant Bisbee received orders to report to Omaha as General Cooke's aide-de-camp. He would depart on December 9 and be promoted to captain shortly after.[26] He and Captain Powell had joined the army as privates and risen through the ranks. As such, one would think that they would appreciate the need for humane treatment of enlisted men. But Carrington later wrote, "Order 38, was enforced, although not according to the acceptance of Brevet Maj. Powell and Capt. W.H. Bisbee."[27] There was also a social divide. Carrington would later write that he "pitied Powell, who married a barefooted camp laundress."[28] Bisbee and Powell had no time for the scholarly and moralistic Carrington, and would do all they could to undermine his reputation following the Fetterman disaster of December 21. But every regiment had its malcontents. Even the dashing, victorious George Custer would have a fractious command. There were officers in the 7th Cavalry who had no confidence in the "boy general" or "Custer's luck."

While dissention permeated the officer ranks within Fort Phil Kearny, the Indians remained active without, despite the onset of chilling winter winds and snow. Indians "crawled up close to the stockade, crawling under wolf skins that covered their body, and a sentry was actually shot from the *banquet* that lay along the stockade, by an arrow,"[29] recalled Frances Grummond, and "once, crawling to the block-house in the Pinery, they sent an arrow through a loop-hole at night, wounding one of it's inmates."[30]

On November 12 Cooke wrote to Carrington that once troops and stores were under shelter, "turn your earnest attention to the possibility of striking the hostile bands by surprise in their winter camps." This would be more successful than a large summer campaign,

Cooke explained, "when the Indians can so easily scatter, and into deserts and mountain hiding places almost beyond pursuit. Four companies of infantry will be available besides some cavalry."[31] But this was the entire garrison of Fort Phil Kearny. What had become of the other troops promised, and who would carry the mails and garrison the post? Frances recalled, even with troops present, "the women, with tearful eyes and shrinking hearts wondered why the War Department and the Commanding General at Omaha, or whoever was responsible, could leave us in such imminent danger during all these dreadful days."[32]

Five enlisted men deserted to seek a better life on the Montana goldfields. With Lieutenant Bradley's return from escort duty, Lieutenant Adair's resignation came into effect, and Bradley did not stay long, ordered to join the 18th's Third Battalion, stationed in Utah.[33] And, as a penny-pinching measure, Carrington was instructed to "discharge James Bridger and all the guides who know the country in which I was operating."[34] Across the back of the order, Carrington wrote, "*impossible of execution.*"[35] Cooke "modified the order," recalled Carrington, "giving me discretion to employ in certain cases." Carrington wrote complaining of the cavalry being issued with Springfields rather than Spencer carbines. And, in any case, 100 replacement Springfields had not arrived to "replace broken and worn out arms" and "I shall look for another company of cavalry soon." But what he got was 45 men under Lieutenant Wilber Arnold detached from "dismounted Co. 'K' 27th U.S. Infantry, being a new company of the reorganized regiment."[36] These and Company C of the 2nd Cavalry would be the only reinforcements he received. He now had five companies of infantry and one of cavalry at Fort Phil Kearny, but was still reliant on teamsters and other civilian employees to carry out military duties. Even before the arrival of Company K on December 2, Cooke had warned Carrington that Major James Van Voast at Fort Laramie had volunteered to lead a punitive expedition from Fort Laramie, thus treading on Carrington's sensitive toes. "I will in person command expeditions when severe weather confines them to their villages," Carrington wrote, "and make the winter one of active operations in different directions, as best affords chance of punishment."

A chance of punishment afforded itself on December 6. At 1 p.m. a messenger arrived saying the wood train was under attack about four miles west of the fort. Carrington consulted Fetterman, and a plan to attack the hostiles was put in action. Fetterman led Lieutenant Bingham, commander of 2nd Cavalry, Company C, and about 30 mounted troopers out to relieve the wood train. They were to "crowd the Indians across Piney Creek" while Carrington led Lieutenant Grummond, three orderlies and 21 mounted infantry north towards Lodge Trail Ridge. Because of the terrain, the Indians would be forced to cross either there or through the nearby valley of Peno Creek to return to their villages on the Tongue River. Carrington would "endeavor to cut off all retreat," the Indians caught between two forces—or so the plan went.[37] The fort gates swung open and Carrington's command rode out first. "Upon reaching the crossing of the Creek," Carrington recalled, "I found ice formed, but pushed on, having to dismount in three feet of water to open the way my horse being thrown in breaking the ice. I pushed on, ascending the eastern slope of Lodge Trail Ridge, making direct for the head of Peno Creek."

Fetterman, meanwhile, had arrived at the corralled wood train to be confronted by about 100 hostiles. He was joined by Frederick Brown, recently promoted to Captain, and "a couple of mounted infantry" who had come along as volunteers.[38] Lieutenant Wands, delayed with a change of horses, also caught up. He was a good man to have along, one of the few who had seen action against Indians before arriving at Fort Phil Kearny. He had fought Seminoles in Florida before the Civil War, and taken part in the wagon fight

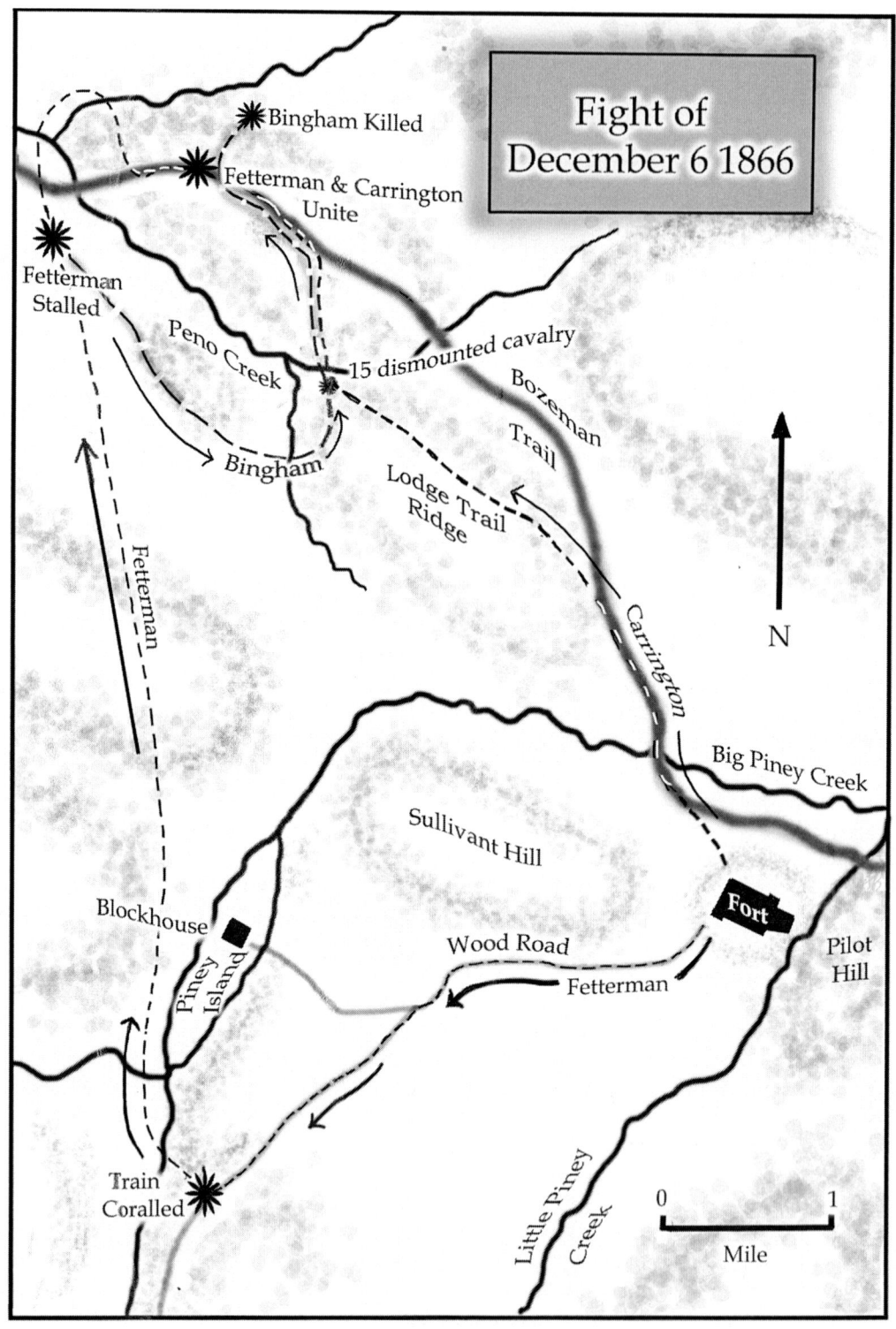

Map by the author.

at Crazy Woman's Fork. Wands had intended to join Carrington but, having been misdirected by a sentry, joined Fetterman by mistake. Such small incidents can have large outcomes. The Henry repeater Wands carried would quite possibly save Fetterman's command.

The Indians fell back to the north, as anticipated, and Fetterman led the pursuit. The enemy kept tantalizingly just out of reach, and five miles later they arrived "in valley through which passed the Big Horn Road (Bozeman Trail)," recalled Fetterman. Here, according to Wands, "they were reinforced by a large number and suddenly turned on us, surrounding us in the shape of a horse shoe."[39] Fetterman called a halt and ordered his men to dismount. They had a better chance of survival by opening fire on foot, their aim steady, and the long barreled Springfields easier to reload. But "about three fourths of the Cavalry dashed off at full speed in the direction the fort, through the opening left in the Indian lines," Wands testified, and Fetterman agreed: "In the most unaccountable manner the cavalry turned and commenced a retreat." Lieutenant Bingham went with them. "His sergeant says his horse ran away with him," recalled Carrington, "and the Lieut. told him he could not hold him."[40] About ten soldiers remained. They looked ready to follow but "were compelled to dismount by the Officers threatening to shoot them if they did not halt and dismount," recalled Wands. Some cavalrymen did return, swelling their numbers to about 14.[41] They dismounted, took cover, and opened fire, keeping the Indians at bay for about 45 minutes. Wands was "grazed by a ball and it was reported that his coolness and Henry rifle saved Fetterman's detachment," Frances Grummond recalled.[42] These Indians saw Carrington's move "about half a mile to our right," to cut them off, and fell back. Fetterman followed, but Carrington did not attack, and many warriors returned to fight Fetterman again. Another stalled fight lasted for 20 minutes before the Indians fell back once more. Fetterman ordered his men to mount up and follow, but they could not keep pace with the fleet footed Indian ponies.

Carrington, meanwhile, had been observed by mounted Indians to their front. They were few in number, but "thirty-two were in a ravine close by them," recalled Carrington. "At the same time I saw on the hills across the Creek, over one hundred Indians descending to the Creek, followed by Lieutenant Colonel Fetterman's command." Grummond proved hard to keep track of during the march, and Carrington sent the following order: "Keep with me and obey orders or return to the post."[43] The colonel's party opened fire on other Indians to their front "who instantly fled, I pushed on at a gallop, west, and along the ridge," and then descended into the Peno Creek valley to cut off those Indians retreating from Fetterman, but "found to my surprise fifteen cavalry dismounted without an officer. I passed through them ordering them to mount up and follow upon the gallop." Only one obeyed, Bugler Adolph Metzger. Carrington's detachment had straggled behind, and he now had only six men with him. Metzger said he had seen Bingham "go down the road around the hill to the right. This seemed impossible," recalled Carrington, "as he belonged to Captain Fetterman's command." The bugler sounded recall, but the missing officers did not appear. Then Private McGuire's horse went down, and an Indian was seen crawling towards the fallen soldier.[44] Carrington ordered his men to dismount and, as one man held the horses, "reserving fire, I succeeded in saving the man and holding the position."

Fetterman, meanwhile, decided to "take the road" and he encountered Carrington's force "a short distance in advance," to the relief, no doubt, of both parties. But Indians were "circling around and yelling, nearly a hundred in number," recalled Carrington, "with one saddle emptied by a single shot fired by myself."[45] The Indians fell back and Carrington, hoping to locate Bingham, led the troops to the right. "For God's sake come down quick!" was heard from the rear. Through a gulch, seven Indians were seen with their spears close to the backs of Lieutenant Grummond and four other men galloping along the road. The Indians veered away when they saw Carrington's troops, and Grummond galloped up to them. He blurted out that Bingham and Sergeant Bowers had been killed.

Bingham, Grummond, Bowers and three others had ridden in pursuit of an Indian party. One brave fell behind the other Indians, and Bingham opened fire with his revolver. His last two bullets brought the Indian's pony down. Throwing his revolver to one side, he and Grummond drew sabers and rode in for the kill, the other soldiers a little behind. They rode around the Indian who avoided their swishing blades by skillfully dodging between and under their horses. Then Bingham suddenly shouted, "We are surrounded." Grummond looked up to see they had ridden into an ambush, Indians closing in from all sides. With swinging sabers they bolted towards the Indian lines. Grummond made it through but Bingham hit the ground, shot through the head. About 20 Indians pursued Grummond who joined Sergeant Bowers and the other three men.[46] Bingham's fate was forgotten as Indians now swarmed around the small, isolated command. They dismounted and opened fire, and the Indians did likewise. Arrows swished through the air wounding two soldiers and one horse, and the soldiers' ammunition began to run out. Flight was the only option. They remounted and charged through the Indian lines. Grummond "shut his eyes and literally slashed his way out," Fessenden later heard. "He could hear his saber 'click' every time he cleaved an Indian's skull" and "the savages attempted to catch several of our boys by trying to put their strung bows over their necks and drag them off."[47] Private John Donovan was a Civil War veteran who had been twice wounded in a previous clash with Indians. Today his Colt's army revolver "was all that saved him," recalled Private Murphy, "when the Indians were on each side trying to pull him off his horse, for just in the nick of time he shot one on each side."[48] Bowers' wounded horse, however, slowed his retreat, and he was dragged to the ground. The others rode for their lives. Grummond later told his wife "that he abandoned the use of spurs and jammed his sword into his weary beast to urge him to greater effort, followed by the chief, in full-war dress, with spear at his back so near that but for his good horse he would then and there have met a terrible fate."[49] When Grummond galloped up to Carrington, he supposedly asked him "if he was a fool or a coward to allow his men to be cut to pieces without offering help." If this was actually said, it defies all logic. Grummond had disobeyed orders and dashed off on his own account putting himself beyond support by Carrington. The originator of this was Lieutenant Bisbee, a Carrington hater who was not present at the time. Neither Carrington's nor Fetterman's reports give any hint of this. Such insubordination would have invited court-martial. Without corroboration, this tale can only be treated as myth.

"After an hour's search," recalled Carrington, "we found Lieutenant Bingham's body, and that of Sergeant Bowers. The latter was still living, but not scalped. He died before an ambulance arrived from the fort, having been cleft to the brain." Bingham had been found slung over a tree stump, his body bristling with arrows, a bullet through his head. At least his death had been swift. There was nothing more to be done. "Severe weather and coming night prevented further pursuit, the Indians breaking for the mountains and Tongue river valley." Carrington abandoned the field and returned to the fort. His wife was distraught to learn that the "gentle, manly and soldierly young officer" had "fallen victim to his ardor and the craft of our foes."[50]

Fetterman had followed his orders to the letter, but "by the death of Bingham all clue was lost," recalled Frances, "and his reason for leaving Fetterman will always be an unsolved mystery."

That may be so, but logic suggests that when the Indians turned on Fetterman's command some troopers, terrified of capture and torture, turned tail and ran, followed by the others. Bingham galloped with them but, looking back, saw the others had stayed to fight, and a few of his men had turned back to join them. Having no explanation for his conduct, he decided, on the spur of the moment, to advance once more, but with Carrington's command. Those left behind may well be killed, and he still had a chance to vindicate himself. He led his troopers north, chancing upon Grummond and a handful of others riding in advance of Carrington. Indians were in sight, decoys, in fact, and Bingham saw a chance to prove he was no coward after all. The reckless Grummond needed little encouragement, and they galloped off followed by Bowers and three others. But 15 of Bingham's command decided they had seen enough Indians for one day. They dismounted and stayed put, to be found shortly afterwards by Carrington's party.

That night Carrington put pen to paper. "Much was done," he optimistically reported. "The loss of Lieutenant Bingham makes all seem lost, but the winter campaign is fairly open and will be met. I do, however, most urgently ask for Officers. As Brevet Captain Bisbee leaves, Captain Brown also, I am to be left again with six officers for six companies, including Adjutant and Commissary.... This is all wrong. There is much at stake." Carrington included a report written by Fetterman, which stated he had seen Carrington pass "along the road about half a mile to our right with the purpose, I hoped, of getting to the rear of the enemy." The Indians retired, "but finding that their rear was not attacked, a large number of them returned. After fighting twenty minutes they again retired, we in pursuit." He makes no mention of any offensive action by Carrington, casting doubt on his performance. Fetterman went on to say, "I cannot speak too highly of the conduct of Captain Brown and Lieutenant Wands, without whose assistance I fear we must have suffered serious disaster."[51]

Carrington's accompanying report stated, "I was confronted by a large force of Indians who, retiring before Captain Fetterman's command, attempted to cut off my detachment or stop its advance." After rescuing the man whose horse had fallen upon him, he succeeded in "holding the position until joined by Fetterman, twenty minutes later," and, furthermore, "by hard riding, I reached the point I had hoped to attain, the Indians fleeing before me."

Much to Carrington's chagrin, a report published by the secretary of war following the disaster of December 21 would include only Fetterman's account, not his own. It would also include comments by Cooke, who had taken on Bisbee as his aide-de-camp. "I am informed that on these occasions it was the custom of officers and men to sally forth, mounted or afoot, much at their discretion.... Colonel Carrington is very plausible—an energetic, industrious man in garrison; but it is too evident that he has not maintained discipline, and that his officers have no confidence in him."[52]

Carrington listed, "One officer killed, One Sergeant killed, One Sergeant and four privates wounded, Three horses were killed and five wounded." He stated that they had confronted "not less than three hundred warriors" of whom at least ten had been killed, and more wounded. Alexander Wands was not impressed with the day's proceedings: "I consider the conduct of the cavalry that day disgraceful, and of such character as to induce the belief on the part of the Indians, that they could overcome the garrison or any party from the garrison, in an open fight."[53]

So ended the fight of December 6, 1866. Bingham and Bowers were buried with full military honors, Chaplain White presiding. Captain Brown placed his own corps badge on the body of Bowers, a Civil War companion and kindred spirit. Perhaps it was the death of Bowers that made him all the more determined to "get Red Cloud's' scalp" before departure to Fort Laramie. If so, it was a fatal mistake.

23

Over Lodge Trail Ridge

In the days following the fight of December 6, Indians were seen by the wood party, and on the bluffs near the fort.[1] There was no attack, but the death of Bingham and Bowers did little for the morale of either the troops or ladies of the garrison. "No sleep came to my weary eyes, except fitfully, for many nights" recalled Frances Grummond. And she had nightmares, seeing her husband "riding madly from me with the Indians in pursuit."[2] The fort's inner structures were still incomplete, and firewood was needed for even colder temperatures to come. The number of men on wood train escort duty was increased, and changes were made in command. Bisbee departed on December 9 to take up his role as Cooke's aide-de-camp. With his wife and son he boarded a "prairie schooner" made as comfortable as possible for winter travel with a stove inside and double-boarded sides for insulation. "My outfit consisted of buffalo skin cap," Bisbee recalled, "two woolen shirts under a heavy blanket suit, buffalo-lined hip boots over two pairs of woolen socks, two pairs of gloves."[3]

On the 13th Grummond replaced Ten Eyck as commander of mounted infantry, and Powell replaced the fallen Bingham as cavalry commander. Fetterman, effectively second-in-command, directed the general infantry. Despite a shortage of officers, this left the troubled Ten Eyck, at one time post commander, in charge of Company H. "This has been a bad day for me," his diary noted. Captain Ten Eyck's fortunes had been in a state of decline for some time. On November 18 he had been placed under arrest for "a mistake made at Dress Parade." As he was not released till November 24, the "mistake" must have been something more serious than tarnished brass, quite possibly being drunk.[4]

Amidst the winter-bound villages along the Tongue River, meanwhile, Red Cloud of the Lakota, Little Wolf of the Cheyenne, Sorrel Horse of the Arapahoe, and other chiefs were formulating plans in a cohesive manner that was unusual for the nomads of the plains. Man for man, the Indian warrior was far superior to the average bluecoat. But it was apparent that small numbers of troops could manage to hold off many times their number with disciplined formations and gunfire. The performance of Fetterman, Brown and Wands on December 6 had proven that. But then there were those other bluecoats who, on the same day, had ridden recklessly to the front in pursuit of a decoy, two of them killed. Here was a lesson to be learned. The Indians must also fight as a well disciplined force. They must follow orders, hold their fire until a signal was given. Rash white officers like Grummond may well provide the opportunity to strike a decisive blow.

On December 19 sentinels peered at the peak of Pilot Hill. Once again the urgent flash of signal flags could be seen, the wood train under attack. Carrington ordered Captain Powell out with a detachment of infantry and cavalry. During the later enquiry, Powell testified that Captain Brown, "being present and mounted, and being desirous to go out," was given command of the cavalry. Brown led the horsemen out with instructions to avoid battle and escort the train back towards the fort while Powell followed with the slower moving infantry. "Upon arriving within a mile and a half of the pinery, Indians were to be seen in every direction except in my rear." Powell had his men hasten to a high point "inaccessible to horses" and sent word for the train to join him at once. The commands united, and they moved back to the safety of the fort. Powell felt that by retiring "I saved the lives of my command.... Col. Carrington approved of the course I had pursued in retiring from the pinery."[5] Following Powell's return, Carrington wrote to Cooke, "No special news since last report. Indians appeared to-day and fired on wood train but were repulsed. They are accomplishing nothing while I am perfecting all details of the post and preparing for active movements."[6] Carrington would regret writing those words. At the enquiry Carrington stated that Powell "did his work," pressing the Indians towards Lodge Trail Ridge, but having "orders not to cross it, he returned with the train, reporting the Indians in large force, and that if he had crossed the ridge, he never would have come back with his command."[7] It was in Carrington's interest to have "orders not to cross it" believed as a precedent for instructions he issued two days later. Powell's testimony made no mention of pressing Indians in any direction, and made no mention of receiving such orders. But Powell had no time for Carrington and proved to be a self-serving witness at the best of times.

December 21, 1866. "The usual 'reveille' broke the stillness of the sunrise hour," recalled Frances Grummond, "to be followed in turn by 'sick call' and 'guard-mounting,' the latter accompanied by the music of the full band, always a grateful and cheering accompaniment."[8] And Margaret Carrington recalled, "Though snow covered the mountains, and there was every indication of the return of severe weather, the morning was quite pleasant. Men only wore blouses at their work."

"About 9 a.m. a party of four Indians appeared on the bluffs opposite the fort," recalled Lieutenant Arnold. They challenged the garrison, in English, "You sons of bitches, come out and fight us."[9] Other Indians could be seen in a thicket near the fort. "A case shot dismounted one and developed nearly thirty more who broke for the hills and ravines to the north," Carrington reported. Soon flags were waving on Pilot Hill. The wood train was corralled and under attack once more, a mile and a half from the fort.

Carrington offered command of an infantry relief force to Powell once more, but "Brevet Lieutenant Colonel Fetterman claimed, by rank to go out," recalled Carrington.[10] This has become a matter of debate. But there was no reason for Carrington to fabricate this, and Powell had led the relief force only two days earlier. Powell stated the command was given directly to Fetterman, but if this was the case why did Carrington not simply say so? Carrington later stated that Powell "*omits the fact*" that it was he who was assigned "to take Co. C. 2nd U.S. Cavalry" and "relieve the train; *that*, Fetterman then present, claimed the command, as Powell's senior officer" and Powell "*did not complain of the substitution of another officer.*"[11] But, in any case, both officers were qualified for the task, and the issue is irrelevant. Fetterman was given command.

George Grummond asked Lieutenant Wands, officer of the day, for permission to take the cavalry along. Wands referred the matter to Carrington who gave his consent. Based on previous experiences, both Fetterman and Grummond were "well admonished, as well as myself," wrote Carrington, "that we were fighting brave and desperate enemies who sought to make up by cunning and deceit, all the advantages which the white man gains by intelligence and better arms." According to Carrington, he instructed Fetterman to "*support the wood train, relieve it and report to me. Do not engage or pursue Indians at its* expense. Under no circumstances pursue over the ridge viz: Lodge Trail Ridge, as per map in your possession."[12] This order has become a matter of debate. Carrington said he gave these orders to Fetterman as infantry companies A, C, E, and H assembled outside the headquarters of Company A, and John Edwards, "Clerk of the Headquarters," heard the orders given. Frances Grummond recalled that she was standing "in front of my door next the commanding officer's headquarters and both saw and heard all that transpired." The instructions to Fetterman were given "within my hearing and were repeated on the parade-ground when then line was formed."[13] The enquiry the following year also backed Carrington's claim.[14]

Fetterman led the infantry out, 49 "choice men, the best of their companies," Carrington recalled. Captain Brown borrowed Calico, a pony he had given to Henry Carrington's sons, Harry and Jimmy, then rode out as a volunteer. Carrington issued Grummond with the same orders and "report to Brevet Colonel Fetterman, implicitly obey orders and not leave him." Carrington then instructed Lieutenant Wands to repeat the order to Grummond. According to Wands, this included "tell Colonel Fetterman, and to remember himself that this command was to go out and succor or relieve the wood train, bring it back if necessary, or if Colonel Fetterman thought best, take the train to the woods (it being then on its way out,) and bring it back and under no circumstances were they to cross the bluff in pursuit of Indians."[15] Then, as the corporal of the guard unlocked the gate, Wands "repeated them, and asked if he thoroughly understood them. He replied he did, and would obey them to the letter." Grummond rode out at the head of 27 cavalry troopers. They were armed with the Spencer repeaters usually held by the regimental band. As they rode off, Carrington mounted a sentinel platform. In a "loud voice," recalled Wands, Carrington repeated the instructions, and asked Grummond "if he understood them. He replied I do."

Thus Grummond was informed four times by two different officers not to cross Lodge Trail Ridge. One might think Carrington had a lack of faith in George Grummond. And one might think that Carrington, having gone to such lengths, was absolved from blame. But "no," say some. There is no proof that Carrington originally issued these same instructions to Fetterman—except the word of Margaret Carrington, Frances Grummond and the "Fetterman Massacre" court of enquiry! And, of course, common sense. Why would Carrington give two different orders to two officers in the same detachment a matter of minutes apart?

But, these orders, once delivered to Grummond, became the standing orders, regardless of what was said beforehand. At Little Bighorn it was Lieutenant William Cooke who carried orders for Major Reno's battalion to attack the Indian village, not Custer personally, and at Balaclava it was Captain Louis Nolan who carried orders for Lord Cardigan's Light Brigade to charge the Russian guns, not Lord Raglan.[16] Interestingly enough, Grummond, Cooke and Nolan all ended up among the dead.

Seeing her husband ride out, Frances "stood for a time, moments indeed, almost dazed, my heart filled with strange forebodings, then turned, entered my little house, and closed my door. The ladies, in turn, soon called to cheer me up.... And yet the recollection of the fateful action of the 6th and the danger experienced at that time came over me with such a tide of apprehension that no reassuring words could dissipate its gloom."[17]

Fetterman, meanwhile, made a surprise move. His command "in place of going to the relief of the wood train filed to the right and went on the Big Horn road," recalled Captain Powell.[18] Fetterman marched directly for the southern slopes of Lodge Trail Ridge. Grummond's faster moving cavalry were seen to join him at the Big Piney ford—but "instead of proceeding to the wood train as ordered," recalled Wands, "the command crossed Piney

Creek to the opposite bank."[19] Lieutenant Arnold recalled that Fetterman proceeded "in an entirely different direction from that which the wood train had taken."[20] Thus Fetterman's move came as a surprise to others who, given the same orders, would not have followed the same course.

Carrington, however, was generous in his assessment: "I remarked the fact that he had deployed his men as skirmishers and was evidently moving wisely up the Creek and along the southern slope of Lodge Trail Ridge with good promise of cutting off the Indians as they should withdraw repulsed at the train, and this position giving him perfect vantage ground to save the train if the Indians pressed the attack." But then Carrington added: "It is true that the usual course was to follow the road directly to the train, but the course adopted was not an error unless there was then a purpose to disobey orders." Carrington found himself obliged to defend Fetterman's surprise move, as he sent no rider to countermand it.

Based on body positions and other factors, it seems quite likely the civilians Wheatley and Fisher sparked the events leading to Fetterman's defeat (author's rendition).

But at no time did Carrington give Fetterman leave to cross Lodge Trail Ridge. It was impossible for Grummond not to have passed Carrington's orders on. At this point the expectation was a return to the fort in a few hours time, and Grummond's insubordination would have been exposed.

But Fetterman could not be to blame for what followed—or so we are told in more recent times. He was a well-liked, true gentleman with an outstanding war record who had shown the stuff he was made of on December 6. Officers like that don't make mistakes— or do they? Was it not a well-liked gentleman with an outstanding war record that ordered Pickett's Charge at Gettysburg? That disaster was the beginning of the end for the Old South. If Robert E. Lee could make such a blunder, perhaps William J. Fetterman could do the same, albeit on a smaller scale.

No doubt the Indians had planned for Carrington to repeat his strategy of December 6, one detachment relieving the train while another headed for Lodge Trail Ridge to cut off the Indians' retreat. They must have been delighted to see them all heading for the ridge. Here was their chance to bag the lot. Had Fetterman simply adopted the "the usual course" and "follow the road directly to the train" there would have been 2,000 disenchanted warriors literally cooling their heals in the snow over Lodge Trail Ridge.

Fetterman crossed Piney Creek, and Captain Ten Eyck recalled: "At this time a few Indians, apparently lookouts or pickets were visible on the hills on the opposite side of the stream from the Fort and about three miles distant. The infantry marched up the Virginia City Road, (Bozeman Trail) which follows a ravine for some miles, being flanked by the cavalry on the ridges."[21] Wands recalled a more dramatic picture: "about forty or fifty Indians riding around the command, firing at them during the march from the crossing of the Creek up the ridges, and the command returning their fire."[22] These may well have been the Indians who fled north after bring shelled, a deliberate ploy to make their appearance seem spontaneous, not decoys.

Both Fetterman and Grummond had received explicit orders not to cross Lodge Trail Ridge. But also present were "two citizen frontiersmen, who were already acting as scouts in the quartermaster's department," recalled Frances. James Wheatley and Isaac Fisher, not being soldiers, would feel less obliged to follow military orders. And, according to Carrington, they "felt invincible" because they carried 16-shot Henry repeaters. Perhaps they believed the advertising for "HENRY'S PATENT REPEATING RIFLE" which a man can "discharge one shot every second so that he is equal to a company every minute, a regiment every ten minutes, a brigade every half hour, and a division every hour." And Wheatley had a score to settle. He had lost both horses and cattle in separate raids during September and November.

The troops ascended the west slope and "they were then seen to halt on the crest of the ridge," recalled Wands. What exactly happened next will never be known, but the following could well be the case: Fetterman ordered a halt, but Wheatley and Fisher continued on, riding over the crest, firing at any Indians in sight. "About the time the troops were seen resting on this ridge," recalled Wands, "pickets reported the wood train had broken coral and had moved on towards the woods."

The civilians may well have mocked the stalled troops. "What's wrong with you lot? Afraid of a good fight?" The hot-headed Grummond could not countenance this. Armed with Spencer repeaters, the cavalry felt they were invincible too. The wood train was safe so, ignoring Fetterman, Grummond rode down the slope after the civilians and the cavalry followed. Had the they been armed with outmoded muzzleloaders, they may well have

SIXTY SHOTS PER MINUTE

HENRY'S PATENT
REPEATING
RIFLE

The Most Effective Weapon in the World.

This Rifle can be discharged 16 times without loading or taking down from the shoulder, or even loosing aim. It is also slung in such a manner, that either on horse or on foot, it can be **Instantly Used**, without taking the strap from the shoulder.

For a House or Sporting Arm, it has no Equal;
IT IS ALWAYS LOADED AND ALWAYS READY.

The size now made is 44-100 inch bore, 24 inch barrel, and carries a conical ball 32 to the pound. The penetration at 100 yards is 8 inches; at 400 yards 5 inches; and it carries with force sufficient to kill at 1,000 yards.

A resolute man, armed with one of these Rifles, particularly if on horseback, **CANNOT BE CAPTURED.**

"We particularly commend it for ARMY USES, as the most effective arm for picket and vidette duty, and to all our citizens in secluded places, as a protection against guerilla attacks and robberies. A man armed with one of these Rifles, can load and discharge one shot every second, so that he is equal to a company every minute, a regiment every ten minutes, a brigade every half hour, and a division every hour."—*Louisville Journal*.

Address **JNO. W. BROWN,**
Gen'l Ag't., Columbus, Ohio.
At Rail Road Building, near the Depot.

Claims made for the Henry repeater may well have contributed to Fetterman's defeat. Wheatley and Fisher carried these rifles, and felt "invincible" as a result (author's collection).

stayed put. Fetterman was astonished to see them move ahead. Should he ride after Grummond and order him back? But Fetterman had Captain Brown alongside. He too had a "perfectly reckless daring in pursuit of Indians," recalled Mrs. Carrington. Only the night before he had "made a call, with spurs fastened in the button-holes of his coat, leggings wrapped, and two revolvers accessible, declaring, by way of explanation, that he was ready by day and night, and must have *one scalp* before leaving for Laramie."[23] Here was Brown's last chance. Damn the orders. Brown rode down the slope in Grummond's wake. Fetterman looked on with dismay, his stomach churning. Shots were being exchanged. The infantry not supporting Grummond's cavalry would appear cowardly. "Discretion is the better part of valor," they say—but not today. He gave his horse a nudge, and led his infantry down the slope.

Thus, like falling dominoes, one failure led to another: Wheatley and Fisher, Grummond, Brown and finally Fetterman took the plunge.

"Colonel Fetterman's command suddenly moved over the ridge and the firing increased," recalled Wands. "In about ten or fifteen minutes, and about 11 o'clock in the day, this firing increased until it was a rapid and continuous fire of musketry."

"At 12 o'clock firing was heard towards Peno Creek, beyond Lodge Trail Ridge," recalled Carrington. "A few shots were followed by constant shots, not to be counted." As no white man lived to tell the tale, Indian testimony and the position of the dead are the only indication of what happened next. The battle took place over one mile, and the Indians could only describe their immediate front through a haze of gunsmoke. As with all battles, this led to conflicting accounts. But, based on the evidence and logic, the battle followed this general path.

Wheatley and Fisher moved ahead exchanging shots with Indians to their front. Grummond and the cavalry followed, leaving the foot soldiers well behind. They rode down a slope into a depression, then rode up once more to join the Bozeman Trail along a ridge top. Sixteen-year-old Lakota warrior Fire Thunder was one of about 2,000 warriors waiting to spring the trap. "We divided into two parts and hid in the gullies on both sides of the ridge and waited," he recalled. "After a long while we heard a shot up over the hill, and we knew the soldiers were coming. So we held the noses of our ponies that they might not whinny at the soldier's horses. Soon we saw our men coming back, and some of them were walking and leading their horses, so that the soldiers would think they were worn out. Then the men we had sent ahead came running down the road between us, and the soldiers on horseback followed, shooting."[24]

Wheatley and Fisher chased the decoys down the trail to more level terrain along Peno Creek, Grummond's cavalry following. The decoys split into two groups and circled around, crossing each others paths, the predetermined signal that the troops were within their grasp. Cheyenne warrior Little Horse burst from cover and the assault began. War whoops and musket fire erupted as gunsmoke billowed and a shower of arrows flew. The soldiers came to a startled halt as the two civilians returned a brisk fire with their repeaters. Grummond and others turned and bolted to the rear. "They began to fight their way back up the hill," recalled Fire Thunder. He shot some soldiers with his "six-shooter," and "there were many bullets, but there were more arrows—so many that it was like a cloud of grasshoppers all above and around the soldiers, and our people, shooting across, hit each other." But Wheatley and Fisher felt they had a better chance by holding their ground. Three or four troopers, armed with Spencers, joined them. This group dismounted and took cover behind a cluster of rocks where they opened fire as the warriors closed in.

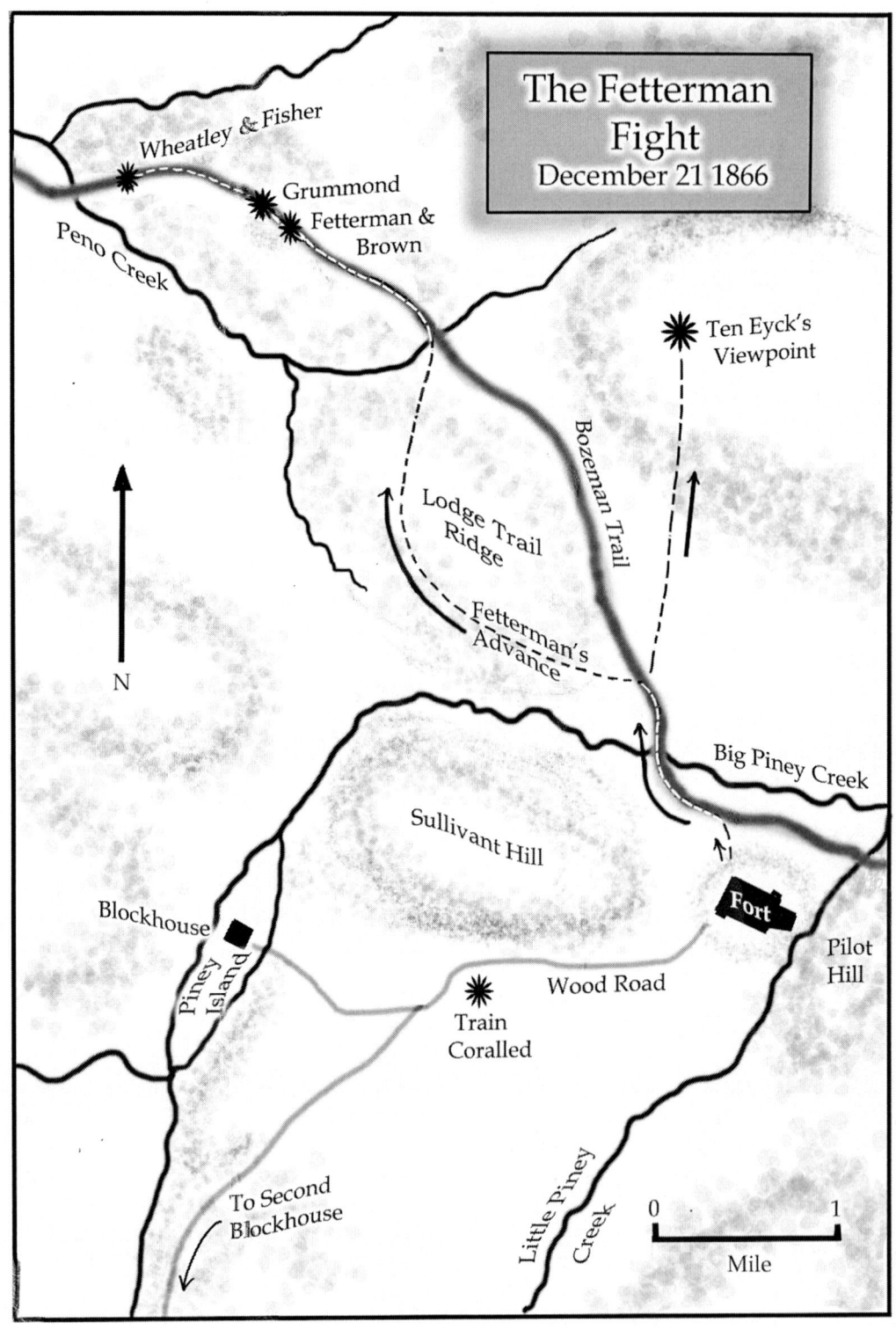

Map by the author.

Numerous cartridge casings were later found around their position, and pools of frozen blood a little way off. But, surrounded and vastly outnumbered, the small group stood no chance against the lethal hail of arrows and bullets.

Lakota warrior White Bull was near Fetterman's infantry further back. When the crash of gunfire was heard from the front, he called out, "Come on! We must start!"[25] Warriors unleashed a shower of arrows on the infantry. Among the hundreds of braves was a young man named Crazy Horse, destined to take a leading role in a bigger battle ten years later. Some say he rode with the decoys, but this is not a proven fact.[26] "All the Indians were shooting, arrows were flying in every direction," recalled White Bull. "Some of the Indians were hit by arrows, among them Thunder Hump and King. The ground was so covered with arrows that a warrior did not have to use his own; he could pick one up almost anywhere."[27]

The infantry began falling back towards the rise, where the stone monument now stands, while Grummond's cavalry fell back in an attempt to reunite. Many dropped from their mounts as arrows struck home. "The soldiers were falling all the while they were fighting back up the hill, and their horses got loose," recalled Fire Thunder. The troopers dismounted on a small plateau that could not been seen from Fetterman's position, and here they made a brief stand. Other's made it back to Fetterman's infantry. "When the soldiers got on top, there were not many of them left and they had no place to hide. They were fighting hard." The chiefs called on their warriors to dismount and crawl towards the bluecoats. Then a cry went up, "Let us go! This is a good day to die.... I was young then and quick on my feet, and I was one of the first to get in among the soldiers. They got up and fought very hard till not one of them was alive.... Dead men and horses and wounded Indians were scattered all the way up the hill."

As the triumphant warriors stripped and mutilated the fallen soldiers, a loud howl was heard. A small dog, brought along by some soldier, now ran back towards the fort. "He was the only one left," recalled Fire Thunder. He thought the animal "sweet," but others felt differently. Arrows cut the cold, afternoon air, and the dog died where it fell.[28]

24

Preparation for an Unparalleled Defense

As Fetterman marched towards the crest of Lodge Trail ridge, Carrington ordered Surgeon Hines to the wood train to tend any wounded, then join Fetterman's command. Hines arrived on horseback with two wagons and a small detachment commanded by Lieutenant Matson. With no casualties to attend, they moved towards Fetterman, but, Hines recalled, "the firing at this time being very rapid, and the Indians appearing on Lodge Trail Ridge, we came to the conclusion the command was surrounded, and rode into the post for reinforcements."

"I received an order from Colonel Carrington," recalled Captain Ten Eyck, "to take command of a detachment of about forty infantry and dismounted cavalry, and proceed as rapidly as possible to the scene of action, and join Col. Fetterman if possible."[1] Captain Powell later claimed Carrington's response had been slack,[2] but Hines testified that this was done "as rapidly as possible."[3]

Surgeon Hines and Lieutenant Matson moved out with Ten Eyck's detachment, and for the second time that day Carrington was surprised by the movement of his troops. As Ten Eyck crossed the ice on Big Piney, the firing tapered off, but instead of heading straight for the scene of action, he led the command to the right up the slope of a hill. They arrived at the crest which gave a clear view of the terrain on the opposite side of Lodge Trail Ridge. Carrington dispatched 40 quartermaster men with ammunition to reinforce Ten Eyck, and the guard house prisoners were released. They were told to report for duty along with every other available man. A courier, meanwhile, rode to the wood train to order them back. Until they returned, "the whole force of armed men at the post, including guard and everything, was but one hundred and nineteen men," recalled Margaret Carrington.[4] Ten Eyck's command could be seen on the heights, and "soon orderly *Sample* was seen to break away from the command and make for the fort, with his horse, on the run. He brought the message that the valleys were full of Indians, and that several hundred were on the road below, yelling and challenging them to come down, but nothing could be seen of Fetterman."[5] Ten Eyck requested more men and a howitzer. Reinforcements were already on the way, but as regards the howitzer, "no one of his company could handle its ammunition and men could not be spared to move it," recalled Frances.[6]

Carrington sent a note to Ten Eyck: "CAPTAIN: Forty well-armed men, with 3000 rounds, ambulance, etc., left before your courier came in. You must unite with Fetterman, fire slowly, and keep men in hand: you could have saved two miles towards the scene of action if you had taken Lodge Trail Ridge. I order the wood train in, which will give fifty more men to spare."[7] Ten Eyck later testified: "I could accomplish the distance sooner, and with less fatigue to my men, there not being as much snow on the road, the ascent being more gradual, and the ridge being intersected by several deep ravines, that were partially filled with snow."[8]

But, like Major Reno after the Little Bighorn, Ten Eyck's reputation would be clouded for years to come. Had he avoided direct action due to cowardice? But "one thing was sure about Ten Eyck," recalled Private Murphy, "there was no cowardice in his make-up. He could not have taken a roundabout way if he wanted to do so, as his command was in plain sight of the fort."[9]

Ten Eyck moved his command towards a pile of large rocks where about 100 mounted Indians could be seen. The hostiles were still firing a few shots which "appeared to be from the arms captured by the Indians," recalled Hines. "We heard a tremendous yell or cry, then the guns were discharged. The rapid firing had ceased half an hour before."[10] Perhaps they were testing the little-known Spencers. Some may have been fired by warriors until the seven-shot magazine was emptied. It would take some experimentation to fathom reloading.

The warriors fell back until only four remained. Then, at a distance, Ten Eyck saw what all dreaded: dead, naked bodies strewn about. A few shots were fired at the four braves, and they rode off, rejoining the main band who moved off along the Bozeman Trail. The 40 civilians joined Ten Eyck with the ambulance and three wagons, and the command moved forward once more. Indians could still be seen in the distance, which Ten Eyck numbered at "not less than 1500 and I think over 2000." They arrived at the main scene of carnage where he estimated the number of bodies at over 60, so some cavalrymen had fallen alongside the infantry. The bodies were "all stripped stark naked, scalped, shot full of arrows and horribly mutilated," recalled Ten Eyck, "some with their skulls mashed in, throats cut of others, thighs ripped open, apparently with knives. Some of their ears were cut off, some with their bowels hanging out, from being cut through the abdomen, and a few with their bodies charred from burning, and some with their noses cut off." He recognized several men among the fallen including Captain Brown.[11] Surgeon Hines remained mounted while he took in the shocking sight: "I should judge in an area of ten or fifteen yards in diameter, there were some fifty or sixty dead men, stripped of everything, their heads apparently radiating out from a common center, with the appearance of having died there."[12]

"The key to the mutilations were startling and impressive," Carrington learned from a warrior years later. "Their idea of the spirit land is that it is a physical paradise; but we enter upon its mysteries just as in the condition we hold when we die. In the Indian paradise every physical taste or longing is promptly met. If he wants food, it is at hand; water springs up and ready for use; ponies and game abound, blossoms, leaves, and fruit never fail; all is perpetual. But what is Indian hell? It is the same in place and profusion of mercies, but the bad cannot partake.... With the muscles of the arms cut out, the victim could not pull a bowstring or trigger, with other muscles gone, he could not put foot in stirrup or stoop to drink; so that, while every sense was in agony for relief from hunger or thirst, there could be no relief at all."[13]

The ghastly job of loading the mutilated corpses into the wagons began. There was not enough room for all, but 49 were put on board, despite trouble from the mules, frightened by the smell of blood. The dejected soldiers made their way back, keeping a sharp eye for any renewed assault. All were fearful of joining their fallen comrades before they could get behind the stockade walls. But would they be safe there? With so many of the garrison killed, could Fort Phil Kearny be taken by storm? It was apparent that the Indians had masterminded a perfect trap for a sizable military detachment. The warriors had maintained a cohesive discipline, none betraying their positions, despite a reputation for individual action. Custer's fall at the Little Bighorn would be the result of spontaneous actions on the day, not a predetermined Indian battle plan.

"The evening gun was fired at sunset as usual," recalled Frances, "but what of us women! Agonizing fear possessed me! The ladies clustered in Mrs. Wands cabin as night drew on, all speechless from absolute stagnation and terror." The fort gates swung open and Ten Eyck's cheerless wagons rolled in. Then soldiers spread the "tenderly whispered" bad news: no survivors. Shockwaves reverberated around the fort. Women wept, including James Wheatley's young wife. Her eventual fate is obscure. Private Murphy claimed she married a man by the name of Breckenridge and lived on a ranch near Fort Laramie.[14] Frontiersman Finn Burnett said she returned to Ohio in company with her brother, possibly confusing her with Frances Grummond who would return to Tennessee with her brother.[15] "Mrs. Carrington herself tenderly took me to her arms and home," recalled Frances, "where in silence we awaited the unfolding of this deadly sorrow."[16]

Carrington's young son Jimmy received an unfortunate lesson in life when he saw the wagons come in. "How many times I awoke in the dark in terror," he recalled years later, "to see again the tortured bodies and bloody arrows of that night."[17]

"A knock at my door brought to me feet," recalled Frances. She was introduced to John Phillips, "a miner and frontiersman, in the employ of the quartermaster, clad in the dress of a scout." With tears in his eyes, Phillips said, "I am going to Laramie for help, with dispatches, as special messenger, if it costs me my life. I am going for your sake! Here is my wolf robe. I brought it for you to keep and remember me by it if you never see me again."[18]

The oblivious wood train from the Pinery rolled train back in. The men were astonished to hear the shocking news. Since the Indians had left their front, all had been peaceful and routine for them. They had not heard a shot fired and had no idea their comrades had fallen only five miles away.

As freezing snow squalls swept across Fort Phil Kearny that evening, Phillips and at least one other man rode out amidst sub zero temperatures. Exactly how many rode out and who they were has been the subject of debate. Phillips may well have been going for Frances Grummond's sake, but the 300 dollars paid was an added inducement.[19] Phillips rode "a fine thoroughbred belonging to the colonel," recalled Frances. "The sally-port gate was unbarred and relocked by the colonel himself, and John Phillips passed out, and beyond."[20] Frances insisted Phillips rode alone, and she was not the only one under this impression: "We never expected to see him again," recalled Fessenden, "but still, there was some hope." Carrington reported, however, "I hired two civilians to take dispatches to Laramie." It seems more than likely another man rode out the same night, but separately, giving two chances rather than one. And perhaps others left of their own accord. Better to ride for help than stay and wait for the Indians to scale the sparsely protected stockade walls.

"As if Nature herself were shocked by the enormity of the Indian torture there inflicted," recalled Mrs. Carrington, "from the very night of December 21st the winter became unmitigated in its severity, requiring guards to be changed at least half hourly, preventing out-of door inspections of the guards, and driving officers, ladies, and men to beaver, buffalo, or wolf skins for protection from the cold."[21]

Phillips rode through these conditions towards Fort Reno. From there he would continue to the Horseshoe Station telegraph to spread the news. Born in the Portuguese colony of the Azores in 1832, he had acquired the nickname "Portugee" Phillips. He carried a dispatch from Carrington which read: "Do send reinforcements forthwith. Expedition now in any force is impossible. I risk everything but the post and its stores. I venture as much as anyone can but I have had a fight today unexampled in Indian warfare, my loss is ninety four killed." Eighty-one had actually died, but Carrington went on to say 49 bodies had been brought in, and another 35 were yet to come, a total of 84. His inability to get basic figures right indicate his agitated state of mind. The letter may well have been written with a trembling hand. He estimated the Indian force at nearly 3,000, and "I hear nothing of my arms that left Leavenworth on September 10th. The additional cavalry ordered to join me has not reported; their arrival would have saved us much loss.... Today I had every teamster on duty, and but one hundred and nineteen men left at post. I hardly need urge this matter, it speaks for itself.... Depend upon it that the Post will be held so long as a round or a man is left."[22]

Eighty-one men killed in one engagement was without precedent when fighting western tribes. It comes as little surprise that all were fearful of a direct assault. With Fetterman's detachment wiped out, how many combatants were left to defend the fort on December 21? The day after receiving the "disastrous news," General Cooke wired Grant. He disputed Carrington's claim of "119" men, writing that his "December 10 report shows an aggregate present of four hundred and seventy five." This included civilian quartermaster employees. In reply Carrington was to write, "*My statement, as already shown officially, was literally true,* and General Cooke could have made no allowance for *wood train* and its guard, *neither* for the dead who fell with Fetterman, nor for any force sent out to support Fetterman."[23] Carrington was responsible for Cooke's confusion. His original hasty response gave the

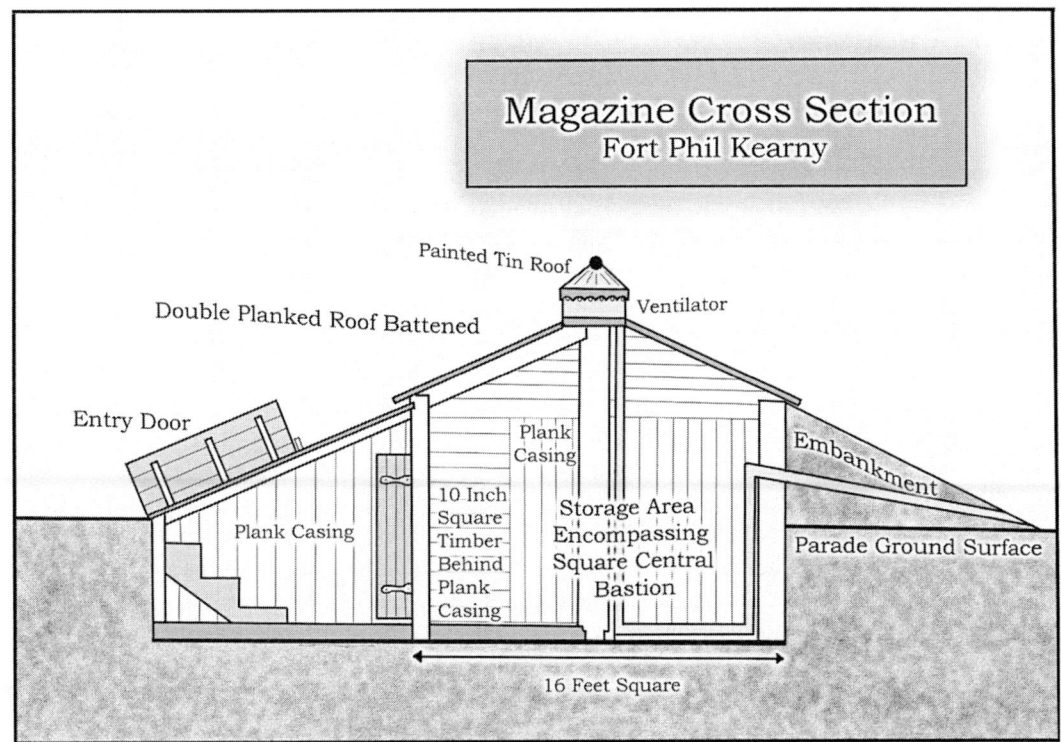

Author's rendition.

impression of 119 men all up, saying nothing of detachments outside the fort. Lieutenant Arnold's detailed list counted only 119 soldiers in the fort and made no mention of civilians willing to fight. Cooke's 475 less Fetterman's 81 dead leaves 394, of which about 300 would have been soldiers.

In any case the "fort proper," being 600 by 800 feet, covered 11 large acres. To properly man the walls against an attack on four sides would entail one soldier standing at each embrasure (called loopholes or portholes) located on every fifth picket join, about four feet apart. Blockhouses would also need to be manned. This would require about 700 defenders for the walls alone, plus more men to service the artillery, distribute ammunition, provide medical aid, etc. And this allows for no defense of the extensive quartermaster's yard, the structures of which would provide cover to an attacking force. The infantry were armed with slow-shooting muzzleloaders, and those Spencer repeaters sent out with Fetterman were now in Indian hands. If the hostiles broke through at any point, a reserve would be required to give support. It would have taken at least 800 soldiers to defend the "fort proper," and many more to defend the six-acre quartermaster's yard.

It comes as little surprise that Captain Powell, "recommended *abandonment of the stockade*," recalled Carrington, "and that each company officer, should upon an attack resort to his separate company quarters and there fire upon the foe." Carrington heartily disapproved. "This plan left the magazine in the public square, abandoned Hospital, warehouses and family quarters, gave the loop-holes to the Indians and left uncertain the effect of fire from four buildings, facing each other, two and two, with magazine between."[24] Carrington, however, came up with another idea. Fessenden recalled that the powder magazine, a half dugout, was "well supported with heavy timbers and covered with earth and sodded over." Carrington ordered this encircled with three rows of wagon boxes placed on their sides, the wheels removed, to form a final redoubt. "We had ten women and several children with us. The colonel gave orders that as soon as the Indians made the expected attack, the women and children should enter the magazine, and the men should hold the fort as long as possible." If forced to fall back from the stockade they were to retreat behind the wagon boxes, "and when the colonel saw that all was lost, he himself would blow up the magazine and take the lives off all."[25] The horrors of the Minnesota uprising only four years earlier were still in people's minds, rape and torture, the result of broken treaty promises by the whites. And the Indians confronting Fort Phil Kearny were in a similar frame of mind.

The morning of the 22nd was bitter cold. Carrington called a council of his remaining officers. The mutilated bodies of 30 soldiers and two civilians still lay on the other side of Lodge Trail Ridge. A force sent out to retrieve them could possibly suffer the same fate, and the fort itself would be vulnerable. Should an attempt to retrieve the dead be risked? "Universal disinclination" was the general feeling, recalled Margaret Carrington. But her husband decided "not to let the Indians have the conviction that the dead could not be rescued." The Indians themselves went to great length lengths to retrieve their fallen. Carrington would show them the white man could show the same resolve. He informed his wife of his decision, and, turning to Frances, said, "'Mrs. Grummond, I shall go in person, and bring back to you the remains of your husband.' I could only reply, 'They are beyond all suffering now. You must not imperil other precious lives and make other women as miserable as myself.' But his decision was fixed, and bidding his wife a tender good-by, and a word of hopeful confidence, he mounted his horse and the bugle sounded 'Forward march' as if on a parade."[26] Captain Ten Eyck, Lieutenant Matson and Dr. Ould also went along with a force of 80 men. "They left with the cheerful Godspeed of every woman and soldier of the garrison," recalled Margaret, "on a holy mission, the pickets, which were distributed on the line of march, indicated their progress, and showed that neither the fort nor the detachment could be threatened without such connection of signals as would advise both and secure co-operation whatever might ensue."[27]

As the column moved towards Lodge Trail Ridge, the ladies watched as work continued around the magazine, "vaguely suspecting" what was going on, recalled Frances, "and a strange hope sprang up, as we watched with calmness and assurance the progress of the work, for it indicated the preparation for an unparalleled defense."[28] A white lamp was placed at the flag staff head. If hostiles appeared a red lamp was to take its place, and the officer of the day was to fire three shots at one minute intervals from the 12-pounder.

Ten Eyck led the column to the ghastly sight. "The seen of action told its story," recalled Carrington. "The road on the little ridge where the final stand took place was strewn with arrow heads, scalps, poles and broken shafts of spears. The arrows that were spent harmlessly from all directions, showed that the command was suddenly overwhelmed, surrounded and cut off while in retreat ... nearly all were heaped near four rocks at the point nearest the Fort, these rocks enclosing a space about six feet square, having been the last refuge for defense.... Fetterman and Brown had each a revolver shot in the left temple. As Brown always reserved a shot for himself as a last resort, so I am convinced that these two brave men fell, each by the other's hand."[29] But coordinating such a move in the heat of battle seems unlikely. It would be far easier to shoot oneself. A warrior named American Horse claimed he knocked Fetterman down with a war club and then slit his throat. This may be the case, as Surgeon Horton's testimony made no mention of a bullet hole, and stated that Fetterman's body "showed his thorax to have been cut crosswise with a knife, deep into the viscera.... I believe that mutilation caused his death." The club alleged to have been used was given to a white rancher, and is now on display at the Agate Fossil Beds National Monument in Nebraska.[30]

As regards Brown's remains, the surgeon confirmed "a hole made in his left temple by a small pistol ball" which probably "caused his death." But the left temple is not the most logical place for a man to shoot himself; further back above the ear is more probable. And Indians carried pistols. Perhaps neither man took his own life. The command moved "about 40 rods" (220 yards), recalled Ten Eyck, where more bodies including that of George Grummond were found.[31] Surgeon Horton testified that the lieutenant's head was "crushed by a club, and his legs were slightly scorched by fire." He believed most men were not tortured, but "were fallen upon by Indians and butchered after they were wounded."[32]

"Pools of blood on the road and sloping sides of the narrow divide showed where Indians bled fatally," recalled Carrington, "but their bodies were carried off. I counted sixty five such pools in the space of an acre, and three within ten feet of Lieutenant Grummond's body." The flying arrows and bullets had killed not only men. "Eleven American horses and nine Indian ponies were on the road, or near the line of bodies, others, crippled, were in the valley." Brown's mount, Calico, was found lying the foot of the hill. "They had even scalped his horse," claimed Fessenden, "their hatred of him was so extreme." If not already dead, Carrington ordered that the pony be mercifully shot.[33]

Carrington moved along the road to the most distant battle point. This was "about one mile"[34] from Fetterman's body, Ten Eyck recalled. Here "five or six" bodies were discovered. Between two rocks, Carrington found "James S. Wheatley and Isaac Fisher of Blue

Springs, Nebraska, who, with 'Henry Rifles,' felt invincible, but fell, one having one hundred and five arrows in his naked body." Numerous cartridge shells were scattered about, which "told how well they fought."

"The "terrible massacre" of Fetterman's detachment "bore marks of great valor," recalled Carrington, "and has demonstrated the force and character of the foe, but no valor could have saved them."[35]

25

Fixing the Blame

At Fort Phil Kearny all dreaded the prospect of hearing gunfire breaking out over lodge Trail Ridge, a repeat of the previous day's disaster. Then the fort itself would almost certainly fall. "We were overjoyed, therefore," Fessenden remembered, "when they came back, but sadness overcame us when, nearing the fort, we saw seven wagons loaded with naked bodies—arms and legs in all shapes, divulging the horrible manner in which our brave comrades had died."[1]

The cheerless command marched back through the gates as twilight set in. "No sight was ever so beautiful to the troops," Carrington recalled, "as that white lantern at masthead, gleaming so like the Star of Bethlehem, guiding to safety and peace." And the ladies felt no sound ever so sweet as Carrington's bugle call, "as if to say, 'Fear not, all is safe.'"[2]

Frances answered a knock at her door. Carrington handed her an envelope, then left her alone. "I opened it with eager but trembling hands," she recalled. "It contained a lock of my husband's hair. He had redeemed his pledge."

The hospital could not accommodate all the frozen bodies, and some were laid out in two hospital tents and a double cabin. Carrington trained additional men "in the shell and gun practice, preparatory for a possible siege," recalled Frances.[3] Plans were put in place to either shoot over the walls, or sweep the fort's interior should the stockade be scaled. "Each company knew its place and the distribution of the loop-holes," recalled Margaret, "the gunners slept in their tents near their guns, and all things were ripe for the destruction of assailants should any venture to attack."[4]

Fessenden, however, was not so sure. "Red Cloud could easily have wiped out every vestige of this fort, had he ever attacked us in full force, and why he did not attempt this is an unanswered question." Fire Thunder provided the answer: "Dead men and horses and wounded Indians were scattered all the way up the hill, and their blood was frozen, for a storm had come up and it was very cold and getting colder all the time … we picked up our wounded and started back; but we lost most of them before we reached our camp at the mouth of the Peno. There was a big blizzard that night; and some of our wounded who did not die on the way, died after we got home." Frances Grummond noted that some in the fort felt "the extraordinary cold and stormy spell" prevented a further assault, while "others argued that the Indian loss must have been so severe that the savages would never risk so wild a venture as to attack the stockade with artillery ready to discharge grape-shot and canister from block-house and parade ground."[5] Despite such thoughts, most feared imminent attack. This included "Mrs. Carrington's colored servant Dennis" who seemed "possessed by a demon," recalled Frances. He would "strike his head with all possible force against the boards of the partition" and continued "this mania by butting his head against the stove-pipe and even the stove itself, like a veritable mad-man. It was not until the appearance of the Colonel with the muzzle of a cocked revolver touching his head that the equilibrium was restored."[6] But Frances had problems of her own: "During the nights I would dream of Indians, of being captured and carried away by Red Cloud himself while frantically screaming for help, and then awaken in terror only to spring from my bed involuntarily to listen if the near-by sentry would still voice the welcome cry, 'All's well.'"[7]

Hammers thumped and saws rasped as pine coffins were assembled. Each case was numbered, and the identity of each fallen man carefully recorded should a later reburial by families or government be required. Many soldiers gave their best uniforms to clothe dead friends. The burial trench, 50 feet long and seven feet deep, was dug in the cemetery at the base of Pilot Hill.[8] The work was hard going, picks and shovels striking frozen ground, and the icy cold required constant 15-minute relays of both diggers and armed guards. Four days of hard work passed before the dead could be interred, "calmly, systematically and safely," recalled Frances.[9]

Wind-driven snow fell and banked against the west stockade wall. Any warriors brave enough to combat both freezing cold and a blast of grapeshot from Carrington's howitzers could simply walk to the top of the palisade and jump within the fort. Men were put to work and cleared a ten-foot-wide trench only to have it filled with snow again by the next icy squall. There was no joy this Christmas season, the usual social gatherings and pleasantries abandoned in memory of the dead. "Present and exacting duty admitted no dalliance with pleasures that were at other times rational and refreshing," recalled Margaret, "and a calm, sedate, but genial sympathy brought most to a closer fraternity, almost confirming the sacred proverb, 'That it is better to go to the house of mourning than to the house of feasting.'"[10]

Even if reinforced, any thoughts of attacking the Tongue River villages was a mere distant memory. The new arms promised, but not delivered, were only outmoded muzzleloaders. Breechloaders or repeaters were required, and the hundreds of tepees along the Tongue River were now seen as sheltering not only vicious warriors, but also Red Cloud's "knifing squaws and shooting papooses," or so Margaret Carrington felt.

But, on the other hand, "it must be the fear I remember most," Black Elk recalled of his childhood. "I was not allowed to play very far away from our tepee, and my mother would say, 'If you are not good the Wasichus will get you.'"[11]

Portugee Phillips meanwhile, arrived at Fort Reno and alerted the garrison. He rested and thawed out as Colonel Wessells wrote a dispatch requesting reinforcements. Phillips and a few other riders pushed on to the Horseshoe Station telegraph office, arriving midmorning, Chrisman Day. Phillips later told Frances Grummond of his ride. She wrote, "he delivered General Wessell's brief dispatch, which reached Fort Laramie at 2 o'clock on Christmas Day." But the telegraph operator "was unwilling to risk so long a dispatch as that of Colonel Carrington, but Phillips pressed on with this dispatch, reaching Fort Laramie at 11 o'clock with icicles hanging from his clothing; both beard and hair matted with snow and ice."[12] Perhaps it was thoughts of the pretty and pregnant Mrs. Grummond under threat that urged Portugee Phillips on.

At Fort Laramie that night officers danced with perfumed ladies beneath softly glowing lanterns, the Christmas ball in full swing. A gust of cold air swept through as the door opened and "a huge form dressed in a buffalo overcoat, pants, gauntlets and cap" walked in with an orderly, recalled Lieutenant David Gordon. The ladies and gents had been "superlatively happy, enjoying the dance," but Phillips' appearance "made a deep impression upon the officers and others that happened to get a glimpse of him, and consequently, and naturally too, excited their curiosity as to his mission in this strange garb, dropping into our full dress garrison ball at the this unseasonable hour."[13]

Phillips' news "created such a gloom over all that the dancing party dispersed early," recalled Colonel Innis Palmer.[14] The colonel had his telegraph operator rattle off a message to General Cooke at Omaha with the bad news and a request for reinforcements.

Cooke's immediate superior in St. Louis, General Sherman, was returning from a trip to Mexico, and Cooke telegraphed Commander-in-Chief Ulysses S. Grant in Washington direct: "On the 21st instant three (3) officers and (90) men, cavalry and infantry, were massacred by Indians near Fort Phil Kearney. Indians reported to be near three thousand (3,000), probable, from the completeness of the massacre. I order up four (4) companies of infantry and two (2) of cavalry from Laramie." Cooke had already been fed anti–Carrington rhetoric by Captain Bisbee, his aide-de-camp, and news of this disaster was the last straw.

Carrington's departure for Fort Casper was already planned, but he expected to retain command at least to the following spring. "I want officers. I want men. Depend on it," he wrote to General Grant directly. "I will operate all winter, whatever the season, if supported; but to redeem my pledge to open and guarantee this line I must have re-enforcements and the best of arms up to my full estimate."

But Cooke wanted Carrington out *now*. He wired Grant. "I order Colonel Carrington to Casper, headquarters of the eighteenth; if not approved I request the assignment of General Wessells at Reno to his brevet rank to command district." Cooke heard back, "Your

The newspapers produced imaginary artwork of the "Fetterman Massacre" based on supposed "actual observer" accounts (*Harper's Weekly*, March 23, 1867).

action in Colonel Carrington's case is approved; and if you deem it necessary you are authorized to assign General Wessells as proposed ... if there has been any fault in the matter, you will have it strictly investigated."[15]

No doubt Cooke congratulated himself on a job well done—but "fault in the matter" meant there was also a Sword of Damocles hanging over his own vulnerable head.

An enquiry into the "Fetterman Massacre" would conclude that Carrington had been denied adequate troops and supplies. Cooke is commonly blamed for this. But he wired Grant on December 27: "You will observe Colonel Carrington asks for Spencer arms for infantry. Some of his men have used them mounted, and have felt since the inferiority of the muzzle-loading arms. In fact, I have had an official report of a cattle guard excusing themselves for not firing on attacking Indians; that if they had fired, the Indians having revolvers, they would be defenseless. They have revolvers, and it comes to this, that the savages are better armed than the troops. I therefore earnestly recommend that breechloading Springfield muskets be now furnished for all these troops. I found that even the cavalry were generally unfurnished with revolvers; and a telegraphic requisition for a supply for five companies, with an implied consent of General Dyer, (Chief of Ordnance) of November 6, has not yet resulted in there being received or heard from."[16] At the later enquiry, Cooke testified that he "had repeatedly urged my superiors to remedy this deficiency of officers in the department, by any and all means possible."[17] According to a clerk in Cooke's office, Alson Ostrander, the general approved and forwarded to Sherman all Carrington's request for more men and supplies.[18]

Grant probably thought the Fetterman defeat was as bad as it could get. If so, he was in for a shock. He would be president of the United States ten years later when Custer was wiped out.

William Sherman returned to his office and heard the bad news. The year before he had written to James Yeatman: "I am sick and tired of war.... It is only those who have not heard a shot nor heard the shrills and groans of the wounded ... that cry aloud for more blood & more vengeance ... so help me God as a man & soldier I will not strike a foe who stands unarmed and submissive before me but will say "Go sin no more.""[19] But on December 28 he wired Grant, "We must act with vindictive earnestness against the Sioux, even to their extermination, men, women and children. Nothing less will reach the root of this case."[20] Two days later, "I am not satisfied with Genl. Cooke—or the two officers now up there, Carrington and Wessells."[21] On January 8 Sherman received a telegram from Grant informing him that Cooke was being replaced with General Christopher Columbus Augur. "You will be much pleased with Augur. He has had long experience with Indians both hostile and peaceable." The 45-year-old Augur had been a classmate of Grant's at West Point. He served with distinction in the Mexican War before spending time on the frontier, and in 1856 fought Indians in Oregon. During the Civil War Augur was wounded at Cedar Mountain, and for gallant service was promoted to Major General of Volunteers.[22] Sherman wired Grant back that Augur was "most acceptable."

Cooke was making plans for a campaign to avenge Fetterman when he received the shattering news. "Shall I work on planning what may be all changed or complained of after the disgrace you put upon me?" he wired Grant. "I certainly do not deserve this inconsiderate action in my case." To Sherman he telegraphed: "You can avert this cruel blow calculated to disgrace me only I fear it may have come from you—I fought and whipped the Sioux and am nearly equal physically to my best day." Sherman later denied any responsibility for Cooke's removal. He wrote to General Grenville Dodge saying the order "came complete without my being consulted, and I do not know what influenced General Grant." Perhaps, however, "I am not satisfied with Genl. Cooke" had something to do with it. Sherman claimed he "never supposed Genl Crooke was in the least to blame for the Fort Phil Kearny Massacre." So who was responsible for troops and modern weapons not being supplied? Secretary of War Edwin Stanton? Grant? Ordnance chief General Dyer, or perhaps Sherman himself? Grant wired Cooke with instructions to follow Sherman's orders regarding the planned campaign, and await Augur's arrival.

Cooke felt he was a being used as a scapegoat. Best to divert the venom in another direction. No doubt Captain Bisbee was only to happy to help. On January 14 Cooke wired Sherman his version of events which stated that Carrington had made no "expedition against Indians; all his skirmishes have been with war parties attacking his supply trains, or appearing in sight of the fort. I am informed that on these occasions it was the custom of officers and men to sally forth, mounted or afoot, much at their discretion." As proof, Cooke included Fetterman's report of the December 6 skirmish which mentioned Brown and some mounted infantry starting out in advance, being joined by Fetterman, and being overtaken by Wands. He did not send Carrington's account of the same action, but did send his dispatch sent only two days before the Fetterman fight stating that the Indians "are accomplishing nothing while I am perfecting all details of the post and preparing for active movements." Cooke went on to point out that many of the men killed had been mounted, while his recommendations to Carrington regarding offensive operations during winter "laid stress upon using infantry ... all the available horses (which I believe were kept saddled) were mounted, and that hastily and irregularly they sallied out to engage or pursue." The Indians then skillfully led the detachment "into ground selected as forbidding escape; and that there, by so greatly superior numbers, the troops were surrounded and massacred, no quarter asked or given."[23]

Five days later a fuming and frustrated Cooke wired the adjutant general's office requesting a court of enquiry into his removal. Grant replied, "The application for a Court of Enquiry is refused. Gen. Cooke was relieved from command of the Dept. of the Platte solely because it was deemed for the good of the service to do so, and he has no right to question the motives which led to his removal."

26

One and All Gloried in Abuse

Carrington, meanwhile, had no idea if help was coming. Had Phillips or anyone else made it through, or were their scalped and frozen bodies lying somewhere in the wilderness? He did not dare send out a "soldier messenger" with an adequate escort to Reno "without precipitating an attack in overwhelming force from the enemy," recalled Frances, "and there was insufficient ammunition in store even for a protracted defense by every one able to assist in its ordeal."[1]

The first troops to reach Carrington arrived on December 27. It was a small force of only 18 men under the command of Captain George Dandy and Lieutenant Alpheus Bowman from Fort Reno escorting the mail wagon.[2] "At last word came that reinforcements had started our way," recalled Fessenden. "How our drooped spirits revived at this joyous news!"[3] Their arrival revealed that Portugee Phillips had made it through the area most frequented by hostiles, and had continued on towards Fort Laramie.

Frances Grummond was astonished to read a letter from Tennessee, written well before December 21. "What can be the matter?" her sister wrote. "I have had such dreadful forebodings, consequent upon dreams that have troubled me. I have witnessed horrible battles with Indians. I have seen them drinking blood from the skulls of the slain. I sincerely hope that such dreams may go by contraries, as we are often reminded, and that you cannot be exposed to such dangers as are suggested by such horrible dreams."

"This letter made me quiver," recalled Frances, "for it really seemed she must have possessed some clairvoyant power thus to interpret so closely the state of affairs."[4]

A sergeant also received mail and wrote to his friend back home, "It is now past tattoo, the night is cold, the men are sleeping in their clothes and accoutrements. Indian signals have been seen, and we don't know at what hour the post may be attacked. Self and two soldiers are keeping watch so as to awaken the men in case of alarm…. Please write soon, and pray God to hasten the day when I shall get out of this horrible place."[5]

On January 1, 1867, Carrington issued General Order No. 1. A military reservation of "twenty five square miles, more or less," was established around the post. Carrington had objected to this proposal, writing that it would preclude the garrison from gathering the best of their own timber and hay, and be reliant on civilian contractors, only to be overruled by Cooke. In reference to the recent disaster, Carrington wrote that he shared "with every officer and man in the deep sorrow which all feel." He praised the three officers who fell, including Grummond: "He was a true man, worthy of higher rank than he held in the army." Brown came in for more subdued admiration: "His daring had been conspicuous in many skirmishes about the post. If he unwisely despised his foe, he fought to the last." And of Fetterman, "his character was pure and without blemish. He was a refined gentleman and had distinguished his regimental record and honored his own name by duty well done."

But only two days later Carrington changed his tone. In the official report he wrote that Fetterman's instructions were "*Support the wood train, relieve it and report to me. Do not engage or pursue Indians at its expense. Under no circumstances pursue over the ridge viz; Lodge Trail Ridge.*" It would take a few weeks for this report to arrive in Omaha, and Carrington arranged for a brief telegram to be sent from Horseshoe Station. The detachment, he wrote, "pushed over Lodge Trail Ridge in ardor of pursuit, after orders three times not to cross that ridge."[6]

Lieutenant Colonel Wessells at Fort Reno, meanwhile, was joined by the four companies of the 18th Infantry and two of the Second Cavalry dispatched from Laramie. Cooke, before removal, had issued orders to "make Reno safe," proceed to Fort Phil Kearny, and replace Carrington as commander of the re-instituted Mountain District. "I hope regular communication can be kept with Fort C. F. Smith, and that we may be able to chastise Indians who may insult the posts; but with great caution. The officers are not equal to their stratagems in the broken ground they know so well; their numbers, it seems now certain, are so very superior."[7] This was a far cry from "strike the hostile bands of Indians by surprise in their winter camps," as pressed less than two months earlier.

Leaving one infantry company at Reno, Wessells, "a soldier with laurels and a gentleman without blemish,"[8] wrote Mrs. Carrington, marched through freezing conditions to arrive at Fort Phil Kearny on January 18, 1867.[9] "The whole story of their march was self-revealed without word of explanation as they entered the main gate," recalled Frances. "They had waded or dug their way through snows, knee deep, and often waist deep, while the mercury ranged from 25 to 40 degrees below zero, and with both hands and feet frostbitten they were as happy as ourselves to reach friends and friendly shelter. Bright fires were blazing in all quarters," and Wessells "spoke of the warmth of his welcome as in double sense most satisfactory." One man had not made it to the warmth, however, having frozen to death in his sleep.[10]

Wessells brought orders from Omaha. No doubt Carrington was most displeased at his abrupt removal from command. He was to move immediately to Fort Casper, through freezing conditions, about 100 miles south of Fort Reno, along with his family and regimental staff. But he would have been delighted to know, no doubt, that the man who had just removed him had been removed himself one week earlier. General Cooke was assigned to "special duties" back east before taking command of the Department of the Cumberland in 1869.

The mail also brought vexing newspaper stories. Once news of the "massacre" had reached Omaha, the story had shot across the country by the "singing wire." Newspapermen and politicians who had come to expect thousands of casualties when white fought white during the Civil War were appalled to learn of Indians wiping out a detachment of 81 men. "It was, of course, to be expected," recalled Margaret Carrington, "that the Illustrated Papers should act promptly and perspicuously, with all the embellishments and accuracy which wood engraving affords ... and it was equally certain and necessary that a 'special artist,' some 'actual observer,' or a 'special correspondent,' should furnish the editor's sanctum with the right material for his use in advance of the mails."[11]

News of the "massacre" was the last thing President Andrew Johnson wanted to hear. On December 3 he had delivered a message to Congress that the Army had been "carefully provided with medical treatment, well sheltered and subsisted, and is to be furnished with breech-loading small arms." And treaties had been concluded with Indians who "have unconditionally submitted to our authority and manifested an earnest desire for a renewal of friendly relations."[12]

There was a long-standing rift between the War Department and the Department of the Interior on how best to manage the western tribes. Officers like William Sherman felt Indians only understood bullet and bayonet, while the Bureau preferred a softly, softly approach. Far better to peacefully Christianize the tribesmen on reservations where they can become farmers and adapt to the white man's way of life. Congress published material on the Fetterman defeat submitted by both departments including the views of Commissioner of Indian Affairs, Lewis Vital Bogy. He stated that an order by Cooke prohibiting the sale of gunpowder and ammunition to Indians "has had a very bad effect." It was "cruel," he asserted, and "Indians are men, and when hungry will, like us, resort to any means to obtain food, and as is the case their only means of subsistence, if you deprive them of the power of procuring it, you certainly produce great dissatisfaction," and, as Indians have "no means of taking care of powder, he will take, if offered to him, but a very limited quantity." Mixed blood frontiersman George Bent, however, stated that Indians preferred arrows for hunting as they were personally marked by warriors which prevented disagreements about who killed what. Indians had survived with arrows before the white mans' arrival, and the lethal shafts had killed most of Fetterman's command. Bogy went on say, "The Indians, almost in a state of starvation, were rendered desperate, and resorted to the stratagem which proved too successful. It seems the commanding officer could have avoided the catastrophe."[13] Bogy said the massacre was triggered by Carrington's troops having fired on peaceful Indians, including women and children, during a visit to the fort, while merely requesting a reversal of Cooke's order. They were in "absolute want of guns and ammunition to make their winter hunt.... Although I regret the unfortunate death of so many brave soldiers, yet there can be no doubt that it is owing to the foolish and rash management of the officer in command of that post."[14]

One Albany newspaper, "from reliable information," wrote, "when the last band of survivors were driven to the gates of the fort, knocking and screaming in vain for submission; when the last cartridge from revolver, carbine, and rifle was expended; when the sabers and butts of the muskets were broken; and when, leaning against the gates, weary and bleeding and all resistance fruitless, all fell in one heap of mangled humanity unsupported and uncared for." And the commanding officer looked on "with two full companies" afraid to "either fire or open the gates lest the garrison within should be massacred by the infuriated savages and the post should be sacked! Block-houses, of course, reserved their fire! Loop-holes shone with the glaring eyes of frightened soldiery, but not with the gleaming rifle! Four howitzers, which could have swept the slope and bottom land, were silent and innocent to harm anybody!"[15]

"One and all gloried in abuse," recalled Margaret Carrington, "and no wonder it is that the hard labor of 1866; its chases and its losses, were never told, lest credit should inure to the pioneer expedition to Absaraka."[16]

On January 23 General Augur arrived at Omaha and assumed command of the Department of the Platte. The day before, Cooke had fired his last salvo. He forwarded Carrington's official report of January 3 which stated that the Fetterman defeat "vindicates my application, so often made, for reinforcements and demonstrates the fact that if I had received those assured to me by telegram and letter, I could have kept up communications and opened a safe route for immigrants next spring,"[17] Cooke accompanied this report with a letter of his own, which included "an officer of high rank, in a letter of January 4, from Phil Kearny, gives the following version: 'The men, as usual, when the wood train was known to be corralled by the Indians, rushed out helter-skelter, some leaping over the stockade, which is in no place over eight feet high. What probability there is of them having had with them a proper supply of ammunition you can judge.' No reinforcements ever 'assured' to Col. C. failed to be sent. Before the Platte was formally put under my command two companies of cavalry were ordered from Fort Laramie, but only one turned out to be disposable; an additional company of cavalry was afterwards sent. November 25 he (Carrington) wrote he would 'make the winter one of active operations in different directions, as best affords chances of punishment.' December 19 telegraphed he was 'preparing for active movements.'"[18]

The officer of "high rank" was the Carrington-hating Captain Powell writing to the Carrington-hating Captain Bisbee. Cooke's letter implied Carrington's lack of discipline had caused the defeat, and Carrington's report blamed Fetterman for disobeying orders. But it was now apparent that Carrington lacked sufficient troops for the job at hand, a problem that came back to Sherman and Grant.

In early February a "Letter of the Secretary of War" appeared "in compliance with a resolution of the Senate of the 30th ultimo, the official reports, papers, and other facts in relation to the causes and extent of the late massacre of United States troops by Indians at Fort Phil Kearny." Included was Carrington's original dispatch of December 21, but missing was his official report of January 3. This would not be forwarded to Secretary of War Edwin Stanton till March 9. Cooke's unfavorable references about Carrington did appear, however. While stating that Carrington was "energetic and industrious" in garrison "it is all to evident he has not maintained discipline, and that his officers have no confidence in him. Some of his acts officially reported, such as shelling woods where Indians had appeared on a previous day may have, by this time, settled his appreciation by Indians."[19]

It comes as little surprise that Carrington was not pleased. At the enquiry he claimed Bisbee, as post adjutant, "never reported 'irregularities' or 'disorder' that he was not at once empowered to correct." But "he differed from *my* views of discipline, in physical and verbal abuse of soldiers, requiring my issue of General Order No. 38 ... *I stand by that order.*" The post was "quiet and orderly at all times.... I had willing, obedient soldiers," and "the want of discipline" was in "officers coming fresh to the command who were unequal to the wiles of the Indians and *despised my caution*, and personal knowledge of the broken ground, which the Indians knew better than all of us, but which I had made my business to study and explore all summer.... Most of those who had no confidence in my judgment, as to Indians, have paid the penalty of their lives, *for their want of confidence.*" Carrington admitted he had shelled woods where Indians had been seen the previous day "*because* the block house of the wood choppers had been besieged the whole night." Men had been killed and wounded, Carrington wrote, and "having been advised by a messenger that Indians were still in the pine woods and thickets.... I *did* go out and shell the forest below, clear it out and restore confidence in the working party."[20]

During Carrington's command, there had been 51 hostile acts by Indians, and most trains on the Bozeman Trail had been attacked. Five officers, 91 enlisted men and 58 civilians had been killed, and many more wounded. Hundreds of horses, oxen, cows and mules had been driven off.[21]

Once Wessells assumed command at Fort Phil Kearny, Carrington made preparations for departure. "It seems very strange that the trip to Fort Caspar, just then," recalled Mrs. Carrington, "was a matter of life and death to the nation, as to make it a question of life or death to us."[22] Captain Dandy, "Chief Quartermaster, with discernment and courtesy, fitted up army wagons for the women and children, and deserves due thanks for our earthly salvation, as that preparation alone secured us a safe deliverance during the trip that ensued."[23] All those making the trek rugged up as best they could. "This was no less marked in the case of Laura, Mrs. Wands' colored maid," recalled Frances, who "improvised for herself a traveling hat, quite unique in its style, made of white rabbit skins but adorned with pink roses, already very much crushed." Mrs. Wands "made no objection to the fur hat proper but drew a decided line as to the roses, greatly to Laura's chagrin and disappointment."[24]

The convoy of troops and wagons set out on the afternoon of January 23. On board were those officers attached to the reorganized 18th Infantry. Women and children, wrapped in furs, were also present. This included "the usual families of band musicians, with their liberal allowance of future trumpeters, flautists and drummers," recalled Margaret. Frank Fessenden, promoted to sergeant, remained behind, as did Captains Powell and Ten Eyck, reassigned to the 27th Infantry. Powell "did not even call to say good bye," recalled Carrington, "when the family started in a snow storm upon a winter's trip of uncertain risk and exposure."[25]

The train crawled south, the Bozeman Trail only just visible "by dint of shoveling and picking at proper intervals." With the convoy was Frances Grummond. "In one sense, that slowly moving train was a funeral procession, for my husband's remains were placed in one wagon, that they might accompany me to my home in Tennessee for a resting place until the final Roll Call."[26]

The train only covered six miles during the next eight hours. Carrington called a halt at 10 p.m., and, amidst wind-driven snow, the wagons were corralled on a hilltop in case of an Indian attack. But it was only a brief rest. The clouds cleared away and the moon rose above the frozen landscape lighting the way ahead. At 1 a.m. a bugle sounded, and two hours later the wagons rolled once more. "I certainly *thanked the stars*, as if they were 'my stars,'" recalled Frances, "for their appearance, and they seemed to twinkle a willing companionship; and the moon, as well, for the storm had ceased and the night was bright at last."

The travelers reached Crazy Woman's Fork on January 25. It was here that Lieutenant Daniels had been killed. The wagons were corralled in a loop of the creek, and a vigilant watch kept during a freezing night. Despite a lit stove in the headquarters wagon, the mercury congealed in the base of the thermometer bulb. But "it *never was red hot*," recalled Margaret, "and its very top would neither thaw nor toast bread, unless when a kettle let down within had contact with the flame that struggled to do its best.... Mrs. Wands and Mrs. Grummond had the same school of practice in keeping up fires, and little Bobby Wands had the same ambition to burn off his buffalo boots as other little boys we know of."[27] Men attempting to warm themselves by fires lit on the open ground saw the melting snow freeze to ice around the base.

Next morning shivering men went to work with axe and pick, and broke through the snow and ice covering the creek. The driver of Mrs. Carrington's wagon asked to be relieved as "his feet had gone to sleep." Once on the ground, he was unable to stand, his feet and legs frozen almost to the knees. As well as the intense cold, there was always that other fear. George Grummond's body was a constant reminder that Indians could be lurking just out of sight. "Mrs. Wands had a curious fancy and would fire up her stove to its utmost capacity when we passed dangerous places under the strange conceit that if the Indians saw the black smoke it indicated that *cannon* were near."[28]

The train set out once more, teams having to be doubled to get the wagons, one by one, up a steep slope. Lieutenant Wands rode up and down the line looking into wagons, checking that all was well with the ladies and children. Then the dreaded cry of "Indians" came down the line. The rear of the train was under threat. "Teams were put to the gallop," recalled Margaret, "the train was closed up, half frozen men in the wagons took their arms, and Lieutenant Wands, with a mounted party, dashed back to bring up the rear, and ascertain the facts."[29] Whips cracked and drivers cursed mules as the forward wagons were moved into corral position. It was a long train including 40 empty wagons to return with supplies from Reno. "Mrs. Wands did not even have the satisfaction of firing up her stove," recalled Frances, "but directed all her energies to holding it in position so as not to lose it altogether, for the door swung wildly on its hinges and there was no time to close it."[30]

But what were thought to be mounted Indians turned out to be an immense herd of buffalo. Carrington ordered the men not to "holler" or crack whips. A stampede of these big animals could do more damage than an Indian attack.

All were thankful when the wagons rolled into Fort Reno. For three days relatively comfortable quarters would be enjoyed before hitting the glacial trail once more. But it was not a pleasant stay for all. "While our wants were being looked after with all promptness," recalled Frances, "it was not long before the surgeons were equally engaged in their merciful ministrations to the men, in some cases requiring the amputation of fingers, toes and even legs, with two fatal results, Mrs. Carrington's driver being one of the fatal cases." More casualties, indirectly, of the Fetterman defeat.

The convoy set out once more with a smaller escort. Soldiers were required to guard the supply wagons returning to Fort Phil Kearny through territory where hostiles were more likely to strike. Lieutenant Joshua Jacobs, who would eventually rise to brigadier general, was in charge of Carrington's new escort. Five days later they arrived at the charred remains of the Deer Creek telegraph station, previously burned by Indians. "In the ruins, however, there was a large fireplace still serviceable," recalled Frances, "and close by it a heap of blocks of tar which had been used for insulation in building the new line between Fort Laramie and Fort Casper." The tar blocks provided "something that would readily burn, and unmindful of both smoke and odor we congratulated ourselves upon its light and warmth."

Up to this point not an Indian had been seen. The following day, however, as they approached Fort Casper, "very suddenly, without a word of warning, I realized that our teams were on the quick trot," recalled Frances. Indians galloped into sight and "dashed between us and the fort." They ran off the army horses grazing outside, and the wagons were formed into "a moving corral with six teams at front, and as many in the rear with flanking teams in single file so that in an emergency all would form a compact hollow square." The Indians did not attack, content to drive their captured horses across the Platte, then disappear into the northern hills. "At any rate we had the excitement of a genuine scare, and groans of relief, not translated into words, came from the women who had to pacify the children."[31]

The travelers entered Fort Casper, disembarked, and settled into their new home—so they thought. "Lieutenant Wands inquired where most would we prefer to go rather than remain at Caspar, the most barren and insignificant post on the plains," recalled Margaret, "for sure enough, General Augur, upon assuming command at Omaha, had changed the headquarters post to McPherson." Fort McPherson was far to the east, on the other side of fort Laramie, and the weary travelers would have to backtrack many miles through the icy conditions they had just endured.

"I am unacquainted, personally, with Colonel Carrington and it is possible that an injustice may be done to him," wrote Augur to Sherman on February 19, "but right or wrong, his reputation in the upper country is such for inefficiency and unfitness for command that I regard it unsafe and unjust to leave him in charge of any post in that country. It is for these reasons that I have brought him to Fort McPherson where the effects of his incapacity, it they exist, may be readily controlled."[32]

The new arrivals at Fort Casper may have been spared the "insignificant and barren post" but, all things considered, they were hardly pleased. In the military, however, "there's not to reason why," and unpacked bags were repacked as all accepted their fate—all except one, that is. Mrs. Wands servant Laura "protested in the most emphatic terms that 'she wouldn't budge another step,'" recalled Francis. There were no regulations for "the punishment of women" so Mrs. Wands asked Mrs. Grummond to witness justice "as she was going to flail Laura with a 'trunk strap.'" Frances felt "gagging would seem to be suitable," but as this might require "more physical force than Mrs. Wands had at her command," the strap seemed a viable alternative. Frances reluctantly agreed to witness the confrontation between mistress and servant. There followed "frequent changes of position from one side of the stage to the other with quite appropriate action something in the nature of sparring.... In military parlance, there was considerable skirmishing for so small a field of action, when, by one supremely misdirected aim, the door was struck instead of Laura, while the enemy hastily retreated through the door, bringing active hostilities to an abrupt close." Frances felt a "moral victory" had been won, because, when departure time came, "Laura was as ready to leave as the rest of the party, only that her rabbit-skin hat was somewhat demoralized though not so seriously as to be unfit for the journey."[33]

Laura had come out unscathed, but Henry Carrington was not to share her luck. On the trek to Fort McPherson, "on the sixth of February," recalled Margaret, "the colonel had the misfortune to be accidently shot while riding rapidly to close up the train, by the discharge of his revolver, which had been badly repaired at Caspar, the ball entering the scarpal space, grazing both femoral artery and sciatic nerve, following the bone around to the outside of the limb, where it lodged."[34] Surgeons, their fingers numb with cold, dare not try and remove the ball. It would have to remain intact till they reached Fort Laramie.

And "In the morning the gloom took on another and deeper shade," recalled Frances. Carrington's fine Kentucky thoroughbred, Grey Eagle, presented to him by the city of Indianapolis, was "loved by every soldier of the command." But "a sergeant unable to control his tears announced that he knew the Colonel never would ride again, for Grey Eagle, who had fed all night from the bark of fallen cottonwood, lay dead from horse-colic.'"[35]

Henry Carrington must have wondered what he had done to deserve such punishment by events beyond his control.

27

The Disaster Probed

On February 18, 1867, President Johnson appointed a commission comprising both civilians and military officers to investigate the events at Fort Philip Kearny.[1] Rejecting Sheridan's desire for wholesale retaliation, he wanted to make good his assurances of peace on the frontier. The commission was headed by General John B. Sanborn, a man well qualified for the task. A lawyer before the Civil War, he saw much action in various campaigns, rising to the rank of brigadier general. In 1865, along with George Bent and Kit Carson, he had negotiated peace treaties with southern plains tribes.

Sitting with him now were General Napoleon B. Buford, General Alfred Sully, Colonel Ely S. Parker, trader George P. Beauvais, and Judge John F. Kinney, the former post sutler at Fort Phil Kearny.[2] The "Sanborn Commission" headed west and found themselves staying in the same hotel at Council Bluffs as Frances Grummond. In company with brother William, she was headed east towards her parent's home in Tennessee. The commissioners "sought an interview, which I declined," Frances recalled. "It seemed a rude shock to my sensibilities that in the presence of strangers I should be called upon to revive the past scenes and give historic details as to events for their enlightenment. Their motive was a proper one and they were good men, but such an interview was ill-timed and they withdrew the request." William informed them of Frances' "own feelings, as the chief surviving sufferer," and "let them know that no censure could attach to the commanding officer."[3]

The Commission commenced operations on March 4, 1867, in Omaha, where they took testimony from Captain Bisbee and General Cooke. Bisbee spoke of "very poor" discipline and, among the officers, and "a general feeling of disgust" towards Carrington."[4] Cooke testified that, based on "official reports" regarding the December 6 skirmish, he was convinced of a "great want of discipline and management" on Carrington's part. "He was out on this occasion, and the circumstances, as detailed to me, indicated misconduct." Strangely though, Bisbee and Cooke did not get their stories synchronized on one point. Bisbee testified that on December 6 the troops "moved out in a body," but before that they had dashed "helter skelter over the stockade whenever an Indian appeared, without regard to orders." But Cooke shifted this conduct to December 21. Fetterman's detachment "was in fact, a disorderly mob, which went out in haste, at their will, and very irregularly."[5] Cooke's charges regarding Carrington's alleged "misconduct" on December 6, and the supposed "disorderly mob" of December 21 did not blend with the facts as told by others who were actually present.

Without hearing Carrington's side of the story, Commissioner Colonel Ely Parker wrote unofficially to Grant's trusted friend and confidante John Rawlins: "Carrington had no sort of discipline in his garrison, and although the Indians had been hostile ever since his arrival there, he took no unusual precautions against them.... Fetterman had disobeyed positive orders in going where he did, yet no one was sent out to ascertain why."[6] Carrington would state that Fetterman could well have been going north to cut off the Indians' retreat, not with the intention of crossing Lodge Trail Ridge.

The Sanborn Commission moved west, and between March 20 and March 27 took testimony from officers at Fort McPherson. Carrington, recuperating from his leg wound, had arrived there on March 2.[7] Well aware that his own reports of the December 6 skirmish and the Fetterman defeat had not been published, he felt he was being set up as a scapegoat by others who wished to clear their own names. But the commission gave him a chance to speak, and he provided much evidence including his suppressed reports. Lieutenant Wands corroborated his claim of orders given to George Grummond, and "Instead of proceeding to the wood train as ordered," Wands recalled, "the command crossed Piney Creek to its opposite bank, and proceeded up the long ridge."[8] Carrington testified that Fetterman "was led off to Peno Valley, perhaps after the party who had been seen at the Ferry crossing, and had attempted precisely the same decoy practiced December 6th 1866."[9] Sanborn and Buford took a supportive view of Carrington's position. Colonel Parker, however, still took a different stance. "In my opinion he is not fit to be in Indian country," he wrote to Rawlins on April 1. "He is no fighter and does not understand the Indian character, or their mode of warfare." And who better to know the "Indian character" than an Indian himself? Ely Parker was of the Seneca tribe. He would later become the first native American to hold the post of Commissioner of Indian Affairs, appointed by Grant following his election as President.[10] But Parker had been born and educated as an engineer in the state of New York, far from the wild tribes of the west, and he now served as Grant's military secretary. As Indians were not recognized as American citizens until 1924, Grant had pulled strings to have him commissioned as an officer during the Civil War. "No organized attempt was ever made to pursue the Indians & bring them to a fight or drive them out of the country," Parker wrote.[11] His conclusions were bound to be what his friend and benefactor, Ulysses S. Grant, wanted to hear. Only two days after Parker wrote these words, even Sherman took a less biased approach: "As to the Sioux of the North Platte it is idle of us to close our eyes to the fact that they are at war. They declare it openly and without reserve. It is hardly fair to attribute the utter annihilation of Colonel Fetterman's party to the misconduct or incapacity of Colonel Carrington."[12]

The small, post–Civil War army was thinly stretched. The former Confederate states had to be policed, and troops, especially cavalry, were in short supply. On April 7 General Pope wrote to Grant that he felt law and order in the South could be maintained, but there were "in the Northern parts of Alabama and Georgia bands of mounted robbers who depredate upon the people & especially upon the Negroes.—These bands are beyond the control of the Civil Authorities and Infantry forces are useless against them—For the same reason that Genl Thomas finds it necessary to keep four companies of Cavalry in Tennessee, I find some companies of Cavalry necessary in Northern Georgia & Alabama & I trust a few companies will be sent to me as soon as possible."[13] Three days later Grant wrote to Secretary of War Edwin Stanton requesting that all regiments west of the Mississippi, or destined to be sent there "be authorized to be filled to the Maximum number of men allowed by law." No troops from the East could be spared "for the defense of the settlements, and lines of travel, in the Indian country. From many quarters the cry is: more protection."[14]

The Sanborn Commission moved to Fort Laramie where they split into three groups, each conferring with Indian leaders from different tribes. But only "friendlies" attended, Red Cloud and other hostile chiefs ignoring their invitation. By early May Sanborn and Buford were prepared to submit a report, but the others were not. "Two of us, General

27. The Disaster Probed

Sanborn and myself," wrote Buford on June 6, "were of the opinion we should have submitted our joint report up to May the 10th, on which day the commission separated ... but could not induce Generals Sully and Parker, and Judge Kinney, to give the matter their attention." Sanborn and Buford traveled to Washington and submitted their own findings,[15] but Judge Kinney in particular stayed on the hunt. Carrington had rejected certain financial claims against the army, so the former post sutler was happy to interview Captain Powell at Fort Phil Kearny on July 24. Powell made outlandish allegations about Carrington's supposed incompetence while painting himself as the garrison's real commander.[16] Kinney dispatched Powell's self-serving testimony directly to the secretary of the interior.

While Sanborn was focused on the general causes of the events at Fort Phil Kearny, and how best to refine Indian policy to avoid a repetition, a second enquiry ordered by Grant was also under way. This was to probe what exactly happened, who did what, and who was to blame. General John Gibbon and Major Van Voast asked the questions, both enquiries lasting from March till the end of May. The inquisition over, Carrington requested a leave of absence for six months on medical grounds. This was approved by Augur and Sherman on June 8, and the Carrington family moved from the barren Nebraska frontier to the green grass and trees of Wallingford, Connecticut, the colonel's hometown. "At the outset so at the close of our trip across the plains and back again," recalled Margaret, "the same kind Providence guided and guarded our footsteps, and more than ever brought home to the soul the sweet assurance of his presence, Wherever we wander, Wherever we roam."[17]

If Carrington really thought kind Providence guided and guarded his footsteps, it is something of a wonder. But to give Providence a helping hand Carrington sought to have his official report on the Fetterman fight released. He felt, once read, those who derided him would understand what had transpired. Jim Bridger, upon hearing of Carrington's plight, felt compelled to join the fray. On May 4 he wrote an article for the *Army and Naval Journal*. "Now as to the Philip Kearny massacre, it has been said that the Indians did not approach with hostile intent, but that the commanding officer, mistaking their intentions, fired upon them, and thus brought on a fight. This is preposterous. Up to that time the Indians had been hanging around the fort every day, stealing stock on every opportunity, attacking the trains going to the woods, and even stealing up at night and shooting men connected with passing trains, while sitting around their camp fires, within one hundred yards of the fort. But a few days before the massacre a train going to the woods was attacked, and in defending it, Lieutenant Bingham, a promising young officer of the 2nd Cavalry, and one sergeant lost their lives. This may be a sign of friendship, but I don't think so." Bridger went on to say that the massacre had been planned by the Indians weeks in advance, and they had gathered 2,200 lodges on the Tongue River. The plan was to wipe out Fort Phil Kearny first, then C.F. Smith. "Friendly Indians report that they are being supplied with ammunition by half-breed traders connected with the Hudson's Bay Company." The Indians would be "willing to enter into any temporary treaty" to resupply themselves with powder "to carry on the war." Bridger wrote that he had "been in this country among these Indians for nearly forty-four years" and "the only way to settle the question is to send out sufficient numbers of troops to completely whip the hostile Sioux, Cheyennes and Arapahoes and make them sue for peace."[18]

At the end of June Sherman sent instructions to terminate the yet to be completed second enquiry. The officers concerned were needed for more pressing duties, he said, and "whatever seeming injustice may result by the present adjournment of the Court, can be rectified at some future more leisure period." He told them to forward what facts were known, and they could give a "qualified opinion" if they wished. Grant would study the material and "apply a remedy, if any is called for, in his own way."

In the meantime the Sanborn Commissioners could not agree on a joint resolution, and each submitted his own report. The conclusions of Generals Sanborn and Buford were published during July in Senate Document 13. Sanborn addressed the Fetterman debacle saying that the Montana road was supposed to have been opened "by compact or treaty" and "not by conquest." The troops furnished Carrington were for building and garrisoning the new posts, not to "carry on systematic and aggressive war against a most powerful tribe of Indians, fighting to maintain possession and control of their own country." Carrington's requests for adequate reinforcements were never fulfilled, and there was never enough ammunition, despite requests, for recruits to have target practice. Sanborn concluded. "The result of all this was that the troops were in no condition to fight successful battles with Indians or other foes, and this from no fault of Colonel Carrington." When Indians attacked the wood train on December 21, Fetterman's command formed "in good order" and he received orders: "Support the wood train, relieve it, and report to me. Do not engage or pursue Indians at its expense; under no circumstances pursue over Lodge Trail Ridge." Fetterman "moved out rapidly to the right of the wood road, for the purpose no doubt of cutting off the retreat of the Indians then attacking the train." He pursued Indians "flitting about him," halted on the crest, then "without regard to orders" led the command over Lodge Trail Ridge. Sanborn described events immediately following, and the difficulty, "in a nutshell," he concluded, was that Carrington "had been furnished no more troops or supplies for this state of war than had been provided and furnished him for a state of profound peace." At Fort Laramie, meanwhile, "where all was peace" 12 companies were stationed "while in regions where all was war, as at Fort Phil Kearney, there were only five companies allowed."[19]

Such a report must have delighted the Carrington ranks—but not Ulysses S. Grant. Senate Document 13 also contained anti–Carrington testimony from the original pamphlet, and there had been, in fact, six companies at Fort Phil Kearny at the time of the Fetterman defeat, not five. As regards the 12 companies at Laramie, according to Lieutenant David Gordon, the garrison at Fort Laramie, "was composed of four troops of cavalry and six companies of the Eighteenth Infantry," a total of ten.[20]

On July 19, 1867, a new post was established on a plateau near Bridger's Ferry on the North Platte River.[21] Only heroes have forts named after them, not those who disobey orders. Carrington, back in Connecticut, was galled when "the post to which my Head Quarters are assigned is named in honor of Fetterman, who, though a gentleman, every inch of him, was over-ruled by others, and in spite of me, caused the Massacre."

But Carrington was to blame, Grant decided. On September 10 he recommended "that the Judge Advocate General be directed to prepare charges against Col. H. B. Carrington." Two years earlier Judge Advocate General Joseph Holt had led the prosecution against the Lincoln assassination conspirators, and four people were hanged, including Mary Surratt, the first woman executed in American legal history. Holt received much criticism for his handling of the case, and in reply issued a pamphlet titled *Vindication of Judge Advocate General Holt From the Foul Slanders of Traitors, Confessed Perjurers and Suborners, Acting in the Interest of Jefferson Davis*. Perhaps Holt identified with Henry Carrington's plight. Grant was miffed when Holt replied that there was no basis for the proposed charges; no action would be taken.[22]

Carrington read the damaging testimony given to Judge Kinney by Captain Powell. This alleged, among numerous other things, "chaotic" discipline among the enlisted men, theft of provisions from the commissary, horse racing, card playing and men getting drunk.[23]

On November 5, 1867, Carrington wrote to O.H. Browning, Secretary of the Interior, "I am mortified that I have to meet such testimony, and more, for the Army, where I have some pride, than for myself." He hotly refuted Powell's charges on all fronts. Discipline was good, he wrote, and there had only been one robbery when the sutler's door was left open, and there was a guard on the Commissary with orders "to shoot whoever attempted to enter." Only a few "cans of blackberries and some syrup" had ever been stolen, thefts "small and rare." One horse race had taken place with betting, which was promptly banned. Drunkenness was rare as there was "almost no liquor of any kind obtainable" and even two officers had been placed under arrest "for undue use of stimulants."[24]

Powell claimed that "Col. Carrington told me he thought I had better take charge of the whole thing or something to that effect. I immediately assumed the duties of executive Officer of the Post, and had all work stopped and prepared the men for action."[25] Carrington hotly refuted this, writing that he only ordered Powell "to organize all unarmed men into permanent gun squads, and take charge of them to divide labor." Powell also claimed to have "thrown a shell beyond Col. Fetterman on the road" to scatter Indians during his march from the fort. Carrington insisted the only shells thrown by Powell were some days later during training, and on December 21, *"he did nothing of the kind."*[26]

Carrington visited Edwin Stanton, saying he wanted his reports published, only to be referred to General Grant. "When I made my statement and he answered that I was making a very grave charge against a brother officer, I stated that 'I was risking my commission as Colonel in the Army and would prefer charges if he so wished'; but on the advice of General Sherman it was allowed to drop as unworthy of notice."[27] What Carrington did not know was that a nomination for Powell to brevet lieutenant colonel was before the Senate. The captain had recently led a heroic defense against Red Cloud's warriors at what became known as the Wagon Box Fight. Carrington departed Grant's office unsatisfied. There was no charge of perjury made, and his reports remained buried. Grant's bid for the presidency was on the horizon. Best to let sleeping dogs lie.

But Margaret Carrington decided to prod the sleeping dog with words of her own. William Sherman had suggested that ladies keep a journal of their "pleasant garrison life" on the Bozeman Trail and, using her notes as a basis, she put pen to paper. *Absaraka, Home of the Crows: Being the Experience of an Officer's Wife on the Plains*, published by J. B. Lippincott of Philadelphia, appeared in 1868. While pointing out Fetterman's gentlemanly qualities, she emphasized his disobedience on December 21. Margaret dedicated her book to General Sherman "whose suggestions at Fort Kearney, in the spring of 1866, were adopted, in preserving a daily record of the events of a peculiarly eventful journey, and whose vigorous policy is as promising of the final settlement of Indian problems and the quick completion of the Union Pacific Railroad as his 'March to the Sea' was signal in crushing the last hope of armed rebellion."[28] Hopefully the "vigorous policy" referred to had softened somewhat from the "extermination" of Sioux "men, women and children."

After one year's leave of absence Henry Carrington resumed command of the 18th at Fort Sedgwick, Nebraska. He finalized his paperwork, and on April 9, 1869, turned over command to Major Van Voast.[29]

What thoughts went through Carrington's mind as he headed back east for a final time, his military career at an end? By that time the Bozeman Trail forts had gone up in flames. Far from being exterminated, the Lakota, Cheyenne and Arapahoe had taken back their land.

28

Red Cloud's Resolve

While Carrington faced trials and other diffculties back east, Colonel Wessell's garrison at Fort Phil Kearny faced problems of its own. The reinforced post now had 18 officers, 657 men and additional stock to feed.¹ The severe winter the Carringtons had escaped continued unabated, temperatures plunging to 40 degrees below zero. "Men could not remain on guard but for a few minutes at a time for fear of being frozen," recalled Fessenden. "Think of men on a platform four feet above the ground and only six feet long—which is where the sentries were stationed—and this space was all the room they had in which to exercise enough to keep themselves from freezing ... horses became so nearly starved that we had to stretch a chain, in place of rope, from post to post, and tie the animals so far apart that they could not reach each other, for they would gnaw the hair from each other's manes and tails.... It was pitiful to witness the suffering of these poor patient animals."²

"Consequently," recalled Lieutenant David Gordon, "we were obliged to turn the animals out and let them forage for themselves or starve. But after consideration the commanding officer thought it best to send Capt. James T. Peale, commanding troop L, Second Cavalry, back to Laramie with the cavalry horses. He made the march all right, but reached there without the animals, 150 in number. As evidence of the march their carcasses could be seen many years afterwards strewn along the road."³ But it was not only the animals who suffered. "Rations for the men were now very scarce," recalled Fessenden, "and we were finally reduced to nothing but a little hardtack and condemned sow-belly ... scurvy broke out, and nearly every man had it, which placed us in sore straits, and made our sufferings doubly hard to bear.... Sick men, poor food, shortage of fuel, zero weather and surrounded by thousands of bloodthirsty savages, eager to lift our scalps!"⁴

Colonel Wessells "had nineteen sentries posted around the stockade every day and night," recalled Private Sam Gibson, "there being three reliefs of the guard. Fifty-nine men mounted guard every day, besides the officer of the day and four non-commissioned officers. This large detail of men for guard duty worked great hardship for us, for in addition, we had to saw wood for our stoves in quarters. Then, many of our comrades were sick with scurvy, and the hospital was filled with invalids, many of whom died."⁵

And what about that isolated post on the Big Horn River 65 miles to the north? Wessells had no idea if the two companies stationed at Fort C.F. Smith were dead or alive. "I am of the opinion," recalled Murphy, "that the officers thought that the men were all killed at the time of the massacre and no one was left."⁶ During January 5 military parties set out from Fort Phil Kearny in an attempt to make contact, only to turn back due to frigid weather conditions or encounters with Indians. Wessells attempted to hire civilians to make the trek, but none would do it for less than $1,000, a fee beyond his purse.

In early February, however, Sergeants George Grant and Joseph Graham volunteered to try their luck. They set out at dawn on February 4. "They went as far as the pinery on mules," recalled Fessenden, "accompanied by two men who were to bring back the mules. They carried rifles and well-filled haversacks, of such provisions as we had, and started from the pinery on foot on that perilous journey over an utterly strange country."[7] The two sergeants trudged north on snow shoes, rejoining the main trail the following day. In order to find the best footing, they were forced to leave the trail on several occasions, but trudged into Fort C.F. Smith at 4 o'clock on the afternoon of February 7.[8] Not only was the post intact, but the troops had fared better than their comrades to the south. While surviving mostly on corn, scurvy had been kept at bay with a supply of cabbage and potatoes supplied from the town of Bozeman the preceding fall.

The two sergeants rested before setting out for Fort Phil Kearny on the evening of February 7. They rode horses for the return trip and led two pack mules carrying mail and provisions. Guiding them was the mixed-blood scout Mitch Bouyer, who would lose his life at the Little Bighorn in 1876.[9] Three days later they were discovered and pursued by hostiles into the Big Horn Mountains. The mules were abandoned, and Grant fell behind as his horse tired. He abandoned the animal and ran for a stand of timber, but fell through a snowdrift onto the ledge of a deep ravine. An Indian came across him but, startled, dropped his gun and fell into the ravine. Then another warrior appeared. Grant shot and killed him before throwing his body over the ledge.[10] As night came on a fog descended, and the Indians gave up the chase. Grant made his way back to lower ground and plodded on towards the fort. Bouyer and Graham had also abandoned their mounts, their provisions and blankets lost. "They managed to kill one rabbit," recalled Fessenden, "and this they ate raw. Their shoes gave out and they were obliged to take their coats and wrap them around their feet."[11] On the evening of February 3, Bouyer and Graham, frozen and starving, staggered into Fort Phil Kearny, then Grant arrived about an hour later, in even worse condition.[12] Grant collapsed with pneumonia and spent some time recuperating in the post hospital. His encounter with the warriors made him the hero of the day, and on May 6, 1871, he was awarded the Medal of Honor for "bravery, energy, and perseverance, involving much suffering and privation through attacks by hostile Indians, deep snows, etc., while voluntarily carrying dispatches."[13]

Even with low morale and scarce rations, work on the construction of Fort Phil Kearny continued. By late February the fifth and sixth barracks had been completed, and two new quartermaster buildings were in service. Despite cold weather, however, the Indians did not only spend all their time by warm fires in cozy tepees. On February 27, three men from Fort Reno's garrison were killed during a hunting foray. At Fort Phil Kearny Wessells and his officers, including Powell and Ten Eyck, reorganized work parties, noted the precise time spent on daily routines, and scheduled regular inspections. Discipline was enforced with court martials, and intensive training, including target practice, commenced during March.[14] With no vegetables on hand, "in the spring when the grass came up there were lots of wild onions," recalled Murphy, "and the scurvy gang was ordered to eat them."[15]

Sergeant Fessenden's enlistment was up, and on April 9 he moved out with his wife and child, along with about a dozen others in a small wagon train. "As much as I wanted to get back to civilization among friends, and away from such a hard life," he recalled, "I disliked to part with the many friends I had made at Fort Phil Kearny."[16]

On April 2, mail carrier Montgomery Van Valsah was killed with four other civilians between Bridger's Ferry and Fort Reno. The Indians even struck as far south as the Platte. Major Van Voast, riding as part of the Fetterman Enquiry, got a first-hand taste of Carrington's problems on April 20 when his small escort beat off an attack. On the same day the man who could be said to have started the war, John Bozeman, met his end, far to the north. Bozeman's business partner, Thomas Cover, arrived with a shoulder wound at a ranch saying they had been attacked by Blackfeet Indians near the Yellowstone River, and Bozeman had been killed. The man who had made the historic cattle drive, Nelson Story, sent out Spanish Joe, his best tracker, to the murder site. He returned and said he saw Bozeman's body, but it was unscalped. There was no sign of Indian tracks, only those of Cover, and a Henry repeater had not been stolen. It is possible that Bozeman's attraction to Cover's wife was behind the murder, but this was never proven, a mystery that remains unsolved to the present day.[17]

One week later skirmishes near Fort Reno saw one soldier killed, and on May 26 hostiles swooped outside Fort Phil Kearny for the first time since the Fetterman defeat. Twenty-four head of government stock were lost. The following month "the school of the soldier" and the "school of the company" were instituted by Wessells as daily routines. Having more troops in a completed fort gave him opportunities for training not enjoyed by the embattled Henry Carrington the year before, and welcome supply train arrived from the south with food for both men and animals.

Summer brought not only warm weather to Fort Phil Kearny, but occasional visits by warriors and families of the Crow tribe. They enjoyed pitching their tepees in their old hunting grounds. Perhaps the enlarged garrison gave them a feeling of security from attack by their old enemies, the Lakota. But during May, 25 ponies and two cavalry horses were driven off. And not only stock disappeared. Two soldiers felt an Indian's life must be better than that of an enlisted man in the U.S. Army. "Painted and dressed in Indian costume," they deserted with a party of Crow on May 9. One, Private Bernard Bravo of the 27th Infantry, never returned to white society, and acted as an interpreter for Lieutenant James Bradley during the Sioux war a decade later.[18]

On May 30 one soldier guarding stock outside Fort Phil Kearny was killed, but the Indians failed to cause a stampede, and during June three Indian raids were beaten off with no loss of life or stock. The training was beginning to pay off, but one man with a hunting party was killed on June 11.

Commissioner Judge Kinney arrived. The former post sutler had sent word that he wished to confer with any friendly Indians who cared to visit the fort. On June 22, 118 Crow and seven Nez Perce lodges sprang up outside the walls. But the eagle-eyed Lakota watched from the hills, and ran off another 25 horses from the village herd. The Crow promptly rode in pursuit, and cavalry rode out in support while an infantry detachment deployed to protect the Crow village. The Crow caught up with the war party and three Lakota warriors were killed in the following skirmish. The others made their escape, but most stolen ponies were recaptured and driven back to the Crow village.[19]

"There were six 6-mule Government teams that arrived with goods for the Indians," recalled Private Murphy. "The goods consisted of beads, calico, blankets, and all kinds of trinkets that an Indian would like…. We thought the goods were to be given to the Indians, but judging from what I saw, the Indians paid several times the value of what they got. For a folding pocket glass about three inches across, a beaver skin or two buckskins was the price…. The six 6-mule teams went back loaded with furs." Murphy observed an example of how the Crow administered justice within the tribe. "They tied an Indian to a tree and the squaws and children with switches, sticks, and stones punished him severely. I only saw the last part of it. The Indian broke loose and the squaws and children scattered. After knocking over some of the squaws he lit out over the bluffs with very little, if any, clothing." "He heap bad Injun," Murphy was told. "He never come back." On another occasion a chief "hit the troublesome Indian on the head with his tomahawk and he was a good Indian, maybe, ever after. The Indians dragged him off to their camp."[20]

On July 3, 1867, Swiss-born Colonel John Eugene Smith arrived. The wagons with him carried not only food and grain, but 700 Springfield breechloaders and 100,000 metallic cartridges to suit. At last the old muzzleloaders could be discarded, and the troops looked forward to trying their new weapons on the wily foe. July 4 saw an Independence Day artillery salvo fired at noon, and Smith assumed command from Henry Wessells the following day.[21]

By July the Bozeman Trail was protected by over 900 soldiers of the 18th and 27th Infantry, and the 2nd Cavalry, and construction of Fort Fetterman near Bridger's Ferry was commenced on July 19. But the undeterred Indians continued their hit-and-run tactics, and the road remained closed to civilian traffic. The warring tribes held their annual Sun Dance, and gathered on the Little Bighorn River where Red Cloud and the other chiefs formulated plans for strikes on Forts Phil Kearny and C. F. Smith.[22] In July Fort C.F. Smith was garrisoned by 350 soldiers under Lieutenant Colonel Luther Bradley, while Fort Phil Kearny had only 269 soldiers on hand.[23] The Indian leaders were unable to agree on which post to hit first, and about 700 warriors, mainly Cheyenne and Arapahoe, rode for Fort C.F. Smith while about 1,000 Lakota and Cheyenne made tracks for Fort Phil Kearny.

A few miles to the northeast of Fort C.F. Smith a hay-mowing camp had been established. It was protected by a 100-by 60-foot breastwork of logs and willow boughs. Inside were tents, wagon boxes and a tethering line for livestock. About 40 feet away, the waters of War Man Creek snaked their way across the grassy plateau.

Those Indians headed for Fort C.F. Smith had only 20 miles to traverse from their camp on the Little Bighorn, and arrived early on August 1. Nine civilians were at work with the mowing machines, protected by a detail of 19 soldiers under Lieutenant Sigismund Sternberg, a veteran of the Prussian and Union Armies. Shots were heard some distance from the camp, and the hay cutters appeared hotly pursued by hostiles. The whooping Indians made a few dashes at the breastwork in an apparent attempt to decoy the troops out, but Sternberg ordered his men to stay put. The Indians withdrew, and Sternberg had his men prepare for defense. It was not long till the Indians reappeared from the northeast and the men took cover, their rifles at the ready. Perhaps inspired by paintings of heroes exposing themselves at the head of their troops, Sternberg, revolver in hand, remained facing the enemy in a standing position. Dust flew as the Indians charged only to be met with a volley from Springfield breechloaders, Henry and Spencer repeaters. The warriors split, galloping down either side of the corral, unleashing a hail of arrows and musket fire as they passed. They rode off out of range, and as the smoke cleared Sternberg was found fallen with a bullet through his head. A quick look around revealed that Private Navin had also been killed, and Sergeant Norton wounded. Command now fell to civilian Don Colvin, an ex-army captain, whose weapon of choice was the Henry repeater.

Surprised by the rapid fire of the modern weapons, the Indians decided to try different tactics, burning the troops out. Dried hay stacks near the corral were put to the torch, and the "fire came on in rolling billows," recalled Private Lockhart, "like the waves of the ocean, the Indians whooping behind. When it arrived within twenty feet of the barricade, it stopped, as though arrested by supernatural power. The flames rose to a perpendicular of at least forty feet, made by one or two undulating movements, and were extinguished with a spanking slap, like the flapping sound of a heavy canvas in a hard gale; the wind, the succeeding instant, carried the smoke ... into the faces of the attacking Indians, who improved the opportunity under cover of it, to carry away their dead and wounded."[24] Squaws watched from hilltops as their men renewed the attack. Bullets and arrows flew, and Sergeant Norton received a second wound, while civilian J. G. Hollister received a mortal wound in the chest. Repulsed again, the Indians settled back for long-range sniping, but then withdrew to reassess the situation. Things were not going to plan; these whites had firepower beyond their small number.

A hot sun beat down and the corral's water supply was replenished from War Man Creek, then the Indians opened fire once more. One warrior, possibly a chief, rode out close to the barricade and was shot from his horse. He fell into the creek where, badly wounded, he struggled and drowned. During the afternoon the warriors charged twice again, and rode back and forth amidst a cloud of gunsmoke along the corral's west barricade. George Duncan hit one warrior, possibly a medicine man, who was picked up by several braves and carried from the field as the others fell back. The Indians' final assault was directed against the south breastwork, this time on foot. The warriors approached the creek under a cover of willows, but were spotted as they waded across. Colvin ordered the defenders to hold their fire till the Indians were in the open, then fired the first shot. A leading warrior fell, probably a chief, the other rifles cracked, and the braves scrambled back through the willows as more were cut down.

The whites were holding their ground, but for how long? Why had no help come from the fort? Although out of sight, the gunfire must have been heard. Late in the day Private Charles Bradley volunteered to ride for help while there was still a horse alive. Most of the livestock had been killed or wounded by arrows and musket fire. The lone soldier galloped out and hostiles gave chase, but he made it safely to the fort.

A detachment of 20 men had been belatedly dispatched under Lieutenant Shurly, only to be stalled by an overwhelming Indian party. Colonel Bradley sent Captain Burrowes to support Shurly with Company G, and reinforced them with Company H and a mountain howitzer. To the relief of the besieged, the column finally arrived during the late afternoon. As the dead and wounded were lifted into wagons, the Indians continued to skirmish from a distance, but a case shot from the howitzer saw them scatter. As the troops moved back towards the fort the Indians closed in again, but another shell saw the column safely withdraw behind the fort's sheltering walls. The whites had lost three killed and two wounded, and the Indian casualties are not known, all but one dead warrior having been carried away. His severed and scalped head was left on a pole in the corral as a warning, proving that the whites could be just as savage as the Indians themselves.[25]

It transpired that Lieutenant Palmer had seen the fight from a distance at about 1 o'clock. Once informed, Colonel Bradley, only concerned for the safety of the fort, had initially refused permission for relief to be sent out, and shut the gates. This caused hostility among the troops, many feeling felt this a cowardly act. Under pressure, he finally gave permission for Shurly's advance.

Bradley's official report read: "Our men fought from behind a light stockade and the Indians charged it several times both mounted and on foot, gaining a position 20 paces of it in considerable numbers while others were circling around it a little distance. They showed a good deal of pluck and were determined to take the stockade. Nothing but the coolness of our men in reserving their fire for close shots saved them. The hay grounds are 2½ miles from the fort and entirely hidden from view by high bluffs. I did not know of the fight until it had been going on for some hours. Very little firing was heard and not a large body of Indians were seen, though a few rode near the fort and harassed the timber train which was over in an opposite direction. Wishing to send out the train of hay wagons in the afternoon I directed 20 mounted men under Mr. Shurly to go in advance and reconnoiter. They intercepted a large number of Indians and were obliged to fall back. I then sent Major Burrowes with companies G and H and a howitzer when the Indians were driven back and the party at the stockade relieved. Maj. Burrowes put a couple of Case shots into their mounted parties and scattered them. He thinks that but for the howitzer he would have had all the fighting he wanted before he got back, and that the Indians had about 800 warriors within reach when he got to the stockade.... The Indians in this attack had but one rifle to two bows, but they used the arrow with great effect."

Captain Burrowes' report stated that he was sent out to relieve Lieutenant Shurly "who was in charge of twenty mounted infantry and sharply engaged with Indians whilst reconnoitering the ground between the garrison and the hayfield." Colonel Bradley, however, made no mention of Private Charles Bradley's ride to get help late in the day, and his report is vague on the timing of events.[26]

29

The Wagon Box Fight

Knowing nothing of the Hayfield Fight the day before, the garrison at Fort Phil Kearny went about their routine duties as a hot summer sun rose on August 2. Henry Carrington's nemesis, Captain James Powell, had moved out two days before with Company C of the 27th Infantry to relieve troops guarding the wood cutting party about five miles to the west. Powell's command consisted of 52 men, including his second-in-command, Lieutenant John Jennes.

As at Fort C.F. Smith, a corral had been established to protect the woodcutters and escort soldiers. But this was of different construction, being oval shaped and consisting of 14 wagon boxes removed from the chassis and wheels. A man could fit through the space between the corralled wagons boxes, but they were narrow enough to avoid the escape of stock contained during the night. Protective canvas canopies were left on two boxes containing provisions, and tents and cooking facilities were placed outside the enclosure.[1]

Upon Powell's arrival, he allocated 14 men to escort the wood train and another 13 to guard the woodcutting camp about one mile to the southwest. All seemed serene, but the following night Private McDonough's pet dog, Jess, seemed unsettled. "Although we could not see or hear anything suspicious," recalled Private Sam Gibson, "the animal would run furiously down the hill toward the Big Piney valley every few minutes, barking and snapping furiously."[2]

At about 7 a.m. the following morning the crack of gunfire echoed across the plain. The soldiers looked around to see and a handful of men running for their lives towards the corral with mounted warriors in close pursuit. Sergeant Max Littman ran out and opened fire with his Springfield breechloader. Some of the Indians "wore gorgeous warbonnets; others had a single feather in their scalp-locks," recalled Gibson. "Their bodies were painted white, green and yellow, which made them look hideous in the extreme." Three soldiers had already been killed when an outlying picket post and a woodcutters' camp had been attacked. Others had fled for safety into the woods. "Captain Powell was down at the creek, taking a bath," recalled Private Frederick Claus. "He came toward the corral on the run, shouting, 'Boys, the Indians are here! It will be a hard day for you all. You know what your orders are!'"[3]

The Indians rode off, but hundreds could be seen gathering in the distance. Ammunition was distributed around the corral as the soldiers prepared their defense. "To my dying day I will never forget the fierce 'do-or-die' look on Captain Powell's face," recalled Gibson. Powell ordered the four civilians and 27 soldiers present to prepare for action.[4] The Indians charged and he shouted, "Men here they come! Take your places and shoot to kill!" The Indians came within range to be met with a blaze of rifle fire. "They were riding madly about," recalled Gibson, "and shooting at us with guns, bows and arrows, first on one side then on the other of the corral. Then they would circle, and each time come in closer, uttering the most piercing and unearthly war cries. Some of the more venturesome would ride in close and throw spears at us. Others would brandish their war-clubs and tomahawks at us, and others, still more daring, would ride within a hundred yards, then suddenly drop off the side of their ponies, and we could see an arm or leg sticking above the pony's back, and 'whizz' would come the arrows! They paid dearly for their daring, for we had a steady rest for our rifles, the Indians were all within easy point blank range, and we simply mowed them down by scores. The tops of the wagon beds were literally ripped and torn to slivers by their bullets." The warriors had expected to be met by muzzleloaders, but "we simply snapped open the breech-blocks of our new rifles to eject the empty shell and slapped in a fresh ones."

"We thought it was some new medicine of great power that they had," recalled Lakota warrior Fire Thunder, "for they shot so fast that it was like tearing a blanket."[5]

The Indians retrieved their casualties whenever possible. "While recovering their injured we witnessed the most magnificent display of horsemanship imaginable," recalled Gibson. "Two mounted Indians would ride like the wind among the dead and wounded, and seeing an arm or leg thrust upward, would ride one on each side of the wounded savage, reach over and pick him up on the run, and carry him to a place of safety. This was done many times, and we could not help but admire their courage and daring."

"I was surrounded by about eight hundred (800) mounted Indians," Powell reported, "but owing to the very effective fire of my small party they were driven back with considerable loss. Finding they could not enter the corral they retired to a hill about six hundred (600) yards distant and there stripped for more determined fighting." The Indians shed not only superfluous clothing, but their ponies as well. According to Fire Thunder, "Our ponies were afraid of the ring of the guns the Wasichus made, and would not go over … we left out horses in the gulch and charged on foot."

One advantage of fighting on foot, however, was a steadier aim. Lieutenant Jennes "had not been in the country very long," recalled Frederick Claus, "and had no experience in fighting Indians. He was instructed also to get into one of the wagon boxes where he would be sheltered from the fire of the Indians, but he replied he knew how to fight redskins as well as anyone." "Boys, look out!" he yelled, recalled Sergeant Littman, "'There are a good many Indians here, but—' The sentence was never finished. A bullet struck him in the head, killing him instantly. I was just at his left, kneeling to fire from behind my salt barrel when he received the fatal shot."[6]

The Indians were driven back, but then flaming arrows arched through the sky. They ignited "scattered bits of hay and dry manure," recalled Littman. "This terrible stench and smoke nearly strangled us at times." The intense summer heat beat down, and the water barrel was virtually dry, having been riddled by bullets. Sam Gibson and Private Grady set out from the corral, crawling close to the ground. They retrieved two water kettles from beneath a wagon some distance away. Despite sniper fire, they made it back alive, but one kettle was punctured twice by flying bullets.

The warriors, "continued to charge us on foot for three consecutive hours," Powell reported, "but were each time repulsed." The attacks were somewhat piecemeal, never the entire force at once. "The Indians were very brave in this fight," Littman remembered, "but seemed to lack good judgment in their attacks." The Indians dashed towards the corral, but fell "like green grass withering in a fire," recalled Fire Thunder. Privates Doyle and Haggerty, however, were killed, and Privates Deming and Somers wounded. "No person inside the corral was killed by an arrow. It was always a bullet that did the deadly work," recalled Littman.

The fight continued on and off through a stifling haze of burning hay, grass, manure and gunsmoke. The blazing sun beat down mercilessly on white and Indian alike. Finally, during early afternoon, "Hark! Did you hear that," one sweating soldier cried out. "We distinctly heard the boom of a big gun to the east of us," recalled Gibson. "It was indeed heavenly music to all of us. It was the sorely needed relief from Fort Phil Kearny." Major Benjamin Smith had marched with over 100 men and a howitzer to the rescue, despite "several hundred" Indians having been seen around the fort.[7] "We threw our caps in the air," recalled Gibson. "We hugged each other in the ecstasy of our joy." The Indians left the field taking most dead and wounded with them. Once they were well clear, 14 soldiers and civilians emerged from sheltering woods to join their comrades in the corral. Powell estimated the Indians loss at 60 killed and 120 wounded, although some others felt this well short of the mark.[8] "I do not know how many of our people were killed," Fire Thunder recalled, "but there were very many. It was bad."[9]

The dead and wounded soldiers were loaded onto wagons, and the column wound its way back to Fort Phil Kearny, the sheltering stockade a welcome sight. "As we approached the commanding officer's quarters," recalled Gibson, "he stepped from the house and halted us." Colonel Smith complimented the men for their splendid victory, and said "he would recommend every one of us for a medal of honor. The recommendation was made, but for some reason none of us ever received the medal."[10]

The Hayfield and Wagon Box victories were welcome news to the military high command, and bolstered the morale of the troops. The Indian warrior was not invincible after all. But the Wagon Box Fight did nothing for Henry Carrington's assertion that James Powell committed perjury. Unlike Carrington, Powell was a hero now, and the army liked those who won.

The Bozeman Trail, however, remained closed to civilian traffic, and the Indians remained a major threat. The forts were now defending nothing but their own existence, and the white mans' determination to prevail, come what may. Word came that the chiefs were prepared to smoke the Peace Pipe, but only if the forts were abandoned, including Fort Reno, a post they had originally been prepared to tolerate. Red Cloud continued his harassing tactics, but avoided a repetition of the Hayfield and Wagon Box fights. "Sioux, Cheyennes and Arrapahoes in great numbers continued around the fort," recalled Lieutenant George Belden, "causing us much uneasiness as we knew, from their sullen deportment, that they were bent on mischief." Belden rode across the ground where Fetterman had fallen: "The ground was still covered with the debris of the fight. Skeletons of horses and mules, human bones, pieces of skulls, knapsacks, torn uniforms, and broken guns lay scattered over the ground for a mile or more.... The stones and rocks were still stained with blood and covered with hair where the Indians had beat out the brains of the white soldiers with their war clubs." He picked up an old flintlock musket, manufactured in London during 1777. "The history of that gun would certainly be curious could it be written how many battles and skirmishes had it been in," recalled Belden. "Where had it traveled, and how many wild animals, Indians, and white men had it slain?"

At the end of October, "the Indians fired the grass all around the post, and for a time we thought we should be burnt up. The slopes of the hills. as far as the eye could reach, were covered with lines of fire, and tall sheets of flame leaped up from the valley or ran crackling through the timber … and then, having consumed all the grass and dry trees, went out, doing us no harm, owing to the streams around the fort, which completely checked the advance of the destroying element."

On the evening of November 5 a runner came into the fort with news that "a severe battle had been fought," recalled Belden. Lieutenant Shurly and others had been wounded during an attack by 200 Indians. Next morning a relief force found "wagons overturned, and sacks of flour, sugar, rice, and bacon scattered over the ground. Boxes of crackers, packages of stationery, pipes, tobacco, books, belts, scabbards, swords, and broken guns lay everywhere. A dead horse, and a mule with a saddle yet on, lay on the road, and further out on the plain were a dozen dead ponies, where the Indians had charged.... One corporal had his thigh broken, and another his hand shattered, rendering amputation necessary in both cases: A soldier was shot through the lungs, another in the knee, another in the shoulder, and still another in the arm. A citizen, who had acted as postilion to a mounted howitzer, received a ball in the thigh. Lieutenant Shurly's wound was very severe and painful, the ball having passed through the instep and flattened against the sole of the boot. Shurly said the principal object of attack by the Indians was the howitzer, they having killed or wounded every man around it in their efforts to capture it. They no doubt wished to secure the piece, so as to shell and annoy the forts with it."[11]

While conflict persisted along the Bozeman Trail, the iron horse pushed westward. The railways brought travelers, settlements and soldiers, all of which would ultimately doom the Indians' way of life. But, ironically, the Union Pacific Railroad that laid track towards Salt Lake City would help Red Cloud win his war some distance to the north. The towns of Cheyenne, Laramie City, Rock River, Medicine Bow, Benton, and Rawlins became, in turn, the railway terminus where road travel began. This made for easier access to the Montana goldfields, so the Bozeman Trail was rapidly becoming obsolete.[12]

President Andrew Johnson wanted peace, and had no desire to continue an expensive and needless war against the Lakota, Cheyenne and Arapahoe. The troops were needed elsewhere, especially protecting the railroad workers from attacks by hostiles further to the south. On March 2, 1868, General Grant ordered that the forts be abandoned once the winter snows had melted, and the roads dried out.[13] Another meeting with Indian leaders at Fort Laramie was arranged for April, and the commissioners arrived with a draft proposal which created the Great Sioux Reservation. This included most of South Dakota west of the Missouri River. Although not part of the reservation proper, the Powder River country was included as "unceded Indian territory" upon which the Indians could hunt. General Sherman and other military minds were displeased with this proposal. To abandon the forts was defeat, they said, and would encourage other tribes to resist.

On April 29 influential peace chief Spotted Tail signed. He believed fighting the white tide was futile. Red Cloud would ultimately agree, but for now, "when we see the soldiers moving away and the forts abandoned," he said, "then I will come down and talk." More chiefs signed during May, and others signed at Fort Rice on July 2. The commissioners now had nearly 200 signatories, but the vital signature of Red Cloud remained on the missing list.

In early August, the Stars and Stripes above the Bozeman Trail forts were lowered for the last time. At Fort Phil Kearny a "monument to the memory of the soldiers killed by Indians" was left in the post cemetery at the base of Pilot Hill.[14] No sooner had the troops marched south than the victorious Indians rode in. Carrington's carefully crafted stockade, blockhouses, barracks, magazine and other structures went up in flames, as had those at Fort William Henry during the same month in 1757. Both posts had survived a scant two years.

But even with the Bozeman Trail forts in ashes, Red Cloud was in no hurry to sign. Perhaps the bluecoats would return with their steam sawmills and the whole saga start over again? It was not until November 6 that Red Cloud put his name to the Fort Laramie Treaty of 1868.

This document, however, was riddled with double speak. It gave the Indians what they wanted on one page, while negating it on another. Whites were not allowed to enter Indian lands, it said, but on the other hand could build roads and forts.[15] With no legal representation, the chiefs really had little idea of what they had signed. The year 1874 would see the War Department order troops under George Custer into the Reservation. Supposedly to find the sight for a fort in the Black Hills, the expedition included newspaper men who spread stories of abundant gold. This would cause the Sioux War of 1876–77, and a far bigger Indian victory than the Fetterman defeat. The Indians won the Battle of the Little Bighorn, but lost the war. Along with that they lost the Powder River country and the Black Hills, the subject of legal disputes to the present day.

30

Finale

One month following her arrival home in Tennessee, Frances Grummond had given birth to a baby boy, William Wands Grummond.[1] He was named for the comfort and friendship given her by the Wands family during her trials at Fort Phil Kearny and the journey home. When Frances applied for her husband's military pension, however, she learned that a claim had already been lodged by Delia, Grummond's former wife. Frances' brother helped sort out the ensuing legal affairs, and she would ultimately receive the pension, having been Grummond's wife at the time of his death.[2]

Following his return from active duty at Fort Sedgwick in April of 1869, Henry Carrington sought a pensioned medical discharge from the army, which was granted the following year. He moved to Crawfordsville, Indiana to take up the position of professor of military science at Wabash College. A second edition of Margaret Carrington's book was published during 1870, one of seven editions to appear over the years, but on May 11, just one day after her 39th birthday, she died of tuberculosis.

Frances Grummond, when visiting her sister in Cincinnati, read *Absaraka, Home of the Crows*, and learned of Carrington's appointment to Wabash College. "Later, when I saw the announcement of the death of a Mrs. Carrington," she recalled, "I wrote to learn if it were indeed, the wife of our old commander. Correspondence ensued that resulted in our marriage in 1871, and my removal to his new home."[3] And it would be "Till Death Do Us Part." At least the trials and tribulations of Fort Phil Kearny days brought some comfort to two of those who had suffered as a result.

Carrington adopted young William as his own, and in the next four years Frances gave birth to three more children, giving a brood of six in total, including Henry's sons Jimmy and Harry. While memory of the Fetterman defeat faded, it remained seared into Carrington's mind, and he kept up pressure on political contacts to have his suppressed report published.

The destruction of Custer's battalion of over 200 men at the Little Bighorn in 1876 must have been a relief for Carrington in many ways; even bigger disasters could overtake battle-hardened Civil War heroes. The three-pronged advance into Indian country had set out to punish the Lakota and their allies with some 2,000 men involved. They were not 700 soldiers with outmoded muzzleloaders attempting to build three forts and protect a wagon road over 500 miles long.

Carrington's military career was well over, but the smell of gunpowder remained in his life. Wabash College was the possessor of a fine field piece used to instruct students in artillery practice. But, lacking horses, it was the young men who had the job of hauling the gun around, a job no more to their taste than Carrington's military instruction in general. The devastating losses of the late Civil War had put an end to combat being seen as romantic and glorious. Also not to the students' taste was the campus privy, nicknamed "Little Egypt." In 1878 this "was spread in fragments scattered half-way to Yountsville," said the report, "and the field-piece was destroyed."[4] The offensive privy had become the students' artillery target. College President Joseph Tuttle directed that military training on the campus cease forthwith. Carrington remained on to teach mathematics, but he departed at the end of the academic year. The Carrington family moved to Boston, Massachusetts, from where he maintained pressure on the government for the release of his suppressed report.

In 1887, two years after Grant's death and three years after Sherman's retirement, Senator Dawes of Massachusetts finally managed to have the Department of War release the report. But Senate Document 97 also included Cooke's damaging telegram regarding troops rushing out "helter-skelter" and Carrington's assurance that he was "preparing for active movements." Carrington had written a reply to Powell's accusations years before, but this was the first time he had seen Cooke's ill-informed endorsement of Powell.[5]

Congress also issued Senate Document 33 which contained Carrington's documents submitted to the Sanborn Commission placing the blame on William Fetterman. Carrington claimed these documents had been found "in a mass of waste-paper in the cellar of the Interior Department.[6]"

Already an author prior to the Civil War, in later years Carrington wrote mainly history books, including *The Indian Question* in 1884, and in 1889 he helped draft a treaty with the Flathead Indians of Montana. In 1890 he carried out a census of the Iroquois in New York, the descendants of those who had fought during the French and Indian War. No doubt he saw certain parallels with Colonel Monro's experience at Fort William Henry in 1757, and his own at Fort Phil Kearny in 1866.

Author Dr. Cyrus Townsend Brady began writing, *Indian Fights and Fighters*, and met with Henry Carrington in 1903. This book revealed that Fetterman and Brown supposedly "offered with eighty men to ride through the whole Sioux nation." A remarkable coincidence that this just happened to be the number killed, which any enquiring mind would have to doubt. But this became part of the standard story, Fetterman, the officer who boasted he could ride through the whole Sioux nation with 80 men. Following authors cast Fetterman as an arrogant and impetuous officer which, based on the facts, does not appear to be true. The blame for this has been cast by some on Frances and Margaret Carrington, one book stating that "both women had personal biases in their descriptions of the actions and ascriptions of responsibility that are reflected in their writings, and thus should be reflected upon by readers of their personal accounts."[7] Another book concludes, "Thus, the Carrington wives changed the history of the Fetterman Massacre to ensure that Fetterman's performance remained shrouded in confusion."[8]

Nothing could be further from the truth. They did not "change" the history in any way. The Sanborn Commission had exonerated Carrington before the women wrote their books. They wrote a forthright and honest account of what transpired, verified by both logic and testimony from others involved. Even James Powell, who would say nothing to help Carrington, testified that Fetterman "instead of going to the relief of the wood train filed to the right and went on the Big Horn road."[9]

Despite writing that Brown led Fetterman astray, Margaret gave a hint that Grummond could well have been at fault. "Lieutenant Wands and other friends urged him, for his family's sake, to avoid all rash movements and any pursuit that would draw them over Lodge Trail Ridge" And "as if peculiarly impressed with some anticipations of rashness in the movement," Carrington "halted the mounted party, and gave additional orders, understood in the garrison, and by those who heard them, to be a substantial repetition of the former."[10]

And Frances paraphrased this in her own account, *My Army Life and the Fort Phil Kearney Massacre*, published in 1910.[11] But there was an alteration—the words "halted the mounted party" were replaced with "halted the column." Only Grummond and the cavalry were halted, the infantry some distance in advance. This change removed the stigma of her former husband being singled out for a repetition of orders.

Both Frances and Margaret come across as puzzled by Fetterman; on one hand a fine gentleman who performed admirably on December 6, but mysteriously disobeyed orders on December 21. Was it Brown who instigated the disaster, or Grummond—or others they did not even consider—Wheatley and Fisher? Applying the same criteria, logic, background and body positions, it appears more than likely that these civilians were the instigators of what came next.

It was Fetterman's decision, however, to march directly towards Lodge Trail Ridge. He had something "clever" in mind from the start, regardless of who led who astray once they reached the top. But, from the fort, Margaret Carrington and Frances Grummond could only repeat what they heard and saw, Fetterman given orders not to cross Lodge Trail Ridge, marching out, and then proceeding to disobey those orders. The ladies simply stated the truth.

Less clear cut was Tenadore Ten Eyck's performance. C. G. Coutant's *History of Wyoming*, published in 1906, the year following Ten Eyck's death, said, "Alas, procrastination robbed Captain Ten Eyck of a victory and permitted the death of many brave men who died after their ammunition had been exhausted." This slight jolted Ten Eyck's daughter, another Frances, into an anxious campaign to clear her father's name. She wrote to Carrington seeking support, and he replied, "Mr. Coutant should not have made surmises, and assumed that which is impossible to determine, absolutely." He stated that Ten Eyck alone supported his decision to ride out and recover the dead, and bravely accompanied the dangerous mission. When Carrington was queried by another historian, Eli S. Ricker, regarding his note to Ten Eyck on the day of the battle, "You would have saved two miles towards the scene of action if you had taken Lodge Trail Ridge," Carrington stated that the captain "could not have done better by doing differently."[12] Perhaps by that time Carrington realized that a direct advance into the hornet's nest could well have led to another dead detachment that day.

On July 4, 1908, a celebration of "Wyoming Opened" took place in Sheridan, about 20 miles from the "beautiful plateau" where Fort Phil Kearny once stood. A handful of survivors were present including Henry and Frances Carrington. Sheridan was a "progressive little city" with electric lighting, telephones and even a sprinkling of those new-fangled contraptions called motor carriages—or motor cars—or automobiles. "The words 'then and now' were constantly recurring to mind," recalled Frances, "and like the swinging of a pendulum indicating the passing years."[13]

On the preceding day, amidst a crowd of dignitaries and the general public, the dedication of the stone monument, built in 1905, at the Fetterman battle site took place. "We gathered clusters of wild flowers, our little party of old soldiers, wherewith to decorate the monument, and some were gathered to bear away in memory of those 'who sleep their last sleep, who have fought their last battle.'" The preceding evening Frances had been shown "a piece of the powder magazine.... One look at this relic awakens the memory of that day when we watched its preparation, as our last refuge, if the fort should be taken by the

The monument built in 1905 where the bodies of most of Fetterman's command were found (author's collection).

Indians." Red Cloud had been invited to attend. Despite expressing a desire to meet the "White Chief," he was unable to come due to ailing health, and would die the following year on December 10.

Henry Carrington, at 85, was the same age as Red Cloud, but made the journey despite his own ailing health. If the crowd expected a general reminisce of "the good old days," they were in for a surprise. Carrington, obviously still seared by the Fetterman affair, gave a lengthy speech recounting the battle and the following events. "Fetterman," he recalled, "gallant through the entire Civil War from the time he joined my regiment in 1861, was impatient and wanted to fight. He said, 'I can take eighty men and go to the Tongue River.' To this my Chief Guide, the veteran James Bridger, replied in my presence, 'Your men who fought down South are crazy! They don't know anything about fighting Indians.'" Fetterman was ordered not to cross Lodge Trail Ridge, Carrington said, and disobeyed that order. But as regards Ten Eyck, he "obeyed my order. He pressed on, kept his men in hand, rescued forty-nine dead bodies, brought them home in safety without the loss of a man." As regards his note to the captain, "You would have saved two miles," Carrington claimed. "This was not a reprimand at all, but suggestive as to the location of the enemy, as he could not otherwise know after the firing had ceased, and he could not judge as I could, on my lookout, of the locality in peril."

Frances Ten Eyck, unable to attend, was delighted by these words.

Carrington went on in some detail explaining his attempts to have his report of January 3 published. "Sometimes very queer things happen in military life," he recalled. Judge Kinney had died in 1902, and Carrington did not spare the rod. Kinney had "bought out the original sutler by paying gold for the same," Carrington said, and soon presented for approval "a large claim of over $1300 for goods alleged to have been stolen from his sutler's stock by my soldiers." An audit, however, revealed that Kinney's original stock, as per invoices, "was less than one-third of the value for which he claimed payment and was rejected." Kinney later used his place on the Sanborn Commission to induce "Captain James Powell to not only approve his claim but to assert under oath," the various false claims such as soldiers robbing the commissary supplies, horse racing, gambling, drinking, etc. Powell had retired from active duty in 1868 and died in 1903 from the combined effects of his old Civil War wounds, and to "general paresis," a disease of the brain on the central nervous system.[14] Carrington said he had visited Powell many years before, was "kindly received," and concluded that the captain's testimony was due to his "mental condition" at the time of the massacre. According to Carrington, Powell said, "It was enough to craze anybody to

Henry and Frances Carrington at the "Wyoming Opened" ceremony in 1908. The Stars and Stripes were raised on a new flagstaff at the original site (author's collection).

hold that Fort when there was everlasting danger with neither men nor ammunition enough to hold our own and save the Fort."

Carrington also recounted a visit to Philip St. George Cooke in Detroit. "In very strong terms he deplored the incident, and giving me a warm congratulation that the true version of the whole campaign had been a complete vindication." Cooke said he had no memory of his endorsement of Powell's account, but he often signed documents prepared by his staff, without reading them, assuming "that they were correct." But the endorsement was "improper" as well as "untrue in fact." Cooke had died in 1895, aged 85, so neither Kinney, Powell nor Cooke could comment on anything Carrington had to say.

Carrington said there was another involved "whose name I have purposely omitted." (William Bisbee, alive and well, who had retired with the rank of brigadier general in 1902. He would die at the age of 102 in 1942, six months after the Japanese bombed Pearl Harbor.)

Henry concluded his lengthy address with "Among the documents before referred to, that I leave behind, are authentic copies of the official statements of all officers who with myself survived the massacre, as to the subject-matter which I have so reluctantly, but impartially and justly, made of record."[15]

"The Closing scene at the monument was one of intensely dramatic interest," recalled Frances. The band played, "then came the final call that melted many to tears; 'Sound Taps,' the usual military order closing the exercises at burial of a soldier." Following the speeches, "the crowd moved to the site of the old fort, at present a luxurious field of alfalfa, where a flag-staff had been erected at the identical spot where, forty-two years ago, the first flag was unfurled in Wyoming." The crowd gathered around and Carrington "again addressed the people, pointing out the boundaries of the stockade; where the gates were located; how and where the Fetterman party left the Fort with orders to succor the wood-train; the direction they took to Sullivant Hill, and where they did go instead of obeying orders."

A reenactment of the battle had been arranged. It comes as little surprise that Frances found this not to her taste. She considered it "a sort of sensational incident ... more as a drawcard, of course, when nothing of the kind could lack the elements of a painful burlesque entirely out of harmony with the feelings of the guests as well as the dignified memorial honors of the celebration itself."

No doubt Henry Carrington had other memories, like the first wife who had stood by him through thick and thin. The following day one of the old soldiers, Samuel Peters, gave a talk and recalled Mrs. Carrington as "our good angel. Her very purpose was for the betterment of the conditions of the command, morally and socially. She was more than the colonel's wife, she was the mother of the regiment, loved by every man, woman and child ... and above all a woman who knew how to suffer, how to sympathize, how to comfort." And Peters felt that Frances was "no less kind, less true, less Christian, or less sympathetic ... and we shared our tears and anguish over the loss of our comrades, with her bereavement, feeling that her grief was our own."[16]

Margaret Carrington had died just two years after the publication of her book. Frances Carrington would die in 1911, aged 66, just one year following her book's release. It was as though fate had decreed that their time had come once their accounts were in print, leaving an invaluable impression of military life and Indian fighting on the American frontier. Henry Carrington died in 1912, aged 88, his name synonymous with the "Fetterman Massacre," one of the most famous episodes of the Old West.

Margaret had wanted the newly opened territory to be called Absaroka, and if others had their way, her wish would have been granted. In 1939 there was a move to take parts of Montana, South Dakota and Wyoming and form the new state of Absaroka. Sheridan was to be the capitol, and street commissioner A. W. Swickard appointed himself the first governor. Many farmers felt their interests were not being represented in the existing state governments, and a visit to Absaroka by the king of Norway led to claims of official recognition. The situation calmed, however, and the proposal was abandoned, despite *Absaroka* car license plates having been issued, and a "Miss Absaroka 1939" competition, won by Dorothy Fellows.

And the spirit still lives on. Nowadays the annual Sheridan *Abraroka State Takeover*

Fort William (later Fort Laramie) as it appeared in 1837. The beginning of the end for the Plains Indians' traditional way of life (author's rendition).

Hot Rod and Custom Car Gathering, complete with a *Miss Absaroka Pin-up Contest*, takes place. "Celebrate the Rebellious Spirit of the State That Never Was," read the posters.

Fort Phil Kearny was the last fort on American soil to be destroyed by enemy hands since Europeans had arrived four centuries earlier. Of prior frontier posts, Fort William Henry is best remembered due to the massacre immortalized in James Fenimore Cooper's novel *The Last of the Mohicans*. This was adapted to a black and white TV series of the 1950s. The impressive title montage showed Indians in canoes, men fighting in the wilderness, a cannon rolled forward through battle smoke. Hawkeye and Chingachgook were embroiled in a different adventure each week. But there had been various feature film versions going back to 1912, culminating in the 1992 epic starring Daniel Day-Lewis. Major Rogers' raid on the Abenakis at St. Francis was the theme of *Northwest Passage*, a big-budget 1940 movie starring Spencer Tracy.

Hollywood has not been so kind to Fort Phil Kearny. An average 1951 movie, *Tomahawk*, starred Van Heflin as a romantically embroiled young Jim Bridger, and Preston Foster as Carrington. *Tomahawk* followed the facts in a very loose manner, a fictional Lieutenant Dancy enticing Captain Fetterman across the ridge. A 1966 TV program, *The Massacre at Fort Phil Kearny*, starring Robert Fuller as Fetterman and Richard Eagan as Carrington, was more realistic, but it would appear a tight budget precluded showing the battle itself. Despite a sympathetic portrayal by Foster and Egan, Henry Carrington would have been most displeased. In both productions Fort Phil Kearny was portrayed as a ramshackle construction with gaps between the uneven pickets that a bullet, or perhaps even an arrow could get through—not the finely crafted post he had actually built.

The American West, a 2016 TV docudrama series executive produced by Robert Redford, portrayed the Fetterman Fight. Crazy Horse is depicted as orchestrating the victory, drawing fire while riding solo in front of the troops on a fine summer's day. Hollywood movies usually take liberties with the facts, but what purports to be factual should stick to the facts instead of perpetuating myths.

Most old forts were either destroyed by fire, left to decay, or became a source of materials for new buildings, the post having provided the roots of a new settlement. Fort Duquesne evolved into the city of Pittsburg, while others, like Fort Ticonderoga, have been restored. In the 1950s Fort William Henry was rebuilt as a tourist attraction, and many years later the Fort Phil Kearny site saw an interpretive center and stockade wall established.

Most 19th century military posts west of the Mississippi had no stockade, being barracks and other structures set around a parade ground. But the Bozeman Trail forts did have their palisade walls and blockhouses. The image of the timber frontier fort has persevered as a symbol of the white man's conquest of North America, while the Indian tepee of the Great Plains tribes has been a poignant reminder of the Indians' fight to preserve their hunting grounds, and way of life.

Appendix
Henry Carrington's Report of January 3, 1867

Head Quarters Post.
Fort Philip Kearney D.T.
January 3rd 1867.
Asst. Adjutant General
Department of the Platte
Omaha N.T.
Sir,

I respectfully state the facts of fight with Indians on the 21st ultimo. This disaster had the effect to confirm my judgment as to the hostility of Indians, solemnly declares by its roll of dead and the number engaged, that my declarations from my arrival at Laramie in June, were not idle conjecture, but true.

It also declares that in Indian warfare there must be perfect coolness, steadiness and judgment. This contest is in their best and almost their last hunting grounds. They cannot be whipped or punished by some dash after a handful, nor by mere resistance of offensive movements. They must be subjected, and made to respect and fear the whites.

It also declares with equal plainness that my letter from Fort Laramie, as to the absolute failure of the treaty, so far as relates to my command, was true.

It also vindicates every report from my pen, and every measure I have taken to secure defensive and tenable posts on this line.

It vindicates my administration of the Mountain District, Department of the Platte, and asserts that the confidence reposed in me by Lieutenant General Sherman, has been fully met.

It vindicates my application, so often made, for reinforcements and demonstrates the fact if I had received those assured to me by telegram and letter, I could have kept up communications and opened a safe route for emigrants next Spring.

It proves correct my report of fifteen hundred lodges of hostile Indians on Tongue river, not many hours ride from this post.

It no less declares that while there has been partial success in impromptu dashes, the Indian, now desperate and bitter, looks upon the rash white man as a sure victim, no less than he does a coward, and that the United States must soon come to the deliberate resolve to send an army equal to a fight with the Indians of the Northwest.

Better to have the expense at once, than to have a lingering provoking war for years. It must be met, and the time is just now. I respectfully refer to my official reports and correspondence from Department Head Quarters for verification of the foregoing propositions, and proceed to the details of Fetterman's massacre.

On the morning of the 21st ultimo at about 11 o'clock a.m. my picket on Pilot hill reported the wood train corralled, and threatened by Indians on Sullivant Hills, a mile and a half from the fort. A few shots were heard. Indians also appeared in the brush at the crossing of Piney, by the Virginia City road. Upon tendering to Brevet Major Powell the command of Company "C," 2nd U.S. Cavalry, then without an Officer, but which he had been drilling, Brevet Lieutenant Colonel Fetterman claimed, by rank, to go out. I acquiesed, giving him the men of his own company, that were for duty, and a portion of "C" company, 2nd Battn. 18th U.S. Infantry.

Lieutenant G.W. Grummond, who had commanded the mounted Infantry, requested to take out the cavalry. He did so. In the previous skirmish Lieutenant Grummond was barely saved from the disaster that befell Lieutenant Bingham, by timely aid.

Brevet Lieutenant Colonel Fetterman also was well admonished, as well as myself, that we were fighting brave and desperate enemies who sought to make up by cunning and deceit, all the advantages which the white man gains by intelligence and better arms.

My instructions were therefore peremtory and explicit. I knew the ambition of each to win honor, but being unprepared for large aggressive action, through want of adequate force (now fully demonstrated) I looked to continuance of timber supplies to prepare for more troops, as the one practical duty. Hence two days before Major Powell, sent out to cover the train under similar circumstances, simply did that duty, when he could have had a fight to any extent.

The day before, viz:—the 20th ultimo, I went to the Pinery and built a bridge of forty five feet span to expedite the passage of wagons from the woods into open ground.

Hence my instructions to Brevet Lieutenant Colonel Fetterman, viz:—"*Support the wood train, relieve it and report to me.* Do not engage or pursue Indians at its expense. Under no circumstances pursue over the ridge viz; Lodge Trail Ridge, as per map in your possession."

To Lieutenant Grummond, I gave orders to report to Brevet Lieutenant Colonel Fetterman, implicitly obey orders and not leave him.

Before the command left, I instructed Lieutenant A.H. Wands, Regimental Quarter Master, and Acting Adjutant, to repeat these orders. He did so. Fearing still that the spirit of ambition might override prudence, (as my refusal to permit sixty mounted men and forty citizens to go for several days down Tongue river valley after villages, had been unfavorably regarded to Brevet Lieutenant Colonel Fetterman and Captain Brown,) I crossed the parade and from a sentry platform, halted the cavalry and again repeated my precise orders.

I knew that the Indians had, for several days, returned each time with increased numbers, to feel our strength and decoy detachments to their sacrifice, and believed to foil their purpose was actual victory until reinforcements should arrive and my preparations were complete.

I was right. Just as the command left, five Indians reappeared at the crossing. The glass revealed others in the thicket, having the apparent object of determining the watchfulness of the garrison, or cutting off any small party that should move out. A case shot dismounted one and developed nearly thirty more who broke for the hills and ravines to the north.

In half an hour the picket reported that the wood train had broken corral and moved on to the Pinery. No report came from the detachment. It was composed of eighty one Officers and men including two citizens, all well armed, the cavalry having new carbines, while the detachment of infantry was of choice men, the pride of their companies.

At 12 o'clock firing was heard towards Peno Creek, beyond Lodge Trail Ridge. A few shots were followed by constant shots, not to be counted. Captain Ten Eyck was immediately dispatched with infantry and the remaining cavalry and two wagons, and ordered to join Colonel Fetterman at all hazards.

The men moved promptly and on the run, but within little more than half an hour from the first shot, and just as the supporting party reached the hill overlooking the scene of action, all firing ceased.

Captain Ten Eyck sent a mounted orderly back with the report that he could see and hear nothing of Fetterman, but that a body of Indians, on the road below him, were challenging him to come down, while larger bodies were in all the valleys for several miles around.

Moving cautiously forward with the wagons, evidently supposed by the enemy to be guns, as mounted men were in advance, he rescued from the spot where the enemy had been nearest, forty nine bodies, including those of Brevet Lieutenant Colonel Fetterman and Captain F.H. Brown. The latter went out without my consent or knowledge, fearless to fight Indians with any adverse odds, and determined to kill one at least before joining his company.

Captain Ten Eyck fell back slowly, but not pressed by the enemy, reaching the fort without loss.

The following morning, finding genuine doubt as to the success of an attempt to recover other bodies, but believing that failure to rescue them would dishearten the command and encourage the Indians who are so particular in this regard, I took eighty men and went to the scene of action, leaving a picket to advise me of any movement in the rear and to keep signal communication with the garrison.

The scene of action told its story. The road on the little ridge where the final stand took place was strewn with arrow heads, scalps, poles and broken shafts of spears. The arrows that were spent harmlessly from all directions, showed that the command was suddenly overwhelmed, surrounded and cut off while in retreat. Not officer or man survived. A few bodies were found at the north end of the divide over which the road runs just below Lodge Trail Ridge.

Nearly all were heaped near four rocks at the point nearest the Fort, these rocks enclosing a space about six feet square, having been the last refuge for defense. Here were also a few unexpended rounds of Spencer cartridge. Fetterman and Brown had each a revolver shot in the left temple. As Brown always declared he would reserve a shot for himself as a last resort, so I am convinced that these two brave men fell, each by the other's hand, rather than undergo the slow torture inflicted upon others.

Lieutenant Grummond's body was on the road between the two extremes, with a few others. This was not far from five miles from the Fort, and nearly as far from the wood train. Neither its own guard nor the detachment could by any possibility have helped each other, and the train was incidentally saved by the fierceness of the fight in the brave but rash impulse of pursuit.

The officers who fell believed that no Indian force could overwhelm that number of troops well held in hand.

Their terrible massacre bore marks of great valor and has demonstrated the force and character of the foe, but no valor could have saved them.

Pools of blood on the road and sloping sides of the narrow divide showed where Indians bled fatally, but their bodies were carried off. I counted sixty five such pools in the space of an acre, and three within ten feet of Lieut. Grummond's body.

Eleven American horses and nine Indian ponies were on the road, or near the line of bodies, others, crippled, were in the valley.

At the northwest or further point, between two rocks, and apparently where the command first fell back from the valley, realizing their danger, I found citizen James S. Wheatly and Isaac Fisher of Blue Springs Nebraska, who, with "Henry rifles," felt invincible, but fell, one having one hundred and five arrows in his naked body.

The widow and family of Wheatly are here. The cartridge shells about him, told how well they fought.

Before closing this report, I wish to say that every man, officer, soldier, or citizen, received burial with such record as to identify each. Fetterman, Brown and Grummond lie in one grave. The remainder also share one tomb, buried, as they fought, together, but the cases in which they were laid, are clearly placed and numbered.

I ask the General Commanding to give my report, in absence of Division Commander, an access to the eye and ear of the General in Chief.

The Department Commander must have more troops and I declare this my judgement, solemnly and for the general public good, without one spark of personal ambition other than to do my duty daily, as it comes, and whether I seem to speak too plainly or not, ever with the purpose to declare the whole truth, and with proper respect to my superior officers who are entitled to the facts, as to scenes remote from their own immediate notice.

I was asked to "send all the bad news." I do it as far as I can. I give some of the facts as to my men whose bodies I found just at dark, resolved to bring all in viz:—

Mutilations

Eyes torn out and laid on the rocks.
Noses cut off.
Ears cut off.
Chins hewn off.
Teeth chopped out.
Joints of fingers.
Brains taken out and placed on rocks with other members of the body.
Entrails taken out and exposed.
Hands cut off.
Feet cut off.
Arms taken out from socket.
Private parts severed and indecently placed on the person.
Eyes, ears, mouth, and arms penetrated with spear heads, sticks and arrows.
Ribs slashed to separation with knifes.
Sculls severed in every form from chin to crown.
Muscles of calves, thighs, stomach, breast, back, arms and cheek, taken out.
Punctures upon every sensitive part of the body, even to the soles of the feet and palms of the hand.

All this only approximates to the whole truth.

Every medical officer was faithful, aided by a large force of men, and all were not buried until Wednesday after the fight.

The great real fact is that these Indians take alive when possible and slowly torture. It is the opinion of Dr. S.M. Horton, Post Surgeon, that not more than six were killed by balls. Of course the "*whole* arrows," hundreds of which were removed from naked bodies, were all used after removal of the clothing.

I have said enough. It is a hard but absolute duty. In the establishment of this post I designed to put it where it fell the heaviest upon the Indian, and therefore the better for the emigrant. My duty will be done when I leave, as ordered to my new Regimental Head Quarters, Fort Casper.

I submit herewith list of casualties marked "A." I shall also, as soon as practicable, make full report for the year 1866, of operations in the establishment of this new line.

I am
Very respectfully
Your Obedient Servant
Henry B. Carrington
Col. 18th Infantry
Comd'g.

Chapter Notes

Chapter 1

1. *Bougainville American Journals*, 142
2. Hughes, *The Siege of Fort William Henry*, 134.
3. *Lloyd's English Post and Evening Chronicle*, September 2, 1757.
4. Roubaud's letter of October 21, 1757.
5. *The Scots Magazine* 19, p. 426.
6. *Bougainville American Journals*, 142.
7. Roubaud's letter of October 21, 1757.
8. *Lloyd's English Post and Evening Chronicle*, September 2, 1757.
9. Castle, *Fort William Henry 1755–57*, 55.
10. Roubaud's letter of October 21, 1757.
11. Parkman, *Montcalm and Wolf*, 279–280.
12. *Bougainville American Journals*, 144.
13. Ibid., 146.
14. *The London Magazine*, Vol. xxvi, 1757, 457.

Chapter 2

1. Hughes, *The Siege of Fort William Henry*, xvii.
2. Bearor, *Leading by Example*, 99.
3. Hughes, *The Siege of Fort William Henry*, xx.
4. Castle, *Fort William Henry 1755–57*, 6.
5. *Origin of the name—Canada*, Canadian Heritage (online).
6. Hughes, *The Siege of Fort William Henry*, xxi.
7. Betts, *The Nine Lives of George Washington*, 34.
8. Hughes, *The Siege of Fort William Henry*, xxii.
9. *Fort Duquesne*, Ohio Central History (online).
10. Parkman, *Montcalm and Wolf*, 121–122.
11. *Fort Necessity*, National Parks Service (online).
12. *Virginia Gazette*, July 9, 1754, 3.
13. Lengel, *General George Washington*, 36.
14. Kopperman, *Braddock at the Monongahela*, 94.
15. Parkman, *Montcalm and Wolf*, 117.
16. Sargent, *The History of an Expedition*, 373.
17. Parkman, *Montcalm and Wolf*, 119.
18. Hughes, *The Siege of Fort William Henry*, xxiv.
19. Shannon, *The Seven Year's War in North America with Documents*, 64.
20. Sargent, *The History of an Expedition*, 385–386.
21. Leslie's letter, July 30 1755, *Graham's Monthly American Magazine*, Vol. xlv, 1854.
22. *Historical Collection of Pennsylvania*, 10–11.
23. Sparks, *The Writings of George Washington*, 87.
24. Tucker, *The Encyclopedia of the North American Indian Wars, 1607–1890*, Vol. 1, 1001.
25. *The Great Cove Massacre*, USGenWeb Archives (online).
26. Shannon, *The Seven Year's War in North America with Documents*, 64.
27. Parkman, *Montcalm and Wolf*, 146.

Chapter 3

1. Castle, *Fort William Henry 1755–57*, 14.
2. Dictionary of Canadian Biography (online).
3. Banks, *Chasing Empire Across the Seas*, 201.
4. Castle, *Fort William Henry 1755–57*, 18.
5. John Henry Lydias, New York State Museum (online).
6. Ibid., 72.
7. Dictionary of Canadian Biography (online).
8. Parkman, *Montcalm and Wolf*, 171.
9. Castle, *Fort William Henry 1755–57*, 21.
10. Parkman, *Montcalm and Wolf*, 101.
11. Letter from Baron de Dieskau to Count d'Argenson, Sept. 14, 1755.
12. Castle, *Fort William Henry 1755–57*, 22.
13. Letter from Baron de Dieskau to Count d'Argenson, Sept. 14, 1755.
14. Johnson's Report on the Battle of Lake George, Sept. 9, 1755.
15. Parkman, *Montcalm and Wolf*, 176.
16. Letter from Baron de Dieskau to Count d'Argenson, Sept. 14, 1755.
17. Johnson's Report on the Battle of Lake George, Sept. 9, 1755.
18. Ibid.
19. Letter from Baron de Dieskau to Count d'Argenson, Sept. 14, 1755.
20. Perry, *Origins in Williamstown*, 366.
21. Sylvester, *Indian Wars of New England*, Vol. 3, 461.
22. Parkman, *Montcalm and Wolf*, 179.
23. Castle, *Fort William Henry 1755–57*, 31.
24. Parkman, *Montcalm and Wolf*, 180.
25. Castle, *Fort William Henry 1755–57*, 35.
26. Dictionary of Canadian Biography (online).

Chapter 4

1. Johnson's Report on the Battle of Lake George, Sept. 9, 1755.
2. Parkman, *Montcalm and Wolfe*, 71.
3. Steele, *Betrayals: Fort William Henry and the Massacre*, 65.
4. Ibid., 38.
5. Castle, *Fort William Henry 1755–57*, 35.
6. Ibid., 36.
7. Hughes, *The Siege of Fort William Henry*, 42.
8. Castle, *Fort William Henry 1755–57*, 37.
9. *Rout of Moy, 1746*, ScotsWars (online).
10. Hughes, *The Siege of Fort William Henry*, 12.
11. Cave, *The French and Indian War*, 14.
12. Dictionary of Canadian Biography (online).
13. Castle, *Fort William Henry 1755–57*, 38.
14. *Bougainville American Journals*, 26.
15. Suthren, *The Sea Has No End*, 49.
16. Travers, *Hodges' Scout*, 55.
17. Starbuck, *Massacre at Fort William Henry*, 8.
18. Castle, *Fort William Henry 1755–57*, 39.
19. Rogers, *Journals of Major Robert Rogers*, 28.
20. Ibid., 30.
21. *Bougainville American Journals*, 81.
22. Brown, *A Plain Narrative of the Sufferings of Thomas Brown*, 6.
23. Rogers, *Journals of Major Robert Rogers*, 31.
24. Castle, *Fort William Henry 1755–57*, 40.

Chapter 5

1. Dictionary of Canadian Biography (online).
2. *Bougainville American Journals*, 86.
3. Castle, *Fort William Henry 1755–57*, 15.
4. Ibid., 87.
5. Castle, *Fort William Henry 1755–57*, 43.
6. Ibid.
7. An Account of Two Attacks on Fort William Henry, Militaryheritage.com.
8. Hughes, *The Siege of Fort William Henry*, 47.
9. An Account of Two Attacks on Fort William Henry, Militaryheritage.com.
10. Castle, *Fort William Henry 1755–57*, 45.
11. *Bougainville American Journals*, 96.
12. An Account of Two Attacks on Fort William Henry, Militaryheritage.com.
13. Castle, *Fort William Henry 1755–57*, 45.
14. *The Universal Magazine of Knowledge and Pleasure*, Vol. xx, Jan. 1757, 293.
15. Steele, *Betrayals: Fort William Henry and the Massacre*, 76.
16. Hughes, *The Siege of Fort William Henry*, 51.
17. An Account of Two Attacks on Fort William Henry, Militaryheritage.com.
18. Castle, *Fort William Henry 1755–57*, 46.
19. Hughes, *The Siege of Fort William Henry*, 52.
20. An Account of Two Attacks on Fort William Henry, Militaryheritage.com.
21. Hughes, *The Siege of Fort William Henry*, 53.
22. Nester, *The First Global War*, 45.
23. Castle, *Fort William Henry 1755–57*, 51.

Chapter 6

1. Castle, *Fort William Henry 1755–57*, 51.
2. Schofield, *The Highland Furies*, 42.
3. Castle, *Fort William Henry 1755–57*, 51.
4. Pargellis, *Lord Loudoun in North America*, 49.
5. Hughes, *The Siege of Fort William Henry*, 3.
6. Ross, *War on the Run*, 139.
7. Castle, *Fort William Henry 1755–57*, 52.
8. *Bougainville American Journals*, 117.
9. Hughes, *The Siege of Fort William Henry*, 132–133.
10. Castle, *Fort William Henry 1755–57*, 53.
11. *Bougainville American Journals*, 119.
12. Letter by Webb to Loudoun, Aug. 1, 1757.
13. Volo, *Daily Life on the Old Colonial Frontier*, 300.
14. Scull, *Montresor Journals*, 24.
15. Lyman/Loudoun *General Orders of 1757*, 56.
16. Castle, *Fort William Henry 1755–57*, 55.
17. *Putnam's Journal*, 38–39.
18. Often referred to as either colonel or lieutenant, Montresor was promoted to major on May 14 1757. He was later promoted to Colonel (Wikisource online), 1757, 496.
19. Hughes, *The Siege of Fort William Henry*, 146
20. Scull, *Montresor Journals*, 22
21. *Letters of George Bartman*, 419
22. *Bougainville American Journals*, 150
23. Hughes, *The Siege of Fort William Henry*, 148
24. Castle, *Fort William Henry 1755–57*, 57

Chapter 7

1. Roubaud's letter of October 21, 1757
2. Castle, *Fort William Henry 1755–57*, 62
3. *Bougainville American Journals*, 146–147
4. Roubaud's letter of October 21, 1757
5. Hughes, *The Siege of Fort William Henry*, 154
6. Ibid., 157
7. *Bougainville American Journals*, 153–154
8. Ibid., 154–155
9. Ibid., 152
10. Ibid., 157
11. Roubaud's letter of October 21, 1757
12. Hughes, *The Siege of Fort William Henry*, 161
13. Roubaud's letter of October 21, 1757
14. *Bougainville American Journals*, 158
15. Castle, *Fort William Henry 1755–57*, 62
16. Frye's Journal, *The Port Folio*, Vol. 7, 1819, 357
17. Hays (author anon.) *A Journal Kept during the Siege of Fort William Henry*, 146
18. Scull, *Montresor Journals*, 25
19. Roubaud's letter of October 21, 1757
20. Hays (author anon.) *A Journal Kept during the Siege of Fort William Henry*, 146
21. Roubaud's letter of October 21, 1757
22. Frye's Journal, *The Port Folio*, Vol. 7, 1819, 367
23. Hughes, *The Siege of Fort William Henry*, 165–166
24. Hays (author anon.) *A Journal Kept during the Siege of Fort William Henry*, 146

25. Castle, *Fort William Henry 1755–57*, 64
26. *The London Magazine or Gentleman's Monthly Intelligencer*, Vol. XXVl, 1757, 496
27. *Bougainville American Journals*, 159
28. Roubaud's letter of October 21, 1757
29. *Bougainville American Journals*, 159–160
30. Hughes, *The Siege of Fort William Henry*, 170
31. Roubaud's letter of October 21, 1757
32. Hughes, *The Siege of Fort William Henry*, 175
33. *Letters of George Bartman*, 419

Chapter 8

1. Castle, *Fort William Henry 1755–57*, 64.
2. *Bougainville American Journals*, 160.
3. *Bougainville American Journals*, 161.
4. Hays (author anon.) *A Journal Kept during the Siege of Fort William Henry*, 146.
5. Castle, *Fort William Henry 1755–57*, 64.
6. *Bougainville American Journals*, 161–162.
7. Hays (author anon.) *A Journal Kept during the Siege of Fort William Henry*, 147–148.
8. *Ibid.*, 162.
9. Roubaud's letter of October 21, 1757.
10. Hughes, *The Siege of Fort William Henry*, 182.
11. *The Universal Magazine of knowledge and Pleasure*, October 1757, 184.
12. Hughes, *The Siege of Fort William Henry*, 186.
13. *Bougainville American Journals*, 162.
14. *Ibid.*, 163.
15. Roubaud's letter of October 21, 1757.
16. Hays (author anon.) *A Journal Kept during the Siege of Fort William Henry*, 148.
17. Castle, *Fort William Henry 1755–57*, 67, 70.
18. *Bougainville American Journals*, 163–164.
19. *Ibid.*, 165.
20. Hughes, *The Siege of Fort William Henry*, 190.
21. Roubaud's letter of October 21, 1757.
22. Castle, *Fort William Henry 1755–57*, 70.
23. *Bougainville American Journals*, 165.

Chapter 9

1. Roubaud's letter of October 21, 1757.
2. Hughes, *The Siege of Fort William Henry*, 191.
3. Frye's Journal, *The Port Folio*, Vol. 7, 1819, 359.
4. Hays (author anon.) *A Journal Kept during the Siege of Fort William Henry*, 147.
5. Frye's Journal, *The Port Folio*, Vol. 7, 1819, 360.
6. Hughes, *The Siege of Fort William Henry*, 192.
7. Hays (author anon.) *A Journal Kept during the Siege of Fort William Henry*, 147.
8. *Bougainville American Journals*, 332.
9. Castle, *Fort William Henry 1755–57*, 70–71.
10. *Daniel Webb ... A General Webb of Deceit?* (Mohican Press online).
11. Hughes, *The Siege of Fort William Henry*, 193.
12. Castle, *Fort William Henry 1755–57*, 75.
13. Hughes, *The Siege of Fort William Henry*, 195.
14. *Bougainville American Journals*, 166.
15. Hughes, *The Siege of Fort William Henry*, 193.
16. Laramie, *The European Invasion of North America*, 308.
17. *Bougainville American Journals*, 166.
18. Roubaud's letter of October 21, 1757.
19. *Ibid.*
20. *Bougainville American Journals*, 166–167.
21. Frye's Journal, *The Port Folio*, Vol. 7, 1819, 361.
22. Roubaud's letter of October 21, 1757.
23. *Bougainville American Journals*, 167.
24. Frye's Journal, *The Port Folio*, Vol. 7, 1819, 361.
25. Hays (author anon.) *A Journal Kept during the Siege of Fort William Henry*, 149.
26. Hughes, *The Siege of Fort William Henry*, 200.
27. Roubaud's letter of October 21, 1757.
28. *Bougainville American Journals*, 168.
29. Hays (author anon.) *A Journal Kept during the Siege of Fort William Henry*, 149.
30. *Bougainville American Journals*, 168.

Chapter 10

1. *Bougainville American Journals*, 168.
2. Hughes, *The Siege of Fort William Henry*, 203.
3. Roubaud's letter of October 21, 1757.
4. *Bougainville American Journals*, 169.
5. Roubaud's letter of October 21, 1757.
6. *Letters of George Bartman*, 423.
7. Gridley, *Diary for 1757*, 14.
8. Steele, *Suppressed British Report on the Siege and Massacre at Fort W. H.*, 347.
9. Roubaud's letter of October 21, 1757.
10. Frye's Journal, *The Port Folio*, Vol. 7, 1819, 363.
11. *Bougainville American Journals*, 169.
12. Hughes, *The Siege of Fort William Henry*, 211.
13. *Bougainville American Journals*, 169.
14. Frye's Journal, *The Port Folio*, Vol. 7, 1819, 364.
15. *Bougainville American Journals*, 170.
16. Roubaud's letter of October 21, 1757.
17. Hays (author anon.) *A Journal Kept during the Siege of Fort William Henry*, 149.
18. *Bougainville American Journals*, 171.
19. Frye's Journal, *The Port Folio*, Vol. 7, 1819, 364.
20. Steele, *Suppressed British Report on the Siege and Massacre at Fort W. H.*, 348–349.
21. Roubaud's letter of October 21, 1757.
22. Starbuck, *Massacre at Fort William Henry*, 64.
23. *Bougainville American Journals*, 170–171.
24. Hughes, *The Siege of Fort William Henry*, 216.
25. Castle, *Fort William Henry 1755–57*, 88.
26. *Letters of George Bartman*, 423.
27. *Bougainville American Journals*, 171.
28. Frye's Journal, *The Port Folio*, Vol. 7, 1819, 365.
29. Roubaud's letter of October 21, 1757.
30. Dictionary of Canadian Biography (online).
31. Frye's Journal, *The Port Folio*, Vol. 7, 1819, 365.

Chapter 11

1. *Bougainville American Journals*, 171–172.
2. Roubaud's letter of October 21, 1757.
3. Ewing, *Eyewitness Account by James Furniss of the Surrender of Fort William Henry*, 313.

4. Frye's Journal, *The Port Folio*, Vol. 7, 1819, 366.
5. Hays (author anon.) *A Journal Kept during the Siege of Fort William Henry*, 150.
6. Parkman, *Montcalm and Wolf*, 560.
7. Hays (author anon.) *A Journal Kept during the Siege of Fort William Henry*, 150.
8. Carver, *Travels Through North America*, 318.
9. Parkman, *Montcalm and Wolf*, 559.
10. *Bougainville American Journals*, 172.
11. Roubaud's letter of October 21, 1757.
12. Carver, *Travels Through North America*, 319.
13. Roubaud's letter of October 21, 1757.
14. Hays (author anon.) *A Journal Kept during the Siege of Fort William Henry*, 150.
15. Bayonet vs. Clubbed Musket—American Civil War forums (online).
16. Carver, *Travels Through North America*, 319.
17. *Bougainville American Journals*, 173.
18. Roubaud's letter of October 21, 1757.
19. Hughes, *The Siege of Fort William Henry*, 227.
20. *Bougainville American Journals*, 173.
21. *Ibid.*
22. Steele, *Betrayals; Fort William Henry and the Massacre*, 119-120.
23. Rogers, *Journals of Major Robert Rogers*, 56.
24. Hughes, *The Siege of Fort William Henry*, 230.
25. Roubaud's letter of October 21, 1757.

Chapter 12

1. *Letters of George Bartman*, 54.
2. Scull, *Montresor Journals*, 28.
3. *Ibid.*
4. *Bougainville American Journals*, 177.
5. Rogers, *Journals of Major Robert Rogers*, 56.
6. *Bougainville American Journals*, 171.
7. *Ibid.*, 172.
8. Gabriel, *Desandrouins*, 97-98.
9. Roubaud's letter of October 21, 1757.
10. *Bougainville American Journals*, 178.
11. Roubaud's letter of October 21, 1757.
12. Scull, *Montresor Journals*, 28.
13. Hughes, *The Siege of Fort William Henry*, 233.
14. Carver, *Travels Through North America*, 319.
15. Gridley, *Diary of 1757*, 49.
16. *Bougainville American Journals*, 173.
17. Mason, *Diary of Jabez Fitch*, 20.
18. *Putnam's Journal*, 43.
19. *Bougainville American Journals*, 177-178.
20. Castle, *Fort William Henry 1755-57*, 78.
21. Parkman, *Montcalm and Wolf*, 303.
22. Hughes, *The Siege of Fort William Henry*, 238.
23. *Bougainville American Journals*, 174.
24. *Ibid.*
25. Parkman, *Montcalm and Wolf*, 306.
26. *Bougainville American Journals*, 174-175.
27. Hughes, *The Siege of Fort William Henry*, 240-241.
28. Castle, *Fort William Henry 1755-57*, 90.
29. Trimen, *A Historical Memoir of the 35th Royal Regiment of Foot*, 40.
30. Hill, *The Life of General Israel Putnam*, 60.
31. *The London Magazine for 1757*, Vol. XXVl, 495.
32. Prebble, *Culloden* (The whole book deals with this affair.)

Chapter 13

1. Hughes, *The Siege of Fort William Henry*, 242.
2. *Albany Chronicles*, pp. 185-187.
3. Hughes, *The Siege of Fort William Henry*, 243.
4. Baugh, *The Global Seven Years War, 1754-1763*, 252.
5. *Bougainville American Journals*, 193.
6. Nester, *The First Global War*, 69.
7. Parkman, *Wolf and Montcalm*, 306-307.
8. *Bougainville American Journals*, 194.
9. Parkman, *Wolf and Montcalm*, 352.
10. *Ibid.*, 374.
11. *Bougainville American Journals*, 193-194.
12. Tomlinson, *The Military Journals of Two Private Soldiers*, 21.
13. Parkman, *Wolf and Montcalm*, 358.
14. Skaarup, *Ticonderoga Soldier: Elijah Estabrooks Journal*, 95.
15. *Bougainville American Journals*, 235.
16. *Ibid.*, 204.
17. *Ibid.*, 232.
18. Parkman, *Wolf and Montcalm*, 358.
19. *Bougainville American Journals*, 238.
20. Fields, *The Seed of a Nation*, 157.
21. *Bougainville American Journals*, 233.
22. Parkman, *Wolf and Montcalm*, 365.
23. *Battle at Fort Carillon*, Canada, a Peoples' History, CBC (online).
24. *Bougainville American Journals*, 238.
25. *Ibid.*, 233.
26. *Ibid.*, 234.
27. Parkman, *Wolf and Montcalm*, 372.
28. Chartrand, *Ticonderoga, Montcalm's Victory Against all Odds*, 86-88.
29. *Bougainville American Journals*, 237.
30. Parkman, *Montcalm and Wolf*, 373.

Chapter 14

1. *Bougainville American Journals*, 269-270.
2. *Ibid.*, 276.
3. Dictionary of Canadian Biography (online).
4. Bearor, *Leading by Example*, 165-170.
5. *Bougainville American Journals*, 294.
6. Stewart, *Letters of General John Forbes*, 35.
7. Parkman, *Montcalm and Wolf*, 383.
8. *Ibid.*, 383-384.
9. *Ibid.*, 384.
10. Stewart, *Letters of General John Forbes*, 59.
11. *Ibid.*, 49.
12. Parkman, *Montcalm and Wolf*, 394.
13. Smith, *Life and Travels of Col. James Smith*, 104-105.
14. Parkman, *Montcalm and Wolf*, 395.
15. *Bougainville American Journals*, 295.
16. Smith, *Life and Travels of Col. James Smith*, 103.

17. Fort Legonier—Fighting Fort in Two Colonial Wars (online).
18. Easton Treaty—The Canadian Encyclopedia (online).
19. Stewart, *Letters of General John Forbes,* 64.
20. *Ibid.,* 75.
21. *Bougainville American Journals,* 322–323.

Chapter 15

1. Hughes, *The Siege of Fort William Henry,* 249.
2. Pouchot, *Memoir on the Late War,* 105.
3. Parkman, *Montcalm and Wolf,* 445.
4. Furness, *Crown Point: An Outline History* (online).
5. Hughes, *The Siege of Fort William Henry,* 251.
6. *Bougainville American Journals,* 90.
7. Dunnigan/Leigh, *Siege-1759: The Campaign Against Niagara,* 146.
8. Parkman, *Montcalm and Wolf,* 448.
9. Porter, *A Brief History of Old Fort Niagara,* 37.
10. Parkman, *Montcalm and Wolf,* 448.
11. Brumwell, *Redcoats: The British Soldier and War in the Americas,* 254.
12. Parkman, *Montcalm and Wolf,* 449.
13. Hughes, *The Siege of Fort William Henry,* 250.
14. *Bougainville American Journals,* 318.
15. Hughes, *The Siege of Fort William Henry,* 251.
16. Gallay, *Colonial Wars of North America, 1512–1763,* 454.
17. Humphreys, *Great Canadian Battles,* 86.
18. Crump, *Canada Under Attack,* 57.
19. Narratives of Early Canada: *Insubordinate Subordinates* (online).
20. Parkman, *Montcalm and Wolf,* 473.
21. Crump, *Canada Under Attack,* 58.
22. Parkman, *Montcalm and Wolf,* 477.
23. *Ibid.,* 478.
24. Hughes, *The Siege of Fort William Henry,* 253, 254.
25. Parkman, *Montcalm and Wolf,* 481.
26. *Bougainville American Journals,* 321.

Chapter 16

1. Rogers, *Journals of Major Robert Rogers,* 142.
2. Brumwell, *White Devil,* 230.
3. *Ibid.,* 240.
4. Manning, *Québec: The Story of Three Sieges,* 113–114.
5. Canadian Encyclopedia (online).
6. Dictionary of Canadian Biography (online).
7. *Bougainville American Journals,* 328.
8. Encyclopedia Britannica (online).

Chapter 17

1. F. Carrington, *My Army Life,* 85–86.
2. Debo, *History of the Indians of the United States,* 91.
3. Utley, *Frontier Regulars,* 13.
4. *Ibid.,* 2.
5. Monnet, *Where a Hundred Soldiers Were Killed,* 36.
6. Wyoming Battles, Skirmishes and Massacres (online).
7. Murray, *Military Posts in the Powder River Country,* 8.
8. Gray, *Custer's Last Campaign,* 42.
9. Olson, *Red Cloud and the Sioux Problem,* 3.
10. M. Carrington, *Absaraka, Home of the Crows,* 41.
11. F. Carrington, *My Army Life,* 68.
12. Wellman, *Death on the Prairie,* 78.
13. Monnet, *Where a Hundred Soldiers Were Killed,* 37.
14. *Ibid.,* 32.
15. Smith, *Give Me Eighty Men,* 17.
16. Monnet, *Where a Hundred Soldiers Were Killed,* 37.
17. McPherson, *Battle Cry of Freedom,* 775–777.
18. M. Carrington, *Absaraka, Home of the Crows,* 45.
19. Brown, *The Fetterman Massacre,* 25.
20. F. Carrington, *My Army Life,* 291.
21. Smith, *Give Me Eighty Men,* 27.
22. Debo, *History of the Indians of the United States,* 191–196.
23. M. Carrington, *Absaraka, Home of the Crows,* 47.
24. Carrington testimony—Ft. P. Kearny Massacre.
25. W. Murphy account—*National Tribune,* June 7, 1928.
26. M. Carrington, *Absaraka, Home of the Crows,* 70.
27. Mattes, *Scotts Bluff,* 49.
28. *Ibid.,* 47.
29. Carrington testimony—Ft. P. Kearny Massacre.
30. W. Murphy account—*National Tribune,* June 7, 1928
31. Lewis, *The West,* 367.
32. Brown, *Bury My Heart at Wounded Knee,* 130.
33. Regier, *Masterpieces of American Indian Literature,* 455.
34. W. Murphy account—*National Tribune,* June 7, 1928.
35. Carrington testimony—Ft. P. Kearny Massacre.
36. F. Carrington, *My Army Life,* 128–129.
37. M. Carrington, *Absaraka, Home of the Crows,* 16.
38. Sajna, *Crazy Horse,* 128.
39. Cozzens, *Eyewitness to the Indian Wars,* 90.
40. Utley, *Frontier Regulars,* 103.

Chapter 18

1. Monnet, *Where a Hundred Soldiers Were Killed,* 42–43.
2. Carrington testimony—Ft. P. Kearny Massacre.
3. Utley, *Frontier Regulars,* 12.
4. M. Carrington, *Absaraka, Home of the Crows,* 80–81.

5. *Ibid.*, 94–95.
6. Jim Bridger, Encyclopedia.com (online).
7. M. Carrington, *Absaraka, Home of the Crows*, 83.
8. F. Carrington, *My Army Life*, 208–209.
9. Brown, *The Fetterman Massacre*, 50.
10. Carrington testimony—Ft. P. Kearny Massacre.
11. Monnett, *Where a Hundred Soldiers Were Killed*, 43.
12. W. Murphy account—*National Tribune*, June 7, 1928.
13. M. Carrington, *Absaraka, Home of the Crows*, 95–96.
14. Carrington testimony—Ft. P. Kearny Massacre.
15. M. Carrington, *Absaraka, Home of the Crows*, 100.
16. *Ibid*.
17. Monnett, *Where a Hundred Soldiers Were Killed*, 42.
18. William Henry Bisbee Papers (online) Archive of California.
19. Carrington testimony—Ft. P. Kearny Massacre.
20. *Ibid*.
21. Regier, *Masterpieces of American Indian Literature*, 458.
22. M. Carrington, *Absaraka, Home of the Crows*, 97.
23. Carrington testimony—Ft. P. Kearny Massacre.
24. W. Murphy account—*National Tribune*, June 7, 1928.
25. M. Carrington, *Absaraka, Home of the Crows*, 94.
26. *Ibid.*, 100.
27. *Ibid.*, 26.
28. McDermott, *The Plains Forts*, Nebraska History (online).
29. M. Carrington, *Absaraka, Home of the Crows*, 102.
30. Carrington testimony—Ft. P. Kearny Massacre.
31. *Ibid*.
32. W. Murphy account—*National Tribune*, June 7, 1928.
33. Monnett, *Where a Hundred Soldiers Were Killed*, 47.
34. F. Carrington, *My Army Life*, 94.
35. Carrington testimony—Ft. P. Kearny Massacre.

Chapter 19

1. Wellman, *Death on the Prairie*, 35.
2. Philip Kearny, Civil War Trust (online).
3. Smith, *Give Me Eighty Men*, 65.
4. M. Carrington, *Absaraka, Home of the Crows*, 106–107.
5. *Ibid.*, 111.
6. Carrington testimony—Ft. P. Kearny Massacre.
7. M. Carrington, *Absaraka, Home of the Crows*, 112.
8. *Ibid.*, 116.
9. Carrington testimony—Ft. P. Kearny Massacre.
10. *Ibid*.
11. Monnett, *Where a Hundred Soldiers Were Killed*, 57.
12. W. Murphy account—*National Tribune*, June 7, 1928.
13. M. Carrington, *Absaraka, Home of the Crows*, 119.
14. Monnett, *Where a Hundred Soldiers Were Killed*, 57.
15. Carrington testimony—Ft. P. Kearny Massacre.
16. W. Murphy account—*National Tribune*, June 7, 1928.
17. Brown, *The Fetterman Massacre*, 78.
18. Carrington testimony—Ft. P. Kearny Massacre.
19. *Ibid*.
20. M. Carrington, *Absaraka, Home of the Crows*, 122.
21. Murray, *Military Post in the Powder River Country*, 33.
22. Fessenden memoir, *The Bozeman Trail; Historical Accounts* (online).
23. Carrington testimony—Ft. P. Kearny Massacre.
24. M. Carrington, *Absaraka*, 146. F. Carrington, *My Army Life*, 93.
25. Murray, *Military Post in the Powder River Country*, 33.
26. *Ibid.*, 38.
27. *Ibid.*, 36.
28. Carrington testimony—Ft. P. Kearny Massacre.
29. Burrowes' Report, July 25, 1866.
30. Fessenden memoir, *The Bozeman Trail; Historical Accounts* (online).
31. Wands testimony—Ft. P. Kearny Massacre.
32. M. Carrington, *Absaraka, Home of the Crows*, 123.
33. Fessenden memoir, *The Bozeman Trail; Historical Accounts* (online).
34. Wands testimony—Ft. P. Kearny Massacre.
35. Brown, *The Fetterman Massacre*, 87.
36. Letter of Sept. 18 to *Leslie's Illustrated Newspaper*.
37. M. Carrington, *Absaraka, Home of the Crows*, 123.
38. F. Carrington, *My Army Life*, 79–80.
39. Burrows Report, July 25, 1866.
40. Wands testimony—Ft. P. Kearny Massacre.
41. Burrows Report, July 25, 1866.

Chapter 20

1. Carrington testimony—Ft. P. Kearny Massacre.
2. M. Carrington, *Absaraka, Home of the Crows*, 166–167.
3. Utley, *Frontier Regulars*, 12.
4. Carrington testimony—Ft. P. Kearny Massacre.
5. Smith, *Give Me Eighty Men*, 13.
6. Carrington testimony—Ft. P. Kearny Massacre.
7. Monnett, *Where a Hundred Soldiers Were Killed*, 49.
8. Carrington testimony—Ft. P. Kearny Massacre.
9. Monnett, *Where a Hundred Soldiers Were Killed*, 89.
10. F. Carrington, *My Army Life*, 114.

11. Murray, *Military Posts in the Powder River Country*, 43.
12. F. Carrington, *My Army Life*, 93.
13. Cooper, *William Babcock Hazen*, 164.
14. Carrington testimony—Ft. P. Kearny Massacre.
15. Murray, *Military Posts in the Powder River Country*, 47, 49.
16. Fessenden memoir, *The Bozeman Trail; Historical Accounts* (online).
17. Murray, *Military Posts in the Powder River Country*, 41.
18. Bisbee testimony—Ft. P. Kearny Massacre.
19. M. Carrington, *Absaraka, Home of the Crows*, 140.
20. Carrington testimony—Ft. P. Kearny Massacre.
21. M. Carrington, *Absaraka, Home of the Crows*, 182, 189.
22. Murray, *Military Posts in the Powder River Country*, 164.
23. Bisbee testimony—Ft. P. Kearny Massacre.
24. Powell testimony—Ft. P. Kearny Massacre.
25. M. Carrington, *Absaraka, Home of the Crows*, 187.
26. Utley, *Frontier Regulars*, 72.
27. Fessenden memoir, *The Bozeman Trail; Historical Accounts* (online).
28. Wands testimony—Ft. P. Kearny Massacre.
29. Brown, *The Fetterman Massacre*, 110–111.
30. Carrington testimony—Ft. P. Kearny Massacre.
31. Cooper, *William Babcock Hazen*, 164.
32. Letter of Sept. 25 to *Leslie's Illustrated Newspaper*.
33. *Ibid*.
34. Brown, *The Fetterman Massacre*, 117.
35. M. Carrington, *Absaraka, Home of the Crows*, 158.
36. Carrington testimony—Ft. P. Kearny Massacre.
37. *Ibid*.
38. Brown, *The Fetterman Massacre*, 120.
39. Carrington testimony—Ft. P. Kearny Massacre.
40. Smith, *Give Me Eighty Men*, 62–63.
41. M. Carrington, *Absaraka, Home of the Crows*, 159–160.
42. Weston testimony—Ft. P. Kearny Massacre.
43. Drimmer, *Captured by the Indians*, 73–104.
44. Williams, *Jackson, Crockett and Houston*, 16–24.
45. M. Carrington, *Absaraka, Home of the Crows*, 163.
46. Carrington testimony—Ft. P. Kearny Massacre.
47. F. Carrington, *My Army Life*, 161.
48. *Ibid*., 163–164.

Chapter 21

1. Carrington testimony—Ft. P. Kearny Massacre.
2. *Ibid*.
3. Monnett, *Where a Hundred Soldiers Were Killed*, 89.
4. Murray, *Military Posts in the Powder River Country*, 51.
5. Monnett, *Where a Hundred Soldiers Were Killed*, 98.
6. F. Carrington, *My Army Life*, 86.
7. *Ibid*., 29, 62.
8. Smith, *Give Me Eighty Men*, 66–67.
9. *Ibid*., 68.
10. Williams, *Jackson, Crockett and Houston*, 109.
11. Monnett, *Where a Hundred Soldiers Were Killed*, 78.
12. Crockett, *A Narrative of the Life of David Crockett*, 147.
13. F. Carrington, *My Army Life*, 30–31.
14. *Ibid*., 68.
15. *Ibid*., 91.
16. *Ibid*., 99.
17. W. Murphy account—*National Tribune*, June 7, 1928.
18. Fessenden memoir, *The Bozeman Trail; Historical Accounts* (online).
19. M. Carrington, *Absaraka, Home of the Crows*, 174.
20. Murray, *Military Posts in the Powder River Country*, 57.
21. State Executive Documents, 1866–1867, Fort P.K. Massacre, 13–14.
22. Smith, *Give Me Eighty Men*, 79.
23. M. Carrington, *Absaraka, Home of the Crows*, 135–136.
24. Brown, *The Fetterman Massacre*, 135.
25. Carrington testimony—Ft. P. Kearny Massacre.
26. M. Carrington, *Absaraka, Home of the Crows*, 149.
27. F. Carrington, *My Army Life*, 113–115.
28. W. Murphy account—*National Tribune*, June 7, 1928.
29. M. Carrington, *Absaraka, Home of the Crows*, 151.
30. F. Carrington, *My Army Life*, 117.
31. Carrington testimony—Ft. P. Kearny Massacre.
32. Cooper, *William Babcock Hazen*, 170.

Chapter 22

1. F. Carrington, *My Army Life*, 118.
2. Carrington testimony—Ft. P. Kearny Massacre.
3. Smith, *Give Me Eighty Men*, 20.
4. Monnett, *Where a Hundred Soldiers Were Killed*, 98.
5. M. Carrington, *Absaraka, Home of the Crows*, 171.
6. F. Carrington, *My Army Life*, 119.
7. *Ibid*., 195.
8. Smith, *Give Me Eighty Men*, 80.
9. F. Carrington, *My Army Life*, 120.
10. Brown, *The Fetterman Massacre*, 152.
11. Ten Eyck testimony—Ft. P. Kearny Massacre.
12. F. Carrington, *My Army Life*, 122, 123.
13. Keenan, *The Wagon Box Fight*, 32.
14. Monnett, *Where a Hundred Soldiers Were Killed*, 97.

15. Carrington's letter to Sec. of the Interior, Nov. 5 1867.
16. Powell testimony—Ft. P. Kearny Massacre.
17. Bisbee testimony—Ft. P. Kearny Massacre.
18. Mackey testimony—Ft. Phil Kearny Massacre.
19. Wands testimony—Ft. P. Kearny Massacre.
20. W. Murphy account—*National Tribune*, June 7, 1928.
21. Carrington testimony—Ft. P. Kearny Massacre.
22. F. Carrington, *My Army Life*, 111.
23. Murray, *Military Posts of the Powder River Country*, 81, 82.
24. Carrington testimony—Ft. P. Kearny Massacre.
25. Murray, *Military Posts of the Powder River Country*, 82.
26. Thrapp, *Encyclopedia of Frontier Biography*, 117.
27. Carrington's letter to Sec. of the Interior, Nov. 5 1867.
28. Smith, *Give Me Eighty Men*, 84.
29. F. Carrington, *My Army Life*, 97.
30. *Ibid.*, 128.
31. Carrington testimony—Ft. P. Kearny Massacre.
32. F. Carrington, *My Army Life*, 119.
33. Brown, *The Fetterman Massacre*, 155.
34. Carrington testimony—Ft. P. Kearny Massacre.
35. F. Carrington, *My Army Life*, 120.
36. Carrington testimony—Ft. P. Kearny Massacre.
37. *Ibid.*
38. Fetterman Report of December 7, 1866.
39. Wands testimony—Ft. P. Kearny Massacre.
40. Carrington testimony—Ft. P. Kearny Massacre.
41. Fetterman Report of December 7, 1866.
42. F. Carrington, *My Army Life*, 132.
43. Carrington testimony—Ft. P. Kearny Massacre.
44. M. Carrington, *Absaraka, Home of the Crows*, 196.
45. Carrington testimony—Ft. P. Kearny Massacre.
46. Smith, *Give Me Eighty Men*, 90.
47. Fessenden memoir, *The Bozeman Trail; Historical Accounts* (online).
48. W. Murphy account—*National Tribune*, June 7, 1928.
49. F. Carrington, *My Army Life*, 134.
50. M. Carrington, *Absaraka, Home of the Crows*, 194.
51. Fetterman Report of December 7, 1866.
52. Report of the Secretary of War, Exec. Document 15, 1867.
53. Wands testimony—Ft. P. Kearny Massacre.

Chapter 23

1. Carrington testimony—Ft. P. Kearny Massacre.
2. F. Carrington, *My Army Life*, 134.
3. Brown, *The Fetterman Massacre*, 168.
4. Smith, *Give Me Eighty Men*, 78.
5. Powell testimony—Ft. P. Kearny Massacre.
6. Senate Executive Documents, 1866-67, 15.
7. Carrington testimony—Ft. P. Kearny Massacre.
8. F. Carrington, *My Army Life*, 142.
9. Arnold testimony—Ft. P. Kearny Massacre.

10. Carrington testimony—Ft. P. Kearny Massacre.
11. Carrington's letter to Sec. of the Interior, Nov. 5 1867.
12. Carrington testimony—Ft. P. Kearny Massacre.
13. F. Carrington, *My Army Life*, 143-144.
14. M. Carrington, *Absaraka, Home of the Crows*, 266-265.
15. Wands testimony—Ft. P. Kearny Massacre.
16. Woodham-Smith, *The Reason Why*, 32-33.
17. F. Carrington, *My Army Life*, 144.
18. Powell testimony—Ft. P. Kearny Massacre.
19. Wands testimony—Ft. P. Kearny Massacre.
20. Arnold testimony—Ft. P. Kearny Massacre.
21. Ten Eyck testimony—Ft. P. Kearny Massacre.
22. Carrington testimony—Ft. P. Kearny Massacre.
23. M. Carrington, *Absaraka, Home of the Crows*, 208-209.
24. Neihardt, *Black Elk Speaks*, 9.
25. Vestal, *Warpath*, 60.
26. Sajna, *Crazy Horse*, 200.
27. Monnet, *Where a Hundred Soldiers Were Killed*, 140.
28. Neihardt, *Black Elk Speaks*, 9.

Chapter 24

1. Ten Eyck testimony—Ft. P. Kearny Massacre.
2. Powell testimony—Ft. P. Kearny Massacre.
3. Hines testimony,—Ft. P. Kearny Massacre.
4. M. Carrington, *Absaraka, Home of the Crows*, 205.
5. *Ibid.*, 205-206.
6. F. Carrington, *My Army Life*, 147.
7. Smith, *Give Me Eighty Men*, 104.
8. Ten Eyck testimony—Ft. P. Kearny Massacre.
9. W. Murphy account—*National Tribune*, June 7, 1928.
10. Hines testimony,—Ft. P. Kearny Massacre.
11. Ten Eyck testimony—Ft. P. Kearny Massacre.
12. Hines testimony—Ft. P. Kearny Massacre.
13. Brown, *The Fetterman Massacre*, 198.
14. W. Murphy account—*National Tribune*, June 7, 1928.
15. David, *Finn Burnett, Frontiersman*, 130.
16. F. Carrington, *My Army Life*, 147-148.
17. Monnet, *Where a Hundred Soldiers Were Killed*, 148.
18. F. Carrington, *My Army Life*, 149.
19. Thrapp, *Encyclopedia of Frontier Biography*, Vol. 3, 1140.
20. F. Carrington, *My Army Life*, 150.
21. M. Carrington, *Absaraka, Home of the Crows*, 212.
22. Carrington testimony—Ft. P. Kearny Massacre.
23. *Ibid.*
24. Carrington's letter to Sec. of the Interior, Nov. 5 1867.
25. Fessenden memoir, *The Bozeman Trail; Historical Accounts* (online).
26. F. Carrington, *My Army Life*, 152.
27. M. Carrington, *Absaraka, Home of the Crows*, 207-208.

28. F. Carrington, *My Army Life*, 153–154.
29. Carrington testimony—Ft. P. Kearny Massacre.
30. Monnet, *Where a Hundred Soldiers Were Killed*, 270.
31. Ten Eyck testimony—Ft. P. Kearny Massacre.
32. Horton testimony—Fort P. Kearny Massacre.
33. F. Carrington, *My Army Life*, 154.
34. Ten Eyck testimony—Ft. P. Kearny Massacre.
35. Carrington testimony—Ft. P. Kearny Massacre.

Chapter 25

1. Fessenden memoir, *The Bozeman Trail; Historical Accounts* (online).
2. F. Carrington, *My Army Life*, 156.
3. *Ibid.*, 156.
4. M. Carrington, *Absaraka, Home of the Crows*, 213.
5. F. Carrington, *My Army Life*, 160.
6. F. Carrington, *My Army Life*, 159.
7. *Ibid.*, 158.
8. M. Carrington, *Absaraka, Home of the Crows*, 212.
9. F. Carrington, *My Army Life*, 155.
10. M. Carrington, *Absaraka, Home of the Crows*, 214–215.
11. Regier, *Masterpieces of American Indian Literature*, 458.
12. F. Carrington, *My Army Life*, 166.
13. Gordon account, The 2nd. Cavalry Assoc. History Center (online).
14. Monnet, *Where a Hundred Soldiers Were Killed*, 184–185.
15. Composite of 2 telegrams of Dec. 26, 1866.
16. Senate Letter of The Secretary of War, Ex. Doc. No. 15.
17. Cooke testimony—Ft. P. Kearny Massacre.
18. Smith, *Give me Eighty Men*, 34.
19. Marszalek, *Sherman: A Soldier's Passion for Order*, 358.
20. Senate Letter of The Secretary of War, Ex. Doc. No. 15.
21. Grant, *The Papers of Ulysses S. Grant*, 423.
22. Arlington National Cemetery Website.
23. Senate Letter of The Secretary of War, Ex. Doc. No. 15.

Chapter 26

1. F. Carrington, *My Army Life*, 169.
2. Murray, *Military Posts in the Powder River Country*, 86.
3. Fessenden memoir, *The Bozeman Trail; Historical Accounts* (online).
4. F. Carrington, *My Army Life*, 174.
5. Senate Letter of The Secretary of War, Ex. Doc. No. 15.
6. Carrington testimony—Ft. P. Kearny Massacre.
7. Senate Letter of The Secretary of War, Ex. Doc. No. 15.
8. M. Carrington, *Absaraka, Home of the Crows*, 226.
9. Murray, *Military Posts in the Powder River Country*, 87.
10. Smith, *Give me Eighty Men*, 125.
11. M. Carrington, *Absaraka, Home of the Crows*, 218–219.
12. Brown, *The Fetterman Massacre*, 159.
13. Monnet, *Where a Hundred Soldiers Were Killed*, 189–190.
14. Smith, *Give me Eighty Men*, 131.
15. M. Carrington, *Absaraka, Home of the Crows*, 220–221.
16. *Ibid.*, 225.
17. Carrington testimony—Ft. P. Kearny Massacre.
18. Smith, *Give me Eighty Men*, 140.
19. Senate Letter of The Secretary of War, Ex. Doc. No. 15.
20. Carrington testimony—Ft. P. Kearny Massacre.
21. Sanborn Report, Senate Document 13.
22. M. Carrington, *Absaraka, Home of the Crows*, 236.
23. *Ibid.*, 226–227.
24. F. Carrington, *My Army Life*, 180.
25. Carrington's letter to Sec. of the Interior, Nov. 5 1867.
26. F. Carrington, *My Army Life*, 182.
27. M. Carrington, *Absaraka, Home of the Crows*, 231–232.
28. F. Carrington, *My Army Life*, 184–185.
29. M. Carrington, *Absaraka, Home of the Crows*, 234–235.
30. F. Carrington, *My Army Life*, 188.
31. *Ibid.*, 196–197.
32. Olson, *Red Cloud and the Sioux Problem*, 55.
33. F. Carrington, *My Army Life*, 199–200.
34. M. Carrington, *Absaraka, Home of the Crows*, 240.
35. F. Carrington, *My Army Life*, 202–203.

Chapter 27

1. Smith, *Give Me Eighty Men*, 149.
2. Murray, *Military Posts in the Powder River Country*, 55.
3. F. Carrington, *My Army Life*, 215.
4. Bisbee testimony—Ft. P. Kearny Massacre.
5. Cooke testimony—Ft. P. Kearny Massacre.
6. Simon, *The Papers of Ulysses S. Grant*, 58.
7. F. Carrington, *My Army Life*, 211.
8. Wands testimony—Ft. P. Kearny Massacre.
9. Carrington Testimony—Ft. P. Kearny Massacre.
10. Brown, *Bury My Heart at Wounded Knee*, 180.
11. Simon, *The Papers of Ulysses S. Grant*, 59.
12. *Ibid.*, 105.
13. *Ibid.*, 102–103.
14. *Ibid.*, 104–105.
15. Olson, *Red Cloud and the Sioux Problem*, 56.
16. Powell testimony—Ft. P. Kearny Massacre.
17. M. Carrington, *Absaraka, Home of the Crows*, 243.
18. Cozzens, *Eyewitness to the Indian Wars*, 91–92.
19. Sanborn Report, Senate Document 13.

20. Gordon account, The 2nd. Cavalry Assoc. History Center (online).
21. Wyoming State Parks—Fort Fetterman website.
22. Smith, *Give Me Eighty Men*, 153–154.
23. Powell testimony—Ft. P. Kearny Massacre.
24. Carrington's letter to Sec. of the Interior, Nov. 5 1867.
25. Powell testimony—Ft. P. Kearny Massacre.
26. Carrington's letter to Sec. of the Interior, Nov. 5 1867.
27. Carrington address, July 3, 1908.
28. M. Carrington, *Absaraka, Home of the Crows*, Dedication.
29. 18th Reg. of Infantry—U.S. Army Center of Military History (online).

Chapter 28

1. Murray, *Military Posts in the Powder River Country*, 86.
2. Fessenden memoir, *The Bozeman Trail; Historical Accounts* (online).
3. Gordon account, The 2nd. Cavalry Assoc. History Center (online).
4. Fessenden memoir, *The Bozeman Trail; Historical Accounts* (online).
5. Keenan, *The Wagon Box Fight*, 64.
6. W. Murphy account—*National Tribune*, June 7, 1928.
7. Fessenden memoir, *The Bozeman Trail; Historical Accounts* (online).
8. Murray, *Military Posts in the Powder River Country*, 88.
9. Williams, *Custer and the Sioux, Durnford and the Zulus*, 108.
10. Gray, *Custer's Last Campaign*, 62.
11. Fessenden memoir, *The Bozeman Trail; Historical Accounts* (online).
12. Murray, *Military Posts in the Powder River Country*, 89.
13. MOH Citation for George Grant—Home of Heroes (online).
14. Murray, *Military Posts in the Powder River Country*, 89–90.
15. W. Murphy account—*National Tribune*, June 7, 1928.
16. Fessenden memoir, *The Bozeman Trail; Historical Accounts* (online).
17. Article by Kent Goodman, *Bozeman Magazine* (online).
18. Murray, *Military Posts in the Powder River Country*, 92.
19. *Ibid.*, 91.
20. W. Murphy account—*National Tribune*, June 7, 1928.
21. Keenan, *The Wagon Box Fight*, 19.
22. Utley, *Frontier Regulars*, 127.
23. Murray, *Military Posts in the Powder River Country*, 165.
24. Brown, *Bury my Heart at Wounded Knee*, 140.
25. Monnett, *Where a Hundred Soldiers Were Killed*, 196.
26. Mattes, *Indians, Infants and Infantry*, 136–137.

Chapter 29

1. Keenan, *The Wagon Box Fight*, 21.
2. Sam Gibson Account.
3. Frederick Claus Account.
4. Captain Powell's report, Aug. 4, 1867.
5. Regier, *Masterpieces of American Indian Literature*, 459.
6. Max Littman Account.
7. Major Smith's report, Aug. 3, 1867.
8. Captain Powell's report, Aug. 4, 1867.
9. Regier, *Masterpieces of American Indian Literature*, 459.
10. Sam Gibson Account.
11. Brisbin, *Belden, The White Chief*, 377–379.
12. Murray, *Military Posts in the Powder River Country*, 105.
13. Utley, *Frontier Regulars*, 139.
14. Murray, *Military Posts in the Powder River Country*, 100.
15. Williams, *Custer and the Sioux, Durnford and the Zulus*, 12.

Chapter 30

1. F. Carrington, *My Army Life*, 216.
2. Monnet, *Where a Hundred Soldiers Were Killed*, 228.
3. F. Carrington, *My Army Life*, 216–217.
4. Local History @ CDPL (online).
5. Smith, *Give Me Eighty Men*, 164.
6. Carrington address, July 3, 1908.
7. Monnet, *Where a Hundred Soldiers Were Killed*, 285.
8. Smith, *Give Me Eighty Men*, 198.
9. Powell testimony—Ft. P. Kearny Massacre.
10. M. Carrington, *Absaraka, Home of the Crows*, 201.
11. F. Carrington, *My Army Life*, 144.
12. Smith, *Give Me Eighty Men*, 177.
13. F. Carrington, *My Army Life*, 241.
14. Keenan, *The Wagon Box Fight*, 25.
15. Carrington address, July 3, 1908.
16. S.S. Peters' address, July 4, 1908.

Bibliography

Archives and Collections

Carrington Papers, Sterling Memorial Library, Yale University, New Haven, CT.
Files of Headquarters, Division of the Missouri, relating to Military Operations, 1865–85, National Archives and Records Administration, Washington, D.C. (NARA).
House Executive Documents, Reports of the Commissioner of Indian Affairs (NARA).
Lord Loudoun Papers, 1755–1758. Huntington Library, San Marino, California.
New York Colonial Manuscripts, 1638–1800, New York State Library, Albany.
Phillip H. Sheridan Papers, William T. Sherman Papers, Library of Congress, Washington, D.C.
Sanborn Commission—Records of the Special Commission to Investigate the Fetterman Massacre and the State of Indian Affairs, 1867 (NARA).
Ten Eyck Diary. Special Collections, University of Arizona Libraries, Tucson.

Online Sources

An Account of Two Attacks on Fort William Henry (www.militaryheritage.com/wm_henry.htm).
Arlington National Cemetery Website (http://www.arlingtoncemetery.mil/#/).
Battle at Fort Carillon, Canada, a Peoples' History, CBC (www.cbc.ca/history/EPCONTENTSE1EP4CH5 PA1LE.html).
Bayonet vs. Clubbed Musket—American Civil War forums (civilwartalk.com › Civil War History—General Discussion).
Burrowes' Report, July 25, 1866 (freepages.history.rootsweb.ancestry.com/~familyinformation/fpk/072566 burrows.html).
Canadian Encyclopedia (www.thecanadianencyclopedia.ca/).
Crown Point: An Outline History (http://www.historiclakes.org/crown_pt/furness.html).
Dictionary of Canadian Biography (www.biographi.ca/index-e.html).
18th Reg. of Infantry—U.S. Army Center of Military History (www.history.army.mil/books/R&H/R&H-18IN.htm).
Encyclopedia Britannica (https://www.britannica.com/).
Fessenden Memoir, The Bozeman Trail; Historical Accounts (https://archive.org/stream/bub_gb_Jc8BAAAA-MAAJ/bub_gb_Jc8BAAAAMAAJ_djvu.txt).
Fort Duquesne, Ohio Central History (www.ohiohistorycentral.org/w/Fort_Duquesne).
Fort Legonier—Fighting Fort in Two Colonial Wars (www.exploringoffthebeatenpath.com/Battlefields/FortLigonier/index.html).
Fort Necessity, National Parks Service (https://www.nps.gov/fone/).
Goodman, Kent. Article in *Bozeman Magazine* (bozemanmagazine.com/contributors/k/74/274_kent_goodman).
Gordon account, The 2nd Cavalry Assoc. History Center (http://www.2dcavalryassociation.com/).
The Great Cove Massacre, USGenWeb Archives (files.usgw archives.net/pa/fulton/areahistory/fultonhist592_606.txt).
Jim Bridger, Encyclopedia.com (www.encyclopedia.com › People › History › U.S. History: Biographies).
John Henry Lydias, New York State Museum (www.nysm.nysed.gov/).
Johnson's Report on the Battle of Lake George, Sept. 9, 1755 (www.americanantiquarian.org/proceedings/44517708.pdf).

Letter from Baron de Dieskau to Count d'Argenson, Sept. 14, 1755 (www.wwnorton.com/college/history/america7_brief/content/.../research_01b.htm).
MOH Citation for George Grant—Home of Heroes (www.homeofheroes.com/moh/citations_1865_ind/grant.html).
Narratives of Early Canada: *Insubordinate Subordinates* (www.uppercanadahistory.ca/wm/wm4r.html).
Origin of the Name—Canada, Canadian Heritage (canada.pch.gc.ca › ... › Canadian identity and society › The creation of Canada).
Philip Kearny, Civil War Trust (www.civilwar.org/education/history/biographies/philip-kearny.htm).
The Plains Forts, Nebraska History (www.nebraskahistory.org/publish/publicat/history/full-text/NH2010Forts.pdf).
Report of the Secretary of War, Exec. Document 15, 1867 (freepages.history.rootsweb.ancestry.com/~familyinformation/fpk/secwar39cong.html).
Roubaud's Letter of Oct. 21, 1757. The Jesuit Relations and Allied Documents Volume 70. (puffin.creighton.edu/jesuit/relations/relations_70.html).
Rout of Moy, 1746, ScotsWars (old.scotwars.com/battle_of_moy.htm).
Senate Executive Document 15 Feb. 2 1867 (freepages.history.rootsweb.ancestry.com/~familyinformation/fpk/secwar39cong.htm).
William Henry Bisbee Papers, Online Archive of California (www.oac.cdlib.org/findaid/ark:/13030/c8f47pzd/).
Wyoming Battles, Skirmishes and Massacres (www.legendsofamerica.com/wy-indian battles.html).

Newspapers and Magazines

Albany Chronicles
Bozeman Daily Chronicle
Graham's Monthly American Magazine
Drewry's Derby Mercury
Frank Leslie's Illustrated Newspaper
Kansas City Star
Lloyd's Evening Post and British Chronicle
London Chronicle
London Magazine
Montana Post
National Tribune
New York Times
Omaha Weekly Herald
The Port Folio
Public Advertiser
Rocky Mountain News
The Scots Magazine
The Universal Magazine of Knowledge and Pleasure
Virginia Gazette

Books

Alter, Cecil J. *Jim Bridger*. Norman: University of Oklahoma Press, 1962.
Anderson, Fred. *Crucible of War: The Seven Years War and the Fate of Empire in British North America, 1754–1766*. London: Faber and Faber, 2001.
_____. *A People's Army: Massachusetts Soldiers and Society in the Seven Years' War*. New York: Norton, 1984.
Athern, Robert. *William Tecumseh Sherman and the Settlement of the West*. Norman: University of Oklahoma Press, 1956.
Banks, Kenneth J. *Chasing Empire Across the Sea*. Montreal: McGill-Queens's University Press, 2006.
Bartman, George, and John A. Schulz. *The Siege of Fort William Henry: Letters of George Bartman*. Philadelphia: University of Pennsylvania Press, 1949.
Baugh, Daniel. *The Global Seven Years War, 1754–1763*. Abingdon: Routledge, 2011.
Bearor, Bob. *Leading by Example: Partisan Fighters and Leaders of New France, 1660 to 1760*. Berwyn Heights: Heritage Books, 2002.
Bellico, Russell P. *Sails and Steam in the Mountains: A Maritime and Military History of Lake George and Lake Champlain*. Fleischmanns: Purple Mountain Press, 2001.
Betts, William W. *The Nine Lives of George Washington*. Bloomingdale: iUniverse, 2013.
Bisbee, William H. *Through Four American Wars*. Boston: Meador Publishers, 1931.

Bougainville, Louis Antoine de. *Adventure in the Wilderness*. Norman: University of Oklahoma Press, 1990.
Brisbin, James S., ed. *Belden, The White Chief*. Aurora: BCR, 2009.
Brown, Dee. *Bury My Heart at Wounded Knee*. London: Vintage, 1991.
_____. *The Fetterman Massacre*. Lincoln: University of Nebraska Press, 1971.
Brown, Thomas, and Edward J. Owen. *A Plain Narrative of the Uncommon Sufferings and Remarkable Deliverance of Thomas Brown, 1757–60*. Whitefish: Kessinger Publishing, 2007.
Brumwell, Stephen. *Redcoats: The British Soldier and War in the Americas, 17766–1763*. New York: Cambridge University Press, 2007.
_____. *White Devil: A True Story of War, Savagery, and Vengeance in Colonial America*. Boston: Da Capo Press, 2007.
Carrington, Frances C. *My Army Life and the Fort Phil Kearney Massacre*. Lincoln: University of Nebraska Press, 2004.
Carrington, Margaret. *Absaraka, Home of the Crows*. New York: Skyhorse Publishing, 2015.
Carroll, Joy. *Wolfe and Montcalm: Their Lives, Their Times and the Fate of a Continent*. Richmond Hill: Firefly, 2004.
Carver, Jonathan. *Travels Through the Interior Parts of North-America*. Walpole: Isiah Thomas, 1813.
Castle, Ian. *Fort William Henry*. Oxford: Osprey Publishing, 2013.
Cave, Alfred A. *The French and Indian War*. Westport: Greenwood Publishing, 2004.
Debo, Angie. *A History of the Indians of the United States*. London: Pimlico, 1995.
Chartrand, René. *Ticonderoga, 1758: Montcalm's Victory Against all Odds*. Oxford: Osprey Publishing, 2000.
Clodfelter, Micheal. *The Dakota War: The United States Army versus the Sioux*. Jefferson: McFarland, 1998.
Cooper, Edward S. *William Babcock Hazen: The Best Hated Man*. Cranbury: AUP, 2005.
Coutant, C.G. *The History of Wyoming*. Laramie: Spafford and Mathison, 1899.
Cozzens, Peter. *Eyewitness to the Indian Wars, 1865–1890*. Mechanicsburg: Stackpole Books, 2004.
Crump, Jennifer. *Canada Under Attack*. Toronto: Dundurn Books, 2010.
David, Robert B. *Finn Burnett, Frontiersman*. Mechanicsburg: Stackpole Books, 2003.
Day, Sherman. *Historical Collection of the State of Pennsylvania*. Philadelphia: George W. Gordon, 1843.
Dodge, Edward J. *Relief Is Greatly Wanted: The Battle of Fort William Henry*. Westminster: Heritage Books, 2009.
Drimmer, Frederick. *Captured by the Indians*. New York: Dover Publications, 1985.
Dunnigan, Brian Leigh. *Siege-1759: The Campaign Against Niagara*. Youngstown: Old Fort Niagara Assoc., 1996.
Fields, Darrell, and Lorrie Fields. *The Seed of a Nation: Rediscovering America*. New York: Morgan James Publishing, 2007.
Fitch, Jabez. *Diary of Captain Jabez Fitch*. Charleston: Nabu Press, 2014.
Ford, C. Worthington, ed. *General Orders of 1757, Issued by the Earl of Loudoun and Phineas Lyman in the Campaign Against the French*. New York: Gillis Press, 1899.
Gabriel, Charles N. *Le Marechal de Camp Desandrouins, 1729–1792*. Charleston: Nabu Press, 2011.
Gallay, Alan. *Colonial Wars of North America, 1512–1763*. London: Routledge, 2015.
Gray, John S. *Custer's Last Campaign: Mitch Boyer and the Little Bighorn Reconstructed*. Lincoln: University of Nebraska Press, 1993.
Gridley, Luke. *Luke Gridley's Diary of 1757 While in Service in French and Indian War*. Hartford: Case, Lockwood and Brainard, 1906.
Griffis, William Elliot. *Sir William Johnson and the Six Nations*. New York: Dodd, Mead, 1891.
Gump, James O. *The Dust Rose Like Smoke: The Subjugation of the Zulu and the Sioux*. Lincoln: University of Nebraska Press, 1994.
Hanson, Joseph M. *The Conquest of the Missouri*. Chicago: A. C. McClurg, 1916.
Hassrick, Royal B. *The Sioux: The Life and Customs of a Warrior Society*. Norman: University of Oklahoma Press, 1964.
Hays, Isaac Minus. *A Journal Kept During the Siege of Fort William Henry, August 1757*. Charleston: BiblioLife, 2009.
Hill, George C. *The Life of General Israel Putnam*. Ann Arbor: Hardpress Publishing, 2012.
Hill, William Henry. *Old Fort Edward Before 1800*. Fort Edward: Honeywood Press, 1956.
Holmes, Richard, *Redcoat: The British Soldier in the Age of Horse and Musket*. New York: Norton, 2002.
Hughes, Ben. *The Siege of Fort William Henry: A Year on the Northeastern Frontier*. Yardley: Westholme Publishing, 2014.
Humphreys, David. *An Essay on the Life of the Honorable Major-General Israel Putnam*. New York: Garland Publishing, 1977.
Humphreys, Edward. *Great Canadian Battles: Heroism and Courage Through the Years*. London: Arcturus Publishing, 2013.
Johnson, Michael G. *American Woodland Indians*. Oxford: Osprey Publishing, 1990.

Keenan, Jerry. *The Wagon Box Fight: An Episode of Red Cloud's War*. Conshohocken: Savas Publishing, 2000.
Kennett, Lee. *The French Armies in the Seven Years' War*. Durham: Duke University Press, 1967.
Kopperman, Paul E. *Braddock at the Monongahela*. Pittsburg: University of Pittsburg Press, 1977.
Larson, Robert W. *Red Cloud: Warrior-Statesman of the Lakota Sioux*. Norman: University of Oklahoma Press, 1997.
Lengel, Edward G. *General George Washington: A Military Life*. New York: Random House, 2007.
Lewis, Jon E. *The Mammoth Book of The West*. London: Robinson Publishing, 1996.
Lewis, Lloyd. *Sherman, Fighting Prophet*. New York: Smithmark Publishers, 1994.
Lewis, Thomas A. *For King and Country: The Maturing of George Washington, 1748–1760*. New York: John Wiley, 1993.
Macleod, Peter D. *The Canadian Iroquois and the Seven Years' War*. Toronto: Durham Press, 1996.
Manning, Stephen. *Québec: The Story of Three Sieges*. Montreal: McGill-Queen's University Press, 2009.
Marszalek, John F. *Sherman: A Soldier's Passion for Order*. Carbondale: Southern Illinois University Press, 2007.
Mattes, Merril J. *Indians, Infants and Infantry. Andrew and Elizabeth Burt on the Frontier*. Lincoln: University of Nebraska Press, 1988.
McPherson, James M. *Battle Cry of Freedom: The American Civil War*. London: Penguin Books, 1990
Monnet, John H. *Where a Hundred Soldiers Were Killed*. Albuquerque: University of New Mexico Press, 2008.
Moore, Jon H. *The Cheyenne Nation: A Social and Demographic History*. Lincoln: University of Nebraska Press, 1987.
Murray, Robert A. *Military Posts in the Powder River Country of Wyoming*. Lincoln: University of Nebraska Press, 1969.
Neihardt, John G. *Black Elk Speaks*. Lincoln: University of Nebraska Press, 2014.
Nester, William R. *The First Global War: Britain, France, and the Fate of North America, 1756–1775*. Westport: Praeger Publishers, 2000.
Olson, James C. *Red Cloud and the Sioux Problem*. Lincoln: University of Nebraska Press, 1989.
Ostrander, Alyson B. *An Army Boy of the Sixties*. Yonkers: World Book Co., 1924.
Pargellis, Stanley M. *Lord Loudoun in North America*. New Haven: Yale University Press, 1933.
Parkman, Francis. *Montcalm and Wolf: The French and Indian War*. New York: Da Capo Press, 1995.
Peckham, Howard H. *The Colonial Wars, 1689–1762*. Chicago: University of Chicago Press, 1964.
Perry, Arthur L. *Origins in Williamstown: A History...* Charleston: Nabu Press, 2011.
Porter, Peter A. *A Brief History of Old Fort Niagara*. Whitefish: Kessinger Publishing, 2008.
Pouchot, Pierre. *Memoir on the Late War in North America Between France and England*. Youngstown: Old Fort Niagara Association, 1994.
Prebble, John. *Culloden*. London: Penguin Books, 1970.
Putnam, Rufus. *Journal of Gen. Rufus Putnam Kept in Northern New York During Four Campaigns of the Old French and Indian War, 1757–1760*. Albany: Joel Munsell's Sons, 1886.
Regier, Willis G. *Masterpieces of American Indian Literature*. Lincoln: University of Nebraska Press, 2005.
Richardson, Heather C. *West from Appomattox: The Reconstruction of America after the Civil War*. New Haven: Yale University Press, 2007.
Rogers, Robert. *Journals of Major Robert Rogers*. Los Angeles: Hardpress Publishing, 2013.
Ross, John F. *War on the Run: The Epic Story of Robert Rogers and the Conquest of America's First Frontier*. New York: Bantam Doubleday Dell, 2011.
Sajna, Mike. *Crazy Horse: The Life Behind the Legend*. New York: John Wiley and Sons, 2000.
Sandoz, Mari. *Crazy Horse: Strange Man of the Oglalas*. Lincoln: University of Nebraska Press, 1942.
Sargent, Winthrop. *The History of an Expedition: Against Fort Du Quesne in 1755*. Carlisle: Applewood Books, 2009
Schofield, Victoria. *The Highland Furies: The Black Watch 1739–1899*. London: Quercus Publishing, 2012.
Scull, Gideon D. *The Montresor Journals*. Charleston: Nabu Press, 2010.
Shannon, Timothy J. *The Seven Years War in North America*. Boston: Bedford/St. Martins, 2014.
Simon, John Y., ed. *The Papers of Ulysses S. Grant*. Carbondale: Southern Illinois University Press, 2006.
Skaarup, *Ticonderoga Soldier: Elijah Estabrooks Journal 1758–1760*. Bloomington: Writers Club Press, 2001.
Smith, James. *Life and Travels of Col. James Smith During His Captivity With the Indians in the Years 1755–1759*. Whitefish: Kessinger Publishing, 2007.
Smith, Shannon D. *Give Me Eighty Men, Women and the Myth of the Fetterman Fight*. Lincoln: University of Nebraska Press, 2008.
Sparks, Jared. *The Writings of George Washington: Life of Washington*. Charleston: Nabu Press, 2012.
Starbuck, David R. *The Legacy of Fort William Henry*. Hanover: University Press of New England, 2014.
Stark, Caleb. *Memoir and Official Correspondence of Gen. John Stark*. Concord: G. Parker Lyon, 1860.
Steele, Ian K. *Fort William Henry & the "Massacre."* New York: Oxford University Press, 1990.
Stewart, Irene, ed. *Letters of General John Forbes: Relating to the Expedition Against Fort Duquesne in 1758*. Philadelphia: Pennsylvania State University Press, 2006.

Stoetzel, Donald I. *Encyclopedia of the French & Indian War in North America, 1754–1763.* Westminster: Heritage Books, 2008.
Suthren, Victor. *The Sea Has No End: The Life of Louis Antoine de Bougainville.* Toronto: Dundurn Press, 2004.
Sylvester, Herbert M. *Indian Wars of New England.* London: Forgotten Books, 2016
Thrapp, Dan L. *Encyclopedia of Frontier Biography.* Lincoln: University of Nebraska Press, 1991.
Tomlinson, Abraham, Lemuel Lyon, and Samuel Haws. *The Military Journals of Two Private Soldiers, 1758–1775.* Charleston: Nabu Press, 2011.
Trask, Kerry A. *Black Hawk: The Battle for the Heart of America.* New York: Owl Books, 2007.
Travers, Len. *Hodges' Scout: A Lost Patrol of the French and Indian War.* Baltimore: John Hopkins University Press, 2015.
Trimen, Richard, ed. *An Historical memoir of the 35th Royal Sussex Regiment of Foot.* Whitefish: Kessinger, 2007.
Tucker, Spencer C., ed. *The Encyclopedia of the North American Indian Wars, 1607–1890.* Oxford: ABC-CLIO, 2011.
Utley, Robert M. *Frontier Regulars, 1866–1891.* New York: Macmillan, 1973.
Vestal, Stanley. *Warpath: The True Story of the Fighting Sioux Told in a Biography of Chief White Bull.* Lincoln: University of Nebraska Press, 1984.
Victor, Francis F. *The River of the West: Life and Adventure in the Rocky Mountains and Oregon.* Hartford: R. W. Bliss, 1970.
Volo, James M., and Dorothy M. Volo. *Daily Life on the Old Colonial Frontier.* Westport: Greenwood Press, 2002.
Wellman, Paul I. *Death on the Prairie.* London: W. Foulsham, 1934.
West, Elliot. *The Contested Plains: Indians, Gold Seekers, and the Rush to Colorado.* Lawrence: University Press of Kansas, 1998.
Windrow, Martin. *Montcalm's Army.* Oxford: Osprey Publishing, 1973.
Woodham-Smith, Cecil. *The Reason Why: A Behind-the-Scenes Account of the Charge of the Light Brigade.* London: Penguin Books, 1977.

Index

Numbers in *bold italics* indicate pages with illustrations

Abercrombie, James 83–88, 94
Acadia 10
Adair, John 137, 140, 151, 153
Albany 9, 19–21, 27, 32, 40, 44, 52, 68, 78, 79, 81, 182
Allegheny River 12, 18
Almstedt, Henry 119
American Horse 137, 173
The American West (TV series) 210
Amherst, Jeffery 81, 83, 88, 94, 97, 100–102
Arbuthnot, William 62
Arnold, Wilber 153, 160, 162, 172
Artillery Cove 56, 76
Atalante (ship) 101
Aubry, Phillipe 96
Augur, Christopher C. 178, 179, 182, 185, 186, 189

Bagley, Jonathan 30
Bailey, George 117
Bailey, William 138
Barnes, Sgt. 147
Barron, Lt. 24
Bartman, George 52, 55, 56, 65, 68
Beasley, Daniel 140
Beaujeu, Lienard de 16
Beauvais, George 187
Beckwourth, James 114
Belden, George 200, 201
Bent, George 182, 187
Berryer, Nicolas 93
Bigot, François 100–102
Bingham, Horatio 153, 156, 189, 212
Bisbee, Lucy 118, 159
Bisbee, William H. 118, 120, 126, 135, 142, 150–152, 156, 157, 159, 177, 179, 183, 187, 208
Black Elk 111, 118, 176
Black Horse 98 121, 123–127, 140, 141

Blackfoot 141
Blanchard, Joseph 23
Bloody Morning Scout 23–25, 27
Bloody Pond 25
Bogy, Lewis V. 182
Bougainville, Louis A. de 3, 6, *7*, 31, 35, 41–43, 46–49, 51, 53–57, 59, 61–63, 65–68, 70, 71–73, 75–79, 82–86, 88–89, 91, 93, 97–99, 102; decorated 93; at Fort William Henry 46–49, 51, 53–57, 59, 61–63, 65–68; at Québec 97–99; at Sabbath Day Point 3, 6, *7*
Bouquet, Henry 90–92
Bourlamaque, François 51, 53, 67, 68, 72, 86, 94, 97
Bouyer, Mitch 193
Bowers, Gideon 156, 157, 158
Bowman, Alpheus 180
Bozeman, John 103, 104, 194
Braddock, Edward 14–21, 24
Bradley, Charles 196, 197
Bradley, James 129, 134, 142, 147, 153, 194
Bradley, Luther 195–197
Bradstreet, John 84
Brady, Cyrus T. 204
Brannan, James 114
Bratt, John 136
Bravo, Bernard 194
Brewer, Lt. 39
Brooks, Private 147
Brown, Frederick 139, 140–142, 150, 153, 157–161, 165, 169, 173, 179, 180, 204, 205, 212, 213
Brown, John 107
Brown, Thomas 33, 34
Browning, O.H. 191
Bridger, Jim 104, 114, 116, 117, 121, 125, 126, 130, 133, 138, 153, 189, 206, 210
Bridger's Ferry 104, 116, 117, 190, 193, 195

Buford, Napoleon 187–190
Bull Run, Battle of 108
Bullitt, Thomas 91
Burke, John 152
Burrowes, Thomas 128–131, 134, 196, 197
Burton, Ralph 32
Byrd (Burd), William 90, 91

Calico (pony) 161, 173
Callery, Terrence 129
Campbell, Duncan 86
Campbell, John *see* Loudoun, Lord
Campbell, Capt. John 86
Cape Breton Island 10
Cardigan, Lord 161
Carrington, Frances (Grummond) 2, 103, 116, 121, 128, 142, 143, *144*, 145–150, 152, 153, 155, 157, 159–161, 163, 168, 170–173, 175, 176, 180, 181, 184–187, 203–205, *207*, 208
Carrington, Harry 107, 108, 161, 203
Carrington, Henry B. 1, 2, 105, *106*, 107–112, 114, 116–128, 130–163, 165, 166, 168–191, 194,198, 200, 201, 203–206, *207*, 208, 210–214; background 107, 108; death 208; Dec. 6 fight 153–157; establishes Fort P.K. 121–123; issues "Bully 38" 152; prevents massacre of Indians 141; removed from command 177, 178, 181; report of Jan. 3, 1866, 211; views battle site 173, 174; visits Stanton and Grant 191; wounded 186
Carrington, James 107, 108, 203
Carrington, Margaret 2, 107–110, *112*, 114, 116, 118–121, 124–128, 130, 132, 135, 136, 138–141, 143, 145–150, 160, 161, 165,

231

168, 170, 172, 173–176, 181–186, 189, 191, 203–205, 208, 209
Carson, Kit 116, 187
Carter, Leviticus 136
Carver, Jonathan 70–73, 77
Champlain, Samuel de 9
Chase, Salmon 107, 108
Chesnaye, Jauques Vaudry de la 51, 55
Chivington, John 109, 134
Claus, Frederick 198, 199
Clear Fork 119, 120, 128, 131
Cleveland, John 83, 86
Collins, Giles 62, 65
Collins, Thomas 49, 53, 54, 59, 75
Collins, William 105, 110
Colvin, Don 195, 196
Connor, Patrick 105, 107, 114, 119, 121
Cooke, John R. 133
Cooke, Philip St. George 132, *133*, 134, 136, 145, 146, 152, 153, 157, 160, 161, 171, 177–183, 187, 208; background 132, 133; issues unrealistic orders to Carrington; 152, 153; removed from command 178
Cooke, William 161
Cooley, C.N. 113
Cooper, James F, 1, 135, 210
Corbiere, Ensign de 6
Coutant, C.G. 205
Cover, Thomas 194
Crazy Horse 167, 210
Crazy Women's Fork 119, 126, 129, 131, 134, 155, 184
Crockett, David 145
Crown Point 21, 32, 41, 95, 100
Cumberland, Duke of 80
Cunningham, Capt. 52, 75
Custard, Amos 107
Custer, George A. 144, 152, 161, 178, 202

Dandy, George 180, 183
Daniels, Napoleon 129–132, 134, 184
Day-Lewis, Daniel 210
Deming, Private 199
Dennison, William 107
Desandrouins, Jean-Nicolas 51, 53, 60, 66, 74
Dieskau, Jean-Armand 20, 21, 23–27, 30, 35, 60
Dinwiddie, Robert 14, 18
Dodge, Grenville 135, 178
Donaldson, Joe 121, 127
Donovan, John 126, 156
Doyle, Private 199
Drummond, Lt. 37
Dumas, Jean-Daniel 16
Dunbar, Thomas 15, 17–19

Duncan, George 196
Dyer, Alexander 178, 179

Eagan, Richard 210
Edwards, John 161
Ethrington, Maj. 140
Eyre, William 21, 28, 32, 36–40

Faesch, Rudolph 66, 77, 79
Fauquier, Francis 92
Fessenden, Frank 121, 129–131, 135–137, 145, 156, 170, 172, 173, 175, 180, 184, 192, 193
Fetterman, William J. 1, 2, 149, 150, *151*–153, 155–157, 159–165, 167, 168, 171–174, 177–183, 185, 187–191, 193–195, 200, 202, 203, 204–206, 208, 210–213; arrives at Fort P.K. 149; background 149; claims command 160; crosses Lodge Trail Ridge 165; death 167, 173
Fire Thunder 165, 167, 175, 199, 200
Fisher, Isaac 162–165, 173, 205, 213
Fitch, Jabez 60, 77, 78
Fletcher, Henry 40
Fontbrune, Capt. 49, 51
Forbes, John 83, 89–93, 95
Fort Anne 42
Fort Beausejour 19, 30
Fort Bull 30, 31
Fort Carillon 3, 6, 8, 28, 32, 33, 35, 36, 38–43, 45, 46, 53, 60, 76, 81, 83–89, 92–96
Fort Casper 142, 177, 181, 183, 185, 186, 214
Fort C.F. Smith 134, 138, 141, 146, 181, 192, 193, 195, 198
Fort Connor 105, 117
Fort Cumberland 14, 15, 17, 18, 90
Fort Detroit 97
Fort Duquesne 12, 14, 15, 17, 18, 20, 83, 88–93, 95, 210
Fort Edward 8, 21, 23, 25, 26, 28, 30, 32, 37, 40–45, 48, 49, 51–57, 59, 60, 63–70, 73–78, 81, 88, 89
Fort Frontenac 32, 88, 91
Fort Granger 143
Fort Herkimer 82
Fort Kearney 108, 110, 191
Fort Laramie 1, 104, 105, 107, 108–111, 114, 118, 126–128, 130, 132, 139, 145, 146, 153, 158, 170, 176, 180, 183, 185, 186, 188, 190, 201, 202, **209**
Fort Leavenworth 112
Fort Ligonier (Loyalhanna) 90–92
Fort Lydias 20

Fort Lyman *see* Fort Edward
Fort Michilimackinac 140
Fort Mims 1, 140
Fort Mitchell 109, **110**
Fort Necessity 12, 46
Fort Niagara 19, 30, 32, 94, 95
Fort Ontario 31
Fort Oswego 31, 35
Fort Pitt 93, 95, 97
Fort Reno 105, 114, 116, 117–119, 121, 128–130, 132–134, 138, 141, 142, 145, 146, 170, 176, 180, 185, 193, 194, 200
Fort Rice 201
Fort Rosalie 1
Fort St. Frédéric 21, 23, 26–28, 30, 32, 94, 95
Fort Sedgwick 109, 116, 191, 203
Fort Ticonderoga 95, 210
Foster, Preston 210
Fouts, William 110
Franklin, Benjamin 14
Frye, Joseph 44, 48, 59, 62, 64, 65, 69, 70, 71, 73, 77–79
Fuller, Robert 210
Furnis, James 73, 75, 78

Gage, Thomas 15
Galvanized Yankees 117
Ganaouske Bay 47
Garrett, Sgt. 152
Gazeau, Pierre (French Pete) 117, 121, 127
Genghis Khan 23
George, King 26, 28, 81
German Flatts 82
Gettysburg 87, 163
Gibbon, John 189
Gibson, Samuel 192, 198, 199, 200
Gilman, George 77
Glover, Ridgeway 114, 129, 130
Gordon, David 176, 190, 192
Gore, George 80, 104
Grady, Private 199
Graham, Joseph 192
Granger, Robert 143, 144
Grant, George 192
Grant, James 90
Grant, Ulysses S. 132, 143, 177, 179, 188, 190, 191, 201
Grattan, John 107, 112
Great Carrying Place 20, 23, 88
Great Sioux Reservation 201
Grey Eagle (horse) 112, 186
Grummond, Delia 143, 144, 203
Grummond, Frances *see* Carrington, Frances
Grummond, George W. 2, 142, **143**–145, 150, 153, 155–157, 159–161, 163, 165–167, 173, 180, 184,188, 203–205, 212, 213; accused of responsibility

2, arrives at Fort P.K. 142; background 143, 144; bigamy 144; death in battle 173, 213; receives orders 161, 212
Grummond, William W. 203

Haggerty, Private 199
Halifax, Lord 18
Hamilton, William 74
Haviland, William 101
Hayfield Fight 195–197
Haymond, Henry 119, 126–128, 134
Heflin, Van 210
Hendrick, King 21, 23–25
Henry, Alexander 140
Henry rifles 129, 132, 155, 163, 162, 174, 194, 195, 213
Hines, C.M. 129, 168, 169
Hitchcock, Capt. 73, 77
Hollister, J.G. 168
Holt, Joseph 190
Horseshoe Bend, Battle of 103
Horseshoe Creek 116
Horton, S.M. 173
Howe, Lord George 83, 84, 98
Howe, William 98
Hudson River 9, 20, 21, 32, 77, 81
Hughes, Robert 110

Isle aux Noix 94

Jackson, Andrew 103, 122, 144
Jacobs, John 104
Jacobs, Joshua 185
Jamestown 9
Jennes, John 198, 199
Jess (dog) 198
Johnson, Andrew 181, 187, 201
Johnson, Private 137
Johnson, William 21, *22*–28, 32, 37, 44, 59, 60, 64, 65, 77, 85, 92, 95, 96
Julesburg 109, 110
Jumonville, Joseph Coulon de 12

Kanectagon, Chief 46, 47
Kearny, Philip 122
Kelly, Fanny 165
Kennedy, Lt. 33
Kinney, John F. 147, 187, 189, 190, 194, 207, 208
Kinney, Nathaniel 128, 131, 133
Kirkwood, Robert 100
Kirtland, Thaddeus 119
Kisensik, Chief 45

la Corne, Luc de 46, 68, 70, 77, 88
La Chute River 20, 28, 46, 83, 84

Langlade, Charles de 10
Lake George, Battle of 22–26
The Last of the Mohicans (novel and films) 1, 135, 210
Latimar, Sarah 105
Laura (maid) 184, 186
Lee, Robert E. 122, 163
Leslie, Captain 16
Lévis, François Gaston de 46, *47*–49, 51, 53, 56, 57, 64, 65, 71, 86, 97, 101, 102
Lewis, Andrew 90
Lignery, Marchand de 89, 91, 95, 96
Lincoln, Abraham 104, 107, 108
Link, Henry 129
Little Dog 109
Little Horse 165
Little Turtle 103
Little Wolf 159
Littman, Max 198, 199, 200
Lockhart, Private 159
Lord Loudoun (sloop) 35, 38, 39, 46
Loudoun, Lord 30–32, 35, 40–42, 77, 81, 83
Louis, King 45, 62
Louisbourg 10, 19, 20, 35, 41, 42, 77, 81, 83, 88, 94, 97
Louisiana 10, 102
Loyalhanna *see* Fort Ligonier
Lydias, John H. 20, 21
Lyman, Phineas 21, 26

MacDonald, Capt. 90, 91
MacKay, George 151
MacLeane, Allan 96
Man-Afraid-of-His-Horses 111
Marin, Joseph 89
The Massacre at Fort Phil Kearny (TV feature) 210
Massey, Eyre 96
Matson, Winfield 138, 168, 172
McCleary, Dr. 147
McClellan, George 107
McCloud, William 49, 77
McDonough, Private 198
McDowell, Irvin 108
McGinnis, Captain 5
Mercer, James 31
Mercier, François le 36, 37, 86
Metzger, Adolph 155
Minnesota Uprising 122, 172
Mitzner, Henry 143
Monckton, Robert 19, 99
Monongahela River 12, 13, 15, 17, 19, 37
Monro, George 8, 41–45, 48, 49, 51, 52, 54–57, 60, 61, 63–67, 69, 70, 72–74, 76–79, 81, 204; arrives at Fort W.H. 40; background 40; death 81; during W.H. massacre 72;

refuses to surrender 61; surrenders 66
Montcalm, Louis Joseph de 6, *7*, 8, 30–32, 35, 36, 39, 41, 43–49, 51–58, 60–62, 64, 65, **66**, 67–77, 79, 81–86, 88, 92–94, 97, 100; arrives in N. America 30; at Battle of Fort Carillon 81–86; captures Fort W.H. 66; captures Oswego 31; death at Québec 99; during W.H. massacre 71, 72
Montgomery, Col. 90, 92, 100
Montréal 7–9, 12, 20, 21, 31, 32, 76, 78, 79, 86, 101, 102
Montresor, James 42–44, 48, 75
Montreuil, Pierre-Andre 20, 25
Moonlight, Thomas 110
Mountain District 105, 108, 116, 122, 142, 181
Murphy, William 108, 109, 111, 117, 119, 121, 126, 145, 147, 151, 156, 169, 170, 192–195
Murray, James 101

New Orleans 87, 102, 103
Nichols, Joseph 85
Nieuw Amsterdam 9
Nolan, Louis 161
North, Bob 138, 139
Northwest Passage (film) 210
Norton, Sgt. 195, 196
Nova Scotia 9, 10, 19, 35, 41, 78, 88

Ohio River territory, 11, 12, 20, 89, 90, 92, 95, 97, 105, 107, 170
Oregon Trail 104, 107, 111, 114, 142
Orme, Robert 17, 18
Ormsby, John 49, 62, 68, 77
Ostrander, Alson 178
Oswego *see* Fort Oswego
Ould, Dr. 172
Overland Trail 104

Palmer, Innis 177
Palmer, Lt. 196
Parker, Ely S. 187–189
Parker, John 3, 5, 6, 8, 42
Peale, James 192
Pennahouel, Chief 8
Perry, David 86
Peters, Samuel 130, 184, 208
Phillips, John (Portugee) 170, 176, 177, 180
Phisterer, Frederick 128, 134
Pickawillany 11
Picquet, Abbe 48, 74
Pierce, Franklin 112
Pilot Hill 121, 124, 136, 138, 140, 159, 160, 176, 201

Pitt, William 40, 83, 90, 94
Pomeroy, Seth 21, 24
Pompadour, Madame de 93
Pontiac 103
Pope, John 105, 188
Potomac River 14
Pouchot, Pierre 94–96
Powell, James 136, 151, 152, 159–161, 168, 172, 183, 184, 189–191, 193, 198–200, 204, 207, 208, 212; accused of perjury 191; claims to have taken command of fort 191; commands at Wagon Box Fight 191–200
Prestre, Sebastian La 28
Prevost, Augustine 75
Prideaux, John 95, 96
Proctor, Joshua 119, 133, 142
Putnam, Israel 42, 43, 51, 52, 55, 78, 80, 84, 89

Québec 9, 10, 12, 19, 20, 30, 41, 79, 88, 93, 94–99, 101

Rae, Caleb 87
Ramezay, Jean-Baptiste de 99
Rattlesnake Mountain 85
Rawlins, John 187, 188
Red Cloud 111, 112, 126, *127*, 131, 138, 141, 146, 158, 159, 175, 176, 188, 191–193, 195, 197, 200, 201, 202, 206
Redford, Robert 210
Reno, Marcus 161, 169
Ricker, Eli S. 205
Rigaud, François-Pierre de 35–40, 42, 55, 57
Rogers, Richard 41, 74
Rogers, Robert 21, 32, *33*, 34, 41, 74, 83, 84, 88, 100, 210
Rotten Tail 141
Roubaud, Pierre 3, 4, 6, 45–49, 51, 55–57, 59, 61, 62, 64, 65, 67–74, 76
Rout of Moy 30
Rover, Private 140
Ryan, John 127

Sabbath Day Point 3–7, 42–48, 79, 84
St. Clair, Arthur 103
Saltonstall, Richard 49
Sanborn, John B. 187, 188–190, 204, 207
Sand Creek Massacre 109, 134
Savournin, Lt. 77
Shaw, John 12
Sherman, William T. 105, 107, 109, 117, 118, 141, 143, 149, 177–179, 182, 183, 186, 188, 189, 191, 201, 204
Shingas, King 18

Shirley, William 19, 27, 30
Shurly, Lnt. 196, 197, 201
Sinclair, John 90
Skinner, Prescott 129
smallpox 36, 41, 79, 84
Smith, Benjamin 200
Smith, James 15, 18, 91
Smith, John E. 195, 198, 200
Smith, Patrick 139
Smith, William 86
Smith, Private William 27
Sokalski, Annie 116
Somers, Private 199
Sorrel Horse, Chief 199
Spencer carbines 108, 136, 149, 153, 161, 163, 165, 169, 172, 178, 195, 210, 213
Spikeman, Capt. 34
Spotted Tail 112, 201
Springfield rifles 108, 129, 136, 137, 140, 149, 153, 155, 178, 195, 198
Standing Elk 111
Stanton, Edwin 179, 183, 188, 191
Stark, John 32, 36
Starr carbines 149
Stead, Jack 121
Sternberg, Sigismund 195
Story, Nelson 146, 147, 194
Stuart, Charles 18
Stuart, Prince Charles E. 30
Stuart, Jeb 133
Sully, Alfred 187, 189
Surratt, Mary 190
Susan (servant) 145
Susquehanna Valley 18
Swanton, Commodore 101

Tanaghrisson 12
Taplin, Jonathan 62
Taylor, E.B. 111, 113
Tecumseh 103
Templeton, George 129, 130, 134
Ten Eyck, Conrad 122
Ten Eyck, Frances 205, 207
Ten Eyck, Tenadore 109, 122, 134, 141, 142, 148–150, 159, 163, 168–170, 172, 173, 184, 193, 205–207, 212, 213; accused of cowardice 169, 205; commands relief party 168, 169; exonerated by Carrington 206
Titcomb, Moses 24
Tomahawk (film) 210
Tracy, Spencer 210
Tuttle, Joseph 204
Two Moons 141

Van Valsah, Montgomery 193
Van Voast, James 153, 189, 191, 193

Vasquez, Louis 116
Vaudreuil-Cavagnial, Pierre François de Rigaud 7, 8, 30, 31, 35, 41, 42, 46, 70, 76, 78, 79, 81, 82, 94, 95, 97, 99, 101
Vauquelin, Jean 101
Vergor, Louis du 98
Victoire (ship) 93
Villiers, Louis Coulon de 12, 13, 14, 46, 53, 62
Virginia City (and Road) 104, 105, 114, 116, 117, 119, 163, 212

Wabash College 203
Wagon Box Fight 198–200
Waldo, Ralph 55
Wallace, William 130
Wands, Alexander 129–131, 136, 142, 151, 153, 155, 157, 159–161, 163, 165, 170, 179, 184, 185, 188, 263, 204, 212
Wands, Mrs. 170, 184–186, 203
Washington, George **11**–15, 17, 18, 46, 90, 92
Washington, D.C. 103, 107, 121, 132, 142, 143, 177, 189
Webb, Daniel 8, 31, 41–44, 49, 51–53, 55–61, 64–66, 68, 69, 75–78, 81
Wessells, Henry 142, 176–178, 181, 183, 192–195
West Point 107, 132, 149, 178
Wheatley, James 134, 150, 162–165, 170, 173, 205, 213
Wheeler, Joseph 144
White, David 129, 130, 137, 141, 145, 147, 158
White, Edward 75
White Bull 167
White Mouth 141
Whiting, Nathan 24
Whitworth, Miles 70
Wild Bill (Indian) 145
Williams, Ephraim 23, 24, 25, 27
Williams, Samuel 49
Williams, Thomas 24
Williamsburg 14
Williamson, Adam 41, 43, 59, 65, 74, 78
Winnebago Indians 116
Winslow, John 32
Wolff, Lt. 38, 46, 47
Wood Creek 42
Woodard, Captain 3

Yellowstone River 104, 194
Young, John 44, 52, 56, 64, 65, 67, 72, 73, 78